Office for Disarmament Affairs
New York, 2022

The United Nations
DISARMAMENT YEARBOOK

Volume 46 (Part I): 2021

Disarmament Resolutions and Decisions
of the Seventy-sixth Session
of the United Nations General Assembly

Guide to the user

To facilitate early analysis of the resolutions and decisions on disarmament adopted at the seventy-sixth session of the General Assembly, the United Nations Office for Disarmament Affairs offers Part I of the Yearbook as a handy, concise reference tool, containing the full texts of all the resolutions and decisions, the date of adoption by the Assembly and the First Committee, the agenda item number, the symbol number of the Report of the Rapporteur, the main sponsors and the voting patterns in the Assembly. For a snapshot of this information in a convenient chart, see "Quick view of votes by cluster". For a list of agenda items and their corresponding reports, see the Annex.

Bold type in the list of sponsors indicates the State(s) that submitted the draft resolution or decision.

Voting statistics in this publication are presented as three sets of numbers separated by two dashes, where the first figure represents the total of votes in favour, followed by votes against and abstentions.

Available in electronic format at:
https://yearbook.unoda.org and www.un.org/disarmament

UNITED NATIONS PUBLICATIONS
405 East 42nd Street, S-09FW001
New York, NY 10017 USA
Email: publications@un.org
Website: shop.un.org

Sales No. E.22.IX.5
ISBN 9789211392142
eISBN 9789210014458
ePUB ISBN 2412-1193

CONTENTS

Preface

The *United Nations Disarmament Yearbook* is now in its forty-sixth year of publication. Part I presents the official texts of the 56 resolutions and 4 decisions related to disarmament, arms control and international security that were debated in the First Committee and forwarded to the General Assembly for adoption at its seventy-sixth session.

Part I is issued as a separate publication to provide early access to the resolutions and decisions, each presented with key information: relevant agenda items, main sponsors and co-sponsors, vote counts, including voting patterns in the First Committee and the General Assembly, adoption and meeting number dates and draft resolution numbers.

A *Quick view by cluster* gives the reader an easy handle (using the First Committee's "cluster" arrangement of agenda items) on resolution numbers, titles and votes in the First Committee and in the Assembly.

We hope that Part I furnishes the reader with a handy, consolidated reference book on multilateral disarmament, in print and electronic form.

Part II of the Yearbook will contain main multilateral issues under consideration, including their trends, summaries of First Committee and General Assembly actions taken on resolutions and a convenient issue-oriented timeline. Part II is forthcoming in October 2022.

Quick view of votes by cluster (56 resolutions and 4 decisions)*

No.	Title	GA action, 6 Dec. (vote)	First Cttee action (vote, date)
Cluster 1: Nuclear weapons			
76/18	African Nuclear-Weapon-Free Zone Treaty	w/o vote	w/o vote 27 Oct.
76/20	Establishment of a nuclear-weapon-free zone in the region of the Middle East	178-1-2	171-1-6 27 Oct.
76/21	Conclusion of effective international arrangements to assure non-nuclear-weapon States against the use or threat of use of nuclear weapons	126-0-59	121-0-62 27 Oct.
76/25	Ethical imperatives for a nuclear-weapon-free world	135-37-14 120-37-16, p.p. 11	129-37-17 113-36-20, p.p. 11 27 Oct.
76/27	Reducing nuclear danger	125-50-14	120-50-13 27 Oct.
76/30	Humanitarian consequences of nuclear weapons	148-12-29	140-12-31 27 Oct.
76/31	Follow-up to nuclear disarmament obligations agreed to at the 1995, 2000 and 2010 Review Conferences of the Parties to the Treaty on the Non-Proliferation of Nuclear Weapons	122-44-17 113-4-54, p.p. 6	108-44-25 109-4-58, p.p. 6 27 Oct.
76/34	Treaty on the Prohibition of Nuclear Weapons	128-42-16	123-42-16 27 Oct.
76/36	Follow-up to the 2013 high-level meeting of the General Assembly on nuclear disarmament	145-34-9 120-37-15, p.p. 14	138-34-11 115-37-17, p.p. 14 27 Oct.
76/44	Nuclear-weapon-free southern hemisphere and adjacent areas	149-5-31 112-38-19, p.p. 6 149-1-26, o.p. 6	143-5-33 111-38-18, p.p. 6 145-1-27, o.p. 6 27 Oct.
76/46	Nuclear disarmament	124-41-22 117-39-16, p.p. 32 169-1-9, o.p. 16	119-41-23 110-39-17, p.p. 32 162-1-9, o.p. 16 27 Oct.
76/48	Universal Declaration on the Achievement of a Nuclear-Weapon-Free World	141-22-24 122-27-23, p.p. 8 141-3-30, p.p. 10	133-24-25 118-27-24, p.p. 8 135-2-32, p.p. 10 27 Oct.

---

* Abbreviations: o.p. = operative paragraph; p.p. = preambular paragraph.

No.	Title	GA action, 6 Dec. (vote)	First Cttee action (vote, date)
76/49	Towards a nuclear-weapon-free world: accelerating the implementation of nuclear disarmament commitments	140-34-15 146-2-28, p.p. 3 115-37-19, p.p. 10 161-4-10, p.p. 25 164-4-9, o.p. 15 118-37-19, o.p. 24	135-34-15 138-2-31, p.p. 3 111-36-18, p.p. 10 152-4-13, p.p. 25 160-4-8, o.p. 15 114-36-17, o.p. 24 27 Oct.
76/51	Treaty banning the production of fissile material for nuclear weapons or other nuclear explosive devices	182-1-5 166-1-11, p.p. 3	177-1-6 162-1-11, p.p. 3 27 Oct.
76/52	Brazilian-Argentine Agency for Accounting and Control of Nuclear Materials	w/o vote	w/o vote 27 Oct.
76/53	Follow-up to the advisory opinion of the International Court of Justice on the legality of the threat or use of nuclear weapons	143-33-14 144-2-29, p.p. 9 116-36-18, p.p. 17 121-36-15, o.p. 2	131-33-17 138-2-30, p.p. 9 110-36-19, p.p. 17 111-36-17, o.p. 2 3 Nov.
76/54	Joint courses of action and future-oriented dialogue towards a world without nuclear weapons	158-4-27 155-2-16, p.p. 2 143-0-28, p.p. 7 160-0-12, p.p. 8 163-1-7, p.p. 10 154-3-16, p.p. 11 168-0-5, p.p. 16 156-1-14, p.p. 17 161-2-6, p.p. 18 156-1-16, p.p. 19 163-2-9, p.p. 20 133-10-24, o.p. 1 129-0-39, o.p. 3 (b) 152-2-17, o.p. 3 (c) 138-2-29, o.p. 3 (d) 147-1-23, o.p. 3 (e) 162-2-9, o.p. 3 (f) 154-0-19, o.p. 5 151-3-19, o.p. 6	152-4-30 150-2-15, p.p. 2 141-0-28, p.p. 7 153-1-15, p.p. 8 163-1-7, p.p. 10 154-2-16, p.p. 11 164-0-6, p.p. 16 155-1-14, p.p. 17 159-2-8, p.p. 18 157-0-14, p.p. 19 160-2-9, p.p. 20 135-10-26, o.p. 1 130-0-39, o.p. 3 (b) 155-2-17, o.p. 3 (c) 138-1-29, o.p. 3 (d) 150-1-22, o.p. 3 (e) 158-2-10, o.p. 3 (f) 154-0-19, o.p. 5 147-3-19, o.p. 6 27 Oct.
76/56	Convention on the Prohibition of the Use of Nuclear Weapons	125-50-13	115-50-16 27 Oct.
76/63	The risk of nuclear proliferation in the Middle East	157-6-24 164-3-7, p.p. 5 165-3-7, p.p. 6	148-6-27 160-3-9, p.p. 5 159-3-6, p.p. 6 27 Oct.

No.	Title	GA action, 6 Dec. (vote)	First Cttee action (vote, date)
76/66	Comprehensive Nuclear-Test-Ban Treaty	182-1-3 176-0-5, p.p. 7	w/o vote 170-0-6, p.p. 7 27 Oct.
76/515	Nuclear disarmament verification (decision)	187-0-2	178-1-4 27 Oct.
76/517	Treaty on the South-East Asia Nuclear-Weapon-Free Zone (Bangkok Treaty) (decision)	w/o vote	w/o vote 27 Oct.

Cluster 2: Other weapons of mass destruction

No.	Title	GA action, 6 Dec. (vote)	First Cttee action (vote, date)
76/28	Measures to prevent terrorists from acquiring weapons of mass destruction	w/o vote	w/o vote 27 Oct.
76/29	Implementation of the Convention on the Prohibition of the Development, Production, Stockpiling and Use of Chemical Weapons and on Their Destruction	154-8-21 130-11-26, p.p. 6 92-15-54, o.p. 2 118-13-34, o.p. 3 111-10-40, o.p. 4 108-12-40, o.p. 5 109-11-42, o.p. 17	147-8-25 116-8-32, p.p. 6 86-12-61, o.p. 2 110-11-38, o.p. 3 105-9-43, o.p. 4 100-12-45, o.p. 5 106-9-44, o.p. 17 27 Oct.
76/35	Prohibition of the dumping of radioactive wastes	w/o vote	w/o vote 27 Oct.
76/67	Convention on the Prohibition of the Development, Production and Stockpiling of Bacteriological (Biological) and Toxin Weapons and on Their Destruction	w/o vote	w/o vote 27 Oct.

Cluster 3: Outer space (disarmament aspects)

No.	Title	GA action, 6 Dec. (vote)	First Cttee action (vote, date)
76/22	Prevention of an arms race in outer space	w/o vote	w/o vote 1 Nov.
76/23	No first placement of weapons in outer space	130-35-20 119-49-6, p.p. 5 123-48-4, p.p. 9 125-31-21, p.p. 11	124-35-22 115-50-7, p.p. 5 118-48-6, p.p. 9 118-33-21, p.p. 11 1 Nov.
76/55	Transparency and confidence-building measures in outer space activities	w/o vote	w/o vote 1 Nov.
76/230	Further practical measures for the prevention of an arms race in outer space	114-9-44 109-46-6, p.p. 5 107-18-35, o.p. 7 24 Dec.	126-9-46 112-47-10, p.p. 5 112-19-38, o.p. 7 1 Nov.

No.	Title	GA action, 6 Dec. (vote)	First Cttee action (vote, date)
76/231	Reducing space threats through norms, rules and principles of responsible behaviours	150-8-7 143-4-13, o.p. 3 143-9-6, o.p. 5 (a) 140-9-7, o.p. 5 (b) 139-9-7, o.p. 5 (c) 24 Dec.	163-8-9 148-3-15, o.p. 3 147-9-9, o.p. 5 (a) 147-9-9, o.p. 5 (b) 146-9-9, o.p. 5 (c) 1 Nov.

Cluster 4: Conventional weapons

No.	Title	GA action, 6 Dec. (vote)	First Cttee action (vote, date)
76/26	Implementation of the Convention on the Prohibition of the Use, Stockpiling, Production and Transfer of Anti-Personnel Mines and on Their Destruction	169-0-19	162-0-20 2 Nov.
76/32	Assistance to States for curbing the illicit traffic in small arms and light weapons and collecting them	w/o vote 150-1-20, p.p. 16	w/o vote 150-0-19, p.p. 16 2 Nov.
76/47	Implementation of the Convention on Cluster Munitions	146-1-37	140-1-39 2 Nov.
76/50	The Arms Trade Treaty	162-0-24 159-1-14, p.p. 9 149-1-21, p.p. 10	151-0-27 149-1-17, p.p. 9 143-0-23, p.p. 10 2 Nov.
76/64	Convention on Prohibitions or Restrictions on the Use of Certain Conventional Weapons Which May Be Deemed to Be Excessively Injurious or to Have Indiscriminate Effects	w/o vote	w/o vote 2 Nov.
76/232	The illicit trade in small arms and light weapons in all its aspects	w/o vote 144-0-16, p.p. 22 24 Dec.	w/o vote 152-0-17, p.p. 22 2 Nov.
76/233	Problems arising from the accumulation of conventional ammunition stockpiles in surplus	159-0-9 24 Dec.	167-0-9 2 Nov.
76/516	Countering the threat posed by improvised explosive devices (decision)	w/o vote	w/o vote 2 Nov.

Cluster 5: Other disarmament measures and international security

No.	Title	GA action, 6 Dec. (vote)	First Cttee action (vote, date)
76/19	Developments in the field of information and telecommunications in the context of international security	w/o vote	w/o vote 3 Nov.
76/24	Role of science and technology in the context of international security and disarmament	w/o vote	w/o vote 3 Nov.

No.	Title	GA action, 6 Dec. (vote)	First Cttee action (vote, date)
76/33	Compliance with non-proliferation, arms limitation and disarmament agreements and commitments	174-3-9	166-3-10 3 Nov.
76/37	Relationship between disarmament and development	w/o vote	w/o vote 3 Nov.
76/39	Observance of environmental norms in the drafting and implementation of agreements on disarmament and arms control	w/o vote	w/o vote 3 Nov.
76/40	Promotion of multilateralism in the area of disarmament and non-proliferation	134-4-51	125-4-51 3 Nov.
76/45	Youth, disarmament and non-proliferation	w/o vote 172-0-4, p.p. 10	w/o vote 168-0-4, p.p. 10 3 Nov.
76/234	Promoting international cooperation on peaceful uses in the context of international security	78-53-32 75-52-27, o.p. 2 74-53-27, o.p. 3 24 Dec.	75-55-43 68-53-37, o.p. 2 69-54-35, o.p. 3 3 Nov.

Cluster 6: Regional disarmament and security

No.	Title	GA action, 6 Dec. (vote)	First Cttee action (vote, date)
76/17	Implementation of the Declaration of the Indian Ocean as a Zone of Peace	133-3-45	135-3-46 3 Nov.
76/41	Regional disarmament	w/o vote	w/o vote 3 Nov.
76/42	Conventional arms control at the regional and subregional levels	186-1-3 173-2-2, p.p. 7 120-1-52, o.p. 2	179-1-4 167-2-4, p.p. 7 116-1-55, o.p. 2 3 Nov.
76/43	Confidence-building measures in the regional and subregional context	w/o vote	w/o vote 3 Nov.
76/65	Strengthening of security and cooperation in the Mediterranean region	182-1-1 173-2-1, o.p. 2 170-2-2, o.p. 5	176-1-2 169-2-0, o.p. 2 167-2-1, o.p. 5 3 Nov.

Cluster 7: Disarmament machinery

No.	Title	GA action, 6 Dec. (vote)	First Cttee action (vote, date)
76/38	Convening of the fourth special session of the General Assembly devoted to disarmament	w/o vote	w/o vote 3 Nov.
76/57	United Nations Regional Centre for Peace and Disarmament in Africa	w/o vote	w/o vote 3 Nov.

No.	Title	GA action, 6 Dec. (vote)	First Cttee action (vote, date)
76/58	United Nations Regional Centre for Peace, Disarmament and Development in Latin America and the Caribbean	w/o vote	w/o vote 3 Nov.
76/59	United Nations Regional Centre for Peace and Disarmament in Asia and the Pacific	w/o vote	w/o vote 3 Nov.
76/60	Regional confidence-building measures: activities of the United Nations Standing Advisory Committee on Security Questions in Central Africa	w/o vote	w/o vote 3 Nov.
76/61	United Nations regional centres for peace and disarmament	w/o vote	w/o vote 3 Nov.
76/62	Report of the Conference on Disarmament	w/o vote	w/o vote 3 Nov.
76/518	Disarmament Commission (decision)	w/o vote	w/o vote 3 Nov.

RESOLUTIONS

Agenda item 93

76/17   Implementation of the Declaration of the Indian Ocean as a Zone of Peace

Text

The General Assembly,

Recalling the Declaration of the Indian Ocean as a Zone of Peace, contained in its resolution 2832 (XXVI) of 16 December 1971, and recalling also its resolutions 54/47 of 1 December 1999, 56/16 of 29 November 2001, 58/29 of 8 December 2003, 60/48 of 8 December 2005, 62/14 of 5 December 2007, 64/23 of 2 December 2009, 66/22 of 2 December 2011, 68/24 of 5 December 2013, 70/22 of 7 December 2015, 72/21 of 4 December 2017 and 74/25 of 12 December 2019 and other relevant resolutions,

Recalling also the report of the Meeting of the Littoral and Hinterland States of the Indian Ocean, held in New York from 2 to 13 July 1979,[1]

Recalling further paragraph 102 of the Final Document of the Thirteenth Conference of Heads of State or Government of Non-Aligned Countries, held in Kuala Lumpur on 24 and 25 February 2003,[2] in which it was noted, inter alia, that the Chair of the Ad Hoc Committee on the Indian Ocean would continue his informal consultations on the future work of the Committee,

Emphasizing the need to foster consensual approaches that are conducive to the pursuit of such endeavours,

Noting the initiatives taken by countries of the region to promote cooperation, in particular economic cooperation, in the Indian Ocean area and the possible contribution of such initiatives to overall objectives of a zone of peace,

Convinced that the participation of all permanent members of the Security Council and the major maritime users of the Indian Ocean in the work of the Ad Hoc Committee is important and would assist the progress of a mutually beneficial dialogue to develop conditions of peace, security and stability in the Indian Ocean region,

---

[1] *Official Records of the General Assembly, Thirty-fourth Session, Supplement No. 45* and corrigendum (A/34/45 and A/34/45/Corr.1).

[2] A/57/759-S/2003/332, annex I.

Considering that greater efforts and more time are required to develop a focused discussion on practical measures to ensure conditions of peace, security and stability in the Indian Ocean region,

Having considered the report of the Ad Hoc Committee,[3]

1. *Takes note* of the report of the Ad Hoc Committee on the Indian Ocean;

2. *Reiterates its conviction* that the participation of all permanent members of the Security Council and the major maritime users of the Indian Ocean in the work of the Ad Hoc Committee is important and would greatly facilitate the development of a mutually beneficial dialogue to advance peace, security and stability in the Indian Ocean region;

3. *Requests* the Chair of the Ad Hoc Committee to continue his informal consultations with the members of the Committee and to report through the Committee to the General Assembly at its seventy-eighth session;

4. *Requests* the Secretary-General to continue to render, within existing resources, all necessary assistance to the Ad Hoc Committee, including the provision of summary records;

5. *Decides* to include in the provisional agenda of its seventy-eighth session the item entitled "Implementation of the Declaration of the Indian Ocean as a Zone of Peace".

Action by the General Assembly

Date: 6 December 2021   Meeting: 45th plenary meeting
Vote: 133-3-45   Report: A/76/437

Sponsors

Indonesia (on behalf of the States Members of the United Nations that are members of the Movement of Non-Aligned Countries)

Recorded vote*

In favour

Afghanistan, Algeria, Angola, Antigua and Barbuda, Argentina, Armenia, Australia, Azerbaijan, Bahamas, Bahrain, Bangladesh, Barbados, Belarus, Belize, Bhutan, Bolivia (Plurinational State of), Botswana, Brazil, Brunei Darussalam, Burkina Faso, Cabo Verde, Cambodia, Cameroon, Central African Republic, Chad, Chile, China, Colombia, Comoros, Congo, Costa Rica, Côte d'Ivoire, Cuba, Democratic People's Republic of Korea,

---

[3] *Official Records of the General Assembly, Seventy-sixth Session, Supplement No. 29* (A/76/29).

* Subsequently, the delegation of Madagascar informed the Secretariat that it had intended to vote in favour.

Djibouti, Dominica, Dominican Republic, Ecuador, Egypt, El Salvador, Equatorial Guinea, Eritrea, Eswatini, Ethiopia, Fiji, Gabon, Gambia, Ghana, Grenada, Guatemala, Guinea, Guinea-Bissau, Guyana, Haiti, Honduras, India, Indonesia, Iran (Islamic Republic of), Iraq, Jamaica, Japan, Jordan, Kazakhstan, Kenya, Kiribati, Kuwait, Kyrgyzstan, Lao People's Democratic Republic, Lebanon, Lesotho, Libya, Malawi, Malaysia, Maldives, Mali, Mauritania, Mauritius, Mexico, Mongolia, Morocco, Mozambique, Namibia, Nepal, Netherlands, New Zealand, Nicaragua, Nigeria, Oman, Pakistan, Palau, Panama, Papua New Guinea, Paraguay, Peru, Philippines, Qatar, Republic of Korea, Russian Federation, Rwanda, Saint Kitts and Nevis, Saint Lucia, Saint Vincent and the Grenadines, Samoa, Sao Tome and Principe, Saudi Arabia, Senegal, Seychelles, Sierra Leone, Singapore, Solomon Islands, South Africa, South Sudan, Sri Lanka, Sudan, Suriname, Syrian Arab Republic, Tajikistan, Thailand, Timor-Leste, Tonga, Trinidad and Tobago, Tunisia, Turkmenistan, Uganda, United Arab Emirates, Uruguay, Uzbekistan, Vanuatu, Venezuela (Bolivarian Republic of), Viet Nam, Yemen, Zambia, Zimbabwe

Against

France, United Kingdom, United States

Abstaining

Albania, Andorra, Austria, Belgium, Bosnia and Herzegovina, Bulgaria, Canada, Croatia, Cyprus, Czechia, Denmark, Estonia, Finland, Georgia, Germany, Greece, Hungary, Iceland, Ireland, Israel, Italy, Latvia, Liechtenstein, Lithuania, Luxembourg, Malta, Marshall Islands, Micronesia (Federated States of), Monaco, Montenegro, North Macedonia, Norway, Poland, Portugal, Republic of Moldova, Romania, San Marino, Serbia, Slovakia, Slovenia, Spain, Sweden, Switzerland, Turkey, Ukraine

Action by the First Committee

Date: 3 November 2021   Meeting: 17th meeting
Vote: 135-3-46   Draft resolution: A/C.1/76/L.22

Agenda item 94

76/18   African Nuclear-Weapon-Free Zone Treaty

Text

The General Assembly,

Recalling its resolutions 51/53 of 10 December 1996 and 56/17 of 29 November 2001 and all its other relevant resolutions, as well as those of the Organization of African Unity and of the African Union,

Recalling also the signing of the African Nuclear-Weapon-Free Zone Treaty (Treaty of Pelindaba) in Cairo on 11 April 1996,[1]

Recalling further the Cairo Declaration adopted on that occasion,[2] in which it was emphasized that nuclear-weapon-free zones, especially in regions of tension, such as the Middle East, enhance global and regional peace and security,

Recalling the statement made by the President of the Security Council on behalf of the members of the Council on 12 April 1996,[3] in which the Council affirmed that the signature of the Treaty constituted an important contribution by the African countries to the maintenance of international peace and security,

Considering that the establishment of nuclear-weapon-free zones, especially in the Middle East, would enhance the security of Africa and the viability of the African nuclear-weapon-free zone,

1.   *Recalls with satisfaction* the entry into force of the African Nuclear-Weapon-Free Zone Treaty (Treaty of Pelindaba) on 15 July 2009;

2.   *Calls upon* African States that have not yet done so to sign and ratify the Treaty as soon as possible;

3.   *Recalls* the convening of the first Conference of States Parties to the African Nuclear-Weapon-Free Zone Treaty (Treaty of Pelindaba), on 4 November 2010, the second Conference of States Parties, on 12 and 13 November 2012, the third Conference of States Parties, on 29 and 30 May 2014, and the fourth Conference of States Parties, on 14 and 15 March 2018, all held in Addis Ababa;

4.   *Expresses its appreciation* to the nuclear-weapon States that have signed the Protocols to the Treaty[4] that concern them, and calls upon those that have not yet ratified the Protocols that concern them to do so as soon as possible;

---

[1] A/50/426, annex.
[2] A/51/113-S/1996/276, annex.
[3] S/PRST/1996/17; see *Resolutions and Decisions of the Security Council*, 1996 (S/INF/52).
[4] See A/50/426, annex.

5. *Calls upon* the States contemplated in Protocol III to the Treaty that have not yet done so to take all measures necessary to ensure the speedy application of the Treaty to territories for which they are, de jure or de facto, internationally responsible and which lie within the limits of the geographical zone established in the Treaty;

6. *Calls upon* the African States parties to the Treaty on the Non-Proliferation of Nuclear Weapons[5] that have not yet done so to conclude comprehensive safeguards agreements with the International Atomic Energy Agency pursuant to the Treaty, thereby satisfying the requirements of article 9 (b) and annex II to the Treaty of Pelindaba, and encourages them to conclude additional protocols to their safeguards agreements on the basis of the model protocol approved by the Board of Governors of the Agency on 15 May 1997;

7. *Expresses its gratitude* to the Secretary-General of the United Nations, the Chairperson of the African Union Commission and the Director General of the International Atomic Energy Agency for the diligence with which they have rendered effective assistance to the signatories to the Treaty;

8. *Decides* to include in the provisional agenda of its seventy-seventh session the item entitled "African Nuclear-Weapon-Free Zone Treaty".

Action by the General Assembly

Date: 6 December 2021   Meeting   45th plenary meeting
Vote: Adopted without a vote   Report: A/76/438

Sponsors

Australia, Austria, Georgia, Kazakhstan, Kyrgyzstan, Mexico, **Nigeria** (on behalf of the States Members of the United Nations that are members of the Group of African States), Portugal, Turkey

Co-sponsors

Azerbaijan, Italy, Malta, Republic of Moldova

Action by the First Committee

Date: 27 October 2021   Meeting: 13th meeting
Vote: Adopted without a vote   Draft resolution: A/C.1/76/L.19

---

[5] United Nations, *Treaty Series*, vol. 729, No. 10485.

Agenda item 95

76/19   Developments in the field of information and telecommunications in the context of international security

Text

The General Assembly,

Recalling its resolutions 43/78 H of 7 December 1988, 53/70 of 4 December 1998, 54/49 of 1 December 1999, 55/28 of 20 November 2000, 56/19 of 29 November 2001, 57/53 of 22 November 2002, 58/32 of 8 December 2003, 59/61 of 3 December 2004, 60/45 of 8 December 2005, 61/54 of 6 December 2006, 62/17 of 5 December 2007, 63/37 of 2 December 2008, 64/25 of 2 December 2009, 65/41 of 8 December 2010, 66/24 of 2 December 2011, 67/27 of 3 December 2012, 68/243 of 27 December 2013, 69/28 of 2 December 2014, 70/237 of 23 December 2015, 71/28 of 5 December 2016, 73/27 of 5 December 2018, 73/266 of 22 December 2018, 74/28 and 74/29 of 12 December 2019, 75/32 of 7 December 2020 and 75/240 of 31 December 2020, as well as its decisions 72/512 of 4 December 2017 and 75/564 of 28 April 2021,

Stressing that it is in the interest of all States to promote the use of information and communications technologies for peaceful purposes and to prevent conflicts arising from the use of information and communications technologies,

Recalling that a number of States are developing information and communications technology capabilities for military purposes and that the use of information and communications technologies in future conflicts between States is becoming more likely,

Noting that considerable progress has been achieved in developing and applying the latest information technologies and means of telecommunication,

Expressing concern that these technologies and means can potentially be used for purposes that are inconsistent with the objectives of maintaining international stability and security and may adversely affect the integrity of the infrastructure of States, to the detriment of their security in both civil and military fields,

Expressing concern also about malicious information and communications technology activities aimed at critical infrastructure and critical information infrastructure facilities supporting essential services to the public,

Considering that it is necessary to prevent the use of information resources or technologies for criminal or terrorist purposes,

Underlining the importance of respect for human rights and fundamental freedoms in the use of information and communications technologies,

Noting that capacity-building is essential for cooperation of States and confidence-building in the field of information and communications technology security,

Reaffirming that voluntary, non-binding norms of responsible State behaviour can reduce risks to international peace, security and stability, and do not seek to limit or prohibit action that is otherwise consistent with international law but nonetheless to set standards for responsible State behaviour, while also reaffirming that, given the unique attributes of information and communications technologies, additional norms could be developed over time and, separately, noting the possibility of future elaboration of additional binding obligations, if appropriate,

Reaffirming also that the United Nations should continue to play a leading role in promoting dialogue on the use of information and communications technologies by States,

Recognizing the importance of the efforts made in this direction by the Group of Governmental Experts and the Open-ended Working Group on Developments in the Field of Information and Telecommunications in the Context of International Security,

Guided by the 2010, 2013 and 2015 reports of the Group of Governmental Experts on Developments in the Field of Information and Telecommunications in the Context of International Security,[1]

1. *Recognizes* the adoption of the consensus final report of the Open-ended Working Group on Developments in the Field of Information and Telecommunications in the Context of International Security;[2]

2. *Welcomes* the consensus final report of the United Nations Group of Governmental Experts on Advancing Responsible State Behaviour in the Context of International Security;[3]

3. *Calls upon* Member States to be guided in their use of information and communications technologies by the 2021 report of the Open-ended Working Group and the 2021 report of the Group of Governmental Experts;

4. *Supports* the open-ended working group on security of and in the use of information and communications technologies 2021–2025, and acknowledges its mandate in accordance with General Assembly resolution 75/240;

5. *Underlines* further that the open-ended working group 2021–2025 should take into account the outcomes of the previous Open-ended Working Group and the Groups of Governmental Experts and add to the efforts undertaken by them, and should be consensus-based and results-oriented;

---

[1] A/65/201, A/68/98 and A/70/174.
[2] A/75/816.
[3] A/76/135.

6.   *Invites* all Member States, taking into account the assessments and recommendations contained in the report of the Open-ended Working Group and the reports of the Group of Governmental Experts, to continue to inform the Secretary-General of their views and assessments on the following questions:

(a)   Efforts taken at the national level to strengthen information security and promote international cooperation in this field;

(b)   The content of the concepts mentioned in the report of the Open-ended Working Group and the reports of the Group of Governmental Experts;

7.   *Decides* to include in the provisional agenda of its seventy-seventh session the item entitled "Developments in the field of information and telecommunications in the context of international security".

Action by the General Assembly

Date: 6 December 2021   Meeting: 45th plenary meeting
Vote: Adopted without a vote   Report: A/76/439

Sponsors

Australia, Austria, Belgium, Brazil, Bulgaria, Croatia, Cyprus, Czechia, Denmark, Ecuador, Equatorial Guinea, Eritrea, Estonia, Eswatini, Finland, France, Germany, Greece, Guatemala, Guinea, Hungary, Iceland, Ireland, Italy, Japan, Lao People's Democratic Republic, Latvia, Lesotho, Lithuania, Luxembourg, Malta, Mauritania, Netherlands, Nicaragua, Nigeria, North Macedonia, Norway, Paraguay, Peru, Poland, Portugal, Republic of Korea, Republic of Moldova, Romania, **Russian Federation**, Slovakia, Slovenia, South Africa, Spain, Sweden, Switzerland, United Kingdom, **United States**, Uzbekistan, Zimbabwe

Co-sponsors

Albania, Algeria, Argentina, Armenia, Belarus, Bolivia (Plurinational State of), Brunei Darussalam, Cabo Verde, Chile, Colombia, Comoros, Costa Rica, Côte d'Ivoire, Ethiopia, Fiji, Ghana, Guinea-Bissau, Honduras, India, Indonesia, Iraq, Jordan, Kazakhstan, Kenya, Kyrgyzstan, Madagascar, Malaysia, Mexico, Montenegro, Morocco, Myanmar, Namibia, Papua New Guinea, Philippines, Samoa, San Marino, Sao Tome and Principe, Senegal, Serbia, Sierra Leone, Singapore, Suriname, Syrian Arab Republic, Tajikistan, Thailand, Togo, Tunisia, Turkey, Turkmenistan, Uganda, Uruguay, Viet Nam, Zambia

Action by the First Committee

Date: 3 November 2021   Meeting: 17th meeting
Vote: Adopted without a vote   Draft resolution: A/C.1/76/L.13

Agenda item 96

76/20   Establishment of a nuclear-weapon-free zone in the region of the Middle East

Text

The General Assembly,

Recalling its resolutions 3263 (XXIX) of 9 December 1974, 3474 (XXX) of 11 December 1975, 31/71 of 10 December 1976, 32/82 of 12 December 1977, 33/64 of 14 December 1978, 34/77 of 11 December 1979, 35/147 of 12 December 1980, 36/87 A and B of 9 December 1981, 37/75 of 9 December 1982, 38/64 of 15 December 1983, 39/54 of 12 December 1984, 40/82 of 12 December 1985, 41/48 of 3 December 1986, 42/28 of 30 November 1987, 43/65 of 7 December 1988, 44/108 of 15 December 1989, 45/52 of 4 December 1990, 46/30 of 6 December 1991, 47/48 of 9 December 1992, 48/71 of 16 December 1993, 49/71 of 15 December 1994, 50/66 of 12 December 1995, 51/41 of 10 December 1996, 52/34 of 9 December 1997, 53/74 of 4 December 1998, 54/51 of 1 December 1999, 55/30 of 20 November 2000, 56/21 of 29 November 2001, 57/55 of 22 November 2002, 58/34 of 8 December 2003, 59/63 of 3 December 2004, 60/52 of 8 December 2005, 61/56 of 6 December 2006, 62/18 of 5 December 2007, 63/38 of 2 December 2008, 64/26 of 2 December 2009, 65/42 of 8 December 2010, 66/25 of 2 December 2011, 67/28 of 3 December 2012, 68/27 of 5 December 2013, 69/29 of 2 December 2014, 70/24 of 7 December 2015, 71/29 of 5 December 2016, 72/24 of 4 December 2017, 73/28 of 5 December 2018, 74/30 of 12 December 2019 and 75/33 of 7 December 2020 on the establishment of a nuclear-weapon-free zone in the region of the Middle East,

Recalling also the recommendations for the establishment of a nuclear-weapon-free zone in the region of the Middle East consistent with paragraphs 60 to 63, and in particular paragraph 63 (d), of the Final Document of the Tenth Special Session of the General Assembly,[1]

Emphasizing the basic provisions of the above-mentioned resolutions, in which all parties directly concerned are called upon to consider taking the practical and urgent steps required for the implementation of the proposal to establish a nuclear-weapon-free zone in the region of the Middle East and, pending and during the establishment of such a zone, to declare solemnly that they will refrain, on a reciprocal basis, from producing, acquiring or in any other way possessing nuclear weapons and nuclear explosive devices and from permitting the stationing of nuclear weapons on their territory by any third party, to agree to place their nuclear facilities under International Atomic Energy Agency safeguards and to declare their support for the establishment

---

[1]   Resolution S-10/2.

of the zone and to deposit such declarations with the Security Council for consideration, as appropriate,

Reaffirming the inalienable right of all States to acquire and develop nuclear energy for peaceful purposes,

Emphasizing the need for appropriate measures on the question of the prohibition of military attacks on nuclear facilities,

Bearing in mind the consensus reached by the General Assembly since its thirty-fifth session that the establishment of a nuclear-weapon-free zone in the region of the Middle East would greatly enhance international peace and security,

Desirous of building on that consensus so that substantial progress can be made towards establishing a nuclear-weapon-free zone in the region of the Middle East,

Welcoming all initiatives leading to general and complete disarmament, including in the region of the Middle East, and in particular on the establishment therein of a zone free of weapons of mass destruction, including nuclear weapons,

Noting the peace negotiations in the Middle East, which should be of a comprehensive nature and represent an appropriate framework for the peaceful settlement of contentious issues in the region,

Recognizing the importance of credible regional security, including the establishment of a mutually verifiable nuclear-weapon-free zone,

Emphasizing the essential role of the United Nations in the establishment of a mutually verifiable nuclear-weapon-free zone,

Having examined the report of the Secretary-General on the implementation of resolution 75/33,[2]

1. *Urges* all parties directly concerned seriously to consider taking the practical and urgent steps required for the implementation of the proposal to establish a nuclear-weapon-free zone in the region of the Middle East in accordance with the relevant resolutions of the General Assembly, and, as a means of promoting this objective, invites the countries concerned to adhere to the Treaty on the Non-Proliferation of Nuclear Weapons;[3]

2. *Calls upon* all countries of the region that have not yet done so, pending the establishment of the zone, to agree to place all their nuclear activities under International Atomic Energy Agency safeguards;

3. *Takes note* of resolution GC(65)/RES/14, adopted on 23 September 2021 by the General Conference of the International Atomic Energy Agency at

---

[2] A/76/190 (Part I).
[3] United Nations, *Treaty Series*, vol. 729, No. 10485.

its sixty-fifth regular session, concerning the application of Agency safeguards in the Middle East;

4.   *Notes* the importance of the ongoing bilateral Middle East peace negotiations and the activities of the multilateral Working Group on Arms Control and Regional Security in promoting mutual confidence and security in the Middle East, including the establishment of a nuclear-weapon-free zone;

5.   *Invites* all countries of the region, pending the establishment of a nuclear-weapon-free zone in the region of the Middle East, to declare their support for establishing such a zone, consistent with paragraph 63 (d) of the Final Document of the Tenth Special Session of the General Assembly, and to deposit those declarations with the Security Council;

6.   *Also invites* those countries, pending the establishment of the zone, not to develop, produce, test or otherwise acquire nuclear weapons or permit the stationing on their territories, or territories under their control, of nuclear weapons or nuclear explosive devices;

7.   *Invites* the nuclear-weapon States and all other States to render their assistance in the establishment of the zone and at the same time to refrain from any action that runs counter to both the letter and the spirit of the present resolution;

8.   *Takes note* of the report of the Secretary-General on the implementation of resolution 75/33;

9.   *Invites* all parties to consider the appropriate means that may contribute towards the goal of general and complete disarmament and the establishment of a zone free of weapons of mass destruction in the region of the Middle East;

10.   *Requests* the Secretary-General to continue to pursue consultations with the States of the region and other concerned States, in accordance with paragraph 7 of resolution 46/30 and taking into account the evolving situation in the region, and to seek from those States their views on the measures outlined in chapters III and IV of the study annexed to the report of the Secretary-General of 10 October 1990[4] or other relevant measures, in order to move towards the establishment of a nuclear-weapon-free zone in the region of the Middle East;

11.   *Also requests* the Secretary-General to submit to the General Assembly at its seventy-seventh session a report on the implementation of the present resolution;

12.   *Decides* to include in the provisional agenda of its seventy-seventh session the item entitled "Establishment of a nuclear-weapon-free zone in the region of the Middle East".

---

[4] A/45/435.

Action by the General Assembly

Date: 6 December 2021   Meeting: 45th plenary meeting
Vote: 178-1-2   Report: A/76/440

Sponsors

Egypt

Recorded vote*

In favour

Afghanistan, Albania, Algeria, Andorra, Angola, Antigua and Barbuda, Argentina, Armenia, Australia, Austria, Azerbaijan, Bahamas, Bahrain, Bangladesh, Barbados, Belarus, Belgium, Belize, Bhutan, Bolivia (Plurinational State of), Bosnia and Herzegovina, Botswana, Brazil, Brunei Darussalam, Bulgaria, Burkina Faso, Cabo Verde, Cambodia, Canada, Chad, Chile, China, Colombia, Comoros, Congo, Costa Rica, Côte d'Ivoire, Croatia, Cuba, Cyprus, Czechia, Democratic People's Republic of Korea, Denmark, Djibouti, Dominica, Dominican Republic, Ecuador, Egypt, El Salvador, Equatorial Guinea, Eritrea, Estonia, Eswatini, Ethiopia, Fiji, Finland, France, Gabon, Gambia, Georgia, Germany, Ghana, Greece, Grenada, Guatemala, Guinea, Guinea-Bissau, Guyana, Haiti, Honduras, Hungary, Iceland, India, Indonesia, Iran (Islamic Republic of), Iraq, Ireland, Italy, Jamaica, Japan, Jordan, Kazakhstan, Kenya, Kiribati, Kuwait, Kyrgyzstan, Lao People's Democratic Republic, Latvia, Lebanon, Lesotho, Liberia, Libya, Liechtenstein, Lithuania, Luxembourg, Malawi, Malaysia, Maldives, Mali, Malta, Mauritania, Mauritius, Mexico, Monaco, Mongolia, Montenegro, Morocco, Mozambique, Myanmar, Namibia, Nepal, Netherlands, New Zealand, Nicaragua, Nigeria, North Macedonia, Norway, Oman, Pakistan, Palau, Panama, Papua New Guinea, Paraguay, Peru, Philippines, Poland, Portugal, Qatar, Republic of Korea, Republic of Moldova, Romania, Russian Federation, Rwanda, Saint Kitts and Nevis, Saint Lucia, Saint Vincent and the Grenadines, Samoa, San Marino, Sao Tome and Principe, Saudi Arabia, Senegal, Serbia, Seychelles, Sierra Leone, Singapore, Slovakia, Slovenia, Solomon Islands, South Africa, South Sudan, Spain, Sri Lanka, Sudan, Suriname, Sweden, Switzerland, Syrian Arab Republic, Tajikistan, Thailand, Timor-Leste, Tonga, Trinidad and Tobago, Tunisia, Turkey, Turkmenistan, Tuvalu, Uganda, Ukraine, United Arab Emirates, United Kingdom, United Republic of Tanzania, Uruguay, Uzbekistan, Vanuatu, Venezuela (Bolivarian Republic of), Viet Nam, Yemen, Zimbabwe

Against

Israel

---

* Subsequently, the delegation of Madagascar informed the Secretariat that it had intended to vote in favour.

Abstaining
Cameroon, United States

Action by the First Committee

Date:	27 October 2021	Meeting:	13th meeting
Vote:	171-1-6	Draft resolution:	A/C.1/76/L.1

Agenda item 97

76/21 Conclusion of effective international arrangements to assure non-nuclear-weapon States against the use or threat of use of nuclear weapons

Text

The General Assembly,

Bearing in mind the need to allay the legitimate concern of the States of the world with regard to ensuring lasting security for their peoples,

Convinced that nuclear weapons pose the greatest threat to humankind and to the survival of civilization,

Noting that the renewed interest in nuclear disarmament should be translated into concrete actions for the achievement of general and complete disarmament under effective international control,

Convinced that nuclear disarmament and the complete elimination of nuclear weapons are essential to remove the danger of nuclear war,

Determined to abide strictly by the relevant provisions of the Charter of the United Nations on the non-use of force or threat of force,

Recognizing that the independence, territorial integrity and sovereignty of non-nuclear-weapon States need to be safeguarded against the use or threat of use of force, including the use or threat of use of nuclear weapons,

Considering that, until nuclear disarmament is achieved on a universal basis, it is imperative for the international community to develop effective measures and arrangements to ensure the security of non-nuclear-weapon States against the use or threat of use of nuclear weapons from any quarter,

Recognizing that effective measures and arrangements to assure non-nuclear-weapon States against the use or threat of use of nuclear weapons can contribute positively to the prevention of the spread of nuclear weapons,

Bearing in mind paragraph 59 of the Final Document of the Tenth Special Session of the General Assembly, the first special session devoted to disarmament,[1] in which it urged the nuclear-weapon States to pursue efforts to conclude, as appropriate, effective arrangements to assure non-nuclear-weapon States against the use or threat of use of nuclear weapons, and desirous of promoting the implementation of the relevant provisions of the Final Document,

---

[1] Resolution S-10/2.

Recalling the relevant parts of the special report of the Committee on Disarmament[2] submitted to the General Assembly at its twelfth special session, the second special session devoted to disarmament,[3] and of the special report of the Conference on Disarmament submitted to the Assembly at its fifteenth special session, the third special session devoted to disarmament,[4] as well as the report of the Conference on its 1992 session,[5]

Recalling also paragraph 12 of the Declaration of the 1980s as the Second Disarmament Decade, contained in the annex to its resolution 35/46 of 3 December 1980, in which it is stated, inter alia, that all efforts should be exerted by the Committee on Disarmament urgently to negotiate with a view to reaching agreement on effective international arrangements to assure non-nuclear-weapon States against the use or threat of use of nuclear weapons,

Noting the in-depth negotiations undertaken in the Conference on Disarmament and its Ad Hoc Committee on Effective International Arrangements to Assure Non-Nuclear-Weapon States against the Use or Threat of Use of Nuclear Weapons,[6] with a view to reaching agreement on this question,

Taking note of the proposals submitted under the item in the Conference on Disarmament, including the drafts of an international convention,

Taking note also of the relevant decision of the Thirteenth Conference of Heads of State or Government of Non-Aligned Countries, held in Kuala Lumpur on 24 and 25 February 2003,[7] which was reiterated at the Seventeenth Conference of Heads of State or Government of Non-Aligned Countries, held on Margarita Island, Bolivarian Republic of Venezuela, from 13 to 18 September 2016, as well as the relevant recommendations of the Organization of Islamic Cooperation,

Taking note further of the unilateral declarations made by all the nuclear-weapon States on their policies of non-use or non-threat of use of nuclear weapons against the non-nuclear-weapon States,

Noting the support expressed in the Conference on Disarmament and in the General Assembly for the elaboration of an international convention to assure non-nuclear-weapon States against the use or threat of use of nuclear weapons, as well as the difficulties pointed out in evolving a common approach acceptable to all,

---

[2] The Committee on Disarmament was redesignated the Conference on Disarmament as from 7 February 1984.

[3] *Official Records of the General Assembly, Twelfth Special Session, Supplement No. 2* (A/S-12/2), sect. III.C.

[4] Ibid., *Fifteenth Special Session, Supplement No. 2* (A/S-15/2), sect. III.F.

[5] Ibid., *Forty-seventh Session, Supplement No. 27* (A/47/27), sect. III.F.

[6] Ibid., *Forty-eighth Session, Supplement No. 27* (A/48/27), sect. III.E.

[7] See A/57/759-S/2003/332, annex I.

Taking note of Security Council resolution 984 (1995) of 11 April 1995 and the views expressed on it,

Recalling its relevant resolutions adopted in previous years, in particular resolutions 45/54 of 4 December 1990, 46/32 of 6 December 1991, 47/50 of 9 December 1992, 48/73 of 16 December 1993, 49/73 of 15 December 1994, 50/68 of 12 December 1995, 51/43 of 10 December 1996, 52/36 of 9 December 1997, 53/75 of 4 December 1998, 54/52 of 1 December 1999, 55/31 of 20 November 2000, 56/22 of 29 November 2001, 57/56 of 22 November 2002, 58/35 of 8 December 2003, 59/64 of 3 December 2004, 60/53 of 8 December 2005, 61/57 of 6 December 2006, 62/19 of 5 December 2007, 63/39 of 2 December 2008, 64/27 of 2 December 2009, 65/43 of 8 December 2010, 66/26 of 2 December 2011, 67/29 of 3 December 2012, 68/28 of 5 December 2013, 69/30 of 2 December 2014, 70/25 of 7 December 2015, 71/30 of 5 December 2016, 72/25 of 4 December 2017, 73/29 of 5 December 2018, 74/31 of 12 December 2019 and 75/34 of 7 December 2020,

1.   *Reaffirms* the urgent need to reach an early agreement on effective international arrangements to assure non-nuclear-weapon States against the use or threat of use of nuclear weapons;

2.   *Notes with satisfaction* that in the Conference on Disarmament there is no objection, in principle, to the idea of an international convention to assure non-nuclear-weapon States against the use or threat of use of nuclear weapons, although the difficulties with regard to evolving a common approach acceptable to all have also been pointed out;

3.   *Appeals* to all States, especially the nuclear-weapon States, to work actively towards an early agreement on a common approach and, in particular, on a common formula that could be included in an international instrument of a legally binding character;

4.   *Recommends* that further intensive efforts be devoted to the search for such a common approach or common formula and that the various alternative approaches, including, in particular, those considered in the Conference on Disarmament, be further explored in order to overcome the difficulties;

5.   *Also recommends* that the Conference on Disarmament actively continue intensive negotiations with a view to reaching early agreement and concluding effective international agreements to assure the non-nuclear-weapon States against the use or threat of use of nuclear weapons, taking into account the widespread support for the conclusion of an international convention and giving consideration to any other proposals designed to secure the same objective;

6.   *Decides* to include in the provisional agenda of its seventy-seventh session the item entitled "Conclusion of effective international arrangements

to assure non-nuclear-weapon States against the use or threat of use of nuclear weapons".

Action by the General Assembly

Date: 6 December 2021   Meeting: 45th plenary meeting
Vote: 126-0-59   Report: A/76/441

Sponsors

Algeria, Bangladesh, Colombia, Cuba, Egypt, Eritrea, Iraq, Kuwait, Nicaragua, **Pakistan**, Saudi Arabia, Uzbekistan

Co-sponsors

Bolivia (Plurinational State of), Iran (Islamic Republic of), Kazakhstan, Kiribati, Kyrgyzstan, Paraguay, Peru, Sri Lanka, Syrian Arab Republic, Venezuela (Bolivarian Republic of)

Recorded vote

In favour

Afghanistan, Algeria, Angola, Antigua and Barbuda, Azerbaijan, Bahamas, Bahrain, Bangladesh, Barbados, Belarus, Belize, Bhutan, Bolivia (Plurinational State of), Botswana, Brazil, Brunei Darussalam, Burkina Faso, Cabo Verde, Cambodia, Cameroon, Central African Republic, Chad, Chile, China, Colombia, Comoros, Congo, Costa Rica, Côte d'Ivoire, Cuba, Democratic People's Republic of Korea, Djibouti, Dominica, Dominican Republic, Ecuador, Egypt, El Salvador, Equatorial Guinea, Eritrea, Eswatini, Ethiopia, Fiji, Gambia, Ghana, Grenada, Guatemala, Guinea, Guinea-Bissau, Guyana, Haiti, Honduras, India, Indonesia, Iran (Islamic Republic of), Iraq, Jamaica, Japan, Jordan, Kazakhstan, Kenya, Kiribati, Kuwait, Kyrgyzstan, Lao People's Democratic Republic, Lebanon, Liberia, Libya, Madagascar, Malawi, Malaysia, Maldives, Mali, Mauritania, Mauritius, Mexico, Mongolia, Morocco, Mozambique, Myanmar, Namibia, Nepal, Nicaragua, Nigeria, Oman, Pakistan, Panama, Papua New Guinea, Paraguay, Peru, Philippines, Qatar, Rwanda, Saint Kitts and Nevis, Saint Lucia, Saint Vincent and the Grenadines, Samoa, Sao Tome and Principe, Saudi Arabia, Senegal, Seychelles, Sierra Leone, Singapore, Solomon Islands, South Sudan, Sri Lanka, Sudan, Suriname, Syrian Arab Republic, Tajikistan, Thailand, Timor-Leste, Tonga, Trinidad and Tobago, Tunisia, Turkmenistan, Uganda, United Arab Emirates, United Republic of Tanzania, Uruguay, Uzbekistan, Vanuatu, Venezuela (Bolivarian Republic of), Viet Nam, Yemen, Zambia, Zimbabwe

Against

None

Abstaining

Albania, Andorra, Argentina, Armenia, Australia, Austria, Belgium, Bosnia and Herzegovina, Bulgaria, Canada, Croatia, Cyprus, Czechia, Denmark, Estonia, Finland, France, Gabon, Georgia, Germany, Greece, Hungary, Iceland, Ireland, Israel, Italy, Latvia, Lesotho, Liechtenstein, Lithuania, Luxembourg, Malta, Marshall Islands, Micronesia (Federated States of), Monaco, Montenegro, Netherlands, New Zealand, North Macedonia, Norway, Palau, Poland, Portugal, Republic of Korea, Republic of Moldova, Romania, Russian Federation, San Marino, Serbia, Slovakia, Slovenia, South Africa, Spain, Sweden, Switzerland, Turkey, Ukraine, United Kingdom, United States

Action by the First Committee

Date:	27 October 2021	Meeting:	13th meeting
Vote:	121-0-62	Draft resolution:	A/C.1/76/L.29

Agenda item 98 (a)

76/22   Prevention of an arms race in outer space

Text

The General Assembly,

Recognizing the common interest of all humankind in the exploration and use of outer space for peaceful purposes,

Reaffirming the will of all States that the exploration and use of outer space, including the Moon and other celestial bodies, shall be for peaceful purposes and shall be carried out for the benefit and in the interest of all countries, irrespective of their degree of economic or scientific development,

Reaffirming also the provisions of articles III and IV of the Treaty on Principles Governing the Activities of States in the Exploration and Use of Outer Space, including the Moon and Other Celestial Bodies,[1]

Recalling the obligation of all States to observe the provisions of the Charter of the United Nations regarding the use or threat of use of force in their international relations, including in their space activities,

Reaffirming paragraph 80 of the Final Document of the Tenth Special Session of the General Assembly,[2] in which it is stated that, in order to prevent an arms race in outer space, further measures should be taken and appropriate international negotiations held in accordance with the spirit of the Treaty,

Recalling its previous resolutions on this issue, the most recent of which is resolution 75/35 of 7 December 2020, and taking note of the proposals submitted to the General Assembly at its tenth special session and at its regular sessions and of the recommendations made to the competent organs of the United Nations and to the Conference on Disarmament,

Recognizing that the prevention of an arms race in outer space would avert a grave danger for international peace and security,

Emphasizing the paramount importance of strict compliance with existing arms limitation and disarmament agreements relevant to outer space, including bilateral agreements, and with the existing legal regime concerning the use of outer space,

Considering that wide participation in the legal regime applicable to outer space could contribute to enhancing its effectiveness,

Noting that the Ad Hoc Committee on the Prevention of an Arms Race in Outer Space, taking into account its previous efforts since its establishment in 1985 and seeking to enhance its functioning in qualitative terms, continued

---

[1] United Nations, *Treaty Series*, vol. 610, No. 8843.
[2] Resolution S-10/2.

the examination and identification of various issues, existing agreements and existing proposals, as well as future initiatives relevant to the prevention of an arms race in outer space, and that this contributed to a better understanding of a number of problems and to a clearer perception of the various positions,

Noting also that there were no objections in principle in the Conference on Disarmament to the re-establishment of the Ad Hoc Committee, subject to reexamination of the mandate contained in the decision of the Conference on Disarmament of 13 February 1992,[3]

Emphasizing the mutually complementary nature of bilateral and multilateral efforts for the prevention of an arms race in outer space, and hoping that concrete results will emerge from those efforts as soon as possible,

Convinced that further measures should be examined in the search for effective and verifiable bilateral and multilateral agreements in order to prevent an arms race in outer space, including the weaponization of outer space,

Stressing that the growing use of outer space increases the need for greater transparency and better information on the part of the international community,

Recalling, in this context, its previous resolutions, in particular resolutions 45/55 B of 4 December 1990, 47/51 of 9 December 1992 and 48/74 A of 16 December 1993, in which, inter alia, it reaffirmed the importance of confidence-building measures as a means conducive to ensuring the attainment of the objective of the prevention of an arms race in outer space,

Conscious of the benefits of confidence- and security-building measures in the military field,

Recognizing that negotiations for the conclusion of an international agreement or agreements to prevent an arms race in outer space remain a priority task of the Conference on Disarmament and that the concrete proposals on confidence-building measures could form an integral part of such agreements,

Noting with satisfaction the constructive, structured and focused debate on the prevention of an arms race in outer space at the Conference on Disarmament each year from 2009 to 2021,

Noting the introduction by China and the Russian Federation at the Conference on Disarmament of the draft treaty on the prevention of the

---

[3] See *Official Records of the General Assembly, Forty-seventh Session, Supplement No. 27* (A/47/27), para. 76.

placement of weapons in outer space and of the threat or use of force against outer space objects in 2008 and the submission of its updated version in 2014,[4]

Recalling the comprehensive and substantive discussions of the Group of Governmental Experts that was convened in 2018 and 2019 pursuant to its resolution 72/250 of 24 December 2017,

Taking note of the decision of the Conference on Disarmament to establish for its 2009 session a working group to discuss, substantially, without limitation, all issues related to the prevention of an arms race in outer space, and the decision to establish for its 2018 session a subsidiary body on the prevention of an arms race in outer space,

1.   *Reaffirms* the importance and urgency of preventing an arms race in outer space and the readiness of all States to contribute to that common objective, in conformity with the provisions of the Treaty on Principles Governing the Activities of States in the Exploration and Use of Outer Space, including the Moon and Other Celestial Bodies;

2.   *Reaffirms its recognition*, as stated in the report of the Ad Hoc Committee on the Prevention of an Arms Race in Outer Space, that the legal regime applicable to outer space by itself does not guarantee the prevention of an arms race in outer space, that the regime plays a significant role in the prevention of an arms race in that environment, that there is a need to consolidate and reinforce that regime and enhance its effectiveness and that it is important to comply strictly with existing agreements, both bilateral and multilateral;

3.   *Emphasizes* the necessity of further measures with appropriate and effective provisions for verification to prevent an arms race in outer space;

4.   *Calls upon* all States, in particular those with major space capabilities, to contribute actively to the objective of the peaceful use of outer space and of the prevention of an arms race in outer space and to refrain from actions contrary to that objective and to the relevant existing treaties in the interest of maintaining international peace and security and promoting international cooperation;

5.   *Reiterates* that the Conference on Disarmament, as the sole multilateral disarmament negotiating forum, has the primary role in the negotiation of a multilateral agreement or agreements, as appropriate, on the prevention of an arms race in outer space in all its aspects;

6.   *Invites* the Conference on Disarmament to establish a working group under its agenda item entitled "Prevention of an arms race in outer space" as early as possible;

---

[4] See CD/1839 and CD/1985.

7.   *Recognizes*, in this respect, the growing convergence of views on the elaboration of measures designed to strengthen transparency, confidence and security in the peaceful uses of outer space, without prejudice to efforts towards the conclusion of an effective and verifiable multilateral agreement or agreements on the prevention of an arms race in outer space;

8.   *Urges* States conducting activities in outer space, as well as States interested in conducting such activities, to keep the Conference on Disarmament informed of the progress of bilateral and multilateral negotiations on the matter, if any, so as to facilitate its work;

9.   *Decides* to include in the provisional agenda of its seventy-seventh session the item entitled "Prevention of an arms race in outer space".

Action by the General Assembly

Date: 6 December 2021   Meeting: 45th plenary meeting
Vote: Adopted without a vote   Report: A/76/442

Sponsors

Algeria, Cuba, **Egypt**, Equatorial Guinea, India, Iraq, Kyrgyzstan, Malaysia, Nepal, Nicaragua, Russian Federation, **Sri Lanka**

Co-sponsors

Armenia, Bangladesh, Belarus, Bolivia (Plurinational State of), China, Ecuador, Eritrea, Indonesia, Iran (Islamic Republic of), Mauritania, Mongolia, Myanmar, Nigeria, Pakistan, Syrian Arab Republic, Thailand, Venezuela (Bolivarian Republic of)

Action by the First Committee

Date: 1 November 2021   Meeting: 15th meeting
Vote: Adopted without a vote   Draft resolution: A/C.1/76/L.3

Agenda item 98 (b)

76/23   No first placement of weapons in outer space

Text

The General Assembly,

Recalling its resolutions 69/32 of 2 December 2014, 70/27 of 7 December 2015, 71/32 of 5 December 2016, 72/27 of 4 December 2017, 73/31 of 5 December 2018 and 74/33 of 12 December 2019, 75/37 of 7 December 2020 and its resolutions 45/55 B of 4 December 1990 and 48/74 B of 16 December 1993, which, inter alia, confirm the importance of transparency and confidence-building measures as a means conducive to ensuring the attainment of the objective of preventing an arms race in outer space,

Recognizing the common interest of all humankind in the exploration and use of outer space for peaceful purposes,

Seriously concerned about the possibility of an arms race in outer space and of outer space turning into an arena for military confrontation, and bearing in mind the importance of articles III and IV of the Treaty on Principles Governing the Activities of States in the Exploration and Use of Outer Space, including the Moon and Other Celestial Bodies,[1]

Conscious that the prevention of an arms race in outer space would avert a grave danger to international peace and security,

Reaffirming that practical measures should be examined and taken in the search for agreements to prevent an arms race in outer space in a common effort towards a community of shared future for humankind,

Emphasizing the paramount importance of strict compliance with the existing legal regime providing for the peaceful use of outer space,

Reaffirming its recognition that the legal regime applicable to outer space by itself does not guarantee prevention of an arms race in outer space and that there is a need to consolidate and reinforce that regime,

Convinced that such measures could critically improve conditions for efficiently addressing the threat of an arms race in outer space, including the placement of weapons in outer space,

Welcoming, in this regard, the draft treaty on the prevention of the placement of weapons in outer space and of the threat or use of force against outer space objects, introduced by China and the Russian Federation at the Conference on Disarmament in 2008,[2] and the submission of its updated version in 2014,[3]

---

[1] United Nations, *Treaty Series*, vol. 610, No. 8843.
[2] See CD/1839.
[3] See CD/1985.

Considering that transparency and confidence-building measures in outer space activities are an integral part of the draft treaty referred to above,

Stressing the importance of the political statements made by a number of States[4] that they would not be the first to place weapons in outer space,

1. *Reaffirms* the importance and urgency of the objective of preventing an arms race in outer space and the willingness of States to contribute to reaching this common goal;

2. *Reiterates* that the Conference on Disarmament, as the single multilateral negotiating forum on this subject,[5] has the primary role in the negotiation of a multilateral agreement, or agreements, as appropriate, on the prevention of an arms race in outer space in all its aspects;

3. *Urges* an early commencement of substantive work based on the updated draft treaty on the prevention of the placement of weapons in outer space and of the threat or use of force against outer space objects, introduced by China and the Russian Federation at the Conference on Disarmament in 2008, under the agenda item entitled "Prevention of an arms race in outer space";

4. *Stresses* that, while such an agreement is not yet concluded, other measures may contribute to ensuring that weapons are not placed in outer space;

5. *Encourages* all States, especially spacefaring nations, to consider the possibility of upholding, as appropriate, a political commitment not to be the first to place weapons in outer space;

6. *Decides* to include in the provisional agenda of its seventy-seventh session, under the item entitled "Prevention of an arms race in outer space", the sub-item entitled "No first placement of weapons in outer space".

Action by the General Assembly

Date:	6 December 2021	Meeting:	45th plenary meeting
Vote:	130-35-20	Report:	A/76/442
	119-49-6, p.p. 5		
	123-48-4, p.p. 9		
	125-31-21, p.p.11		

---

[4] Argentina, Armenia, Belarus, Bolivia (Plurinational State of), Brazil, Burundi, Cambodia, Congo, Cuba, Ecuador, Guatemala, Indonesia, Kazakhstan, Kyrgyzstan, Myanmar, Nicaragua, Pakistan, Russian Federation, Seychelles, Sierra Leone, Sri Lanka, Suriname, Syrian Arab Republic, Tajikistan, Togo, Turkmenistan, Uruguay, Uzbekistan, Venezuela (Bolivarian Republic of) and Viet Nam.

[5] See resolution S-10/2.

Sponsors

Algeria, Armenia, Cambodia, Cuba, Egypt, Eritrea, Kyrgyzstan, Lao People's Democratic Republic, Nicaragua, **Russian Federation**, Syrian Arab Republic, Uzbekistan, Viet Nam, Zimbabwe

Co-sponsors

Argentina, Bangladesh, Belarus, Bolivia (Plurinational State of), China, Comoros, Democratic People's Republic of Korea, Dominica, Equatorial Guinea, Eswatini, Ethiopia, Indonesia, Kazakhstan, Madagascar, Morocco, Pakistan, Somalia, Tajikistan, Thailand, Turkmenistan, Venezuela (Bolivarian Republic of), Zambia

Recorded vote

As a whole

In favour

Afghanistan, Algeria, Angola, Antigua and Barbuda, Argentina, Armenia, Azerbaijan, Bahamas, Bahrain, Bangladesh, Barbados, Belarus, Belize, Bhutan, Bolivia (Plurinational State of), Botswana, Brazil, Brunei Darussalam, Burkina Faso, Burundi, Cabo Verde, Cambodia, Cameroon, Central African Republic, Chad, Chile, China, Colombia, Comoros, Congo, Costa Rica, Cuba, Democratic People's Republic of Korea, Djibouti, Dominica, Dominican Republic, Ecuador, Egypt, El Salvador, Equatorial Guinea, Eritrea, Eswatini, Ethiopia, Fiji, Gambia, Ghana, Grenada, Guatemala, Guinea, Guinea-Bissau, Guyana, Haiti, Honduras, India, Indonesia, Iran (Islamic Republic of), Iraq, Jamaica, Jordan, Kazakhstan, Kenya, Kiribati, Kuwait, Kyrgyzstan, Lao People's Democratic Republic, Lebanon, Lesotho, Libya, Madagascar, Malawi, Malaysia, Maldives, Mali, Mauritania, Mauritius, Mexico, Mongolia, Morocco, Mozambique, Myanmar, Namibia, Nauru, Nepal, Nicaragua, Nigeria, Oman, Pakistan, Panama, Papua New Guinea, Paraguay, Peru, Philippines, Qatar, Russian Federation, Rwanda, Saint Kitts and Nevis, Saint Lucia, Saint Vincent and the Grenadines, Samoa, Sao Tome and Principe, Saudi Arabia, Senegal, Serbia, Seychelles, Sierra Leone, Singapore, South Africa, South Sudan, Sri Lanka, Sudan, Suriname, Syrian Arab Republic, Tajikistan, Thailand, Timor-Leste, Togo, Trinidad and Tobago, Tunisia, Turkmenistan, Uganda, United Arab Emirates, United Republic of Tanzania, Uruguay, Uzbekistan, Vanuatu, Venezuela (Bolivarian Republic of), Viet Nam, Yemen, Zambia, Zimbabwe

Against

Albania, Australia, Bulgaria, Canada, Croatia, Czechia, Denmark, Estonia, Finland, France, Georgia, Germany, Iceland, Israel, Japan, Latvia, Lithuania, Luxembourg, Marshall Islands, Micronesia (Federated States of), Monaco, Montenegro, Netherlands, New Zealand, North Macedonia, Norway, Poland, Republic of Korea, Romania, Slovakia, Slovenia, Sweden, Ukraine, United Kingdom, United States

Abstaining

Andorra, Austria, Belgium, Bosnia and Herzegovina, Côte d'Ivoire, Cyprus, Gabon, Greece, Hungary, Ireland, Italy, Liechtenstein, Malta, Portugal, Republic of Moldova, San Marino, Spain, Switzerland, Tonga, Turkey

Fifth preambular paragraph*

In favour

Algeria, Angola, Antigua and Barbuda, Argentina, Armenia, Azerbaijan, Bahamas, Bahrain, Bangladesh, Barbados, Belarus, Belize, Bhutan, Bolivia (Plurinational State of), Botswana, Brazil, Brunei Darussalam, Cabo Verde, Cambodia, Cameroon, Central African Republic, Chad, Chile, China, Colombia, Comoros, Congo, Costa Rica, Côte d'Ivoire, Cuba, Democratic People's Republic of Korea, Djibouti, Dominica, Dominican Republic, Ecuador, Egypt, El Salvador, Equatorial Guinea, Eritrea, Eswatini, Ethiopia, Fiji, Gambia, Ghana, Grenada, Guatemala, Guinea, Guinea-Bissau, Guyana, Honduras, Indonesia, Iran (Islamic Republic of), Iraq, Jamaica, Jordan, Kazakhstan, Kenya, Kuwait, Kyrgyzstan, Lao People's Democratic Republic, Lebanon, Lesotho, Libya, Madagascar, Malawi, Malaysia, Maldives, Mali, Mauritius, Mexico, Mongolia, Morocco, Mozambique, Myanmar, Namibia, Nepal, Nicaragua, Oman, Pakistan, Panama, Papua New Guinea, Paraguay, Peru, Philippines, Qatar, Russian Federation, Rwanda, Saint Kitts and Nevis, Saint Lucia, Saint Vincent and the Grenadines, Samoa, Sao Tome and Principe, Saudi Arabia, Senegal, Seychelles, Singapore, South Africa, South Sudan, Sri Lanka, Sudan, Suriname, Syrian Arab Republic, Tajikistan, Thailand, Timor-Leste, Trinidad and Tobago, Tunisia, Turkmenistan, Uganda, United Arab Emirates, United Republic of Tanzania, Uruguay, Uzbekistan, Vanuatu, Venezuela (Bolivarian Republic of), Viet Nam, Yemen, Zambia, Zimbabwe

Against

Albania, Andorra, Australia, Austria, Belgium, Bulgaria, Canada, Croatia, Cyprus, Czechia, Denmark, Estonia, Finland, France, Georgia, Germany, Greece, Hungary, Iceland, India, Ireland, Israel, Italy, Japan, Latvia, Liechtenstein, Lithuania, Luxembourg, Malta, Marshall Islands, Monaco, Montenegro, Netherlands, New Zealand, North Macedonia, Norway, Poland, Portugal, Republic of Korea, Republic of Moldova, Romania, San Marino, Slovakia, Slovenia, Spain, Sweden, Ukraine, United Kingdom, United States

Abstaining

Bosnia and Herzegovina, Gabon, Haiti, Mauritania, Switzerland, Turkey

---

* Subsequently, the delegation of Gabon informed the Secretariat that it had not intended to participate; the delegation of Togo informed the Secretariat that it had intended to vote in favour.

Ninth preambular paragraph*

In favour

Afghanistan, Algeria, Angola, Antigua and Barbuda, Argentina, Armenia, Azerbaijan, Bahamas, Bahrain, Bangladesh, Barbados, Belarus, Belize, Bhutan, Bolivia (Plurinational State of), Botswana, Brazil, Brunei Darussalam, Burkina Faso, Cabo Verde, Cambodia, Cameroon, Central African Republic, Chad, Chile, China, Colombia, Comoros, Congo, Costa Rica, Côte d'Ivoire, Cuba, Democratic People's Republic of Korea, Djibouti, Dominica, Dominican Republic, Ecuador, Egypt, El Salvador, Equatorial Guinea, Eritrea, Eswatini, Ethiopia, Fiji, Gambia, Ghana, Grenada, Guatemala, Guinea, Guinea-Bissau, Guyana, Haiti, Honduras, India, Indonesia, Iran (Islamic Republic of), Iraq, Jamaica, Jordan, Kazakhstan, Kenya, Kuwait, Kyrgyzstan, Lao People's Democratic Republic, Lebanon, Lesotho, Libya, Madagascar, Malawi, Malaysia, Maldives, Mali, Mauritania, Mauritius, Mexico, Mongolia, Morocco, Mozambique, Myanmar, Namibia, Nepal, Nicaragua, Oman, Pakistan, Panama, Paraguay, Peru, Philippines, Qatar, Russian Federation, Rwanda, Saint Kitts and Nevis, Saint Lucia, Saint Vincent and the Grenadines, Samoa, Sao Tome and Principe, Saudi Arabia, Senegal, Seychelles, Singapore, South Africa, South Sudan, Sri Lanka, Sudan, Suriname, Syrian Arab Republic, Tajikistan, Thailand, Timor-Leste, Trinidad and Tobago, Tunisia, Turkmenistan, Uganda, United Arab Emirates, United Republic of Tanzania, Uruguay, Uzbekistan, Vanuatu, Venezuela (Bolivarian Republic of), Viet Nam, Yemen, Zambia, Zimbabwe

Against

Albania, Andorra, Australia, Austria, Belgium, Bulgaria, Canada, Croatia, Cyprus, Czechia, Denmark, Estonia, Finland, France, Georgia, Germany, Greece, Hungary, Iceland, Ireland, Israel, Italy, Japan, Latvia, Liechtenstein, Lithuania, Luxembourg, Malta, Marshall Islands, Monaco, Montenegro, Netherlands, New Zealand, North Macedonia, Norway, Poland, Portugal, Republic of Korea, Republic of Moldova, Romania, San Marino, Slovakia, Slovenia, Spain, Sweden, Ukraine, United Kingdom, United States

Abstaining

Bosnia and Herzegovina, Gabon, Switzerland, Turkey

---

* Subsequently, the delegation of Gabon informed the Secretariat that it had not intended to participate.

Eleventh preambular paragraph*

In favour
Afghanistan, Algeria, Angola, Antigua and Barbuda, Argentina, Armenia, Azerbaijan, Bahamas, Bahrain, Bangladesh, Barbados, Belarus, Belize, Bhutan, Bolivia (Plurinational State of), Botswana, Brazil, Brunei Darussalam, Burkina Faso, Cabo Verde, Cambodia, Cameroon, Central African Republic, Chad, Chile, China, Colombia, Comoros, Congo, Costa Rica, Côte d'Ivoire, Cuba, Democratic People's Republic of Korea, Djibouti, Dominica, Dominican Republic, Ecuador, Egypt, El Salvador, Equatorial Guinea, Eritrea, Eswatini, Ethiopia, Fiji, Gambia, Ghana, Grenada, Guatemala, Guinea, Guinea-Bissau, Guyana, Haiti, Honduras, India, Indonesia, Iran (Islamic Republic of), Iraq, Jamaica, Jordan, Kazakhstan, Kenya, Kuwait, Kyrgyzstan, Lao People's Democratic Republic, Lebanon, Lesotho, Libya, Madagascar, Malawi, Malaysia, Maldives, Mali, Mauritania, Mauritius, Mexico, Mongolia, Morocco, Mozambique, Myanmar, Namibia, Nepal, Nicaragua, Nigeria, Oman, Pakistan, Panama, Papua New Guinea, Paraguay, Peru, Philippines, Qatar, Russian Federation, Rwanda, Saint Kitts and Nevis, Saint Lucia, Saint Vincent and the Grenadines, Samoa, Sao Tome and Principe, Saudi Arabia, Senegal, Seychelles, Singapore, South Africa, South Sudan, Sri Lanka, Sudan, Suriname, Syrian Arab Republic, Tajikistan, Thailand, Timor-Leste, Trinidad and Tobago, Tunisia, Turkmenistan, Uganda, United Arab Emirates, United Republic of Tanzania, Uruguay, Uzbekistan, Vanuatu, Venezuela (Bolivarian Republic of), Viet Nam, Yemen, Zambia, Zimbabwe

Against
Albania, Australia, Croatia, Czechia, Denmark, Estonia, Finland, France, Georgia, Germany, Iceland, Ireland, Israel, Japan, Latvia, Lithuania, Luxembourg, Marshall Islands, Monaco, Montenegro, Netherlands, North Macedonia, Norway, Poland, Romania, Slovakia, Slovenia, Sweden, Ukraine, United Kingdom, United States

Abstaining
Andorra, Austria, Belgium, Bosnia and Herzegovina, Bulgaria, Canada, Cyprus, Gabon, Greece, Hungary, Italy, Liechtenstein, Malta, New Zealand, Portugal, Republic of Korea, Republic of Moldova, San Marino, Spain, Switzerland, Turkey

Action by the First Committee

Date:	1 November 2021	Meeting:	15th meeting
Vote:	124-35-22	Draft resolution:	A/C.1/76/L.50
	115-50-7, p.p. 5		
	118-48-6, p.p. 9		
	118-33-21, p.p. 11		

---

* Subsequently, the delegation of Gabon informed the Secretariat that it had not intended to participate.

Agenda item 99

76/24 Role of science and technology in the context of international security and disarmament

Text

The General Assembly,

Recognizing that scientific and technological developments can have both civilian and military applications and that progress in science and technology for civilian applications needs to be maintained and encouraged,

Underlining the keen interest of the international community to keep abreast of the latest developments in science and technology of relevance to international security and disarmament and to channel scientific and technological developments for beneficial purposes,

Mindful of the need to regulate the transfer of technologies for peaceful uses, in accordance with relevant international obligations, to address the risk of proliferation by States or non-State actors,

Acknowledging the need to continue the exchange of technologies for peaceful uses, including in accordance with relevant international obligations,

Mindful of the rights of States, reflected in relevant international agreements, regarding the development, production, transfer and use of technologies for peaceful purposes, in accordance with relevant international obligations, as well as the need for all Member States to fulfil their obligations in relation to arms control and disarmament and to prevent proliferation in all its aspects of all weapons of mass destruction and their means of delivery,

Cognizant of the discussions on developments in science and technology at the International Atomic Energy Agency and the Organisation for the Prohibition of Chemical Weapons and within the meetings of experts on science and technology under the 2018–2020 intersessional programme established by the 2017 Meeting of the States Parties to the Convention on the Prohibition of the Development, Production and Stockpiling of Bacteriological (Biological) and Toxin Weapons and on Their Destruction,

Cognizant also of the discussions in the Conference on Disarmament in 2018 under its subsidiary body 5,

Mindful of the discussions in other forums, such as the Committee on the Peaceful Uses of Outer Space, on the long-term sustainability of outer space activities and on the prevention of an arms race in outer space in the United Nations disarmament machinery,

Noting the discussions on various dimensions of emerging technologies under the framework of the Convention on Prohibitions or Restrictions on the Use of Certain Conventional Weapons Which May Be Deemed to Be

Excessively Injurious or to Have Indiscriminate Effects,[1] and recalling the discussions and progress made by the Group of Governmental Experts on lethal autonomous weapons systems during its sessions held from 2018 to 2021,

Noting also the discussions within the United Nations and the specialized agencies on developments in the field of information and communications technologies, including in the context of international security,

Acknowledging that the accelerating pace of technological change necessitates a system-wide assessment of the potential impact of developments in science and technology on international security and disarmament, with due regard to avoiding duplication and complementing efforts already under way in United Nations entities and in the framework of the relevant international conventions,

Noting the discussions on current developments in science and technology and their potential impact on international security and disarmament efforts in the Advisory Board on Disarmament Matters,

1. *Invites* Member States to continue efforts to apply developments in science and technology for disarmament-related purposes, including the verification of disarmament, arms control and non-proliferation instruments, and to make disarmament-related technologies available to interested States;

2. *Calls upon* Member States to remain vigilant in understanding new and emerging developments in science and technology that could imperil international security, and underlines the importance of Member States engaging with experts from industry, the research community and civil society in addressing this challenge;

3. *Takes note* of the updated report of the Secretary-General on current developments in science and technology and their potential impact on international security and disarmament efforts;[2]

4. *Requests* the Secretary-General to submit to the General Assembly at its seventy-seventh session an updated report on the matter;

5. *Encourages* the Advisory Board on Disarmament Matters to continue its discussions on current developments in science and technology and their potential impact on international security and disarmament efforts;

6. *Encourages* Member States to organize events such as conferences, seminars, workshops and exhibitions, at the national, regional and international levels, on the role of science and technology in the context of international security and disarmament, in order to facilitate multilateral dialogue, as well as dialogue among relevant stakeholders, on current developments in science

---

[1] United Nations, *Treaty Series*, vol. 1342, No. 22495.
[2] A/76/182.

and technology and their potential impact on international security and disarmament efforts;

7. *Decides* to include in the provisional agenda of its seventy-seventh session the item entitled "Role of science and technology in the context of international security and disarmament".

Action by the General Assembly

Date: 6 December 2021	Meeting: 45th plenary meeting
Vote: Adopted without a vote	Report: A/76/443

Sponsors

Australia, Austria, Bangladesh, Bhutan, Brazil, Croatia, Equatorial Guinea, Eswatini, Finland, Germany, **India**, Israel, Italy, Kiribati, Netherlands, Nicaragua, Norway, Portugal, Republic of Moldova, Spain, Sweden, Vanuatu

Co-sponsors

Afghanistan, Bolivia (Plurinational State of), Ethiopia, Hungary, Japan, Kazakhstan, Kenya, Kyrgyzstan, Maldives, Malta, Mauritius, Montenegro, North Macedonia, Paraguay, Republic of Korea, Singapore, Slovenia, Switzerland, Zambia

Action by the First Committee

Date: 3 November 2021	Meeting: 17th meeting
Vote: Adopted without a vote	Draft resolution: A/C.1/76/L.6

Agenda item 100 (ee)

76/25   Ethical imperatives for a nuclear-weapon-free world

Text

The General Assembly,

Recalling its resolution 75/73 of 7 December 2020, adopted on the occasion of the seventy-fifth anniversary of the United Nations, which was established to save succeeding generations from the untold suffering of the scourge of war, and its resolution 74/47 of 12 December 2019,

Recalling also that the United Nations emerged at the time of the immense trail of death and destruction resulting from the Second World War, over 75 years ago,

Recalling further the noble principles of the Charter of the United Nations, which enjoin the international community, individually and collectively, to spare no effort in promoting the ethical imperative of "in larger freedom", so that all peoples may enjoy freedom from want, freedom from fear and the freedom to live in dignity,

Convinced that, given the catastrophic humanitarian consequences and risks associated with a nuclear weapon detonation, Member States have long envisaged nuclear disarmament and nuclear non-proliferation as urgent and interlinked ethical imperatives in achieving the objectives of the Charter, which is reflected in the first resolution, resolution 1 (I), adopted by the General Assembly on 24 January 1946, aimed at the elimination from national armaments of atomic weapons and of all other major weapons adaptable to mass destruction,

Acknowledging, in this connection, the ethical imperatives outlined in the provisions of its resolutions and reports and those of other related international initiatives on the catastrophic humanitarian consequences and risks posed by a nuclear weapon detonation, including the declaration that the use of nuclear weapons would cause indiscriminate suffering and as such is a violation of the Charter and the laws of humanity and international law,[1] the condemnation of nuclear war as contrary to human conscience and a violation of the fundamental right to life,[2] the threat to the very survival of humankind posed by the existence of nuclear weapons,[3] the detrimental environmental effects of the use of nuclear weapons,[4] and the disquiet that was expressed

---

[1] See resolution 1653 (XVI).
[2] See resolution 38/75.
[3] See resolution S-10/2.
[4] See resolution 50/70 M.

at the continued spending on the development and maintenance of nuclear arsenals,[5]

Acknowledging also the preamble to and article VI of the Treaty on the Non-Proliferation of Nuclear Weapons[6] and the advisory opinion of the International Court of Justice on the legality of the threat or use of nuclear weapons,[7] in which the Court unanimously concluded that there exists an obligation to pursue in good faith and bring to a conclusion negotiations leading to nuclear disarmament in all its aspects under strict and effective international control,

Acknowledging further the United Nations Millennium Declaration,[8] in which Heads of State and Government resolved to strive for the elimination of weapons of mass destruction, particularly nuclear weapons, and to keep all options open for achieving that aim, including the possibility of convening an international conference to identify ways of eliminating nuclear dangers,

Concerned that, despite the long-standing recognition that it has accorded to these ethical imperatives and while much effort has been directed to addressing nuclear non-proliferation, limited progress has been made in meeting the nuclear disarmament obligations required to achieve and maintain the nuclear-weapon-free world that the international community demands,

Disappointed at the continued absence of progress towards multilateral negotiations on nuclear disarmament in the Conference on Disarmament, despite unrelenting efforts of Member States towards this end,

Noting with satisfaction the increasing awareness, renewed attention and growing momentum that has been generated by Member States and the international community since 2010 regarding the catastrophic humanitarian consequences and risks associated with nuclear weapons, which underpin the ethical imperatives for nuclear disarmament and the urgency of achieving and maintaining a nuclear-weapon-free world, together with all related international initiatives,

Recalling the adoption on 7 July 2017 of the Treaty on the Prohibition of Nuclear Weapons,[9] in which the ethical imperatives for nuclear disarmament are acknowledged, and welcoming its entry into force on 22 January 2021,

Conscious of the absolute validity of multilateral diplomacy in relation to nuclear disarmament, and determined to promote multilateralism as essential to nuclear disarmament negotiations,

---

[5] See A/59/119.
[6] United Nations, *Treaty Series*, vol. 729, No. 10485.
[7] A/51/218, annex.
[8] Resolution 55/2.
[9] A/CONF.229/2017/8.

1.   *Calls upon* all States to acknowledge the catastrophic humanitarian consequences and risks posed by a nuclear weapon detonation, whether by accident, miscalculation or design;

2.   *Acknowledges* the ethical imperatives for nuclear disarmament and the urgency of achieving and maintaining a nuclear-weapon-free world, which is a "global public good of the highest order", serving both national and collective security interests;

3.   *Declares* that:

(a)   The global threat posed by nuclear weapons must urgently be eliminated;

(b)   Discussions, decisions and actions on nuclear weapons must focus on the effects of these weapons on human beings and the environment and must be guided by the unspeakable suffering and unacceptable harm that they cause;

(c)   Greater attention must be given to the impact of a nuclear weapon detonation on women and the importance of their participation in discussions, decisions and actions on nuclear weapons;

(d)   Nuclear weapons serve to undermine collective security, heighten the risk of nuclear catastrophe, aggravate international tension and make conflict more dangerous;

(e)   Arguments in favour of the retention of nuclear weapons have a negative impact on the credibility of the nuclear disarmament and non-proliferation regime;

(f)   The long-term plans for the modernization of nuclear weapons arsenals run contrary to commitments and obligations to nuclear disarmament and engender perceptions of the indefinite possession of these weapons;

(g)   In a world where basic human needs have not yet been met, the vast resources allocated to the modernization of nuclear weapons arsenals could instead be redirected to meeting the Sustainable Development Goals;[10]

(h)   Given the humanitarian impact of nuclear weapons, it is inconceivable that any use of nuclear weapons, irrespective of the cause, would be compatible with the requirements of international humanitarian law or international law, or the laws of morality, or the dictates of public conscience;

(i)   Given their indiscriminate nature and potential to annihilate humanity, nuclear weapons are inherently immoral;

4.   *Notes* that all responsible States have a solemn duty to take decisions that serve to protect their people and each other from the ravages

---

[10]   See resolution 70/1.

of a nuclear weapon detonation, and that the only way for States to do so is through the total elimination of nuclear weapons;

5. *Stresses* that all States share an ethical responsibility to act with urgency and determination, with the support of all relevant stakeholders, to take the effective measures, including legally binding measures, necessary to eliminate and prohibit all nuclear weapons, given their catastrophic humanitarian consequences and associated risks;

6. *Decides* to include in the provisional agenda of its seventy-seventh session, under the item entitled "General and complete disarmament", the sub-item entitled "Ethical imperatives for a nuclear-weapon-free world".

Action by the General Assembly

Date: 6 December 2021   Meeting: 45th plenary meeting
Vote: 135-37-14   Report: A/76/444
       120-37-16, p.p. 11

Sponsors

Algeria, Austria, Chile, Costa Rica, Democratic Republic of the Congo, Egypt, Equatorial Guinea, Eswatini, Ireland, Lesotho, Mexico, Mozambique, Nicaragua, Nigeria, Philippines, **South Africa**, Thailand, Viet Nam, Zimbabwe

Co-sponsors

Brazil, Dominican Republic, Ecuador, Ghana, Guatemala, Guinea-Bissau, Namibia, Palau, Peru, Turkmenistan, Uruguay

Recorded vote

As a whole

In favour

Afghanistan, Algeria, Andorra, Angola, Antigua and Barbuda, Argentina, Austria, Azerbaijan, Bahamas, Bahrain, Bangladesh, Barbados, Belarus, Belize, Bhutan, Bolivia (Plurinational State of), Botswana, Brazil, Brunei Darussalam, Burkina Faso, Burundi, Cabo Verde, Cambodia, Chad, Chile, Colombia, Comoros, Congo, Costa Rica, Côte d'Ivoire, Cuba, Djibouti, Dominica, Dominican Republic, Ecuador, Egypt, El Salvador, Equatorial Guinea, Eritrea, Eswatini, Ethiopia, Fiji, Gabon, Gambia, Ghana, Grenada, Guatemala, Guinea, Guinea-Bissau, Guyana, Honduras, Indonesia, Iran (Islamic Republic of), Iraq, Ireland, Jamaica, Jordan, Kazakhstan, Kenya, Kiribati, Kuwait, Kyrgyzstan, Lao People's Democratic Republic, Lebanon, Lesotho, Libya, Liechtenstein, Madagascar, Malawi, Malaysia, Maldives, Mali, Malta, Marshall Islands, Mauritania, Mauritius, Mexico, Mongolia, Morocco, Mozambique, Myanmar, Namibia, Nauru, Nepal, New Zealand,

Nicaragua, Niger, Nigeria, Oman, Palau, Panama, Papua New Guinea, Paraguay, Peru, Philippines, Qatar, Republic of Moldova, Rwanda, Saint Kitts and Nevis, Saint Lucia, Saint Vincent and the Grenadines, Samoa, San Marino, Sao Tome and Principe, Saudi Arabia, Senegal, Seychelles, Sierra Leone, Singapore, South Africa, South Sudan, Sri Lanka, Sudan, Suriname, Syrian Arab Republic, Tajikistan, Thailand, Timor-Leste, Togo, Tonga, Trinidad and Tobago, Tunisia, Turkmenistan, Tuvalu, Uganda, United Arab Emirates, United Republic of Tanzania, Uruguay, Uzbekistan, Vanuatu, Venezuela (Bolivarian Republic of), Viet Nam, Yemen, Zambia, Zimbabwe

Against

Albania, Australia, Belgium, Bulgaria, Canada, Croatia, Czechia, Denmark, Estonia, Finland, France, Germany, Greece, Hungary, Iceland, Israel, Italy, Latvia, Lithuania, Luxembourg, Monaco, Montenegro, Netherlands, North Macedonia, Norway, Poland, Portugal, Republic of Korea, Romania, Russian Federation, Slovakia, Slovenia, Spain, Turkey, Ukraine, United Kingdom, United States

Abstaining

Armenia, Bosnia and Herzegovina, Cameroon, China, Cyprus, Democratic People's Republic of Korea, Georgia, Haiti, India, Japan, Pakistan, Serbia, Sweden, Switzerland

Eleventh preambular paragraph*

In favour

Afghanistan, Algeria, Andorra, Angola, Antigua and Barbuda, Argentina, Austria, Azerbaijan, Bahamas, Bahrain, Bangladesh, Barbados, Belize, Bhutan, Bolivia (Plurinational State of), Botswana, Brazil, Brunei Darussalam, Burkina Faso, Burundi, Cabo Verde, Cambodia, Chad, Chile, Colombia, Comoros, Costa Rica, Côte d'Ivoire, Cuba, Cyprus, Djibouti, Dominica, Dominican Republic, Ecuador, Egypt, El Salvador, Eritrea, Ethiopia, Fiji, Gambia, Ghana, Grenada, Guatemala, Guinea, Guinea-Bissau, Guyana, Honduras, Indonesia, Iran (Islamic Republic of), Iraq, Ireland, Jamaica, Jordan, Kazakhstan, Kenya, Kiribati, Kuwait, Lao People's Democratic Republic, Lebanon, Lesotho, Liberia, Libya, Liechtenstein, Madagascar, Malawi, Malaysia, Maldives, Mali, Malta, Mauritania, Mauritius, Mexico, Mongolia, Morocco, Mozambique, Myanmar, Namibia, Nepal, New Zealand, Nicaragua, Niger, Nigeria, Oman, Panama, Papua New Guinea, Paraguay, Peru, Philippines, Qatar, Republic of Moldova, Rwanda, Saint Lucia, Saint Vincent and the Grenadines, Samoa, San Marino, Sao Tome and Principe, Senegal, Seychelles, Singapore, South Africa, South Sudan, Sri Lanka, Sudan,

---

* Subsequently, the delegation of Gabon informed the Secretariat that it had not intended to participate.

Suriname, Thailand, Timor-Leste, Togo, Trinidad and Tobago, Tunisia, Turkmenistan, Uganda, United Arab Emirates, United Republic of Tanzania, Uruguay, Vanuatu, Venezuela (Bolivarian Republic of), Viet Nam, Yemen, Zambia, Zimbabwe

Against

Albania, Australia, Belgium, Bosnia and Herzegovina, Bulgaria, Canada, China, Croatia, Czechia, Denmark, Estonia, France, Germany, Greece, Hungary, Iceland, Israel, Italy, Latvia, Lithuania, Luxembourg, Monaco, Montenegro, North Macedonia, Norway, Poland, Portugal, Republic of Korea, Romania, Russian Federation, Slovakia, Slovenia, Spain, Turkey, Ukraine, United Kingdom, United States

Abstaining

Armenia, Belarus, Cameroon, Finland, Gabon, Georgia, Haiti, India, Japan, Marshall Islands, Netherlands, Pakistan, Saudi Arabia, Serbia, Sweden, Switzerland

Action by the First Committee

Date: 27 October 2021	Meeting: 13th meeting
Vote: 129-37-17	Draft resolution: A/C.1/76/L.4
113-36-20, p.p. 11	

Agenda item 100 (m)

76/26 Implementation of the Convention on the Prohibition of the Use, Stockpiling, Production and Transfer of Anti-Personnel Mines and on Their Destruction

Text

The General Assembly,

Recalling its resolutions 54/54 B of 1 December 1999, 55/33 V of 20 November 2000, 56/24 M of 29 November 2001, 57/74 of 22 November 2002, 58/53 of 8 December 2003, 59/84 of 3 December 2004, 60/80 of 8 December 2005, 61/84 of 6 December 2006, 62/41 of 5 December 2007, 63/42 of 2 December 2008, 64/56 of 2 December 2009, 65/48 of 8 December 2010, 66/29 of 2 December 2011, 67/32 of 3 December 2012, 68/30 of 5 December 2013, 69/34 of 2 December 2014, 70/55 of 7 December 2015, 71/34 of 5 December 2016, 72/53 of 4 December 2017, 73/61 of 5 December 2018, 74/61 of 12 December 2019 and 75/52 of 7 December 2020,

Reaffirming its determination to put an end to the suffering and casualties caused by anti-personnel mines, which kill or injure thousands of people – women, girls, boys and men – every year, and which place people living in affected areas at risk and hinder the development of their communities,

Believing it necessary to do the utmost to contribute in an efficient and coordinated manner to facing the challenge of removing anti-personnel mines placed throughout the world and to assure their destruction,

Wishing to do the utmost to ensure assistance for the care and rehabilitation, including the social and economic reintegration, of mine victims,

Noting with satisfaction the work undertaken to implement the Convention on the Prohibition of the Use, Stockpiling, Production and Transfer of Anti-Personnel Mines and on Their Destruction[1] and the substantial progress made towards addressing the global anti-personnel landmine problem,

Recalling the first to eighteenth meetings of the States parties to the Convention, held in Maputo (1999), Geneva (2000), Managua (2001), Geneva (2002), Bangkok (2003), Zagreb (2005), Geneva (2006), the Dead Sea (2007), Geneva (2008 and 2010), Phnom Penh (2011), Geneva (2012, 2013 and 2015), Santiago (2016), Vienna (2017) and Geneva (2018 and 2020), and the First, Second, Third and Fourth Review Conferences of the States Parties to

---

[1] United Nations, *Treaty Series*, vol. 2056, No. 35597.

the Convention, held in Nairobi (2004), Cartagena, Colombia (2009), Maputo (2014) and Oslo (2019),

Recalling also that, at the Fourth Review Conference of the States Parties to the Convention, the international community reviewed the implementation of the Convention and the States parties adopted a declaration and an action plan for the period 2020–2024 to support the enhanced implementation and promotion of the Convention,

Underlining the importance of cooperation and assistance in the implementation of the Convention, including through the so-called individualized approach, which offers mine-affected countries a platform for presenting their challenges,

Stressing the need to take into account gender aspects in mine action,

Noting with satisfaction that 164 States have ratified or acceded to the Convention and have formally accepted the obligations of the Convention,

Emphasizing the desirability of attracting the adherence of all States to the Convention, and determined to work strenuously towards the promotion of its universalization and norms,

Noting with regret that anti-personnel mines continue to be used in some conflicts around the world, causing human suffering and impeding post-conflict development,

1.	*Invites* all States that have not signed the Convention on the Prohibition of the Use, Stockpiling, Production and Transfer of Anti-Personnel Mines and on Their Destruction to accede to it without delay;

2.	*Urges* the one remaining State that has signed but has not ratified the Convention to ratify it without delay;

3.	*Stresses* the importance of the full and effective implementation of and compliance with the Convention, including through the continued implementation of the action plans under the Convention;

4.	*Expresses strong concern* regarding the use of anti-personnel mines in various parts of the world, including use highlighted in recent allegations, reports and documented evidence;

5.	*Urges* all States parties to provide the Secretary-General with complete and timely information as required under article 7 of the Convention in order to promote transparency and compliance with the Convention;

6.	*Invites* all States that have not ratified the Convention or acceded to it to provide, on a voluntary basis, information to make global mine action efforts more effective;

7.	*Renews its call upon* all States and other relevant parties to work together to promote, support and advance the care, rehabilitation and social and economic reintegration of mine victims, mine risk education and reduction programmes and the removal and destruction of anti-personnel mines placed or stockpiled throughout the world;

8.   *Urges* all States to remain seized of the issue at the highest political level and, where in a position to do so, to promote adherence to the Convention through bilateral, subregional, regional and multilateral contacts, outreach, seminars and other means;

9.   *Invites and encourages* all interested States, the United Nations, other relevant international organizations or institutions, regional organizations, the International Committee of the Red Cross and relevant non-governmental organizations to attend the Nineteenth Meeting of the States Parties to the Convention, to be held in The Hague from 15 to 19 November 2021, and to participate in the future programme of meetings of the States parties to the Convention;

10.   *Requests* the Secretary-General, in accordance with article 12, paragraph 1, of the Convention, to undertake the preparations necessary to convene the Twentieth Meeting of the States Parties to the Convention and, on behalf of the States parties and in accordance with article 12, paragraph 3, of the Convention, to invite States not parties to the Convention, as well as the United Nations, other relevant international organizations or institutions, regional organizations, the International Committee of the Red Cross and relevant non-governmental organizations, to attend the Twentieth Meeting of the States Parties as observers;

11.   *Calls upon* States parties and States participating in meetings to address issues arising from outstanding dues and to proceed promptly with the payment of their share of the estimated costs;

12.   *Decides* to include in the provisional agenda of its seventy-seventh session, under the item entitled "General and complete disarmament", the sub-item entitled "Implementation of the Convention on the Prohibition of the Use, Stockpiling, Production and Transfer of Anti-Personnel Mines and on Their Destruction".

Action by the General Assembly

Date: 6 December 2021	Meeting: 45th plenary meeting
Vote: 169-0-19	Report: A/76/444

Sponsors

Netherlands, Sudan

Recorded vote

In favour

Afghanistan, Albania, Algeria, Andorra, Angola, Argentina, Armenia, Australia, Austria, Azerbaijan, Bahamas, Bahrain, Bangladesh, Barbados,

Belarus, Belgium, Belize, Bhutan, Bolivia (Plurinational State of), Bosnia and Herzegovina, Botswana, Brazil, Brunei Darussalam, Bulgaria, Burkina Faso, Burundi, Cabo Verde, Cambodia, Cameroon, Canada, Central African Republic, Chad, Chile, China, Colombia, Comoros, Congo, Costa Rica, Côte d'Ivoire, Croatia, Cyprus, Czechia, Denmark, Djibouti, Dominica, Dominican Republic, Ecuador, El Salvador, Equatorial Guinea, Eritrea, Estonia, Eswatini, Ethiopia, Fiji, Finland, France, Gabon, Gambia, Georgia, Germany, Ghana, Greece, Grenada, Guatemala, Guinea, Guinea-Bissau, Guyana, Haiti, Honduras, Hungary, Iceland, Indonesia, Iraq, Ireland, Italy, Jamaica, Japan, Jordan, Kazakhstan, Kenya, Kiribati, Kuwait, Kyrgyzstan, Lao People's Democratic Republic, Latvia, Lebanon, Lesotho, Liberia, Libya, Liechtenstein, Lithuania, Luxembourg, Madagascar, Malawi, Malaysia, Maldives, Mali, Malta, Marshall Islands, Mauritania, Mauritius, Mexico, Micronesia (Federated States of), Monaco, Mongolia, Montenegro, Morocco, Mozambique, Namibia, Nauru, Netherlands, New Zealand, Nicaragua, Niger, Nigeria, North Macedonia, Norway, Oman, Palau, Panama, Papua New Guinea, Paraguay, Peru, Philippines, Poland, Portugal, Qatar, Republic of Moldova, Romania, Rwanda, Saint Kitts and Nevis, Saint Lucia, Saint Vincent and the Grenadines, Samoa, San Marino, Sao Tome and Principe, Senegal, Seychelles, Sierra Leone, Singapore, Slovakia, Slovenia, South Africa, South Sudan, Spain, Sri Lanka, Sudan, Suriname, Sweden, Switzerland, Tajikistan, Thailand, Timor-Leste, Togo, Tonga, Trinidad and Tobago, Tunisia, Turkey, Turkmenistan, Tuvalu, Uganda, Ukraine, United Arab Emirates, United Kingdom, United Republic of Tanzania, Uruguay, Vanuatu, Venezuela (Bolivarian Republic of), Yemen

Against

None

Abstaining

Cuba, Democratic People's Republic of Korea, Egypt, India, Iran (Islamic Republic of), Israel, Myanmar, Nepal, Pakistan, Republic of Korea, Russian Federation, Saudi Arabia, Serbia, Syrian Arab Republic, United States, Uzbekistan, Viet Nam, Zambia, Zimbabwe

Action by the First Committee

Date: 2 November 2021   Meeting: 16th meeting
Vote: 162-0-20   Draft resolution: A/C.1/76/L.5

Agenda item 100 (o)

76/27   Reducing nuclear danger

Text

The General Assembly,

Bearing in mind that the use of nuclear weapons poses the most serious threat to humankind and to the survival of civilization,

Reaffirming that any use or threat of use of nuclear weapons would constitute a violation of the Charter of the United Nations,

Convinced that the proliferation of nuclear weapons in all its aspects would seriously enhance the danger of nuclear war,

Convinced also that nuclear disarmament and the complete elimination of nuclear weapons are essential to remove the danger of nuclear war,

Considering that, until nuclear weapons cease to exist, it is imperative on the part of the nuclear-weapon States to adopt measures that assure non-nuclear-weapon States against the use or threat of use of nuclear weapons,

Considering also that the hair-trigger alert of nuclear weapons carries unacceptable risks of unintentional or accidental use of nuclear weapons, which would have catastrophic consequences for all humankind,

Emphasizing the need to adopt measures to avoid accidental, unauthorized or unexplained incidents arising from computer anomalies or other technical malfunctions,

Conscious that limited steps relating to de-alerting and de-targeting have been taken by the nuclear-weapon States and that further practical, realistic and mutually reinforcing steps are necessary to contribute to the improvement in the international climate for negotiations leading to the elimination of nuclear weapons,

Mindful that a diminishing role for nuclear weapons in the security policies of nuclear-weapon States would have a positive impact on international peace and security and improve the conditions for the further reduction and the elimination of nuclear weapons,

Reiterating the highest priority accorded to nuclear disarmament in the Final Document of the Tenth Special Session of the General Assembly[1] and by the international community,

Recalling the advisory opinion of the International Court of Justice on the legality of the threat or use of nuclear weapons[2] that there exists an obligation for all States to pursue in good faith and bring to a conclusion

---

[1] Resolution S-10/2.
[2] A/51/218, annex.

negotiations leading to nuclear disarmament in all its aspects under strict and effective international control,

Recalling also the call, in the United Nations Millennium Declaration,[3] to seek to eliminate the dangers posed by weapons of mass destruction and the resolve to strive for the elimination of weapons of mass destruction, particularly nuclear weapons, including the possibility of convening an international conference to identify ways of eliminating nuclear dangers,

1.   *Calls for* a review of nuclear doctrines and, in this context, immediate and urgent steps to reduce the risks of unintentional and accidental use of nuclear weapons, including through de-alerting and de-targeting nuclear weapons;

2.   *Requests* the five nuclear-weapon States to take measures towards the implementation of paragraph 1 above;

3.   *Calls upon* Member States to take the measures necessary to prevent the proliferation of nuclear weapons in all its aspects and to promote nuclear disarmament, with the objective of eliminating nuclear weapons;

4.   *Takes note* of the report of the Secretary-General submitted pursuant to paragraph 5 of its resolution 75/57 of 7 December 2020;[4]

5.   *Requests* the Secretary-General to intensify efforts and support initiatives that would contribute to the full implementation of the seven recommendations identified in the report of the Advisory Board on Disarmament Matters that would significantly reduce the risk of nuclear war,[5] and also to continue to encourage Member States to consider the convening of an international conference, as proposed in the United Nations Millennium Declaration, to identify ways of eliminating nuclear dangers, and to report thereon to the General Assembly at its seventy-seventh session;

6.   *Decides* to include in the provisional agenda of its seventy-seventh session, under the item entitled "General and complete disarmament", the sub-item entitled "Reducing nuclear danger".

Action by the General Assembly

Date: 6 December 2021   Meeting: 45th plenary meeting
Vote: 125-50-14   Report: A/76/444

Sponsors

Bangladesh, Bhutan, Cuba, **India**, Nepal, Nicaragua, Vanuatu, Viet Nam

Co-sponsors

Afghanistan, Indonesia, Kazakhstan, Kiribati, Malaysia, Maldives, Mauritius, Myanmar, Palau, Sri Lanka, Venezuela (Bolivarian Republic of), Zambia

---

[3] Resolution 55/2.
[4] A/76/117.
[5] A/56/400, para. 3.

Recorded vote

In favour
> Afghanistan, Algeria, Angola, Antigua and Barbuda, Azerbaijan, Bahamas, Bahrain, Bangladesh, Barbados, Belize, Bhutan, Bolivia (Plurinational State of), Botswana, Brazil, Brunei Darussalam, Burkina Faso, Burundi, Cabo Verde, Cambodia, Cameroon, Central African Republic, Chad, Chile, Colombia, Comoros, Congo, Costa Rica, Côte d'Ivoire, Cuba, Djibouti, Dominica, Dominican Republic, Ecuador, Egypt, El Salvador, Equatorial Guinea, Eritrea, Eswatini, Ethiopia, Fiji, Gabon, Gambia, Ghana, Grenada, Guatemala, Guinea, Guinea-Bissau, Guyana, Honduras, India, Indonesia, Iran (Islamic Republic of), Iraq, Jamaica, Jordan, Kazakhstan, Kenya, Kiribati, Kuwait, Kyrgyzstan, Lao People's Democratic Republic, Lebanon, Lesotho, Libya, Madagascar, Malaysia, Maldives, Mali, Mauritania, Mauritius, Mexico, Mongolia, Morocco, Mozambique, Myanmar, Namibia, Nauru, Nepal, Nicaragua, Niger, Nigeria, Oman, Palau, Panama, Papua New Guinea, Paraguay, Peru, Philippines, Qatar, Rwanda, Saint Kitts and Nevis, Saint Lucia, Saint Vincent and the Grenadines, Samoa, Sao Tome and Principe, Saudi Arabia, Senegal, Seychelles, Sierra Leone, Singapore, Solomon Islands, South Africa, South Sudan, Sri Lanka, Sudan, Suriname, Syrian Arab Republic, Tajikistan, Thailand, Timor-Leste, Togo, Tonga, Trinidad and Tobago, Tunisia, Turkmenistan, Tuvalu, Uganda, United Arab Emirates, United Republic of Tanzania, Uruguay, Uzbekistan, Vanuatu, Venezuela (Bolivarian Republic of), Viet Nam, Yemen

Against
> Albania, Andorra, Australia, Austria, Belgium, Bosnia and Herzegovina, Bulgaria, Canada, Croatia, Cyprus, Czechia, Denmark, Estonia, Finland, France, Germany, Greece, Hungary, Iceland, Ireland, Israel, Italy, Latvia, Liechtenstein, Lithuania, Luxembourg, Malta, Marshall Islands, Micronesia (Federated States of), Monaco, Montenegro, Netherlands, New Zealand, North Macedonia, Norway, Poland, Portugal, Republic of Korea, Republic of Moldova, Romania, San Marino, Slovakia, Slovenia, Spain, Sweden, Switzerland, Turkey, Ukraine, United Kingdom, United States

Abstaining
> Argentina, Armenia, Belarus, China, Democratic People's Republic of Korea, Georgia, Haiti, Japan, Malawi, Pakistan, Russian Federation, Serbia, Zambia, Zimbabwe

Action by the First Committee

Date:	27 October 2021	Meeting:	13th meeting
Vote:	120-50-13	Draft resolution:	A/C.1/76/L.7

Agenda item 100 (s)

76/28   Measures to prevent terrorists from acquiring weapons of mass destruction

Text

The General Assembly,

Recalling its resolution 75/58 of 7 December 2020,

Recognizing the determination of the international community to combat terrorism, as evidenced in relevant General Assembly and Security Council resolutions,

Deeply concerned by the growing risk of linkages between terrorism and weapons of mass destruction, and in particular by the fact that terrorists may seek to acquire weapons of mass destruction,

Cognizant of the steps taken by States to implement Security Council resolution 1540 (2004) of 28 April 2004 on the non-proliferation of weapons of mass destruction,

Recalling Security Council resolution 2325 (2016) of 15 December 2016 on the non-proliferation of weapons of mass destruction,

Recalling also the entry into force on 7 July 2007 of the International Convention for the Suppression of Acts of Nuclear Terrorism,[1]

Recalling further the adoption, by consensus, of amendments to strengthen the Convention on the Physical Protection of Nuclear Material[2] by the International Atomic Energy Agency on 8 July 2005, and their entry into force on 8 May 2016,

Recalling the support expressed in the Final Document of the Eighteenth Summit of Heads of State or Government of Non-Aligned Countries, held in Baku on 25 and 26 October 2019,[3] for measures to prevent terrorists from acquiring weapons of mass destruction,

Recalling also that the Group of Eight, the European Union, the Regional Forum of the Association of Southeast Asian Nations and others have taken into account in their deliberations the dangers posed by the likely acquisition by terrorists of weapons of mass destruction and the need for international cooperation in combating it, and that the Global Initiative to Combat Nuclear Terrorism has been launched jointly by the Russian Federation and the United States of America,

---

[1] United Nations, *Treaty Series*, vol. 2445, No. 44004.
[2] Ibid., vol. 1456, No. 24631.
[3] See A/74/548, annex.

Recalling further the holding of the Nuclear Security Summit on 12 and 13 April 2010 in Washington, D.C., on 26 and 27 March 2012 in Seoul, on 24 and 25 March 2014 in The Hague and on 31 March and 1 April 2016 in Washington, D.C.,

Recalling the holding of the high-level meeting on countering nuclear terrorism, with a focus on strengthening the legal framework, in New York on 28 September 2012,

Acknowledging the consideration of issues relating to terrorism and weapons of mass destruction by the Advisory Board on Disarmament Matters,[4]

Taking note of the holding by the International Atomic Energy Agency of the third International Conference on Nuclear Security: Sustaining and Strengthening Efforts, in Vienna in February 2020, the second International Conference on Nuclear Security: Commitments and Actions, in Vienna in December 2016, and the first International Conference on Nuclear Security: Enhancing Global Efforts, in Vienna in July 2013, and the relevant resolutions adopted by the General Conference of the Agency at its sixty-fifth regular session,

Recalling the Code of Conduct on the Safety and Security of Radioactive Sources, approved by the Board of Governors of the International Atomic Energy Agency on 8 September 2003, and the supplementary Guidance on the Management of Disused Radioactive Sources, approved by the Board of Governors of the Agency on 11 September 2017,

Recalling also the 2005 World Summit Outcome adopted at the high-level plenary meeting of the General Assembly on 16 September 2005[5] and the adoption of the United Nations Global Counter-Terrorism Strategy on 8 September 2006,[6]

Taking note of the report of the Secretary-General submitted pursuant to paragraph 5 of resolution 75/58,[7]

Mindful of the urgent need for addressing, within the United Nations framework and through international cooperation, this threat to humanity,

Emphasizing that progress is urgently needed in the area of disarmament and non-proliferation in order to maintain international peace and security and to contribute to global efforts against terrorism,

1.   *Calls upon* all Member States to support international efforts to prevent terrorists from acquiring weapons of mass destruction and their means of delivery;

---

[4] See A/59/361.
[5] Resolution 60/1.
[6] Resolution 60/288.
[7] A/76/189.

2.   *Appeals* to all Member States to consider early accession to and ratification of the International Convention for the Suppression of Acts of Nuclear Terrorism, and encourages States parties to the Convention to review its implementation;

3.   *Urges* all Member States to take and strengthen national measures, as appropriate, to prevent terrorists from acquiring weapons of mass destruction, their means of delivery and materials and technologies related to their manufacture;

4.   *Encourages* cooperation among and between Member States and relevant regional and international organizations for strengthening national capacities in this regard;

5.   *Requests* the Secretary-General to compile a report on measures already taken by international organizations on issues relating to the linkage between the fight against terrorism and the proliferation of weapons of mass destruction and to seek the views of Member States on additional relevant measures, including national measures, for tackling the global threat posed by the acquisition by terrorists of weapons of mass destruction and to report to the General Assembly at its seventy-seventh session;

6.   *Decides* to include in the provisional agenda of its seventy-seventh session, under the item entitled "General and complete disarmament", the sub-item entitled "Measures to prevent terrorists from acquiring weapons of mass destruction".

Action by the General Assembly

Date: 6 December 2021   Meeting: 45th plenary meeting
Vote: Adopted without a vote   Report: A/76/444

Sponsors

Armenia, Australia, Austria, Bangladesh, Belgium, Bhutan, Bosnia and Herzegovina, Bulgaria, Chile, Costa Rica, Croatia, Czechia, Democratic Republic of the Congo, Denmark, Estonia, Finland, Georgia, Germany, Greece, Hungary, **India**, Iraq, Ireland, Italy, Latvia, Lithuania, Luxembourg, Malta, Mauritius, Mongolia, Nepal, Netherlands, New Zealand, Norway, Philippines, Poland, Portugal, Republic of Moldova, San Marino, Slovakia, Spain, Sweden, Turkey, United States, Vanuatu

Co-sponsors

Afghanistan, Albania, Angola, Argentina, Azerbaijan, Burkina Faso, Cyprus, Eritrea, France, Ghana, Guatemala, Guinea-Bissau, Guyana, Haiti, Honduras, Jamaica, Kazakhstan, Kenya, Kiribati, Kyrgyzstan, Liechtenstein, Madagascar, Maldives, Monaco, Montenegro, Morocco, Mozambique, Myanmar, Nicaragua, Nigeria, North Macedonia, Palau, Papua New Guinea, Paraguay, Republic of Korea, Romania, Samoa,

Senegal, Serbia, Singapore, Slovenia, Somalia, Sri Lanka, Thailand, Tunisia, United Kingdom, Uruguay, Zambia

Action by the First Committee

Date:	27 October 2021	Meeting:	14th meeting
Vote:	Adopted without a vote	Draft resolution:	A/C.1/76/L.8

Agenda item 100 (l)

76/29 Implementation of the Convention on the Prohibition of the Development, Production, Stockpiling and Use of Chemical Weapons and on Their Destruction

Text

The General Assembly,

Recalling its previous resolutions on the subject of chemical weapons, in particular resolution 75/55 of 7 December 2020,

Determined to achieve the effective prohibition of the development, production, acquisition, transfer, stockpiling and use of chemical weapons and their destruction,

Honouring the memory of and paying tribute to all victims of chemical weapons,

Reaffirming its strong support for the Convention on the Prohibition of the Development, Production, Stockpiling and Use of Chemical Weapons and on Their Destruction[1] and for the Organisation for the Prohibition of Chemical Weapons and its deep appreciation of the Organisation, which was awarded the Nobel Peace Prize for 2013 for its extensive efforts to eliminate chemical weapons,

Welcoming decisions C-24/DEC.4 and C-24/DEC.5 of 27 November 2019 adopted by the Conference of the States Parties at its twenty-fourth session, introducing changes to schedules 1 (A) and 1, respectively, of the Annex on Chemicals to the Convention,

Re-emphasizing its unequivocal support for the decision of the Director General of the Organisation for the Prohibition of Chemical Weapons to continue the mission to establish the facts surrounding the allegations of the use of chemical weapons, including toxic chemicals, for hostile purposes in the Syrian Arab Republic, while stressing that the safety and security of mission personnel remains the top priority, and recalling the work, pursuant to Security Council resolutions 2235 (2015) of 7 August 2015 and 2319 (2016) of 17 November 2016, of the Joint Investigative Mechanism of the Organisation for the Prohibition of Chemical Weapons and the United Nations,

Noting the work related to the Fourth Special Session of the Conference of the States Parties to Review the Operation of the Chemical Weapons Convention, held in The Hague from 21 to 30 November 2018,

Reaffirming the importance of the outcome of the Third Special Session of the Conference of the States Parties to Review the Operation of the

---

[1] United Nations, *Treaty Series*, vol. 1974, No. 33757.

Chemical Weapons Convention, held in The Hague from 8 to 19 April 2013 (the Third Review Conference), including its consensus final report, in which the Conference addressed all aspects of the Convention and made important recommendations on its continued implementation,

Emphasizing that the Third Review Conference welcomed the fact that the Convention is a unique multilateral agreement banning an entire category of weapons of mass destruction in a non-discriminatory and verifiable manner under strict and effective international control and noted with satisfaction that the Convention continues to be a remarkable success and an example of effective multilateralism,

Convinced that the Convention, 24 years after its entry into force, has reinforced its role as the international norm against chemical weapons, and that it constitutes a major contribution to:

(a)   International peace and security,

(b)   Eliminating chemical weapons and preventing their re-emergence,

(c)   The ultimate objective of general and complete disarmament under strict and effective international control,

(d)   Excluding completely, for the sake of all mankind, the possibility of the use of chemical weapons,

(e)   Promoting international cooperation and exchange in scientific and technical information in the field of chemical activities among States parties for peaceful purposes in order to enhance the economic and technological development of all States parties,

Noting the impact of the coronavirus disease (COVID-19) on the work of the Organisation for the Prohibition of Chemical Weapons and all efforts to ensure its effectiveness,

1.   *Reaffirms its condemnation in the strongest possible terms* of the use of chemical weapons by anyone under any circumstances, emphasizing that any use of chemical weapons anywhere, at any time, by anyone, under any circumstances is unacceptable and is and would be a violation of international law and expressing its strong conviction that those individuals responsible for the use of chemical weapons must and should be held accountable;

2.   *Condemns in the strongest possible terms* the use of a toxic chemical as a weapon against Alexei Navalny in the Russian Federation, and notes with grave concern the note by the Technical Secretariat of the Organisation for the Prohibition of Chemical Weapons of 6 October 2020 on the summary of the report on activities carried out in support of a request for technical assistance by Germany;[2]

---

[2]   S/1906/2020.

3.   *Also condemns in the strongest possible terms* that chemical weapons have since 2012 been used in Iraq, Malaysia, the Syrian Arab Republic and the United Kingdom of Great Britain and Northern Ireland, including as reported by the Joint Investigative Mechanism of the Organisation for the Prohibition of Chemical Weapons and the United Nations and by the Investigation and Identification Team of the Organisation for the Prohibition of Chemical Weapons in:

(a)   The reports of the Joint Investigative Mechanism of 24 August 2016[3] and 21 October 2016,[4] which concluded that there was sufficient information to determine that the Syrian Arab Armed Forces were responsible for the attacks which released toxic substances in Talmenes, Syrian Arab Republic, on 21 April 2014, in Sarmin, Syrian Arab Republic, on 16 March 2015, and in Qmenas, Syrian Arab Republic, also on 16 March 2015, and that the so-called "Islamic State in Iraq and the Levant" used sulfur mustard in Marea, Syrian Arab Republic, on 21 August 2015;

(b)   The report of the Joint Investigative Mechanism of 26 October 2017,[5] which concluded that there was sufficient information to be confident that Islamic State in Iraq and the Levant was responsible for the use of sulfur mustard at Umm Hawsh on 15 and 16 September 2016 and that the Syrian Arab Republic was responsible for the release of sarin at Khan Shaykhun on 4 April 2017;

(c)   The first report of the Investigation and Identification Team, of 8 April 2020,[6] which concluded that there were reasonable grounds to believe that the Syrian Arab Air Force used chemical weapons in Ltamenah on 24, 25 and 30 March 2017;

(d)   The second report of the Investigation and Identification Team, of 12 April 2021,[7] which concluded that there were reasonable grounds to believe that a military helicopter of the Syrian Arab Air Force carried out a chemical weapons attack on Saraqib on 4 February 2018; and demands that the perpetrators immediately desist from any further use of chemical weapons;

4.   *Takes note with great concern in that regard* of the reports of the fact-finding mission of the Organisation for the Prohibition of Chemical Weapons regarding alleged incidents in Ltamenah, Syrian Arab Republic,[8] and regarding an alleged incident in Saraqib, Syrian Arab Republic,[9] as well as the final report of the fact-finding mission of the Organisation regarding the incident of alleged use of toxic chemicals as a weapon in Douma, Syrian Arab

---

[3]   See S/2016/738/Rev.1.

[4]   See S/2016/888.

[5]   See S/2017/904, annex.

[6]   See S/2020/310, annex.

[7]   See S/2021/371, annex.

[8]   See S/2017/931, annex, and S/2018/620, annex.

[9]   See S/2018/478, annex.

Republic, which concluded there were reasonable grounds that the use of a toxic chemical as a weapon took place;[10]

5. *Recalls* the adoption of:

(a) Decision C-SS-4/DEC.3 of the Fourth Special Session of the Conference of the States Parties, entitled "Addressing the threat from chemical weapons use", of 27 June 2018;

(b) Decision EC-94/DEC.2 of the Executive Council, entitled "Addressing the possession and use of chemical weapons by the Syrian Arab Republic", of 9 July 2020;

(c) Decision C-25/DEC.9 of the Conference of the States Parties, entitled "Addressing the possession and use of chemical weapons by the Syrian Arab Republic", of 21 April 2021;

and stresses the importance of their implementation, in accordance with the Convention, and, accordingly, expresses concern with the conclusions contained in the report of the Director General of the Organisation for the Prohibition of Chemical Weapons of 14 October 2020 on the implementation of decision EC-94/DEC.2;[11]

6. *Emphasizes* that the universality of the Convention is essential to achieving its object and purpose and to enhancing the security of States parties, as well as to international peace and security, underlines the fact that the objectives of the Convention will not be fully realized as long as there remains even a single State not party to the Convention that could possess or acquire such weapons, calls upon all States that have not yet done so to become parties to the Convention without delay, and in this regard recalls the outcome of the Third Special Session of the Conference of the States Parties to Review the Operation of the Chemical Weapons Convention (the Third Review Conference);

7. *Underlines* the fact that the full, effective and non-discriminatory implementation of all articles of the Convention makes a major contribution to international peace and security through the elimination of existing stockpiles of chemical weapons and the prohibition of their acquisition and use, and provides for assistance and protection in the event of use or threat of use of chemical weapons and for international cooperation for peaceful purposes in the field of chemical activities;

8. *Notes* the impact of scientific and technological progress on the effective implementation of the Convention and the importance for the Organisation for the Prohibition of Chemical Weapons and its policymaking organs of taking due account of such developments;

---

[10] See S/2019/208, annex.
[11] EC-96/DG.1.

9. *Reaffirms* that the obligation of the States parties to complete the destruction of chemical weapons stockpiles and the destruction or conversion of chemical weapons production facilities in accordance with the provisions of the Convention and the Annex on Implementation and Verification (Verification Annex) and under the verification of the Technical Secretariat of the Organisation for the Prohibition of Chemical Weapons is essential for the realization of the object and purpose of the Convention;

10. *Stresses* the importance to the Convention that all possessors of chemical weapons, chemical weapons production facilities or chemical weapons development facilities, including previously declared possessor States, should be among the States parties to the Convention, and welcomes progress to that end;

11. *Recalls* that the Third Review Conference expressed concern regarding the statement made by the Director General of the Organisation for the Prohibition of Chemical Weapons in his report to the Executive Council of the Organisation at its sixty-eighth session, provided in accordance with paragraph 2 of decision C-16/DEC.11 of 1 December 2011 adopted by the Conference of the States Parties at its sixteenth session, that three possessor States parties, namely, Libya, the Russian Federation and the United States of America, had been unable to fully meet the final extended deadline of 29 April 2012 for the destruction of their chemical weapons stockpiles, and also expressed determination that the destruction of all categories of chemical weapons should be completed in the shortest time possible in accordance with the provisions of the Convention and the Verification Annex, and with the full application of the relevant decisions that have been taken;

12. *Welcomes* the confirmation by the Director General of the Organisation for the Prohibition of Chemical Weapons expressed in his report of 5 October 2017,[12] based upon information received from the Russian Federation and independent information received from the inspectors of the Organisation, regarding the completion of the full destruction of chemical weapons declared by the Russian Federation;

13. *Also welcomes* the completed destruction of Libya's remaining category 2 chemical weapons, as reported by the Director General of the Organisation for the Prohibition of Chemical Weapons in his report of 22 December 2017,[13] as well as the completed destruction by Iraq of its entire declared stockpile of chemical weapons remnants, as reported by the Director General in his report of 28 February 2018;[14]

14. *Notes with concern* that, along with the threat of the possible production, acquisition and use of chemical weapons by States, the

---

[12] EC-86/DG.31.
[13] EC-87/DG.6.
[14] EC-87/DG.18.

international community also faces the danger of the production, acquisition and use of chemical weapons by non-State actors, including terrorists, concerns which have highlighted the necessity of achieving universal adherence to the Convention, as well as the high level of readiness of the Organisation for the Prohibition of Chemical Weapons, and stresses that the full and effective implementation of all provisions of the Convention, including those on national implementation (article VII) and assistance and protection (article X), constitutes an important contribution to the efforts of the United Nations in the global fight against terrorism in all its forms and manifestations;

15. *Notes* that the effective application of the verification system builds confidence in compliance with the Convention by States parties;

16. *Stresses* the importance of the Organisation for the Prohibition of Chemical Weapons in verifying compliance with the provisions of the Convention as well as in promoting the timely and efficient accomplishment of all its objectives;

17. *Expresses grave concern* that, despite the verified destruction of all 27 chemical weapons production facilities declared by the Syrian Arab Republic, the Technical Secretariat, as recently reported by the Director General in his report of 24 September 2021,[15] cannot fully verify that the Syrian Arab Republic has submitted a declaration that can be considered accurate and complete in accordance with the Convention or Executive Council decision EC-M-33/DEC.1 as well as with the conclusion of decision C-SS-4/DEC.3, of the Fourth Review Conference, that the Syrian Arab Republic failed to declare and destroy all of its chemical weapons and chemical weapons production facilities, and underscores the importance of such full verification;

18. *Urges* all States parties to the Convention to meet in full and on time their obligations under the Convention and to support the Organisation for the Prohibition of Chemical Weapons in its implementation activities;

19. *Welcomes* the progress made in the national implementation of article VII obligations, commends the States parties and the Technical Secretariat for assisting other States parties, on request, with the implementation of the follow-up to the plan of action regarding article VII obligations, urges States parties that have not fulfilled their obligations under article VII to do so without further delay, in accordance with their constitutional processes, and in this context reaffirms that full, effective and non-discriminatory implementation of article VII is essential for the realization of the object and purpose of the Convention;

---

[15] EC-98/DG.24.

20. *Emphasizes* the continuing relevance and importance of the provisions of article X of the Convention, welcomes the activities of the Organisation for the Prohibition of Chemical Weapons in relation to assistance and protection against chemical weapons, supports further efforts by both States parties and the Technical Secretariat to promote a high level of readiness to respond to chemical weapons threats as articulated in article X, and welcomes the effectiveness and efficiency of the increased focus on making full use of regional and subregional capacities and expertise, including taking advantage of established training centres;

21. *Reaffirms* that the provisions of the Convention shall be implemented in a manner that avoids hampering the economic or technological development of States parties and international cooperation in the field of chemical activities for purposes not prohibited under the Convention, including the international exchange of scientific and technical information, and chemicals and equipment for the production, processing or use of chemicals for purposes not prohibited under the Convention;

22. *Emphasizes* the importance of the provisions of article XI of the Convention relating to the economic and technological development of States parties, recalls that the full, effective and non-discriminatory implementation of those provisions contributes to universality, and reaffirms the undertaking of the States parties to foster international cooperation for peaceful purposes in the field of chemical activities of the States parties and the importance of that cooperation and its contribution to the promotion of the Convention as a whole;

23. *Notes with appreciation* the ongoing work of the Organisation for the Prohibition of Chemical Weapons to achieve the object and purpose of the Convention, to ensure the full implementation of its provisions, including those for international verification of compliance with it, and to provide a forum for consultation and cooperation among States parties;

24. *Welcomes* the cooperation between the United Nations and the Organisation for the Prohibition of Chemical Weapons within the framework of the relationship agreement between the United Nations and the Organisation,[16] in accordance with the provisions of the Convention;

25. *Decides* to include in the provisional agenda of its seventy-seventh session, under the item entitled "General and complete disarmament", the sub-item entitled "Implementation of the Convention on the Prohibition of the Development, Production, Stockpiling and Use of Chemical Weapons and on Their Destruction".

---

[16] United Nations, *Treaty Series*, vol. 2160, No. 1240.

Action by the General Assembly

Date: 6 December 2021   Meeting: 45th plenary meeting
Vote: 154-8-21   Report: A/76/444
  130-11-26, p.p. 6
  92-15-54, o.p. 2
  118-13-34, o.p. 3
  111-10-40, o.p. 4
  108-12-40, o.p. 5
  109-11-42, o.p. 17

Sponsors

Poland

Recorded vote

As a whole

In favour

Afghanistan, Albania, Andorra, Angola, Antigua and Barbuda, Argentina, Australia, Austria, Bahamas, Bahrain, Bangladesh, Barbados, Belgium, Belize, Bhutan, Bosnia and Herzegovina, Botswana, Brazil, Brunei Darussalam, Bulgaria, Burkina Faso, Cabo Verde, Cameroon, Canada, Central African Republic, Chad, Chile, Colombia, Congo, Costa Rica, Côte d'Ivoire, Croatia, Cyprus, Czechia, Denmark, Dominica, Dominican Republic, Ecuador, El Salvador, Equatorial Guinea, Estonia, Eswatini, Ethiopia, Fiji, Finland, France, Gabon, Gambia, Georgia, Germany, Ghana, Greece, Grenada, Guatemala, Guinea, Guinea-Bissau, Guyana, Haiti, Honduras, Hungary, Iceland, India, Indonesia, Iraq, Ireland, Israel, Italy, Jamaica, Japan, Jordan, Kiribati, Kuwait, Lao People's Democratic Republic, Latvia, Lesotho, Liberia, Libya, Liechtenstein, Lithuania, Luxembourg, Madagascar, Malawi, Malaysia, Maldives, Malta, Marshall Islands, Mauritania, Mauritius, Mexico, Micronesia (Federated States of), Monaco, Montenegro, Morocco, Mozambique, Myanmar, Namibia, Nauru, Nepal, Netherlands, New Zealand, Niger, Nigeria, North Macedonia, Norway, Oman, Pakistan, Palau, Panama, Papua New Guinea, Paraguay, Peru, Philippines, Poland, Portugal, Qatar, Republic of Korea, Republic of Moldova, Romania, Saint Kitts and Nevis, Saint Lucia, Saint Vincent and the Grenadines, Samoa, San Marino, Sao Tome and Principe, Saudi Arabia, Senegal, Sierra Leone, Singapore, Slovakia, Slovenia, Solomon Islands, South Africa, Spain, Sri Lanka, Suriname, Sweden, Switzerland, Thailand, Timor-Leste, Togo, Tonga, Trinidad and Tobago, Turkey, Tuvalu, Ukraine, United Arab Emirates, United Kingdom, United Republic of Tanzania, United States, Uruguay, Vanuatu, Viet Nam, Yemen, Zambia

Against

Cambodia, China, Iran (Islamic Republic of), Nicaragua, Russian Federation, Syrian Arab Republic, Venezuela (Bolivarian Republic of), Zimbabwe

Abstaining

Algeria, Armenia, Belarus, Bolivia (Plurinational State of), Burundi, Cuba, Djibouti, Egypt, Eritrea, Kazakhstan, Kenya, Kyrgyzstan, Lebanon, Mali, Mongolia, Rwanda, Sudan, Tajikistan, Tunisia, Uganda, Uzbekistan

Sixth preambular paragraph*

In favour

Afghanistan, Albania, Andorra, Angola, Antigua and Barbuda, Argentina, Australia, Austria, Bahamas, Bahrain, Barbados, Belgium, Belize, Bhutan, Bosnia and Herzegovina, Brazil, Brunei Darussalam, Bulgaria, Canada, Chad, Chile, Colombia, Costa Rica, Côte d'Ivoire, Croatia, Cyprus, Czechia, Denmark, Djibouti, Dominican Republic, Ecuador, El Salvador, Estonia, Eswatini, Ethiopia, Fiji, Finland, France, Gambia, Georgia, Germany, Ghana, Greece, Guatemala, Guinea, Guinea-Bissau, Guyana, Haiti, Honduras, Hungary, Iceland, India, Ireland, Israel, Italy, Jamaica, Japan, Kazakhstan, Kiribati, Kuwait, Latvia, Lesotho, Liberia, Libya, Liechtenstein, Lithuania, Luxembourg, Madagascar, Malawi, Malaysia, Maldives, Malta, Marshall Islands, Mauritania, Mauritius, Mexico, Micronesia (Federated States of), Monaco, Mongolia, Montenegro, Mozambique, Myanmar, Namibia, Netherlands, New Zealand, Niger, North Macedonia, Norway, Oman, Pakistan, Palau, Panama, Papua New Guinea, Paraguay, Peru, Poland, Portugal, Qatar, Republic of Korea, Republic of Moldova, Romania, Saint Lucia, Samoa, San Marino, Sao Tome and Principe, Saudi Arabia, Sierra Leone, Singapore, Slovakia, Slovenia, South Africa, South Sudan, Spain, Sri Lanka, Sweden, Switzerland, Thailand, Timor-Leste, Togo, Turkey, Ukraine, United Arab Emirates, United Kingdom, United Republic of Tanzania, United States, Uruguay, Vanuatu, Viet Nam, Yemen, Zambia

Against

Belarus, Cuba, Democratic People's Republic of Korea, Eritrea, Iran (Islamic Republic of), Mali, Nicaragua, Russian Federation, Syrian Arab Republic, Venezuela (Bolivarian Republic of), Zimbabwe

Abstaining

Algeria, Armenia, Bangladesh, Bolivia (Plurinational State of), Botswana, Burkina Faso, Burundi, China, Egypt, Gabon, Indonesia, Iraq, Jordan, Kenya, Kyrgyzstan, Lebanon, Nepal, Nigeria, Philippines, Saint Vincent

---

* Subsequently, the delegation of Gabon informed the Secretariat that it had not intended to participate.

and the Grenadines, Senegal, Sudan, Suriname, Trinidad and Tobago, Tunisia, Uzbekistan

Operative paragraph 2*

In favour

Afghanistan, Albania, Andorra, Angola, Antigua and Barbuda, Argentina, Australia, Austria, Bahamas, Barbados, Belgium, Belize, Bhutan, Bosnia and Herzegovina, Bulgaria, Canada, Chad, Chile, Colombia, Costa Rica, Croatia, Cyprus, Czechia, Denmark, Dominican Republic, El Salvador, Estonia, Eswatini, Fiji, Finland, France, Georgia, Germany, Greece, Guyana, Haiti, Honduras, Hungary, Iceland, Ireland, Israel, Italy, Jamaica, Japan, Kazakhstan, Latvia, Lebanon, Liberia, Liechtenstein, Lithuania, Luxembourg, Madagascar, Maldives, Malta, Marshall Islands, Mauritania, Micronesia (Federated States of), Monaco, Montenegro, Myanmar, Netherlands, New Zealand, North Macedonia, Norway, Palau, Panama, Papua New Guinea, Paraguay, Poland, Portugal, Republic of Korea, Republic of Moldova, Romania, Saint Lucia, Samoa, San Marino, Sao Tome and Principe, Sierra Leone, Slovakia, Slovenia, Spain, Sri Lanka, Sweden, Switzerland, Timor-Leste, Turkey, Ukraine, United Kingdom, United Republic of Tanzania, United States, Uruguay, Vanuatu

Against

Armenia, Belarus, China, Cuba, Democratic People's Republic of Korea, Eritrea, Ethiopia, Iran (Islamic Republic of), Kyrgyzstan, Mali, Nicaragua, Russian Federation, Syrian Arab Republic, Venezuela (Bolivarian Republic of), Zimbabwe

Abstaining

Algeria, Bahrain, Bangladesh, Bolivia (Plurinational State of), Botswana, Brazil, Brunei Darussalam, Burkina Faso, Burundi, Djibouti, Ecuador, Egypt, Gabon, Ghana, Guatemala, Guinea, India, Indonesia, Iraq, Jordan, Kenya, Kuwait, Lao People's Democratic Republic, Lesotho, Malaysia, Mexico, Mongolia, Morocco, Mozambique, Namibia, Nepal, Niger, Nigeria, Oman, Pakistan, Peru, Philippines, Qatar, Saint Vincent and the Grenadines, Saudi Arabia, Senegal, Singapore, South Africa, Sudan, Suriname, Thailand, Togo, Trinidad and Tobago, Tunisia, United Arab Emirates, Uzbekistan, Viet Nam, Yemen, Zambia

---

* Subsequently, the delegation of Gabon informed the Secretariat that it had not intended to participate; the delegation of Kazakhstan informed the Secretariat that it had intended to vote against.

Operative paragraph 3*

In favour

> Afghanistan, Albania, Andorra, Angola, Antigua and Barbuda, Argentina, Australia, Austria, Bahamas, Bahrain, Barbados, Belgium, Belize, Bhutan, Bosnia and Herzegovina, Brazil, Brunei Darussalam, Bulgaria, Canada, Chad, Chile, Colombia, Costa Rica, Côte d'Ivoire, Croatia, Cyprus, Czechia, Denmark, Dominican Republic, El Salvador, Estonia, Eswatini, Ethiopia, Fiji, Finland, France, Georgia, Germany, Ghana, Greece, Guatemala, Guinea, Guyana, Haiti, Honduras, Hungary, Iceland, Iraq, Ireland, Israel, Italy, Jamaica, Japan, Kazakhstan, Kiribati, Kuwait, Latvia, Lesotho, Liberia, Libya, Liechtenstein, Lithuania, Luxembourg, Madagascar, Malawi, Maldives, Malta, Marshall Islands, Mauritius, Mexico, Micronesia (Federated States of), Monaco, Mongolia, Montenegro, Morocco, Mozambique, Myanmar, Namibia, Netherlands, New Zealand, North Macedonia, Norway, Oman, Palau, Panama, Papua New Guinea, Paraguay, Peru, Poland, Portugal, Qatar, Republic of Korea, Republic of Moldova, Romania, Saint Lucia, Samoa, San Marino, Sao Tome and Principe, Saudi Arabia, Sierra Leone, Singapore, Slovakia, Slovenia, South Africa, Spain, Sri Lanka, Sweden, Switzerland, Thailand, Timor-Leste, Turkey, Ukraine, United Kingdom, United Republic of Tanzania, United States, Uruguay, Vanuatu, Yemen

Against

> Belarus, China, Cuba, Democratic People's Republic of Korea, Eritrea, Iran (Islamic Republic of), Kyrgyzstan, Mali, Nicaragua, Russian Federation, Syrian Arab Republic, Venezuela (Bolivarian Republic of), Zimbabwe

Abstaining

> Algeria, Armenia, Bangladesh, Bolivia (Plurinational State of), Botswana, Burkina Faso, Burundi, Djibouti, Ecuador, Egypt, Gabon, India, Indonesia, Jordan, Kenya, Lebanon, Malaysia, Mauritania, Nepal, Niger, Nigeria, Pakistan, Philippines, Saint Vincent and the Grenadines, Senegal, Sudan, Suriname, Togo, Trinidad and Tobago, Tunisia, United Arab Emirates, Uzbekistan, Viet Nam, Zambia

Operative paragraph 4**

In favour

> Afghanistan, Albania, Andorra, Angola, Antigua and Barbuda, Argentina, Australia, Austria, Bahamas, Bahrain, Barbados, Belgium, Belize, Bhutan, Bosnia and Herzegovina, Brazil, Brunei Darussalam, Bulgaria,

---

* Subsequently, the delegation of Gabon informed the Secretariat that it had not intended to participate; the delegation of Kazakhstan informed the Secretariat that it had intended to vote against.

** Subsequently, the delegation of Bangladesh informed the Secretariat that it had intended to vote in favour; the delegation of Gabon informed the Secretariat that it had not intended to

Canada, Chad, Chile, Colombia, Costa Rica, Côte d'Ivoire, Croatia, Cyprus, Czechia, Denmark, Dominican Republic, Ecuador, El Salvador, Estonia, Eswatini, Ethiopia, Fiji, Finland, France, Georgia, Germany, Greece, Guatemala, Guyana, Haiti, Honduras, Hungary, Iceland, Ireland, Israel, Italy, Jamaica, Japan, Kazakhstan, Kuwait, Latvia, Liberia, Libya, Liechtenstein, Lithuania, Luxembourg, Madagascar, Malaysia, Maldives, Malta, Marshall Islands, Mauritania, Mauritius, Mexico, Micronesia (Federated States of), Monaco, Mongolia, Montenegro, Myanmar, Netherlands, New Zealand, North Macedonia, Norway, Oman, Palau, Panama, Papua New Guinea, Paraguay, Peru, Poland, Portugal, Qatar, Republic of Korea, Republic of Moldova, Romania, Saint Lucia, Samoa, San Marino, Sao Tome and Principe, Saudi Arabia, Sierra Leone, Singapore, Slovakia, Slovenia, Spain, Sri Lanka, Sweden, Switzerland, Thailand, Timor-Leste, Turkey, Ukraine, United Kingdom, United States, Uruguay, Vanuatu, Yemen, Zambia

Against

Belarus, China, Cuba, Democratic People's Republic of Korea, Iran (Islamic Republic of), Mali, Nicaragua, Russian Federation, Syrian Arab Republic, Venezuela (Bolivarian Republic of)

Abstaining

Algeria, Armenia, Bangladesh, Bolivia (Plurinational State of), Botswana, Burkina Faso, Burundi, Djibouti, Egypt, Eritrea, Gabon, Ghana, Guinea, India, Indonesia, Iraq, Jordan, Kenya, Kyrgyzstan, Lebanon, Lesotho, Malawi, Mozambique, Namibia, Nepal, Niger, Nigeria, Pakistan, Philippines, Saint Vincent and the Grenadines, Senegal, South Africa, Sudan, Suriname, Togo, Trinidad and Tobago, Tunisia, United Arab Emirates, Uzbekistan, Viet Nam

Operative paragraph 5*

In favour

Albania, Andorra, Angola, Antigua and Barbuda, Argentina, Australia, Austria, Bahamas, Bahrain, Barbados, Belgium, Belize, Bhutan, Bosnia and Herzegovina, Brazil, Bulgaria, Canada, Chad, Chile, Colombia, Costa Rica, Côte d'Ivoire, Croatia, Cyprus, Czechia, Denmark, Djibouti, Dominican Republic, Ecuador, El Salvador, Estonia, Eswatini, Fiji, Finland, France, Georgia, Germany, Ghana, Greece, Guatemala, Guinea, Guyana, Haiti, Honduras, Hungary, Iceland, Ireland, Israel, Italy, Jamaica, Japan, Kuwait, Latvia, Liberia, Libya, Liechtenstein, Lithuania, Luxembourg,

---

participate; the delegation of Kazakhstan informed the Secretariat that it had intended to vote against.

* Subsequently, the delegation of Gabon informed the Secretariat that it had not intended to participate; the delegation of Kazakhstan informed the Secretariat that it had intended to vote against.

Madagascar, Malawi, Maldives, Malta, Marshall Islands, Mauritius, Micronesia (Federated States of), Monaco, Montenegro, Netherlands, New Zealand, North Macedonia, Norway, Oman, Palau, Panama, Papua New Guinea, Paraguay, Peru, Philippines, Poland, Portugal, Qatar, Republic of Korea, Republic of Moldova, Romania, Saint Lucia, Samoa, San Marino, Sao Tome and Principe, Saudi Arabia, Sierra Leone, Singapore, Slovakia, Slovenia, Spain, Sri Lanka, Sweden, Switzerland, Timor-Leste, Togo, Turkey, Ukraine, United Kingdom, United Republic of Tanzania, United States, Uruguay, Vanuatu, Yemen, Zambia

Against

Belarus, China, Cuba, Democratic People's Republic of Korea, Iran (Islamic Republic of), Kyrgyzstan, Lao People's Democratic Republic, Mali, Nicaragua, Russian Federation, Syrian Arab Republic, Venezuela (Bolivarian Republic of)

Abstaining

Algeria, Bangladesh, Bolivia (Plurinational State of), Botswana, Brunei Darussalam, Burkina Faso, Burundi, Egypt, Eritrea, Ethiopia, Gabon, India, Indonesia, Iraq, Jordan, Kazakhstan, Lebanon, Lesotho, Malaysia, Mauritania, Mexico, Mongolia, Mozambique, Myanmar, Namibia, Nepal, Niger, Nigeria, Pakistan, Saint Vincent and the Grenadines, Senegal, South Africa, Sudan, Suriname, Thailand, Trinidad and Tobago, Tunisia, United Arab Emirates, Uzbekistan, Viet Nam

Operative paragraph 17*

In favour

Albania, Andorra, Angola, Antigua and Barbuda, Argentina, Australia, Austria, Bahamas, Bahrain, Barbados, Belgium, Belize, Bhutan, Bosnia and Herzegovina, Botswana, Brazil, Bulgaria, Canada, Chad, Chile, Colombia, Costa Rica, Côte d'Ivoire, Croatia, Cyprus, Czechia, Denmark, Dominican Republic, Ecuador, El Salvador, Estonia, Eswatini, Fiji, Finland, France, Georgia, Germany, Greece, Guatemala, Guyana, Haiti, Honduras, Hungary, Iceland, Ireland, Israel, Italy, Jamaica, Japan, Kuwait, Latvia, Lesotho, Liberia, Libya, Liechtenstein, Lithuania, Luxembourg, Madagascar, Maldives, Malta, Marshall Islands, Mauritius, Mexico, Micronesia (Federated States of), Monaco, Montenegro, Mozambique, Namibia, Netherlands, New Zealand, North Macedonia, Norway, Oman, Palau, Panama, Papua New Guinea, Paraguay, Peru, Philippines, Poland, Portugal, Qatar, Republic of Korea, Republic of Moldova, Romania, Saint Lucia, Samoa, San Marino, Sao Tome and Principe, Saudi Arabia, Sierra Leone, Singapore, Slovakia, Slovenia, South Africa, Spain, Sri Lanka,

---

* Subsequently, the delegation of Gabon informed the Secretariat that it had not intended to participate; the delegation of Kazakhstan informed the Secretariat that it had intended to vote against.

Sweden, Switzerland, Timor-Leste, Turkey, Ukraine, United Kingdom, United Republic of Tanzania, United States, Uruguay, Vanuatu, Yemen, Zambia

Against

Belarus, China, Cuba, Democratic People's Republic of Korea, Iran (Islamic Republic of), Mali, Nicaragua, Russian Federation, Syrian Arab Republic, Venezuela (Bolivarian Republic of), Zimbabwe

Abstaining

Algeria, Bangladesh, Bolivia (Plurinational State of), Brunei Darussalam, Burkina Faso, Burundi, Djibouti, Egypt, Eritrea, Ethiopia, Gabon, Ghana, Guinea, India, Indonesia, Iraq, Jordan, Kazakhstan, Kenya, Kyrgyzstan, Lao People's Democratic Republic, Lebanon, Malawi, Malaysia, Mauritania, Mongolia, Myanmar, Nepal, Niger, Nigeria, Pakistan, Saint Vincent and the Grenadines, Senegal, Sudan, Suriname, Thailand, Togo, Trinidad and Tobago, Tunisia, United Arab Emirates, Uzbekistan, Viet Nam

Action by the First Committee

Date: 27 October 2021   Meeting: 14th meeting
Vote: 147-8-25   Draft resolution: A/C.1/76/L.10
      116-8-32, p.p. 6
      86-12-61, o.p. 2
      110-11-38, o.p. 3
      105-9-43, o.p. 4
      100-12-45, o.p. 5
      106-9-44, o.p. 17

Agenda item 100 (dd)

76/30   Humanitarian consequences of nuclear weapons

Text

The General Assembly,

Recalling its resolutions 70/47 of 7 December 2015, 71/46 of 5 December 2016, 72/30 of 4 December 2017, 73/47 of 5 December 2018, 74/42 of 12 December 2019 and 75/39 of 7 December 2020,

Reiterating the deep concern about the catastrophic consequences of nuclear weapons,

Stressing that the immense and uncontrollable destructive capability and indiscriminate nature of nuclear weapons cause unacceptable humanitarian consequences, as has been demonstrated through their past use and testing,

Recalling that concern about the humanitarian consequences of nuclear weapons has been reflected in numerous United Nations resolutions, including the first resolution adopted by the General Assembly, on 24 January 1946,

Recalling also that at the first special session of the General Assembly devoted to disarmament, in 1978, the Assembly stressed that nuclear weapons posed the greatest danger to mankind and to the survival of civilization,[1]

Welcoming the renewed interest and resolve of the international community, together with the International Committee of the Red Cross and international humanitarian organizations, to address the catastrophic consequences of nuclear weapons,

Recalling that the 2010 Review Conference of the Parties to the Treaty on the Non-Proliferation of Nuclear Weapons expressed deep concern at the catastrophic humanitarian consequences of any use of nuclear weapons,[2]

Noting the resolution of 26 November 2011 of the Council of Delegates of the International Red Cross and Red Crescent Movement entitled "Working towards the elimination of nuclear weapons",

Recalling the joint statements on the humanitarian consequences of nuclear weapons delivered to the General Assembly and during the 2010–2015 cycle of the review of the Treaty on the Non-Proliferation of Nuclear Weapons,[3]

Welcoming the facts-based discussions on the effects of a nuclear weapon detonation that were held at the conferences on the humanitarian impact of

---

[1] See resolution S-10/2.
[2] See *2010 Review Conference of the Parties to the Treaty on the Non-Proliferation of Nuclear Weapons, Final Document*, vol. I (NPT/CONF.2010/50 (Vol. I)), part I, *Conclusions and recommendations for follow-on actions*.
[3] United Nations, *Treaty Series*, vol. 729, No. 10485.

nuclear weapons, convened by Norway, on 4 and 5 March 2013, Mexico, on 13 and 14 February 2014, and Austria, on 8 and 9 December 2014,

Cognizant that a key message from experts and international organizations at those conferences was that no State or international body could address the immediate humanitarian emergency caused by a nuclear weapon detonation or provide adequate assistance to victims,

Firmly believing that it is in the interest of all States to engage in discussions on the humanitarian consequences of nuclear weapons with the aim of further broadening and deepening the understanding of this matter, and welcoming civil society's ongoing engagement,

Reaffirming the role of civil society, in partnership with Governments, in raising awareness about the unacceptable humanitarian consequences of nuclear weapons,

Emphasizing that the catastrophic consequences of nuclear weapons affect not only Governments but each and every citizen of our interconnected world and have deep implications for human survival, for the environment, for socioeconomic development, for our economies and for the health of future generations,

1.   *Stresses* that it is in the interest of the very survival of humanity that nuclear weapons never be used again, under any circumstances;

2.   *Emphasizes* that the only way to guarantee that nuclear weapons will never be used again is their total elimination;

3.   *Stresses* that the catastrophic effects of a nuclear weapon detonation, whether by accident, miscalculation or design, cannot be adequately addressed;

4.   *Expresses its firm belief* that awareness of the catastrophic consequences of nuclear weapons must underpin all approaches and efforts towards nuclear disarmament;

5.   *Calls upon* all States, in their shared responsibility, to prevent the use of nuclear weapons, to prevent their vertical and horizontal proliferation and to achieve nuclear disarmament;

6.   *Urges* States to exert all efforts to totally eliminate the threat of these weapons of mass destruction;

7.   *Decides* to include in the provisional agenda of its seventy-seventh session, under the item entitled "General and complete disarmament", the sub-item entitled "Humanitarian consequences of nuclear weapons".

Action by the General Assembly

Date: 6 December 2021   Meeting: 45th plenary meeting
Vote: 148-12-29   Report: A/76/444

Sponsors

Algeria, Andorra, Antigua and Barbuda, **Austria**, Bahrain, Brazil, Brunei Darussalam, Chile, Colombia, Comoros, Congo, Costa Rica, Côte d'Ivoire, Democratic Republic of the Congo, Ecuador, Egypt, Equatorial Guinea, Eritrea, Eswatini, Ghana, Guatemala, Indonesia, Iraq, Ireland, Jamaica, Kiribati, Lao People's Democratic Republic, Lebanon, Lesotho, Libya, Liechtenstein, Malaysia, Malta, Mauritania, Mexico, Nepal, New Zealand, Nicaragua, Nigeria, Paraguay, Peru, Philippines, Republic of Moldova, San Marino, Saudi Arabia, South Africa, Sweden, Switzerland, Thailand, Trinidad and Tobago, Viet Nam

Co-sponsors

Angola, Bahamas, Bangladesh, Belize, Bolivia (Plurinational State of), Burkina Faso, Cabo Verde, Dominican Republic, El Salvador, Fiji, Guinea-Bissau, Guyana, Honduras, Kazakhstan, Madagascar, Maldives, Marshall Islands, Mongolia, Morocco, Mozambique, Myanmar, Namibia, Palau, Papua New Guinea, Saint Kitts and Nevis, Saint Lucia, Samoa, Senegal, Singapore, Suriname, Togo, Tunisia, Tuvalu, Uganda, United Republic of Tanzania, Uruguay, Venezuela (Bolivarian Republic of), Zimbabwe

Recorded vote

In favour

Afghanistan, Algeria, Andorra, Angola, Antigua and Barbuda, Argentina, Austria, Azerbaijan, Bahamas, Bahrain, Bangladesh, Barbados, Belarus, Belize, Bhutan, Bolivia (Plurinational State of), Botswana, Brazil, Brunei Darussalam, Burkina Faso, Burundi, Cabo Verde, Cambodia, Cameroon, Central African Republic, Chad, Chile, Colombia, Comoros, Congo, Costa Rica, Côte d'Ivoire, Cuba, Cyprus, Djibouti, Dominica, Dominican Republic, Ecuador, Egypt, El Salvador, Equatorial Guinea, Eritrea, Eswatini, Ethiopia, Fiji, Finland, Gabon, Gambia, Ghana, Greece, Grenada, Guatemala, Guinea, Guinea-Bissau, Guyana, Haiti, Honduras, India, Indonesia, Iran (Islamic Republic of), Iraq, Ireland, Jamaica, Japan, Jordan, Kazakhstan, Kenya, Kiribati, Kuwait, Kyrgyzstan, Lao People's Democratic Republic, Lebanon, Lesotho, Liberia, Libya, Liechtenstein, Madagascar, Malawi, Malaysia, Maldives, Mali, Malta, Marshall Islands, Mauritania, Mauritius, Mexico, Mongolia, Morocco, Mozambique, Myanmar, Namibia, Nauru, Nepal, New Zealand, Nicaragua, Niger, Nigeria, North Macedonia, Oman, Palau, Panama, Papua New Guinea, Paraguay, Peru, Philippines, Qatar, Republic of Moldova, Rwanda, Saint Kitts and Nevis, Saint Lucia, Saint Vincent and the Grenadines, Samoa, San Marino, Sao Tome and Principe, Saudi Arabia, Senegal, Seychelles, Sierra Leone, Singapore, Solomon Islands, South Africa, South Sudan, Sri Lanka, Sudan, Suriname, Sweden, Switzerland, Syrian Arab Republic, Tajikistan, Thailand, Timor-Leste, Togo, Tonga, Trinidad and Tobago, Tunisia,

Turkmenistan, Tuvalu, Uganda, United Arab Emirates, United Republic of Tanzania, Uruguay, Uzbekistan, Vanuatu, Venezuela (Bolivarian Republic of), Viet Nam, Yemen, Zambia, Zimbabwe

Against

Czechia, Estonia, France, Hungary, Israel, Latvia, Lithuania, Poland, Romania, Russian Federation, United Kingdom, United States

Abstaining

Albania, Armenia, Australia, Belgium, Bosnia and Herzegovina, Bulgaria, Canada, China, Croatia, Democratic People's Republic of Korea, Denmark, Georgia, Germany, Iceland, Italy, Luxembourg, Monaco, Montenegro, Netherlands, Norway, Pakistan, Portugal, Republic of Korea, Serbia, Slovakia, Slovenia, Spain, Turkey, Ukraine

Action by the First Committee

Date:	27 October 2021	Meeting:	13th meeting
Vote:	140-12-31	Draft resolution:	A/C.1/76/L.11

Agenda item 100 (w)

76/31 Follow-up to nuclear disarmament obligations agreed to at the 1995, 2000 and 2010 Review Conferences of the Parties to the Treaty on the Non-Proliferation of Nuclear Weapons

Text

The General Assembly,

Recalling its various resolutions in the field of nuclear disarmament, including resolutions 60/72 of 8 December 2005, 62/24 of 5 December 2007, 64/31 of 2 December 2009, 66/28 of 2 December 2011, 68/35 of 5 December 2013, 69/43 and 69/48 of 2 December 2014, 70/38 of 7 December 2015, 72/29 of 4 December 2017 and 74/36 of 12 December 2019,

Bearing in mind its resolution 2373 (XXII) of 12 June 1968, the annex to which contains the Treaty on the Non-Proliferation of Nuclear Weapons,[1]

Noting the provisions of article VIII, paragraph 3, of the Treaty regarding the convening of review conferences at five-year intervals,

Recalling its resolution 50/70 Q of 12 December 1995, in which the General Assembly noted that the States parties to the Treaty affirmed the need to continue to move with determination towards the full realization and effective implementation of the provisions of the Treaty, and accordingly adopted a set of principles and objectives,

Recalling also that, on 11 May 1995, the 1995 Review and Extension Conference of the Parties to the Treaty on the Non-Proliferation of Nuclear Weapons adopted three decisions on, respectively, strengthening the review process for the Treaty, principles and objectives for nuclear non-proliferation and disarmament, and extension of the Treaty,[2]

Reaffirming the resolution on the Middle East adopted on 11 May 1995 by the 1995 Review and Extension Conference, in which the Conference reaffirmed the importance of the early realization of universal adherence to the Treaty and placement of nuclear facilities under full-scope International Atomic Energy Agency safeguards,

Reaffirming also its resolution 55/33 D of 20 November 2000, in which the General Assembly welcomed the adoption by consensus on 19 May 2000 of the Final Document of the 2000 Review Conference of the Parties to the

---

[1] See also United Nations, *Treaty Series*, vol. 729, No. 10485.
[2] See *1995 Review and Extension Conference of the Parties to the Treaty on the Non-Proliferation of Nuclear Weapons, Final Document, Part I* (NPT/CONF.1995/32 (Part I) and NPT/CONF.1995/32 (Part I)/Corr.2), annex.

Treaty on the Non-Proliferation of Nuclear Weapons,[3] including, in particular, the documents entitled "Review of the operation of the Treaty, taking into account the decisions and the resolution adopted by the 1995 Review and Extension Conference" and "Improving the effectiveness of the strengthened review process for the Treaty",[4]

Taking into consideration the unequivocal undertaking by the nuclear-weapon States, in the Final Document of the 2000 Review Conference, to accomplish the total elimination of their nuclear arsenals leading to nuclear disarmament, to which all States parties to the Treaty are committed under article VI of the Treaty,

Expressing concern that the ninth Review Conference of the Parties to the Treaty on the Non-Proliferation of Nuclear Weapons, held from 27 April to 22 May 2015, was not able to reach agreement on a substantive final document,

1.   *Recalls* that the 2010 Review Conference of the Parties to the Treaty on the Non-Proliferation of Nuclear Weapons reaffirmed the continued validity of the practical steps agreed to in the Final Document of the 2000 Review Conference of the Parties to the Treaty on the Non-Proliferation of Nuclear Weapons;[5]

2.   *Determines* to pursue practical steps for systematic and progressive efforts to implement article VI of the Treaty on the Non-Proliferation of Nuclear Weapons and paragraphs 3 and 4 (c) of the decision on principles and objectives for nuclear non-proliferation and disarmament of the 1995 Review and Extension Conference of the Parties to the Treaty on the Non-Proliferation of Nuclear Weapons;

3.   *Calls for* practical steps, as agreed to at the 2000 Review Conference of the Parties to the Treaty on the Non-Proliferation of Nuclear Weapons, to be taken by all nuclear-weapon States, that would lead to nuclear disarmament in a way that promotes international stability and, based on the principle of undiminished security for all:

(a)   Further efforts to be made by the nuclear-weapon States to reduce their nuclear arsenals unilaterally;

(b)   Increased transparency by the nuclear-weapon States with regard to nuclear weapons capabilities and the implementation of agreements pursuant to article VI of the Treaty and as a voluntary confidence-building measure to support further progress in nuclear disarmament;

---

[3]   *2000 Review Conference of the Parties to the Treaty on the Non-Proliferation of Nuclear Weapons, Final Document*, vols. I–III (NPT/CONF.2000/28 (Parts I and II), NPT/CONF.2000/28 (Part III) and NPT/CONF.2000/28 (Part IV)).

[4]   Ibid., vol. I (NPT/CONF.2000/28 (Parts I and II)), part I.

[5]   Ibid., section entitled "Article VI and eighth to twelfth preambular paragraphs", para. 15.

(c)   The further reduction of non-strategic nuclear weapons, based on unilateral initiatives and as an integral part of the nuclear arms reduction and disarmament process;

(d)   Concrete agreed measures to reduce further the operational status of nuclear weapons systems;

(e)   A diminishing role for nuclear weapons in security policies so as to minimize the risk that these weapons will ever be used and to facilitate the process of their total elimination;

(f)   The engagement, as soon as appropriate, of all the nuclear-weapon States in the process leading to the total elimination of their nuclear weapons;

4.   *Notes* that the 2000 and 2010 Review Conferences agreed that legally binding security assurances by the five nuclear-weapon States to the non-nuclear-weapon States parties to the Treaty strengthen the nuclear non-proliferation regime;

5.   *Urges* the States parties to the Treaty to follow up on the implementation of the nuclear disarmament obligations under the Treaty agreed to at the 1995, 2000 and 2010 Review Conferences within the framework of review conferences and their preparatory committees;

6.   *Decides* to include in the provisional agenda of its seventy-eighth session, under the item entitled "General and complete disarmament", the sub-item entitled "Follow-up to nuclear disarmament obligations agreed to at the 1995, 2000 and 2010 Review Conferences of the Parties to the Treaty on the Non-Proliferation of Nuclear Weapons".

Action by the General Assembly

Date: 6 December 2021   Meeting: 45th plenary meeting
Vote: 122-44-17   Report: A/76/444
      113-4-54, p.p. 6

Sponsors

Iran (Islamic Republic of)

Recorded vote

As a whole

In favour

Afghanistan, Algeria, Angola, Antigua and Barbuda, Argentina, Azerbaijan, Bahamas, Bahrain, Bangladesh, Barbados, Belarus, Belize, Bhutan, Bolivia (Plurinational State of), Botswana, Brazil, Brunei Darussalam, Burkina Faso, Burundi, Cabo Verde, Cambodia, Cameroon, Central African Republic, Chad, Chile, Colombia, Congo, Costa Rica, Côte d'Ivoire, Cuba, Djibouti, Dominica, Dominican Republic, Ecuador, Egypt,

El Salvador, Equatorial Guinea, Eritrea, Eswatini, Ethiopia, Fiji, Gambia, Ghana, Grenada, Guatemala, Guinea, Guinea-Bissau, Guyana, Haiti, Honduras, Indonesia, Iran (Islamic Republic of), Iraq, Jamaica, Jordan, Kazakhstan, Kiribati, Kuwait, Kyrgyzstan, Lao People's Democratic Republic, Lebanon, Lesotho, Libya, Madagascar, Malawi, Malaysia, Maldives, Mali, Marshall Islands, Mauritania, Mauritius, Mexico, Mongolia, Morocco, Mozambique, Myanmar, Namibia, Nepal, Nicaragua, Niger, Nigeria, Oman, Palau, Panama, Papua New Guinea, Paraguay, Peru, Philippines, Qatar, Rwanda, Saint Lucia, Saint Vincent and the Grenadines, Sao Tome and Principe, Senegal, Seychelles, Sierra Leone, Singapore, Solomon Islands, South Africa, South Sudan, Sri Lanka, Sudan, Suriname, Syrian Arab Republic, Tajikistan, Thailand, Timor-Leste, Togo, Trinidad and Tobago, Tunisia, Turkmenistan, Uganda, United Arab Emirates, United Republic of Tanzania, Uruguay, Uzbekistan, Vanuatu, Venezuela (Bolivarian Republic of), Viet Nam, Yemen, Zambia, Zimbabwe

Against

Albania, Australia, Belgium, Bosnia and Herzegovina, Bulgaria, Canada, Croatia, Cyprus, Czechia, Denmark, Estonia, Finland, France, Germany, Greece, Hungary, Iceland, Ireland, Israel, Italy, Latvia, Lithuania, Luxembourg, Malta, Micronesia (Federated States of), Monaco, Montenegro, Netherlands, New Zealand, North Macedonia, Norway, Poland, Portugal, Republic of Korea, Republic of Moldova, Romania, Russian Federation, Slovakia, Slovenia, Spain, Sweden, Ukraine, United Kingdom, United States

Abstaining

Andorra, Armenia, Austria, China, Georgia, India, Japan, Kenya, Liechtenstein, Pakistan, Samoa, San Marino, Saudi Arabia, Serbia, Switzerland, Tonga, Turkey

Sixth preambular paragraph*

In favour

Afghanistan, Algeria, Angola, Antigua and Barbuda, Argentina, Azerbaijan, Bahamas, Bahrain, Bangladesh, Barbados, Belarus, Belize, Bolivia (Plurinational State of), Botswana, Brazil, Brunei Darussalam, Burkina Faso, Burundi, Cambodia, Chad, Chile, Colombia, Costa Rica, Côte d'Ivoire, Cuba, Djibouti, Dominica, Dominican Republic, Ecuador, Egypt, El Salvador, Eritrea, Eswatini, Ethiopia, Fiji, Gambia, Ghana, Grenada, Guatemala, Guinea, Guinea-Bissau, Guyana, Haiti, Honduras, Indonesia, Iran (Islamic Republic of), Iraq, Jamaica, Japan, Jordan, Kazakhstan, Kuwait, Kyrgyzstan, Lao People's Democratic Republic, Lebanon, Lesotho, Libya, Malaysia, Maldives, Mali, Mauritania, Mauritius, Mexico,

---

* Subsequently, the delegation of Madagascar informed the Secretariat that it had intended to vote in favour.

Mongolia, Morocco, Mozambique, Myanmar, Namibia, Nepal, Nicaragua, Niger, Nigeria, Oman, Panama, Papua New Guinea, Paraguay, Peru, Philippines, Russian Federation, Rwanda, Saint Lucia, Saint Vincent and the Grenadines, Sao Tome and Principe, Saudi Arabia, Senegal, Seychelles, Sierra Leone, Singapore, South Africa, South Sudan, Sri Lanka, Sudan, Suriname, Switzerland, Syrian Arab Republic, Tajikistan, Thailand, Timor-Leste, Togo, Trinidad and Tobago, Tunisia, Turkey, Turkmenistan, Uganda, United Arab Emirates, United Republic of Tanzania, Uruguay, Uzbekistan, Venezuela (Bolivarian Republic of), Viet Nam, Yemen, Zambia, Zimbabwe

Against

Canada, India, Israel, Micronesia (Federated States of)

Abstaining

Albania, Andorra, Armenia, Australia, Austria, Belgium, Bhutan, Bosnia and Herzegovina, Bulgaria, Croatia, Cyprus, Czechia, Denmark, Estonia, Finland, France, Gabon, Georgia, Germany, Greece, Hungary, Iceland, Ireland, Italy, Kenya, Latvia, Liechtenstein, Lithuania, Luxembourg, Madagascar, Malawi, Malta, Monaco, Montenegro, Netherlands, New Zealand, North Macedonia, Norway, Pakistan, Poland, Portugal, Republic of Korea, Republic of Moldova, Romania, Samoa, San Marino, Serbia, Slovakia, Slovenia, Spain, Sweden, Ukraine, United Kingdom, United States

Action by the First Committee

Date:	27 October 2021	Meeting:	13th meeting
Vote:	108-44-25	Draft resolution:	A/C.1/76/L.14
	109-4-58, p.p. 6		

Agenda item 100 (n)

76/32 Assistance to States for curbing the illicit traffic in small arms and light weapons and collecting them

Text

The General Assembly,

Recalling its resolution 75/56 of 7 December 2020,

Deeply concerned by the magnitude of human casualty and suffering, especially among children, caused by the illicit proliferation and use of small arms and light weapons,

Concerned by the negative impact that the illicit proliferation and use of those weapons continue to have on the efforts of States in the Sahelo-Saharan subregion in the areas of poverty eradication, sustainable development and the maintenance of peace, security and stability,

Bearing in mind the Bamako Declaration on an African Common Position on the Illicit Proliferation, Circulation and Trafficking of Small Arms and Light Weapons, adopted in Bamako on 1 December 2000,[1]

Recalling the report of the Secretary-General entitled "In larger freedom: towards development, security and human rights for all",[2] in which he emphasized that States must strive just as hard to eliminate the threat of small arms and light weapons as they do to eliminate the threat of weapons of mass destruction,

Recalling also the International Instrument to Enable States to Identify and Trace, in a Timely and Reliable Manner, Illicit Small Arms and Light Weapons, adopted on 8 December 2005,[3]

Recalling further the expression of support in the 2005 World Summit Outcome for the implementation of the Programme of Action to Prevent, Combat and Eradicate the Illicit Trade in Small Arms and Light Weapons in All Its Aspects,[4]

Recalling the adoption, on 14 June 2006 in Abuja at the thirtieth ordinary summit of the Economic Community of West African States, of the Convention on Small Arms and Light Weapons, Their Ammunition and Other Related Materials, in replacement of the moratorium on the importation, exportation and manufacture of small arms and light weapons in West Africa,

Recalling also the entry into force of the Convention on 29 September 2009,

---

[1] A/CONF.192/PC/23, annex.
[2] A/59/2005.
[3] See decision 60/519 and A/60/88 and A/60/88/Corr.2, annex.
[4] Resolution 60/1, para. 93.

Recalling further the decision taken by the Economic Community to establish the Small Arms Unit, responsible for advocating appropriate policies and developing and implementing programmes, as well as the establishment of the Economic Community's Small Arms Control Programme, launched on 6 June 2006 in Bamako, in replacement of the Programme for Coordination and Assistance for Security and Development,

Taking note of the latest report of the Secretary-General on the illicit trade in small arms and light weapons in all its aspects and assistance to States for curbing the illicit traffic in small arms and light weapons and collecting them,[5]

Recalling, in that regard, the decision of the European Union to significantly support the Economic Community in its efforts to combat the illicit proliferation of small arms and light weapons,

Recognizing the important role that civil society organizations play, by raising public awareness, in efforts to curb the illicit traffic in small arms and light weapons,

Recalling the report of the Seventh Biennial Meeting of States to Consider the Implementation of the Programme of Action to Prevent, Combat and Eradicate the Illicit Trade in Small Arms and Light Weapons in All Its Aspects, held in New York from 26 to 30 July 2021,[6]

Recalling also the report of the third United Nations Conference to Review Progress Made in the Implementation of the Programme of Action to Prevent, Combat and Eradicate the Illicit Trade in Small Arms and Light Weapons in All Its Aspects, held in New York from 18 to 29 June 2018,[7]

Welcoming the inclusion of small arms and light weapons in the scope of the Arms Trade Treaty,[8] as well as the inclusion of international assistance in its provisions,

1. *Commends* the United Nations and international, regional and other organizations for their assistance to States for curbing the illicit traffic in small arms and light weapons and collecting them;

2. *Encourages* the Secretary-General to pursue his efforts in the context of the implementation of General Assembly resolution 49/75 G of 15 December 1994 and the recommendations of the United Nations advisory missions aimed at curbing the illicit circulation of small arms and light weapons and collecting them in the affected States that so request, with the support of the United Nations Regional Centre for Peace and Disarmament in Africa and in close cooperation with the African Union;

---

[5] A/76/284.
[6] A/CONF.192/BMS/2021/1.
[7] A/CONF.192/2018/RC/3.
[8] United Nations, *Treaty Series*, vol. 3013, No. 52373.

3.   *Encourages* the international community to support the implementation of the Economic Community of West African States Convention on Small Arms and Light Weapons, Their Ammunition and Other Related Materials;

4.   *Encourages* the countries of the Sahelo-Saharan subregion to facilitate the effective functioning of national commissions to combat the illicit proliferation of small arms and light weapons, and in that regard invites the international community to lend its support wherever possible;

5.   *Encourages* the collaboration of civil society organizations and associations in the efforts of the national commissions to combat the illicit traffic in small arms and light weapons and in the implementation of the Programme of Action to Prevent, Combat and Eradicate the Illicit Trade in Small Arms and Light Weapons in All Its Aspects;[9]

6.   *Encourages* cooperation among State organs, international organizations and civil society in support of programmes and projects aimed at combating the illicit traffic in small arms and light weapons and collecting them;

7.   *Calls upon* the international community to provide technical and financial support to strengthen the capacity of civil society organizations to take action to help to combat the illicit trade in small arms and light weapons;

8.   *Invites* the Secretary-General and those States and organizations that are in a position to do so to continue to provide assistance to States for curbing the illicit traffic in small arms and light weapons and collecting them;

9.   *Requests* the Secretary-General to continue to consider the matter and to report to the General Assembly at its seventy-seventh session on the implementation of the present resolution;

10.   *Decides* to include in the provisional agenda of its seventy-seventh session, under the item entitled "General and complete disarmament", the sub-item entitled "Assistance to States for curbing the illicit traffic in small arms and light weapons and collecting them".

Action by the General Assembly

Date:	6 December 2021	Meeting:	45th plenary meeting
Vote:	Adopted without a vote 150-1-20, p.p. 16	Report:	A/76/444

---

[9] *Report of the United Nations Conference on the Illicit Trade in Small Arms and Light Weapons in All Its Aspects, New York, 9–20 July 2001* (A/CONF.192/15), chap. IV, para. 24.

Sponsors

Antigua and Barbuda, Australia, Austria, Belgium, Bosnia and Herzegovina, Bulgaria, Colombia, Croatia, Czechia, Democratic Republic of the Congo, Denmark, Estonia, Finland, France, Georgia, Germany, Greece, Hungary, Iceland, Ireland, Italy, Latvia, Lesotho, Lithuania, Luxembourg, **Mali** (on behalf of the States Members of the United Nations that are members of the Economic Community of West African States), Malta, Netherlands, Norway, Poland, Portugal, Republic of Moldova, Slovakia, Spain, Sweden, Turkey, United Kingdom

Co-sponsors

Albania, Andorra, Chad, Cyprus, Equatorial Guinea, Eritrea, Eswatini, Guatemala, Guyana, Haiti, Honduras, Kyrgyzstan, Lebanon, Madagascar, Maldives, Mauritania, Monaco, Montenegro, Morocco, Namibia, New Zealand, North Macedonia, Romania, San Marino, Sao Tome and Principe, Serbia, Slovenia, Somalia, Thailand, Tunisia, Uruguay

Recorded vote

Sixteenth preambular paragraph

In favour

Afghanistan, Albania, Andorra, Angola, Antigua and Barbuda, Argentina, Australia, Austria, Bahamas, Bahrain, Bangladesh, Barbados, Belgium, Belize, Bosnia and Herzegovina, Botswana, Brazil, Brunei Darussalam, Bulgaria, Burkina Faso, Burundi, Cabo Verde, Cambodia, Canada, Chad, Chile, China, Colombia, Congo, Costa Rica, Côte d'Ivoire, Croatia, Cyprus, Czechia, Denmark, Djibouti, Dominica, Dominican Republic, Ecuador, El Salvador, Estonia, Eswatini, Ethiopia, Fiji, Finland, France, Gambia, Georgia, Germany, Ghana, Greece, Grenada, Guatemala, Guinea, Guinea-Bissau, Guyana, Haiti, Honduras, Hungary, Iceland, Iraq, Ireland, Israel, Italy, Jamaica, Japan, Jordan, Kazakhstan, Kenya, Kuwait, Kyrgyzstan, Latvia, Lebanon, Lesotho, Liberia, Libya, Liechtenstein, Lithuania, Luxembourg, Madagascar, Malawi, Malaysia, Maldives, Mali, Malta, Marshall Islands, Mauritius, Mexico, Micronesia (Federated States of), Monaco, Mongolia, Montenegro, Morocco, Mozambique, Myanmar, Namibia, Nepal, Netherlands, New Zealand, Niger, Nigeria, North Macedonia, Norway, Pakistan, Panama, Papua New Guinea, Paraguay, Peru, Philippines, Poland, Portugal, Republic of Korea, Republic of Moldova, Romania, Rwanda, Saint Lucia, Saint Vincent and the Grenadines, Samoa, San Marino, Sao Tome and Principe, Senegal, Serbia, Sierra Leone, Singapore, Slovakia, Slovenia, South Africa, South Sudan, Spain, Sri Lanka, Sudan, Suriname, Sweden, Switzerland, Thailand, Timor-Leste, Togo, Trinidad and Tobago, Tunisia, Turkey, Uganda, Ukraine,

United Arab Emirates, United Kingdom, United Republic of Tanzania, United States, Uruguay, Vanuatu, Zambia, Zimbabwe

Against
Nauru

Abstaining
Algeria, Armenia, Belarus, Bhutan, Bolivia (Plurinational State of), Cuba, Egypt, Eritrea, India, Indonesia, Iran (Islamic Republic of), Mauritania, Nicaragua, Oman, Qatar, Russian Federation, Saudi Arabia, Syrian Arab Republic, Venezuela (Bolivarian Republic of), Yemen

Action by the First Committee

Date: 2 November 2021   Meeting: 16th meeting
Vote: Adopted without a vote Draft resolution: A/C.1/76/L.15
         150-0-19, p.p. 16

Agenda item 100 (aa)

76/33 Compliance with non-proliferation, arms limitation and disarmament agreements and commitments

Text

The General Assembly,

Recalling its decision 75/517 of 7 December 2020 and relevant resolutions on the question,

Recognizing the abiding concern of all Member States for ensuring respect for the rights and obligations arising from treaties to which they are parties and from other sources of international law,

Convinced that observance by Member States of the Charter of the United Nations and compliance with non-proliferation, arms limitation and disarmament agreements to which they are parties and with other agreed obligations are essential for regional and global peace, security and stability,

Stressing that failure by States parties to comply with such agreements and with other agreed obligations not only adversely affects the security of States parties but also can create security risks for other States relying on the constraints and commitments stipulated in those agreements,

Stressing also that the viability and effectiveness of non-proliferation, arms limitation and disarmament agreements and of other agreed obligations require that those agreements be fully complied with and enforced,

Concerned by non-compliance by some States with their respective obligations,

Noting that verification and compliance, and enforcement in a manner consistent with the Charter, are integrally related,

Recognizing the importance of and support for effective national, regional and international capacities for such verification, compliance and enforcement,

Recognizing also that full compliance by States with all their respective Non-Proliferation, arms limitation and disarmament agreements and with other agreed obligations they have undertaken contributes to efforts to prevent the development and proliferation, contrary to international obligations, of weapons of mass destruction, related technologies and means of delivery, as well as to efforts to deny non-State actors access to such capabilities,

1. *Underscores* the contribution that compliance with non-proliferation, arms limitation and disarmament agreements and with other agreed obligations makes to enhancing confidence and to strengthening international security and stability;

2. *Urges* all States to implement and to comply fully with their respective obligations;

3. *Welcomes* efforts by all States to pursue additional areas of cooperation, as appropriate, that can increase confidence in compliance with existing Non-Proliferation, arms limitation and disarmament agreements and commitments and reduce the possibility of misinterpretation and misunderstanding;

4. *Calls upon* all States to include and empower women, including through capacity-building efforts, as appropriate, as full, equal and meaningful participants in the design and implementation of disarmament, non-proliferation and arms control efforts;

5. *Calls upon* all Member States to encourage and, for those States in a position to do so, to appropriately help States that request assistance to increase their capacity to implement fully their obligations;

6. *Calls upon* Member States to support efforts aimed at the resolution of compliance questions by means consistent with such agreements and other applicable international law;

7. *Welcomes* the role that the United Nations has played and continues to play in maintaining the integrity of certain arms limitation, disarmament and non-proliferation agreements and in addressing threats to international peace and security;

8. *Calls upon* all concerned States to take concerted action, in a manner consistent with relevant international law, to encourage, through bilateral and multilateral means, the compliance by all States with their respective non-proliferation, arms limitation and disarmament agreements and with other agreed obligations, and to hold those not in compliance with such agreements or obligations accountable for their non-compliance in a manner consistent with the Charter of the United Nations;

9. *Urges* those States not currently in compliance with their respective obligations and commitments to make the strategic decision to come back into compliance;

10. *Encourages* efforts by all States, the United Nations and other international organizations, pursuant to their respective mandates, to take action, consistent with the Charter, to prevent serious damage to international security and stability arising from non-compliance by States with their existing non-proliferation, arms limitation and disarmament obligations;

11. *Decides* to include in the provisional agenda of its seventy-ninth session, under the item entitled "General and complete disarmament", the sub-item entitled "Compliance with non-proliferation, arms limitation and disarmament agreements and commitments".

Action by the General Assembly

Date: 6 December 2021   Meeting: 45th plenary meeting
Vote: 174-3-9   Report: A/76/444

Sponsors

Albania, Andorra, Argentina, Australia, Belgium, Bosnia and Herzegovina, Bulgaria, Canada, Croatia, Czechia, Democratic Republic of the Congo, Denmark, Estonia, Finland, Georgia, Germany, Hungary, Iceland, Israel, Italy, Japan, Kiribati, Latvia, Liberia, Lithuania, Luxembourg, Monaco, Montenegro, New Zealand, Niger, North Macedonia, Norway, Palau, Panama, Poland, Portugal, Republic of Korea, Republic of Moldova, Romania, San Marino, Slovakia, Spain, Sweden, Turkey, Ukraine, United Kingdom, **United States**

Co-sponsors

Afghanistan, Angola, Austria, Burkina Faso, Colombia, Côte d'Ivoire, Cyprus, Dominican Republic, El Salvador, Eswatini, Fiji, France, Greece, Guinea-Bissau, Guyana, Haiti, Honduras, Ireland, Lebanon, Lesotho, Liechtenstein, Madagascar, Maldives, Mauritania, Morocco, Myanmar, Netherlands, Slovenia, Suriname, Switzerland, Uruguay, Zambia

Recorded vote

In favour

Afghanistan, Albania, Algeria, Andorra, Angola, Antigua and Barbuda, Argentina, Armenia, Australia, Austria, Azerbaijan, Bahamas, Bahrain, Bangladesh, Barbados, Belgium, Belize, Bhutan, Bosnia and Herzegovina, Botswana, Brazil, Brunei Darussalam, Bulgaria, Burkina Faso, Burundi, Cabo Verde, Cambodia, Cameroon, Canada, Central African Republic, Chad, Chile, Colombia, Comoros, Congo, Costa Rica, Côte d'Ivoire, Croatia, Cyprus, Czechia, Denmark, Djibouti, Dominica, Dominican Republic, Ecuador, El Salvador, Equatorial Guinea, Eritrea, Estonia, Eswatini, Ethiopia, Fiji, Finland, France, Gabon, Gambia, Georgia, Germany, Ghana, Greece, Grenada, Guatemala, Guinea, Guinea-Bissau, Guyana, Haiti, Honduras, Hungary, Iceland, India, Indonesia, Iraq, Ireland, Israel, Italy, Jamaica, Japan, Jordan, Kazakhstan, Kenya, Kiribati, Kuwait, Kyrgyzstan, Lao People's Democratic Republic, Latvia, Lebanon, Lesotho, Liberia, Libya, Liechtenstein, Lithuania, Luxembourg, Madagascar, Malawi, Malaysia, Maldives, Mali, Malta, Marshall Islands, Mauritania, Mauritius, Mexico, Micronesia (Federated States of), Monaco, Mongolia, Montenegro, Morocco, Mozambique, Myanmar, Namibia, Nepal, Netherlands, New Zealand, Niger, Nigeria, North Macedonia, Norway, Oman, Pakistan, Palau, Panama, Papua New Guinea, Paraguay, Peru, Philippines, Poland, Portugal, Qatar, Republic of Korea, Republic of Moldova, Romania, Rwanda, Saint Kitts and Nevis, Saint Lucia, Saint

> Vincent and the Grenadines, Samoa, San Marino, Sao Tome and Principe, Saudi Arabia, Senegal, Serbia, Seychelles, Sierra Leone, Singapore, Slovakia, Slovenia, Solomon Islands, South Africa, South Sudan, Spain, Sri Lanka, Sudan, Suriname, Sweden, Switzerland, Thailand, Timor-Leste, Togo, Tonga, Trinidad and Tobago, Tunisia, Turkey, Tuvalu, Uganda, Ukraine, United Arab Emirates, United Kingdom, United Republic of Tanzania, United States, Uruguay, Vanuatu, Viet Nam, Yemen, Zambia

Against
> China, Democratic People's Republic of Korea, Iran (Islamic Republic of)

Abstaining
> Belarus, Bolivia (Plurinational State of), Cuba, Egypt, Nicaragua, Russian Federation, Syrian Arab Republic, Venezuela (Bolivarian Republic of), Zimbabwe

Action by the First Committee

Date:	3 November 2021	Meeting:	17th meeting
Vote:	166-3-10	Draft resolution:	A/C.1/76/L.16

Agenda item 100 (ii)

76/34 Treaty on the Prohibition of Nuclear Weapons

Text

The General Assembly,

Recalling its resolutions 72/31 of 4 December 2017, 73/48 of 5 December 2018, 74/41 of 12 December 2019 and 75/40 of 7 December 2020,

1. *Recalls* the adoption of the Treaty on the Prohibition of Nuclear Weapons[1] on 7 July 2017;

2. *Welcomes* the entry into force of the Treaty on 22 January 2021;

3. *Notes* that the Treaty has been open for signature at United Nations Headquarters in New York since 20 September 2017;

4. *Welcomes* that already 86 States had signed the Treaty and 55 States had become parties to it as at 6 October 2021;

5. *Confirms* that the Secretary-General of the United Nations is no longer required to convene the first Meeting of States Parties within one year of the entry into force of the Treaty in accordance with article 8, paragraph 2, thereof;

6. *Also confirms* that the first Meeting of States Parties will be held from 22 to 24 March 2022 at the United Nations Office at Vienna, and requests the Secretary-General to convene the first Meeting on those dates and the Secretariat to make the appropriate arrangements to that end;

7. *Invites* States not party to the Treaty, as well as the relevant entities of the United Nations system, other relevant international organizations or institutions, regional organizations, the International Committee of the Red Cross, the International Federation of Red Cross and Red Crescent Societies and relevant non-governmental organizations to attend the first Meeting of States Parties as observers;

8. *Calls upon* all States that have not yet done so to sign, ratify, accept, approve or accede to the Treaty at the earliest possible date;

9. *Calls upon* those States in a position to do so to promote adherence to the Treaty through bilateral, subregional, regional and multilateral contacts, outreach and other means;

10. *Requests* the Secretary-General, as depositary of the Treaty, to report to the General Assembly at its seventy-seventh session on the status of signature and ratification, acceptance, approval or accession of the Treaty;

---

[1] A/CONF.229/2017/8.

11. *Decides* to include in the provisional agenda of its seventy-seventh session, under the item entitled "General and complete disarmament", the sub-item entitled "Treaty on the Prohibition of Nuclear Weapons".

Action by the General Assembly

Date: 6 December 2021   Meeting: 45th plenary meeting
Vote: 128-42-16   Report: A/76/444

Sponsors

Algeria, Antigua and Barbuda, **Austria**, Bangladesh, Botswana, Brazil, Chile, Congo, Costa Rica, Côte d'Ivoire, Cuba, Democratic Republic of the Congo, Ecuador, Equatorial Guinea, Eritrea, Eswatini, Ghana, Guatemala, Indonesia, Ireland, Jamaica, Kazakhstan, Kiribati, Lao People's Democratic Republic, Lesotho, Liechtenstein, Malaysia, Malta, Mauritania, Mexico, Nepal, New Zealand, Nicaragua, Nigeria, Paraguay, Peru, Philippines, San Marino, South Africa, Thailand, Togo, Trinidad and Tobago, Viet Nam, Zimbabwe

Co-sponsors

Angola, Bahamas, Belize, Bolivia (Plurinational State of), Cabo Verde, Dominican Republic, El Salvador, Guinea-Bissau, Guyana, Honduras, Maldives, Mongolia, Mozambique, Myanmar, Namibia, Nauru, Palau, Saint Kitts and Nevis, Saint Lucia, Samoa, Senegal, Turkmenistan, Tuvalu, Uruguay, Venezuela (Bolivarian Republic of), Zambia

Recorded vote

In favour

Afghanistan, Algeria, Andorra, Angola, Antigua and Barbuda, Austria, Azerbaijan, Bahamas, Bahrain, Bangladesh, Barbados, Belize, Bhutan, Bolivia (Plurinational State of), Botswana, Brazil, Brunei Darussalam, Burkina Faso, Burundi, Cabo Verde, Cambodia, Chile, Colombia, Comoros, Congo, Costa Rica, Côte d'Ivoire, Cuba, Cyprus, Dominica, Dominican Republic, Ecuador, Egypt, El Salvador, Equatorial Guinea, Eritrea, Eswatini, Ethiopia, Fiji, Gabon, Gambia, Ghana, Grenada, Guatemala, Guinea, Guinea-Bissau, Guyana, Haiti, Honduras, Indonesia, Iran (Islamic Republic of), Iraq, Ireland, Jamaica, Jordan, Kazakhstan, Kenya, Kiribati, Kuwait, Lao People's Democratic Republic, Lebanon, Lesotho, Liberia, Libya, Liechtenstein, Madagascar, Malawi, Malaysia, Maldives, Mali, Malta, Mauritania, Mauritius, Mexico, Mongolia, Morocco, Mozambique, Myanmar, Namibia, Nauru, Nepal, New Zealand, Nicaragua, Niger, Nigeria, Oman, Palau, Panama, Papua New Guinea, Paraguay, Peru, Philippines, Qatar, Republic of Moldova, Rwanda, Saint Kitts and Nevis, Saint Lucia, Saint Vincent and the Grenadines, Samoa, San Marino, Sao Tome and Principe, Senegal, Seychelles, Sierra Leone,

Solomon Islands, South Africa, South Sudan, Sri Lanka, Sudan, Suriname, Thailand, Timor-Leste, Togo, Trinidad and Tobago, Tunisia, Turkmenistan, Tuvalu, Uganda, United Arab Emirates, United Republic of Tanzania, Uruguay, Uzbekistan, Vanuatu, Venezuela (Bolivarian Republic of), Viet Nam, Yemen, Zambia, Zimbabwe

Against

Albania, Australia, Belgium, Bosnia and Herzegovina, Bulgaria, Canada, China, Croatia, Czechia, Democratic People's Republic of Korea, Denmark, Estonia, France, Germany, Greece, Hungary, Iceland, India, Israel, Italy, Japan, Latvia, Lithuania, Luxembourg, Micronesia (Federated States of), Monaco, Montenegro, Netherlands, North Macedonia, Norway, Pakistan, Poland, Portugal, Republic of Korea, Romania, Russian Federation, Slovakia, Slovenia, Spain, Turkey, United Kingdom, United States

Abstaining

Argentina, Armenia, Belarus, Djibouti, Finland, Georgia, Kyrgyzstan, Marshall Islands, Saudi Arabia, Serbia, Singapore, Sweden, Switzerland, Tajikistan, Tonga, Ukraine

Action by the First Committee

Date: 27 October 2021 Meeting: 13th meeting
Vote: 123-42-16 Draft resolution: A/C.1/76/L.17

Agenda item 100 (e)

76/35   Prohibition of the dumping of radioactive wastes

Text

The General Assembly,

Bearing in mind resolutions CM/Res.1153 (XLVIII) of 1988[1] and CM/Res.1225 (L) of 1989,[2] adopted by the Council of Ministers of the Organization of African Unity, concerning the dumping of nuclear and industrial wastes in Africa,

Recalling resolution GC(XXXIV)/RES/530 establishing the Code of Practice on the International Transboundary Movement of Radioactive Waste, adopted on 21 September 1990 by the General Conference of the International Atomic Energy Agency at its thirty-fourth regular session,

Taking note of the commitment made by the participants in the Summit on Nuclear Safety and Security, held in Moscow on 19 and 20 April 1996, to ban the dumping at sea of radioactive wastes,[3]

Considering its resolution 2602 C (XXIV) of 16 December 1969, in which the General Assembly requested the Conference of the Committee on Disarmament,[4] inter alia, to consider effective methods of control against the use of radiological methods of warfare,

Aware of the potential hazards underlying any use of radioactive wastes that would constitute radiological warfare and its implications for regional and international security, in particular for the security of developing countries,

Recalling all its resolutions on the matter since its forty-third session in 1988, including its resolution 51/45 J of 10 December 1996,

Recalling also resolution GC(45)/RES/10, adopted by consensus on 21 September 2001 by the General Conference of the International Atomic Energy Agency at its forty-fifth regular session, in which States shipping radioactive materials are invited to provide, as appropriate, assurances to concerned States, upon their request, that the national regulations of the shipping State take into account the Agency's transport regulations and to provide them with relevant information relating to the shipment of such materials, with the information provided being in no case contradictory to the measures of physical security and safety,

---

[1]   See A/43/398, annex I.

[2]   See A/44/603, annex I.

[3]   A/51/131, annex I, para. 20.

[4]   The Conference of the Committee on Disarmament became the Committee on Disarmament as from the tenth special session of the General Assembly. The Committee on Disarmament was redesignated the Conference on Disarmament as from 7 February 1984.

Recalling further the adoption, in Vienna on 5 September 1997, of the Joint Convention on the Safety of Spent Fuel Management and on the Safety of Radioactive Waste Management,[5] as recommended by the participants in the Summit on Nuclear Safety and Security,

Recalling the convening by the International Atomic Energy Agency of the Ministerial Conference on Nuclear Safety, in Vienna from 20 to 24 June 2011, and its outcome, the Declaration of the International Atomic Energy Agency Ministerial Conference on Nuclear Safety, as well as the Action Plan on Nuclear Safety, endorsed by the General Conference of the Agency at its fifty-fifth regular session,

Noting the convening by the Secretary-General of the high-level meeting on nuclear safety and security, in New York on 22 September 2011,

Noting with satisfaction that the Joint Convention entered into force on 18 June 2001,

Noting that the first Review Meeting of the Contracting Parties to the Joint Convention on the Safety of Spent Fuel Management and on the Safety of Radioactive Waste Management was convened in Vienna from 3 to 14 November 2003,

Desirous of promoting the implementation of paragraph 76 of the Final Document of the Tenth Special Session of the General Assembly, the first special session devoted to disarmament,[6]

1.   *Takes note* of the part of the report of the Conference on Disarmament relating to radiological weapons;[7]

2.   *Also takes note* of the Declaration of the International Atomic Energy Agency Ministerial Conference on Nuclear Safety, the Action Plan on Nuclear Safety and the high-level meeting on nuclear safety and security convened by the Secretary-General;

3.   *Expresses grave concern* regarding any use of nuclear wastes that would constitute radiological warfare and have grave implications for the national security of all States;

4.   *Calls upon* all States to take appropriate measures with a view to preventing any dumping of nuclear or radioactive wastes that would infringe upon the sovereignty of States;

5.   *Requests* the Conference on Disarmament to take into account, in any negotiations for a convention on the prohibition of radiological weapons, radioactive wastes as part of the scope of such a convention;

---

[5] United Nations, *Treaty Series*, vol. 2153, No. 37605.
[6] Resolution S-10/2.
[7] *Official Records of the General Assembly, Seventy-sixth Session, Supplement No. 27* (A/76/27), sect. III.E.

6.   *Also requests* the Conference on Disarmament to continue to consider such a convention and to include in its report to the General Assembly at its seventy-seventh session the progress recorded in the negotiations on this subject;

7.   *Takes note* of resolution CM/Res.1356 (LIV) of 1991, adopted by the Council of Ministers of the Organization of African Unity,[8] on the Bamako Convention on the Ban of the Import into Africa and the Control of Transboundary Movement and Management of Hazardous Wastes within Africa;[9]

8.   *Expresses the hope* that the effective implementation of the International Atomic Energy Agency Code of Practice on the International Transboundary Movement of Radioactive Waste will enhance the protection of all States from the dumping of radioactive wastes on their territories;

9.   *Appeals* to all Member States that have not yet taken the steps necessary to become party to the Joint Convention on the Safety of Spent Fuel Management and on the Safety of Radioactive Waste Management to do so as soon as possible;

10.   *Decides* to include in the provisional agenda of its seventy-eighth session, under the item entitled "General and complete disarmament", the sub-item entitled "Prohibition of the dumping of radioactive wastes".

Action by the General Assembly

Date: 6 December 2021   Meeting: 45th plenary meeting
Vote: Adopted without a vote   Report: A/76/444

Sponsors

Nigeria (on behalf of the States Members of the United Nations that are members of the Group of African States)

Co-sponsors

Maldives

Action by the First Committee

Date: 27 October 2021   Meeting: 13th meeting
Vote: Adopted without a vote   Draft resolution: A/C.1/76/L.20

---

[8]   See A/46/390, annex I.
[9]   United Nations, *Treaty Series*, vol. 2101, No. 36508.

Agenda item 100 (bb)

76/36 Follow-up to the 2013 high-level meeting of the General Assembly on nuclear disarmament

Text

The General Assembly,

Recalling its resolutions 67/39 of 3 December 2012, 68/32 of 5 December 2013, 69/58 of 2 December 2014, 70/34 of 7 December 2015, 71/71 of 5 December 2016, 72/251 of 24 December 2017, 73/40 of 5 December 2018, 74/54 of 12 December 2019 and 75/45 of 7 December 2020,

Welcoming the convening of the high-level meeting of the General Assembly on nuclear disarmament, on 26 September 2013, and recognizing its contribution to furthering the objective of the total elimination of nuclear weapons,

Emphasizing the importance of seeking a safer world for all and achieving peace and security in a world without nuclear weapons,

Reaffirming that effective measures of nuclear disarmament have the highest priority, as affirmed at the first special session of the General Assembly devoted to disarmament,

Convinced that nuclear disarmament and the total elimination of nuclear weapons are the only absolute guarantee against the use or threat of use of nuclear weapons,

Acknowledging the significant contribution made by a number of countries towards realizing the objective of nuclear disarmament by the establishment of nuclear-weapon-free zones, as well as by the voluntary renunciation of nuclear weapon programmes or withdrawal of all nuclear weapons from their territories, and strongly supporting the speedy establishment of a nuclear-weapon-free zone in the Middle East,

Recalling the resolve of the Heads of State and Government, as contained in the United Nations Millennium Declaration,[1] to strive for the elimination of weapons of mass destruction, particularly nuclear weapons, and to keep all options open for achieving this aim, including the possibility of convening an international conference to identify ways of eliminating nuclear dangers,

Reaffirming the central role of the United Nations in the field of disarmament, and reaffirming also the continued importance and relevance of multilateral disarmament machinery as mandated by the General Assembly at its first special session devoted to disarmament,

---

[1] Resolution 55/2.

Acknowledging the important role of civil society, including non-governmental organizations, academia, parliamentarians and the mass media, in advancing the objective of nuclear disarmament,

Sharing the deep concern at the catastrophic humanitarian consequences of any use of nuclear weapons, and in this context reaffirming the need for all States at all times to comply with applicable international law, including international humanitarian law,

Taking note of the report of the Secretary-General submitted pursuant to resolution 75/45,[2] and welcoming the fact that a large number of Member States contributed their views to this report,

Noting the adoption, with a vote, of the Treaty on the Prohibition of Nuclear Weapons[3] on 7 July 2017 at the United Nations conference to negotiate a legally binding instrument to prohibit nuclear weapons, leading towards their total elimination, and its entry into force on 22 January 2021,

Mindful of the solemn obligations of States parties, undertaken in article VI of the Treaty on the Non-Proliferation of Nuclear Weapons,[4] particularly to pursue negotiations in good faith on effective measures relating to the cessation of the nuclear arms race at an early date and to nuclear disarmament,

Expressing its concern that improvements in existing nuclear weapons and the development of new types of nuclear weapons, as provided for in the military doctrines of some nuclear-weapon States, violate their legal obligations on nuclear disarmament, as well as the commitments made to diminish the role of nuclear weapons in their military and security policies, and contravene the negative security assurances provided by the nuclear-weapon States,

Expressing its deep concern that the negotiations in the Conference on Disarmament for the conclusion of a comprehensive convention on nuclear weapons have not yet commenced,

Determined to work collectively towards the realization of nuclear disarmament,

1.   *Underlines* the strong support, expressed at the high-level meeting of the General Assembly on nuclear disarmament, held on 26 September 2013, for taking urgent and effective measures to achieve the total elimination of nuclear weapons;

2.   *Calls for* urgent compliance with the legal obligations and the fulfilment of the commitments undertaken on nuclear disarmament;

---

[2] A/76/125.
[3] A/CONF.229/2017/8.
[4] United Nations, *Treaty Series*, vol. 729, No. 10485.

3. *Endorses* the wide support expressed at the high-level meeting for a comprehensive convention on nuclear weapons;

4. *Calls for* the urgent commencement of negotiations in the Conference on Disarmament on effective nuclear disarmament measures to achieve the total elimination of nuclear weapons, including, in particular, on a comprehensive convention on nuclear weapons;

5. *Decides* to convene, in New York, on a date to be decided later, a United Nations high-level international conference on nuclear disarmament to review the progress made in this regard;

6. *Takes note* of the views provided by Member States with regard to achieving the objective of the total elimination of nuclear weapons, in particular on the elements of a comprehensive convention on nuclear weapons, as reflected in the report submitted by the Secretary-General pursuant to resolution 75/45, and requests the Secretary-General to forward this report to the Conference on Disarmament and the Disarmament Commission for their early consideration;

7. *Welcomes* the commemoration and promotion of 26 September as the International Day for the Total Elimination of Nuclear Weapons devoted to furthering this objective;

8. *Expresses its appreciation* to Member States, the United Nations system and civil society, including non-governmental organizations, academia, parliamentarians, the mass media and individuals that developed activities in promotion of the International Day for the Total Elimination of Nuclear Weapons;

9. *Reiterates its request* to the President of the General Assembly to organize, on 26 September every year, a one-day high-level plenary meeting of the Assembly to commemorate and promote the International Day for the Total Elimination of Nuclear Weapons;

10. *Decides* that the aforementioned high-level plenary meeting shall be held with the participation of Member and observer States, represented at the highest possible level, as well as with the participation of the President of the General Assembly and the Secretary-General;

11. *Requests* the Secretary-General to continue to update the platform for the promotion of these activities and to undertake all the arrangements, providing all the necessary resources and services, including webcasts, to commemorate and promote the International Day for the Total Elimination of Nuclear Weapons, including through the United Nations Offices at Geneva and Vienna, as well as the United Nations regional centres for peace and disarmament;

12. *Calls upon* Member States, the United Nations system and civil society, including non-governmental organizations, academia,

parliamentarians, the mass media and individuals, to commemorate and promote the International Day for the Total Elimination of Nuclear Weapons through all means of educational and public awareness-raising activities about the threat posed to humanity by nuclear weapons and the necessity for their total elimination in order to mobilize international efforts towards achieving the common goal of a nuclear-weapon-free world;

13.   *Requests* the Secretary-General to seek the views of Member States with regard to achieving the objective of the total elimination of nuclear weapons, in particular on effective nuclear disarmament measures, including elements of a comprehensive convention on nuclear weapons, and to submit a report thereon to the General Assembly at its seventy-seventh session, and also to transmit the report to the Conference on Disarmament;

14.   *Also requests* the Secretary-General to report on the implementation of the present resolution to the General Assembly at its seventy-seventh session;

15.   *Decides* to include in the provisional agenda of its seventy-seventh session, under the item entitled "General and complete disarmament", the sub-item entitled "Follow-up to the 2013 high-level meeting of the General Assembly on nuclear disarmament".

Action by the General Assembly

Date: 6 December 2021	Meeting: 45th plenary meeting
Vote: 145-34-9	Report: A/76/444
120-37-15, p.p. 14	

Sponsors

Indonesia (on behalf of the States Members of the United Nations that are members of the Movement of Non-Aligned Countries)

Recorded vote

As a whole

In favour

Afghanistan, Algeria, Andorra, Angola, Antigua and Barbuda, Argentina, Armenia, Austria, Azerbaijan, Bahamas, Bahrain, Bangladesh, Barbados, Belarus, Belize, Bhutan, Bolivia (Plurinational State of), Botswana, Brazil, Brunei Darussalam, Burkina Faso, Burundi, Cabo Verde, Cambodia, Cameroon, Central African Republic, Chad, Chile, China, Colombia, Comoros, Congo, Costa Rica, Côte d'Ivoire, Cuba, Cyprus, Democratic People's Republic of Korea, Djibouti, Dominica, Dominican Republic, Ecuador, Egypt, El Salvador, Equatorial Guinea, Eritrea, Eswatini, Ethiopia, Fiji, Gabon, Gambia, Ghana, Grenada, Guatemala, Guinea, Guinea-Bissau, Guyana, Haiti, Honduras, India, Indonesia, Iran (Islamic

Republic of), Iraq, Ireland, Jamaica, Jordan, Kazakhstan, Kenya, Kiribati, Kuwait, Kyrgyzstan, Lao People's Democratic Republic, Lebanon, Lesotho, Liberia, Libya, Liechtenstein, Madagascar, Malawi, Malaysia, Maldives, Mali, Malta, Marshall Islands, Mauritania, Mauritius, Mexico, Mongolia, Morocco, Mozambique, Myanmar, Namibia, Nauru, Nepal, New Zealand, Nicaragua, Niger, Nigeria, Oman, Pakistan, Palau, Panama, Papua New Guinea, Paraguay, Peru, Philippines, Qatar, Republic of Moldova, Rwanda, Saint Kitts and Nevis, Saint Lucia, Saint Vincent and the Grenadines, Samoa, San Marino, Sao Tome and Principe, Saudi Arabia, Senegal, Seychelles, Sierra Leone, Singapore, South Africa, South Sudan, Sri Lanka, Sudan, Suriname, Syrian Arab Republic, Tajikistan, Thailand, Timor-Leste, Togo, Tonga, Trinidad and Tobago, Tunisia, Turkmenistan, Tuvalu, Uganda, United Arab Emirates, United Republic of Tanzania, Uruguay, Uzbekistan, Vanuatu, Venezuela (Bolivarian Republic of), Viet Nam, Yemen, Zambia, Zimbabwe

Against

Albania, Australia, Belgium, Bulgaria, Croatia, Czechia, Denmark, Estonia, France, Germany, Greece, Hungary, Iceland, Israel, Italy, Latvia, Lithuania, Luxembourg, Monaco, Montenegro, Netherlands, North Macedonia, Norway, Poland, Portugal, Republic of Korea, Romania, Russian Federation, Slovakia, Slovenia, Spain, Turkey, United Kingdom, United States

Abstaining

Bosnia and Herzegovina, Canada, Finland, Georgia, Japan, Serbia, Sweden, Switzerland, Ukraine

Fourteenth preambular paragraph

In favour

Afghanistan, Algeria, Angola, Antigua and Barbuda, Argentina, Azerbaijan, Bahamas, Bahrain, Bangladesh, Barbados, Belarus, Belize, Bhutan, Bolivia (Plurinational State of), Botswana, Brazil, Brunei Darussalam, Burkina Faso, Burundi, Cabo Verde, Cambodia, Chad, Chile, China, Colombia, Comoros, Costa Rica, Côte d'Ivoire, Cuba, Democratic People's Republic of Korea, Djibouti, Dominica, Dominican Republic, Ecuador, Egypt, El Salvador, Equatorial Guinea, Eritrea, Eswatini, Ethiopia, Fiji, Gambia, Ghana, Grenada, Guatemala, Guinea, Guinea-Bissau, Guyana, Haiti, Honduras, India, Indonesia, Iran (Islamic Republic of), Iraq, Jamaica, Jordan, Kazakhstan, Kenya, Kiribati, Kuwait, Lao People's Democratic Republic, Lebanon, Lesotho, Liberia, Libya, Madagascar, Malawi, Malaysia, Maldives, Mali, Mauritania, Mauritius, Mexico, Mongolia, Morocco, Mozambique, Myanmar, Namibia, Nauru, Nepal, Nicaragua, Niger, Nigeria, Oman, Pakistan, Panama, Papua New Guinea, Paraguay, Peru, Philippines, Qatar, Saint Lucia, Saint Vincent and the Grenadines, Samoa, Sao Tome and Principe, Saudi Arabia, Senegal, Seychelles, Singapore, South Africa, Sri Lanka, Sudan, Suriname, Syrian Arab Republic, Thailand, Timor-Leste, Togo, Trinidad and Tobago, Tunisia, Turkmenistan, Uganda, United Arab Emirates, United Republic of Tanzania, Uruguay, Vanuatu, Venezuela (Bolivarian Republic of), Viet Nam, Yemen, Zambia, Zimbabwe

Against

Albania, Australia, Belgium, Bulgaria, Canada, Croatia, Czechia, Denmark, Estonia, Finland, France, Germany, Greece, Hungary, Iceland, Israel, Italy, Latvia, Lithuania, Luxembourg, Monaco, Montenegro, Netherlands, North Macedonia, Norway, Poland, Portugal, Republic of Korea, Romania, Russian Federation, Slovakia, Slovenia, Spain, Turkey, Ukraine, United Kingdom, United States

Abstaining

Andorra, Armenia, Austria, Bosnia and Herzegovina, Cyprus, Georgia, Ireland, Japan, Liechtenstein, Malta, New Zealand, Republic of Moldova, San Marino, Sweden, Switzerland

Action by the First Committee

Date:	27 October 2021	Meeting:	13th meeting
Vote:	138-34-11	Draft resolution:	A/C.1/76/L.23
	115-37-17, p.p. 14		

Agenda item 100 (d)

76/37   Relationship between disarmament and development

Text

The General Assembly,

Recalling that the Charter of the United Nations envisages the establishment and maintenance of international peace and security with the least diversion for armaments of the world's human and economic resources,

Recalling also the provisions of the Final Document of the Tenth Special Session of the General Assembly concerning the relationship between disarmament and development,[1] as well as the adoption on 11 September 1987 of the Final Document of the International Conference on the Relationship between Disarmament and Development,[2]

Recalling further its resolutions 49/75 J of 15 December 1994, 50/70 G of 12 December 1995, 51/45 D of 10 December 1996, 52/38 D of 9 December 1997, 53/77 K of 4 December 1998, 54/54 T of 1 December 1999, 55/33 L of 20 November 2000, 56/24 E of 29 November 2001, 57/65 of 22 November 2002, 59/78 of 3 December 2004, 60/61 of 8 December 2005, 61/64 of 6 December 2006, 62/48 of 5 December 2007, 63/52 of 2 December 2008, 64/32 of 2 December 2009, 65/52 of 8 December 2010, 66/30 of 2 December 2011, 67/40 of 3 December 2012, 68/37 of 5 December 2013, 69/56 of 2 December 2014, 70/32 of 7 December 2015, 71/62 of 5 December 2016, 72/46 of 4 December 2017, 73/37 of 5 December 2018, 74/57 of 12 December 2019 and 75/43 of 7 December 2020 and its decision 58/520 of 8 December 2003,

Bearing in mind the Final Document of the Eighteenth Summit of Heads of State or Government of Non-Aligned Countries, held in Baku on 25 and 26 October 2019,[3]

Mindful of the changes in international relations that have taken place since the adoption in 1987 of the Final Document of the International Conference on the Relationship between Disarmament and Development, including the development agenda that has emerged over the past decade,

Bearing in mind the new challenges for the international community in the fields of development, poverty eradication and the elimination of the diseases that afflict humanity,

Stressing the importance of the symbiotic relationship between disarmament and development and the important role of security in this

---

[1]   See resolution S-10/2.
[2]   See *Report of the International Conference on the Relationship between Disarmament and Development, New York, 24 August–11 September 1987* (A/CONF.130/39).
[3]   A/74/548, annex.

connection, and concerned at increasing global military expenditure, which could otherwise be spent on development needs,

Recalling the report of the Group of Governmental Experts on the relationship between disarmament and development[4] and its reappraisal of this significant issue in the current international context,

Bearing in mind the importance of following up on the implementation of the action programme adopted at the 1987 International Conference on the Relationship between Disarmament and Development,

Taking note of the report of the Secretary-General submitted pursuant to resolution 75/43,[5]

1.   *Stresses* the central role of the United Nations in the relationship between disarmament and development, and requests the Secretary-General to strengthen further the role of the Organization in this field, in particular the high-level Steering Group on Disarmament and Development, in order to ensure continued and effective coordination and close cooperation between the relevant United Nations departments, agencies and subagencies;

2.   *Requests* the Secretary-General to continue to take action, through appropriate organs and within available resources, for the implementation of the action programme adopted on 11 September 1987 at the International Conference on the Relationship between Disarmament and Development;

3.   *Urges* the international community to devote part of the resources made available by the implementation of disarmament and arms limitation agreements to economic and social development, with a view to reducing the ever-widening gap between developed and developing countries;

4.   *Encourages* the international community to achieve the Sustainable Development Goals[6] and to make reference to the contribution that disarmament could provide in meeting them when it reviews its progress towards this purpose, as well as to make greater efforts to integrate disarmament, humanitarian and development activities;

5.   *Encourages* the relevant regional and subregional organizations and institutions, non-governmental organizations and research institutes to incorporate issues related to the relationship between disarmament and development into their agendas and, in this regard, to take into account the report of the Group of Governmental Experts on the relationship between disarmament and development;

6.   *Reiterates its invitation* to Member States to provide the Secretary-General with information regarding measures and efforts to devote part of the

---

[4] See A/59/119.
[5] A/76/88.
[6] See resolution 70/1.

resources made available by the implementation of disarmament and arms limitation agreements to economic and social development, with a view to reducing the ever-widening gap between developed and developing countries;

7.   *Requests* the Secretary-General to report to the General Assembly at its seventy-seventh session on the implementation of the present resolution, including the information provided by Member States pursuant to paragraph 6 above;

8.   *Decides* to include in the provisional agenda of its seventy-seventh session, under the item entitled "General and complete disarmament", the sub-item entitled "Relationship between disarmament and development".

Action by the General Assembly

Date: 6 December 2021   Meeting: 45th plenary meeting
Vote: Adopted without a vote   Report: A/76/444

Sponsors

Indonesia (on behalf of the States Members of the United Nations that are members of the Movement of Non-Aligned Countries)

Action by the First Committee

Date: 3 November 2021   Meeting: 17th meeting
Vote: Adopted without a vote   Draft resolution: A/C.1/76/L.24

Agenda item 100 (h)

76/38   Convening of the fourth special session of the General Assembly devoted to disarmament

Text

The General Assembly,

Recalling its resolutions 49/75 I of 15 December 1994, 50/70 F of 12 December 1995, 51/45 C of 10 December 1996, 52/38 F of 9 December 1997, 53/77 AA of 4 December 1998, 54/54 U of 1 December 1999, 55/33 M of 20 November 2000, 56/24 D of 29 November 2001, 57/61 of 22 November 2002, 59/71 of 3 December 2004, 61/60 of 6 December 2006, 62/29 of 5 December 2007, 65/66 of 8 December 2010, 72/49 of 4 December 2017, 73/42 of 5 December 2018, 74/56 of 12 December 2019 and 75/44 of 7 December 2020, as well as its decisions 58/521 of 8 December 2003, 60/518 of 8 December 2005, 60/559 of 6 June 2006, 63/519 of 2 December 2008, 64/515 of 2 December 2009 and 70/551 of 23 December 2015,

Recalling also that, there being a consensus to do so in each case, three special sessions of the General Assembly devoted to disarmament were held in 1978, 1982 and 1988, respectively,

Bearing in mind the Final Document of the Tenth Special Session of the General Assembly, adopted by consensus at the first special session devoted to disarmament,[1]

Bearing in mind also the ultimate objective of general and complete disarmament under effective international control,

Reiterating its conviction that a special session of the General Assembly devoted to disarmament can set the future course of action in the fields of disarmament, arms control, non-proliferation and related international security matters,

Emphasizing the importance of multilateralism in the process of disarmament, arms control, non-proliferation and related international security matters,

Recalling the conclusion of the work of the Open-ended Working Group on the fourth special session of the General Assembly devoted to disarmament to consider the objectives and agenda of the fourth special session, and to adopt its report and substantive recommendations by consensus,

Recalling also the report of the Open-ended Working Group and the recommendations contained therein,[2]

---

[1]   Resolution S-10/2.
[2]   A/AC.268/2017/2.

1.   *Recalls* the adoption by consensus of the recommendations on the objectives and agenda of the fourth special session of the General Assembly devoted to disarmament by the Open-ended Working Group on the fourth special session of the General Assembly devoted to disarmament, which was established by the Assembly by its resolution 65/66 and its decision 70/551 and which met in New York in 2016 and 2017;

2.   *Also recalls* the report of the Open-ended Working Group and the substantive recommendations contained therein;

3.   *Reiterates its appreciation* to the participants of the Open-ended Working Group for their constructive contribution to its work;

4.   *Encourages* Member States to continue consultations on the next steps for the convening of the fourth special session of the General Assembly devoted to disarmament;

5.   *Decides* to include in the provisional agenda of its seventy-seventh session, under the item entitled "General and complete disarmament", the sub-item entitled "Convening of the fourth special session of the General Assembly devoted to disarmament".

Action by the General Assembly

Date: 6 December 2021   Meeting: 45th plenary meeting
Vote: Adopted without a vote   Report: A/76/444

Sponsors

Indonesia (on behalf of the States Members of the United Nations that are members of the Movement of Non-Aligned Countries)

Action by the First Committee

Date: 3 November 2021   Meeting: 17th meeting
Vote: Adopted without a vote   Draft resolution: A/C.1/76/L.25

Agenda item 100 (j)

76/39   Observance of environmental norms in the drafting and implementation of agreements on disarmament and arms control

Text

The General Assembly,

Recalling its resolutions 50/70 M of 12 December 1995, 51/45 E of 10 December 1996, 52/38 E of 9 December 1997, 53/77 J of 4 December 1998, 54/54 S of 1 December 1999, 55/33 K of 20 November 2000, 56/24 F of 29 November 2001, 57/64 of 22 November 2002, 58/45 of 8 December 2003, 59/68 of 3 December 2004, 60/60 of 8 December 2005, 61/63 of 6 December 2006, 62/28 of 5 December 2007, 63/51 of 2 December 2008, 64/33 of 2 December 2009, 65/53 of 8 December 2010, 66/31 of 2 December 2011, 67/37 of 3 December 2012, 68/36 of 5 December 2013, 69/55 of 2 December 2014, 70/30 of 7 December 2015, 71/60 of 5 December 2016, 72/47 of 4 December 2017, 73/39 of 5 December 2018, 74/52 of 12 December 2019 and 75/53 of 7 December 2020,

Emphasizing the importance of the observance of environmental norms in the preparation and implementation of disarmament and arms limitation agreements,

Recognizing that it is necessary to take duly into account the agreements adopted at the United Nations Conference on Environment and Development, as well as prior relevant agreements, in the drafting and implementation of agreements on disarmament and arms limitation,

Taking note of the report of the Secretary-General submitted pursuant to resolution 75/53,[1]

Noting that the Eighteenth Summit of Heads of State or Government of Non-Aligned Countries, held in Baku on 25 and 26 October 2019, welcomed the adoption by the General Assembly, without a vote, of resolution 73/39 on the observance of environmental norms in the drafting and implementation of agreements on disarmament and arms control,[2]

Mindful of the detrimental environmental effects of the use of nuclear weapons,

1.   *Reaffirms* that international disarmament forums should take fully into account the relevant environmental norms in negotiating treaties and agreements on disarmament and arms limitation and that all States, through their actions, should contribute fully to ensuring compliance with the

---

[1]   A/76/113.

[2]   See A/74/548, annex.

aforementioned norms in the implementation of treaties and conventions to which they are parties;

2. *Calls upon* States to adopt unilateral, bilateral, regional and multilateral measures so as to contribute to ensuring the application of scientific and technological progress within the framework of international security, disarmament and other related spheres, without detriment to the environment or to its effective contribution to attaining sustainable development;

3. *Welcomes* the information provided by Member States on the implementation of the measures that they have adopted to promote the objectives envisaged in the present resolution;

4. *Invites* all Member States to communicate to the Secretary-General information on the measures that they have adopted to promote the objectives envisaged in the present resolution, and requests the Secretary-General to submit a report containing that information to the General Assembly at its seventy-seventh session;

5. *Decides* to include in the provisional agenda of its seventy-seventh session, under the item entitled "General and complete disarmament", the sub-item entitled "Observance of environmental norms in the drafting and implementation of agreements on disarmament and arms control".

Action by the General Assembly

Date: 6 December 2021	Meeting: 45th plenary meeting
Vote: Adopted without a vote	Report: A/76/444

Sponsors

Indonesia (on behalf of the States Members of the United Nations that are members of the Movement of Non-Aligned Countries)

Action by the First Committee

Date: 3 November 2021	Meeting: 17th meeting
Vote: Adopted without a vote	Draft resolution: A/C.1/76/L.26

Agenda item 100 (r)

76/40 Promotion of multilateralism in the area of disarmament and non-proliferation

Text

The General Assembly,

Determined to foster strict respect for the purposes and principles enshrined in the Charter of the United Nations,

Recalling its resolution 56/24 T of 29 November 2001 on multilateral cooperation in the area of disarmament and non-proliferation and global efforts against terrorism and other relevant resolutions, as well as its resolutions 57/63 of 22 November 2002, 58/44 of 8 December 2003, 59/69 of 3 December 2004, 60/59 of 8 December 2005, 61/62 of 6 December 2006, 62/27 of 5 December 2007, 63/50 of 2 December 2008, 64/34 of 2 December 2009, 65/54 of 8 December 2010, 66/32 of 2 December 2011, 67/38 of 3 December 2012, 68/38 of 5 December 2013, 69/54 of 2 December 2014, 70/31 of 7 December 2015, 71/61 of 5 December 2016, 72/48 of 4 December 2017, 73/41 of 5 December 2018, 74/55 of 12 December 2019 and 75/47 of 7 December 2020 on the promotion of multilateralism in the area of disarmament and non-proliferation,

Recalling also the purpose of the United Nations to maintain international peace and security and, to that end, to take effective collective measures for the prevention and removal of threats to the peace and for the suppression of acts of aggression or other breaches of the peace, and to bring about by peaceful means, and in conformity with the principles of justice and international law, adjustment or settlement of international disputes or situations which might lead to a breach of the peace, as enshrined in the Charter,

Recalling further the United Nations Millennium Declaration,[1] in which it is stated, inter alia, that the responsibility for managing worldwide economic and social development, as well as threats to international peace and security, must be shared among the nations of the world and should be exercised multilaterally and that, as the most universal and most representative organization in the world, the United Nations must play the central role,

Convinced that, in the globalization era and with the information revolution, arms regulation, non-proliferation and disarmament problems are more than ever the concern of all countries in the world, which are affected in one way or another by these problems and therefore should have the possibility to participate in the negotiations that arise to tackle them,

---

[1] Resolution 55/2.

Bearing in mind the existence of a broad structure of disarmament and arms regulation agreements resulting from non-discriminatory and transparent multilateral negotiations with the participation of a large number of countries, regardless of their size and power,

Aware of the need to advance further in the field of arms regulation, Non-Proliferation and disarmament on the basis of universal, multilateral, non-discriminatory and transparent negotiations with the goal of reaching general and complete disarmament under strict international control,

Recognizing the complementarity of bilateral, plurilateral and multilateral negotiations on disarmament,

Recognizing also that the proliferation and development of weapons of mass destruction, including nuclear weapons, are among the most immediate threats to international peace and security which need to be dealt with, with the highest priority,

Considering that the multilateral disarmament agreements provide the mechanism for States parties to consult one another and to cooperate in solving any problems which may arise in relation to the objective of, or in the application of, the provisions of the agreements and that such consultations and cooperation may also be undertaken through appropriate international procedures within the framework of the United Nations and in accordance with the Charter,

Stressing that international cooperation, the peaceful settlement of disputes, dialogue and confidence-building measures would make an essential contribution to the creation of multilateral and bilateral friendly relations among peoples and nations,

Being gravely concerned at the continuous and progressive erosion of multilateralism in the field of arms regulation, non-proliferation and disarmament, and recognizing that the abrogation of major instruments of the arms control and Non-Proliferation architecture as a result of unilateral actions by Member States in resolving their security concerns would jeopardize international peace and security and undermine confidence in the international security system as well as the foundations of the United Nations itself,

Noting that the Eighteenth Summit of Heads of State or Government of Non-Aligned Countries, held in Baku on 25 and 26 October 2019, welcomed the adoption of resolution 73/41 on the promotion of multilateralism in the area of disarmament and non-proliferation and underlined the fact that multilateralism and multilaterally agreed solutions, in accordance with the Charter, provide the only sustainable method of addressing disarmament and international security issues,[2]

---

[2] See A/74/548, annex.

Reaffirming the absolute validity of multilateral diplomacy in the field of disarmament and non-proliferation, and determined to promote multilateralism as an essential way to develop arms regulation and disarmament negotiations,

1. *Reaffirms* multilateralism as the core principle in negotiations in the area of disarmament and non-proliferation with a view to maintaining and strengthening universal norms and enlarging their scope;

2. *Also reaffirms* multilateralism as the core principle in resolving disarmament and non-proliferation concerns;

3. *Urges* the participation of all interested States in multilateral negotiations on arms regulation, non-proliferation and disarmament in a non-discriminatory and transparent manner;

4. *Underlines* the importance of preserving the existing agreements on arms regulation and disarmament and the multilateral disarmament forums, which constitute an expression of the results of international cooperation and multilateral negotiations in response to the challenges facing humankind;

5. *Calls once again upon* all Member States to renew and fulfil their individual and collective commitments to multilateral cooperation as an important means of pursuing and achieving their common objectives in the area of disarmament and non-proliferation;

6. *Requests* the States parties to the relevant instruments on weapons of mass destruction to consult and cooperate among themselves in resolving their concerns with regard to cases of non-compliance as well as on implementation, in accordance with the procedures defined in those instruments, and to refrain from resorting or threatening to resort to unilateral actions or directing unverified non-compliance accusations against one another to resolve their concerns;

7. *Takes note* of the report of the Secretary-General containing the replies of Member States on the promotion of multilateralism in the area of disarmament and non-proliferation, submitted pursuant to resolution 75/47;[3]

8. *Requests* the Secretary-General to seek the views of Member States on the issue of the promotion of multilateralism in the area of disarmament and Non-Proliferation and to submit a report thereon to the General Assembly at its seventy-seventh session;

9. *Decides* to include in the provisional agenda of its seventy-seventh session, under the item entitled "General and complete disarmament", the sub-item entitled "Promotion of multilateralism in the area of disarmament and non-proliferation".

---

[3] A/76/90.

Action by the General Assembly

Date: 6 December 2021   Meeting: 45th plenary meeting

Vote: 134-4-51   Report: A/76/444

Sponsors

Indonesia (on behalf of the States Members of the United Nations that are members of the Movement of Non-Aligned Countries)

Recorded vote

In favour

Afghanistan, Algeria, Angola, Antigua and Barbuda, Argentina, Azerbaijan, Bahamas, Bahrain, Bangladesh, Barbados, Belarus, Belize, Bhutan, Bolivia (Plurinational State of), Botswana, Brazil, Brunei Darussalam, Burkina Faso, Burundi, Cabo Verde, Cambodia, Cameroon, Central African Republic, Chad, Chile, China, Colombia, Comoros, Congo, Costa Rica, Côte d'Ivoire, Cuba, Democratic People's Republic of Korea, Djibouti, Dominica, Dominican Republic, Ecuador, Egypt, El Salvador, Equatorial Guinea, Eritrea, Eswatini, Ethiopia, Fiji, Gabon, Gambia, Ghana, Grenada, Guatemala, Guinea, Guinea-Bissau, Guyana, Haiti, Honduras, India, Indonesia, Iran (Islamic Republic of), Iraq, Jamaica, Jordan, Kazakhstan, Kenya, Kiribati, Kuwait, Kyrgyzstan, Lao People's Democratic Republic, Lebanon, Lesotho, Liberia, Libya, Madagascar, Malawi, Malaysia, Maldives, Mali, Marshall Islands, Mauritania, Mauritius, Mexico, Mongolia, Morocco, Mozambique, Myanmar, Namibia, Nauru, Nepal, Nicaragua, Niger, Nigeria, Oman, Pakistan, Palau, Panama, Papua New Guinea, Paraguay, Peru, Philippines, Qatar, Russian Federation, Rwanda, Saint Kitts and Nevis, Saint Lucia, Saint Vincent and the Grenadines, Sao Tome and Principe, Saudi Arabia, Senegal, Seychelles, Sierra Leone, Singapore, Solomon Islands, South Africa, South Sudan, Sri Lanka, Sudan, Suriname, Syrian Arab Republic, Tajikistan, Thailand, Timor-Leste, Togo, Trinidad and Tobago, Tunisia, Turkmenistan, Uganda, United Arab Emirates, United Republic of Tanzania, Uruguay, Uzbekistan, Vanuatu, Venezuela (Bolivarian Republic of), Viet Nam, Yemen, Zambia, Zimbabwe

Against

Israel, Micronesia (Federated States of), United Kingdom, United States

Abstaining

Albania, Andorra, Armenia, Australia, Austria, Belgium, Bosnia and Herzegovina, Bulgaria, Canada, Croatia, Cyprus, Czechia, Denmark, Estonia, Finland, France, Georgia, Germany, Greece, Hungary, Iceland, Ireland, Italy, Japan, Latvia, Liechtenstein, Lithuania, Luxembourg, Malta, Monaco, Montenegro, Netherlands, New Zealand, North Macedonia, Norway, Poland, Portugal, Republic of Korea, Republic of Moldova,

Romania, Samoa, San Marino, Serbia, Slovakia, Slovenia, Spain, Sweden, Switzerland, Tonga, Turkey, Ukraine

Action by the First Committee

Date:	3 November 2021	Meeting:	17th meeting
Vote:	125-4-51	Draft resolution:	A/C.1/76/L.27

Agenda item 100 (f)

76/41   Regional disarmament

Text

The General Assembly,

Recalling its resolutions 45/58 P of 4 December 1990, 46/36 I of 6 December 1991, 47/52 J of 9 December 1992, 48/75 I of 16 December 1993, 49/75 N of 15 December 1994, 50/70 K of 12 December 1995, 51/45 K of 10 December 1996, 52/38 P of 9 December 1997, 53/77 O of 4 December 1998, 54/54 N of 1 December 1999, 55/33 O of 20 November 2000, 56/24 H of 29 November 2001, 57/76 of 22 November 2002, 58/38 of 8 December 2003, 59/89 of 3 December 2004, 60/63 of 8 December 2005, 61/80 of 6 December 2006, 62/38 of 5 December 2007, 63/43 of 2 December 2008, 64/41 of 2 December 2009, 65/45 of 8 December 2010, 66/36 of 2 December 2011, 67/57 of 3 December 2012, 68/54 of 5 December 2013, 69/45 of 2 December 2014, 70/43 of 7 December 2015, 71/40 of 5 December 2016, 72/34 of 4 December 2017, 73/33 of 5 December 2018, 74/37 of 12 December 2019 and 75/49 of 7 December 2020 on regional disarmament,

Believing that the efforts of the international community to move towards the ideal of general and complete disarmament are guided by the inherent human desire for genuine peace and security, the elimination of the danger of war and the release of economic, intellectual and other resources for peaceful pursuits,

Affirming the abiding commitment of all States to the purposes and principles enshrined in the Charter of the United Nations in the conduct of their international relations,

Noting that essential guidelines for progress towards general and complete disarmament were adopted at the tenth special session of the General Assembly,[1]

Recalling the guidelines and recommendations for regional approaches to disarmament within the context of global security adopted by the Disarmament Commission at its 1993 substantive session,[2]

Welcoming the prospects of genuine progress in the field of disarmament engendered in recent years as a result of negotiations between the two super-Powers,

Taking note of the recent proposals for disarmament at the regional and subregional levels,

---

[1] Resolution S-10/2.
[2] *Official Records of the General Assembly, Forty-eighth Session, Supplement No. 42* (A/48/42), annex II.

Recognizing the importance of confidence-building measures for regional and international peace and security,

Convinced that endeavours by countries to promote regional disarmament, taking into account the specific characteristics of each region and in accordance with the principle of undiminished security at the lowest level of armaments, would enhance the security of all States and would thus contribute to international peace and security by reducing the risk of regional conflicts,

1.   *Stresses* that sustained efforts are needed, within the framework of the Conference on Disarmament and under the umbrella of the United Nations, to make progress on the entire range of disarmament issues;

2.   *Affirms* that global and regional approaches to disarmament complement each other and should therefore be pursued simultaneously to promote regional and international peace and security;

3.   *Calls upon* States to conclude agreements, wherever possible, for nuclear non-proliferation, disarmament and confidence-building measures at the regional and subregional levels;

4.   *Welcomes* the initiatives towards disarmament, nuclear non-proliferation and security undertaken by some countries at the regional and subregional levels;

5.   *Supports and encourages* efforts aimed at promoting confidence-building measures at the regional and subregional levels to ease regional tensions and to further disarmament and nuclear non-proliferation measures at the regional and subregional levels;

6.   *Decides* to include in the provisional agenda of its seventy-seventh session, under the item entitled "General and complete disarmament", the sub-item entitled "Regional disarmament".

Action by the General Assembly

Date: 6 December 2021   Meeting: 45th plenary meeting
Vote: Adopted without a vote   Report: A/76/444

Sponsors

Bangladesh, Egypt, Eritrea, Iraq, Kuwait, Nepal, Nicaragua, Nigeria, **Pakistan**, Saudi Arabia, Turkey

Co-sponsors

Bolivia (Plurinational State of), Peru, Sri Lanka, Tunisia

Action by the First Committee

Date: 3 November 2021   Meeting: 17th meeting
Vote: Adopted without a vote   Draft resolution: A/C.1/76/L.30

Agenda item 100 (g)

76/42 Conventional arms control at the regional and subregional levels

Text

The General Assembly,

Recalling its resolutions 48/75 J of 16 December 1993, 49/75 O of 15 December 1994, 50/70 L of 12 December 1995, 51/45 Q of 10 December 1996, 52/38 Q of 9 December 1997, 53/77 P of 4 December 1998, 54/54 M of 1 December 1999, 55/33 P of 20 November 2000, 56/24 I of 29 November 2001, 57/77 of 22 November 2002, 58/39 of 8 December 2003, 59/88 of 3 December 2004, 60/75 of 8 December 2005, 61/82 of 6 December 2006, 62/44 of 5 December 2007, 63/44 of 2 December 2008, 64/42 of 2 December 2009, 65/46 of 8 December 2010, 66/37 of 2 December 2011, 67/62 of 3 December 2012, 68/56 of 5 December 2013, 69/47 of 2 December 2014, 70/44 of 7 December 2015, 71/41 of 5 December 2016, 72/35 of 4 December 2017, 73/34 of 5 December 2018, 74/38 of 12 December 2019 and 75/50 of 7 December 2020,

Recognizing the crucial role of conventional arms control in promoting regional and international peace and security,

Recognizing also the importance of equitable representation of women in arms control discussions and negotiations,

Convinced that conventional arms control needs to be pursued primarily in the regional and subregional contexts since most threats to peace and security in the post-cold-war era arise mainly among States located in the same region or subregion,

Aware that the preservation of a balance in the defence capabilities of States at the lowest level of armaments would contribute to peace and stability and should be a prime objective of conventional arms control,

Desirous of promoting agreements to strengthen regional peace and security at the lowest possible level of armaments and military forces,

Noting with particular interest the initiatives taken in this regard in different regions of the world, in particular the commencement of consultations among a number of Latin American countries and the proposals for conventional arms control made in the context of South Asia, and recognizing, in the context of this subject, the relevance and value of the Treaty on Conventional Armed Forces in Europe,[1] which is a cornerstone of European security,

---

[1] See CD/1064.

Believing that militarily significant States and States with larger military capabilities have a special responsibility in promoting such agreements for regional security,

Believing also that an important objective of conventional arms control in regions of tension should be to prevent the possibility of military attack launched by surprise and to avoid aggression,

1.   *Decides* to give urgent consideration to the issues involved in conventional arms control at the regional and subregional levels;

2.   *Requests* the Conference on Disarmament to consider the formulation of principles that can serve as a framework for regional agreements on conventional arms control, and looks forward to a report of the Conference on this subject;

3.   *Requests* the Secretary-General, in the meantime, to seek the views of Member States on the subject and to submit a report to the General Assembly at its seventy-seventh session;

4.   *Decides* to include in the provisional agenda of its seventy-seventh session, under the item entitled "General and complete disarmament", the sub-item entitled "Conventional arms control at the regional and subregional levels".

Action by the General Assembly

Date: 6 December 2021   Meeting: 45th plenary meeting
Vote: 186-1-3   Report: A/76/444
       173-2-2, p.p. 7
       120-1-52, o.p. 2

Sponsors

Bangladesh, Eritrea, **Pakistan**

Co-sponsors

Belarus, Mozambique, Peru, Syrian Arab Republic

Recorded vote

As a whole

In favour

Afghanistan, Albania, Algeria, Andorra, Angola, Antigua and Barbuda, Argentina, Armenia, Australia, Austria, Azerbaijan, Bahamas, Bahrain, Bangladesh, Barbados, Belarus, Belgium, Belize, Bolivia (Plurinational State of), Bosnia and Herzegovina, Botswana, Brazil, Brunei Darussalam, Bulgaria, Burkina Faso, Burundi, Cabo Verde, Cambodia, Cameroon, Canada, Central African Republic, Chad, Chile, China, Colombia,

Comoros, Congo, Costa Rica, Côte d'Ivoire, Croatia, Cuba, Cyprus, Czechia, Democratic People's Republic of Korea, Denmark, Djibouti, Dominica, Dominican Republic, Ecuador, Egypt, El Salvador, Equatorial Guinea, Eritrea, Estonia, Eswatini, Ethiopia, Fiji, Finland, France, Gabon, Gambia, Georgia, Germany, Ghana, Greece, Grenada, Guatemala, Guinea, Guinea-Bissau, Guyana, Haiti, Honduras, Hungary, Iceland, Indonesia, Iran (Islamic Republic of), Iraq, Ireland, Israel, Italy, Jamaica, Japan, Jordan, Kazakhstan, Kenya, Kiribati, Kuwait, Kyrgyzstan, Lao People's Democratic Republic, Latvia, Lebanon, Lesotho, Liberia, Libya, Liechtenstein, Lithuania, Luxembourg, Madagascar, Malawi, Malaysia, Maldives, Mali, Malta, Marshall Islands, Mauritania, Mauritius, Mexico, Micronesia (Federated States of), Monaco, Mongolia, Montenegro, Morocco, Mozambique, Myanmar, Namibia, Nauru, Nepal, Netherlands, New Zealand, Nicaragua, Niger, Nigeria, North Macedonia, Norway, Oman, Pakistan, Palau, Panama, Papua New Guinea, Paraguay, Peru, Philippines, Poland, Portugal, Qatar, Republic of Korea, Republic of Moldova, Romania, Rwanda, Saint Kitts and Nevis, Saint Lucia, Saint Vincent and the Grenadines, Samoa, San Marino, Sao Tome and Principe, Saudi Arabia, Senegal, Serbia, Seychelles, Sierra Leone, Singapore, Slovakia, Slovenia, Solomon Islands, South Africa, South Sudan, Spain, Sri Lanka, Sudan, Suriname, Sweden, Switzerland, Syrian Arab Republic, Tajikistan, Thailand, Timor-Leste, Togo, Tonga, Trinidad and Tobago, Tunisia, Turkey, Turkmenistan, Tuvalu, Uganda, Ukraine, United Arab Emirates, United Kingdom, United Republic of Tanzania, United States, Uruguay, Uzbekistan, Vanuatu, Venezuela (Bolivarian Republic of), Viet Nam, Yemen, Zambia

Against
India

Abstaining
Bhutan, Russian Federation, Zimbabwe

Seventh preambular paragraph*

In favour
Afghanistan, Albania, Algeria, Andorra, Angola, Antigua and Barbuda, Argentina, Armenia, Australia, Austria, Azerbaijan, Bahamas, Bahrain, Bangladesh, Barbados, Belarus, Belgium, Belize, Bhutan, Bolivia (Plurinational State of), Bosnia and Herzegovina, Botswana, Brazil, Brunei Darussalam, Bulgaria, Burkina Faso, Burundi, Cabo Verde, Cambodia, Canada, Chad, Chile, China, Colombia, Comoros, Costa Rica, Côte d'Ivoire, Croatia, Cuba, Cyprus, Czechia, Democratic People's Republic of Korea, Denmark, Djibouti, Dominica, Dominican Republic,

---

* Subsequently, the delegation of Gabon informed the Secretariat that it had not intended to participate.

Ecuador, Egypt, El Salvador, Eritrea, Estonia, Eswatini, Ethiopia, Fiji, Finland, France, Gambia, Georgia, Germany, Ghana, Greece, Grenada, Guatemala, Guinea, Guinea-Bissau, Guyana, Haiti, Honduras, Hungary, Iceland, Indonesia, Iran (Islamic Republic of), Iraq, Ireland, Israel, Italy, Jamaica, Japan, Jordan, Kazakhstan, Kenya, Kuwait, Kyrgyzstan, Lao People's Democratic Republic, Latvia, Lebanon, Lesotho, Liberia, Libya, Liechtenstein, Lithuania, Luxembourg, Madagascar, Malawi, Malaysia, Maldives, Mali, Malta, Mauritania, Mexico, Monaco, Mongolia, Montenegro, Morocco, Mozambique, Myanmar, Namibia, Nepal, Netherlands, New Zealand, Nicaragua, Niger, Nigeria, North Macedonia, Norway, Oman, Pakistan, Palau, Panama, Papua New Guinea, Paraguay, Peru, Philippines, Poland, Portugal, Qatar, Republic of Korea, Republic of Moldova, Romania, Rwanda, Saint Lucia, Saint Vincent and the Grenadines, Samoa, San Marino, Sao Tome and Principe, Saudi Arabia, Senegal, Serbia, Seychelles, Sierra Leone, Singapore, Slovakia, Slovenia, South Africa, South Sudan, Spain, Sri Lanka, Sudan, Suriname, Sweden, Switzerland, Syrian Arab Republic, Tajikistan, Thailand, Timor-Leste, Togo, Trinidad and Tobago, Tunisia, Turkey, Turkmenistan, Uganda, Ukraine, United Arab Emirates, United Kingdom, United Republic of Tanzania, United States, Uruguay, Uzbekistan, Vanuatu, Venezuela (Bolivarian Republic of), Viet Nam, Yemen, Zambia

Against
India, Russian Federation

Abstaining
Gabon, Zimbabwe

Operative paragraph 2

In favour
Algeria, Angola, Antigua and Barbuda, Argentina, Azerbaijan, Bahamas, Bahrain, Bangladesh, Barbados, Belarus, Belize, Bolivia (Plurinational State of), Botswana, Brazil, Brunei Darussalam, Burkina Faso, Burundi, Cabo Verde, Cambodia, Chad, Chile, China, Colombia, Comoros, Costa Rica, Côte d'Ivoire, Cuba, Democratic People's Republic of Korea, Djibouti, Dominica, Dominican Republic, Ecuador, Egypt, El Salvador, Eritrea, Eswatini, Ethiopia, Fiji, Gambia, Georgia, Ghana, Grenada, Guatemala, Guinea, Guinea-Bissau, Guyana, Haiti, Honduras, Iran (Islamic Republic of), Iraq, Jamaica, Japan, Jordan, Kazakhstan, Kenya, Kuwait, Kyrgyzstan, Lao People's Democratic Republic, Lebanon, Lesotho, Liberia, Libya, Madagascar, Malawi, Malaysia, Mali, Mauritania, Mongolia, Morocco, Mozambique, Myanmar, Namibia, Nepal, Nicaragua, Niger, Nigeria, Oman, Pakistan, Palau, Panama, Papua New Guinea, Paraguay, Peru, Philippines, Qatar, Rwanda, Saint Lucia, Saint Vincent and the Grenadines, Samoa, Sao Tome and Principe, Saudi Arabia, Senegal,

Serbia, Seychelles, Sierra Leone, Singapore, South Sudan, Sri Lanka, Sudan, Suriname, Syrian Arab Republic, Tajikistan, Thailand, Timor-Leste, Togo, Trinidad and Tobago, Tunisia, Turkey, Turkmenistan, Uganda, United Arab Emirates, United Republic of Tanzania, United States, Uruguay, Uzbekistan, Vanuatu, Venezuela (Bolivarian Republic of), Viet Nam, Yemen, Zambia

Against

India

Abstaining

Albania, Andorra, Australia, Austria, Belgium, Bhutan, Bosnia and Herzegovina, Bulgaria, Canada, Croatia, Cyprus, Czechia, Denmark, Estonia, Finland, France, Germany, Greece, Hungary, Iceland, Indonesia, Ireland, Israel, Italy, Latvia, Liechtenstein, Lithuania, Luxembourg, Malta, Mexico, Monaco, Montenegro, Netherlands, New Zealand, North Macedonia, Norway, Poland, Portugal, Republic of Korea, Republic of Moldova, Romania, Russian Federation, San Marino, Slovakia, Slovenia, South Africa, Spain, Sweden, Switzerland, Ukraine, United Kingdom, Zimbabwe

Action by the First Committee

Date:	3 November 2021	Meeting:	17th meeting
Vote:	179-1-4	Draft resolution:	A/C.1/76/L.31
	167-2-4, p.p. 7		
	116-1-55, o.p. 2		

Agenda item 100 (t)

76/43　Confidence-building measures in the regional and subregional context

Text

The General Assembly,

Guided by the purposes and principles enshrined in the Charter of the United Nations,

Recalling its resolutions 58/43 of 8 December 2003, 59/87 of 3 December 2004, 60/64 of 8 December 2005, 61/81 of 6 December 2006, 62/45 of 5 December 2007, 63/45 of 2 December 2008, 64/43 of 2 December 2009, 65/47 of 8 December 2010, 66/38 of 2 December 2011, 67/61 of 3 December 2012, 68/55 of 5 December 2013, 69/46 of 2 December 2014, 70/42 of 7 December 2015, 71/39 of 5 December 2016, 72/33 of 4 December 2017, 73/35 of 5 December 2018, 74/39 of 12 December 2019 and 75/51 of 7 December 2020 on confidence-building measures in the regional and subregional context,

Recalling also its resolution 57/337 of 3 July 2003 on the prevention of armed conflict, in which the General Assembly calls upon Member States to settle their disputes by peaceful means, as set out in Chapter VI of the Charter, inter alia, by any procedures adopted by the parties,

Recalling further the resolutions and guidelines adopted by consensus by the General Assembly and the Disarmament Commission relating to confidence-building measures and their implementation at the global, regional and subregional levels,

Considering the importance and effectiveness of confidence-building measures taken at the initiative and with the agreement of all States concerned, and taking into account the specific characteristics of each region, since such measures can contribute to regional stability,

Convinced that resources released by disarmament, including regional disarmament, can be devoted to economic and social development and to the protection of the environment for the benefit of all peoples, in particular those of the developing countries,

Recognizing the need for meaningful dialogue among States concerned to avert conflict,

Welcoming the peace processes already initiated by States concerned to resolve their disputes through peaceful means bilaterally or through mediation, inter alia, by third parties, regional organizations or the United Nations,

Recognizing that States in some regions have already taken steps towards confidence-building measures at the bilateral, subregional and regional levels in the political and military fields, including arms control and disarmament, and noting that such confidence-building measures have improved peace and security in those regions and contributed to progress in the socioeconomic conditions of their people,

Concerned that the continuation of disputes among States, particularly in the absence of an effective mechanism to resolve them through peaceful means, may contribute to the arms race and endanger the maintenance of international peace and security and the efforts of the international community to promote arms control and disarmament,

1.   *Calls upon* Member States to refrain from the use or threat of use of force in accordance with the purposes and principles of the Charter of the United Nations;

2.   *Reaffirms its commitment* to the peaceful settlement of disputes under Chapter VI of the Charter, in particular Article 33, which provides for a solution by negotiation, enquiry, mediation, conciliation, arbitration, judicial settlement, resort to regional agencies or arrangements or other peaceful means chosen by the parties;

3.   *Reaffirms* the ways and means regarding confidence- and security-building measures set out in the report of the Disarmament Commission on its 1993 session;[1]

4.   *Calls upon* Member States to pursue these ways and means through sustained consultations and dialogue, while at the same time avoiding actions that may hinder or impair such a dialogue;

5.   *Urges* States to comply strictly with all bilateral, regional and international agreements, including arms control and disarmament agreements, to which they are party;

6.   *Emphasizes* that the objective of confidence-building measures should be to help to strengthen international peace and security and to be consistent with the principle of undiminished security at the lowest level of armaments;

7.   *Encourages* the promotion of bilateral and regional confidence-building measures, with the consent and participation of the parties concerned, to avoid conflict and prevent the unintended and accidental outbreak of hostilities;

8.   *Requests* the Secretary-General to submit a report to the General Assembly at its seventy-seventh session containing the views of Member States on confidence-building measures in the regional and subregional context;

---

[1] *Official Records of the General Assembly, Forty-eighth Session, Supplement No. 42* (A/48/42), annex II, sect. III.A.

9.   *Decides* to include in the provisional agenda of its seventy-seventh session, under the item entitled "General and complete disarmament", the sub-item entitled "Confidence-building measures in the regional and subregional context".

Action by the General Assembly

Date: 6 December 2021   Meeting: 45th plenary meeting
Vote: Adopted without a vote   Report: A/76/444

Sponsors

Bangladesh, Egypt, Eritrea, **Pakistan**

Co-sponsors

Cameroon, Syrian Arab Republic

Action by the First Committee

Date: 3 November 2021   Meeting: 17th meeting
Vote: Adopted without a vote   Draft resolution: A/C.1/76/L.32

Agenda item 100 (i)

76/44 Nuclear-weapon-free southern hemisphere and adjacent areas

Text

The General Assembly,

Recalling its resolutions 51/45 B of 10 December 1996, 52/38 N of 9 December 1997, 53/77 Q of 4 December 1998, 54/54 L of 1 December 1999, 55/33 I of 20 November 2000, 56/24 G of 29 November 2001, 57/73 of 22 November 2002, 58/49 of 8 December 2003, 59/85 of 3 December 2004, 60/58 of 8 December 2005, 61/69 of 6 December 2006, 62/35 of 5 December 2007, 63/65 of 2 December 2008, 64/44 of 2 December 2009, 65/58 of 8 December 2010, 67/55 of 3 December 2012, 69/35 of 2 December 2014, 70/45 of 7 December 2015, 71/51 of 5 December 2016, 72/45 of 4 December 2017 and 74/48 of 12 December 2019,

Recalling also the provisions on nuclear-weapon-free zones of the Final Document of the Tenth Special Session of the General Assembly, the first special session devoted to disarmament,[1]

Recalling further the adoption by the Disarmament Commission at its 1999 substantive session of a text entitled "Establishment of nuclear-weapon-free zones on the basis of arrangements freely arrived at among the States of the region concerned",[2]

Determined to pursue the total elimination of nuclear weapons,

Determined also to continue to contribute to the prevention of the proliferation of nuclear weapons in all its aspects and to the process of general and complete disarmament under strict and effective international control, in particular in the field of nuclear weapons and other weapons of mass destruction, with a view to strengthening international peace and security, in accordance with the purposes and principles of the Charter of the United Nations,

Welcoming the entry into force on 22 January 2021 of the Treaty on the Prohibition of Nuclear Weapons[3] and its reaffirmation of the conviction that the establishment of the internationally recognized nuclear-weapon-free zones on the basis of arrangements freely arrived at among the States of the region concerned enhances global and regional peace and security, strengthens the nuclear non-proliferation regime and contributes towards realizing the objective of nuclear disarmament,

---

[1] Resolution S-10/2.

[2] *Official Records of the General Assembly, Fifty-fourth Session, Supplement No. 42* (A/54/42), annex I.

[3] A/CONF.229/2017/8.

Recalling the Final Document of the 2010 Review Conference of the Parties to the Treaty on the Non-Proliferation of Nuclear Weapons,[4] which reaffirmed the conviction that the establishment of nuclear-weapon-free zones contributes towards realizing the objectives of nuclear disarmament,

Stressing the importance of the treaties of Tlatelolco,[5] Rarotonga,[6] Bangkok[7] and Pelindaba[8] establishing nuclear-weapon-free zones, as well as the Antarctic Treaty,[9] inter alia, for achieving a world entirely free of nuclear weapons,

Recalling resolution 75/312 of 29 July 2021, in which it stressed the role of the zone of peace and cooperation of the South Atlantic as a forum for increased interaction, coordination and cooperation among its member States,

Underlining the importance of convening the fourth Conference of Nuclear-Weapon-Free Zones and Mongolia at the earliest possible date,

Noting that 115 States are currently parties and signatories to nuclear-weapon-free zone treaties,

Underlining the value of enhancing cooperation among the nuclear-weapon-free zone treaty members by means of mechanisms such as joint meetings of States parties, signatories and observers to those treaties, and recalling with appreciation in this regard the seminar on fostering cooperation and enhancing consultation mechanisms among the existing nuclear-weapon-free zones, held in Kazakhstan on 28 and 29 August 2019,

Reaffirming the applicable principles and rules of international law relating to the freedom of the high seas and the rights of passage through maritime space, including those of the United Nations Convention on the Law of the Sea,[10]

1.   *Reaffirms its conviction* of the important role of nuclear-weapon-free zones in strengthening the nuclear non-proliferation regime and in extending the areas of the world that are nuclear-weapon-free, and calls for greater progress towards the total elimination of all nuclear weapons;

2.   *Welcomes* the continued contribution that the Antarctic Treaty and the treaties of Tlatelolco, Rarotonga, Bangkok and Pelindaba are making

---

[4] *2010 Review Conference of the Parties to the Treaty on the Non-Proliferation of Nuclear Weapons, Final Document*, vols. I–III (NPT/CONF.2010/50 (Vol. I), NPT/CONF.2010/50 (Vol. II) and NPT/CONF.2010/50 (Vol. III)).

[5] United Nations, *Treaty Series*, vol. 634, No. 9068.

[6] *The United Nations Disarmament Yearbook*, vol. 10: 1985 (United Nations publication, Sales No. E.86.IX.7), appendix VII.

[7] United Nations, *Treaty Series*, vol. 1981, No. 33873.

[8] A/50/426, annex.

[9] United Nations, *Treaty Series*, vol. 402, No. 5778.

[10] Ibid., vol. 1833, No. 31363.

towards freeing the southern hemisphere and adjacent areas covered by those treaties from nuclear weapons;

3.   *Notes with satisfaction* that all nuclear-weapon-free zones in the southern hemisphere and adjacent areas are now in force;

4.   *Calls upon* all States concerned to continue to work together in order to facilitate adherence to the protocols to nuclear-weapon-free zone treaties by all relevant States that have not yet done so, in this regard recalls with appreciation the ratification by China, France, the Russian Federation and the United Kingdom of Great Britain and Northern Ireland of the Protocol to the Treaty on a Nuclear-Weapon-Free Zone in Central Asia[11] and the steps taken by the United States of America towards the ratification of the protocols to the Treaty on a Nuclear-Weapon-Free Zone in Central Asia, to the Treaty of Pelindaba and to the Treaty of Rarotonga, and encourages progress with a view to concluding consultations between the nuclear-weapon States and the parties to the Bangkok Treaty on the Protocol to that Treaty;

5.   *Calls upon* the nuclear-weapon States to withdraw any reservations or interpretive declarations contrary to the object and purpose of the treaties establishing nuclear-weapon-free zones;

6.   *Welcomes* the steps taken to conclude further nuclear-weapon-free zone treaties on the basis of arrangements freely arrived at among the States of the region concerned, including the steps taken towards the establishment of a nuclear-weapon-free zone in the Middle East;

7.   *Congratulates* the States parties and signatories to the treaties of Tlatelolco, Rarotonga, Bangkok and Pelindaba, as well as of Central Asia and Mongolia, for their efforts to pursue the common goals envisaged in those treaties and to promote the nuclear-weapon-free status of the southern hemisphere and adjacent areas, and calls upon them to explore and implement further ways and means of cooperation among themselves and their treaty agencies;

8.   *Encourages* efforts to reinforce coordination among nuclear-weapon-free zones;

9.   *Encourages* the competent authorities of the nuclear-weapon-free zone treaties to provide assistance to the States parties and signatories to those treaties so as to facilitate the accomplishment of the goals of the treaties;

10.   *Decides* to include in the provisional agenda of its seventy-seventh session, under the item entitled "General and complete disarmament", the sub-item entitled "Nuclear-weapon-free southern hemisphere and adjacent areas".

---

[11]   Ibid., vol. 2970, No. 51633.

Action by the General Assembly

Date: 6 December 2021   Meeting: 45th plenary meeting
Vote: 149-5-31   Report: A/76/444
      112-38-19, p.p. 6
      149-1-26, o.p. 6

Sponsors

Austria, Bolivia (Plurinational State of), **Brazil**, Chile, Cuba, Indonesia, Ireland, Kiribati, Lesotho, Malta, Mexico, Mongolia, Namibia, New Zealand, Nicaragua, Paraguay, Peru, Philippines, South Africa, Vanuatu

Co-sponsors

Argentina, Brunei Darussalam, Ecuador, Ghana, Malaysia, Papua New Guinea, Samoa, Suriname, Thailand, Uruguay

Recorded vote

As a whole*

In favour

Afghanistan, Algeria, Andorra, Angola, Antigua and Barbuda, Argentina, Armenia, Austria, Azerbaijan, Bahamas, Bahrain, Bangladesh, Barbados, Belarus, Belgium, Belize, Bhutan, Bolivia (Plurinational State of), Botswana, Brazil, Brunei Darussalam, Burkina Faso, Burundi, Cabo Verde, Cambodia, Canada, Chad, Chile, China, Colombia, Comoros, Congo, Costa Rica, Côte d'Ivoire, Cuba, Cyprus, Democratic People's Republic of Korea, Djibouti, Dominica, Dominican Republic, Ecuador, Egypt, El Salvador, Equatorial Guinea, Eswatini, Ethiopia, Fiji, Finland, Gabon, Gambia, Ghana, Grenada, Guatemala, Guinea, Guinea-Bissau, Guyana, Haiti, Honduras, India, Indonesia, Iran (Islamic Republic of), Iraq, Ireland, Jamaica, Japan, Jordan, Kazakhstan, Kenya, Kiribati, Kuwait, Kyrgyzstan, Lao People's Democratic Republic, Lebanon, Lesotho, Liberia, Libya, Liechtenstein, Malawi, Malaysia, Maldives, Mali, Malta, Mauritania, Mauritius, Mexico, Mongolia, Morocco, Mozambique, Myanmar, Namibia, Nepal, Netherlands, New Zealand, Nicaragua, Niger, Nigeria, Oman, Pakistan, Palau, Panama, Papua New Guinea, Paraguay, Peru, Philippines, Qatar, Republic of Moldova, Rwanda, Saint Kitts and Nevis, Saint Lucia, Saint Vincent and the Grenadines, Samoa, San Marino, Sao Tome and Principe, Saudi Arabia, Senegal, Serbia, Seychelles, Sierra Leone, Singapore, Slovenia, Solomon Islands, South Africa, South Sudan, Sri Lanka, Sudan, Suriname, Sweden, Switzerland, Syrian Arab Republic, Tajikistan, Thailand, Timor-Leste, Togo, Tonga, Trinidad and

---

* Subsequently, the delegation of Madagascar informed the Secretariat that it had intended to vote in favour.

Tobago, Tunisia, Turkmenistan, Tuvalu, Uganda, United Arab Emirates, United Republic of Tanzania, Uruguay, Uzbekistan, Vanuatu, Venezuela (Bolivarian Republic of), Viet Nam, Yemen, Zambia, Zimbabwe

Against

France, Israel, Russian Federation, United Kingdom, United States

Abstaining

Albania, Australia, Bosnia and Herzegovina, Bulgaria, Cameroon, Croatia, Czechia, Denmark, Estonia, Georgia, Germany, Greece, Hungary, Iceland, Italy, Latvia, Lithuania, Luxembourg, Madagascar, Monaco, Montenegro, North Macedonia, Norway, Poland, Portugal, Republic of Korea, Romania, Slovakia, Spain, Turkey, Ukraine

Sixth preambular paragraph*

In favour

Afghanistan, Algeria, Andorra, Angola, Antigua and Barbuda, Argentina, Austria, Azerbaijan, Bahamas, Bahrain, Bangladesh, Barbados, Belize, Bolivia (Plurinational State of), Botswana, Brazil, Brunei Darussalam, Burkina Faso, Cabo Verde, Cambodia, Chad, Chile, Colombia, Costa Rica, Côte d'Ivoire, Cuba, Cyprus, Djibouti, Dominica, Dominican Republic, Ecuador, Egypt, El Salvador, Eritrea, Eswatini, Ethiopia, Fiji, Gambia, Ghana, Grenada, Guatemala, Guinea-Bissau, Guyana, Haiti, Honduras, Indonesia, Iran (Islamic Republic of), Iraq, Ireland, Jamaica, Jordan, Kazakhstan, Kenya, Kuwait, Lao People's Democratic Republic, Lebanon, Lesotho, Libya, Liechtenstein, Malawi, Malaysia, Maldives, Malta, Mauritania, Mauritius, Mexico, Mongolia, Morocco, Mozambique, Myanmar, Namibia, Nepal, New Zealand, Nicaragua, Niger, Nigeria, Oman, Panama, Papua New Guinea, Paraguay, Peru, Philippines, Qatar, Republic of Moldova, Saint Lucia, Saint Vincent and the Grenadines, Samoa, San Marino, Sao Tome and Principe, Senegal, Seychelles, Singapore, South Africa, South Sudan, Sri Lanka, Sudan, Suriname, Thailand, Timor-Leste, Togo, Trinidad and Tobago, Tunisia, Turkmenistan, Tuvalu, Uganda, United Arab Emirates, United Republic of Tanzania, Uruguay, Vanuatu, Venezuela (Bolivarian Republic of), Viet Nam, Yemen

Against

Albania, Australia, Belgium, Bosnia and Herzegovina, Bulgaria, Canada, China, Croatia, Czechia, Denmark, Estonia, France, Germany, Greece, Hungary, Iceland, Israel, Italy, Latvia, Lithuania, Luxembourg, Monaco, Montenegro, Netherlands, North Macedonia, Norway, Poland, Portugal, Republic of Korea, Romania, Russian Federation, Slovakia, Slovenia, Spain, Turkey, Ukraine, United Kingdom, United States

---

* Subsequently, the delegation of Gabon informed the Secretariat that it had not intended to participate; the delegation of Madagascar informed the Secretariat that it had intended to vote in favour.

Abstaining
> Armenia, Belarus, Bhutan, Burundi, Finland, Gabon, Georgia, Guinea, India, Japan, Madagascar, Mali, Marshall Islands, Pakistan, Saudi Arabia, Serbia, Sweden, Switzerland, Zambia

Operative paragraph 6*

In favour
> Afghanistan, Algeria, Andorra, Angola, Antigua and Barbuda, Argentina, Armenia, Austria, Azerbaijan, Bahamas, Bahrain, Bangladesh, Barbados, Belarus, Belgium, Belize, Bolivia (Plurinational State of), Bosnia and Herzegovina, Botswana, Brazil, Brunei Darussalam, Burkina Faso, Burundi, Cabo Verde, Cambodia, Canada, Chad, Chile, China, Colombia, Comoros, Costa Rica, Côte d'Ivoire, Cuba, Cyprus, Democratic People's Republic of Korea, Djibouti, Dominica, Dominican Republic, Ecuador, Egypt, El Salvador, Eritrea, Eswatini, Ethiopia, Fiji, Finland, Gambia, Germany, Ghana, Greece, Grenada, Guatemala, Guinea, Guinea-Bissau, Guyana, Haiti, Honduras, Iceland, India, Indonesia, Iran (Islamic Republic of), Iraq, Ireland, Jamaica, Japan, Jordan, Kazakhstan, Kenya, Kiribati, Kuwait, Kyrgyzstan, Lao People's Democratic Republic, Lebanon, Lesotho, Libya, Liechtenstein, Malawi, Malaysia, Maldives, Mali, Malta, Mauritania, Mauritius, Mexico, Mongolia, Montenegro, Morocco, Mozambique, Myanmar, Namibia, Nepal, Netherlands, New Zealand, Nicaragua, Niger, Nigeria, North Macedonia, Norway, Oman, Pakistan, Palau, Panama, Papua New Guinea, Paraguay, Peru, Philippines, Qatar, Republic of Korea, Republic of Moldova, Russian Federation, Saint Lucia, Saint Vincent and the Grenadines, Samoa, San Marino, Sao Tome and Principe, Saudi Arabia, Senegal, Serbia, Seychelles, Singapore, Slovenia, South Africa, South Sudan, Spain, Sri Lanka, Sudan, Suriname, Sweden, Switzerland, Syrian Arab Republic, Thailand, Timor-Leste, Togo, Trinidad and Tobago, Tunisia, Turkey, Turkmenistan, Tuvalu, Uganda, United Arab Emirates, United Republic of Tanzania, Uruguay, Uzbekistan, Vanuatu, Venezuela (Bolivarian Republic of), Viet Nam, Yemen, Zambia

Against
> Israel

Abstaining
> Albania, Australia, Bhutan, Bulgaria, Croatia, Czechia, Denmark, Estonia, France, Gabon, Georgia, Hungary, Italy, Latvia, Lithuania, Luxembourg, Madagascar, Monaco, Poland, Portugal, Romania, Slovakia, Ukraine, United Kingdom, United States, Zimbabwe

---

* Subsequently, the delegation of Gabon informed the Secretariat that it had not intended to participate; the delegation of Madagascar informed the Secretariat that it had intended to vote in favour.

Action by the First Committee

Date: 27 October 2021
Vote: 143-5-33
     111-38-18, p.p. 6
     145-1-27, o.p. 6

Meeting: 13th meeting
Draft resolution: A/C.1/76/L.34/Rev.1

Agenda item 100 (jj)

76/45   Youth, disarmament and non-proliferation

Text

The General Assembly,

Recalling its resolution 74/64 of 12 December 2019,

Recalling also its resolution 75/1 of 21 September 2020 on the declaration on the commemoration of the seventy-fifth anniversary of the United Nations, in which the Heads of State and Government representing the peoples of the world have committed to listen to and work with youth,

Recognizing that young people in all countries are key agents for social change, economic development and technological innovation,

Reaffirming the important and positive contribution that young people can make to the promotion and attainment of sustainable peace and security,

Noting that engagement with young people can provide opportunities to benefit from their views, insights and ideas,

Bearing in mind its resolution 75/61 of 7 December 2020, which highlights the need for disarmament and non-proliferation education, particularly among youth,

Recalling its resolution 75/48 of 7 December 2020, in which it reaffirmed that the equal, full and effective participation of both women and men is one of the essential factors for the promotion and attainment of sustainable peace and security,

Recalling also relevant General Assembly and Security Council resolutions on the issue of youth, peace and security,

Noting the launch on 24 September 2018 of Youth 2030: The United Nations Youth Strategy, which includes peace and security as a thematic priority area,

Noting also action 38 of the disarmament agenda put forward by the Secretary-General, in which he describes the young generation as the ultimate force for change and proposes actions to promote youth engagement,

Mindful of the initiatives and activities undertaken by Member States, the United Nations entities and relevant civil society organizations for the implementation of the World Programme of Action for Youth[1] and the achievement of the Sustainable Development Goals,[2]

---

[1] Resolution 50/81, annex, and resolution 62/126, annex.
[2] See resolution 70/1.

Acknowledging the initiatives and activities undertaken by Member States, the United Nations, other relevant international and regional organizations, and civil society organizations to engage, educate and empower youth in the field of disarmament and non-proliferation,

Recognizing the role of civil society in promoting the engagement of young people in the field of disarmament and non-proliferation,

1. *Encourages* Member States, the United Nations, relevant specialized agencies and regional and subregional organizations to continue to promote the meaningful and inclusive participation of young people in discussions in the field of disarmament and non-proliferation, including through dialogue platforms, mentoring, internships, fellowships, scholarships, model events and youth group activities;

2. *Calls upon* Member States, the United Nations, relevant specialized agencies and regional and subregional organizations to consider developing and implementing policies and programmes for young people to increase and facilitate their constructive engagement in the field of disarmament and non-proliferation;

3. *Stresses* the importance of realizing the full potential of young people through education and capacity-building, bearing in mind the ongoing efforts and the need to promote the sustainable entry of young people into the field of disarmament and non-proliferation;

4. *Notes* the holding of a formal plenary meeting on youth and disarmament by the Conference on Disarmament on 12 August 2021, during which youth participants expressed their readiness to contribute to the consideration of issues of disarmament and non-proliferation, including those on the agenda of the Conference;

5. *Requests* the Secretary-General to seek specific measures to promote the meaningful and inclusive participation and empowerment of youth on disarmament and non-proliferation issues, including through the effective utilization of the dedicated digital platform Youth4Disarmament,[3] and through token grants and awards supported by voluntary contributions;

6. *Also requests* the Secretary-General to seek the views of Member States, the United Nations, other relevant international and regional organizations and civil society organizations on the issue of the promotion of youth engagement and empowerment activities in the area of disarmament and non-proliferation and to submit a report thereon to the General Assembly at its seventy-eighth session;

---

[3] https://youth4disarmament.org.

7. *Encourages* Member States to continue efforts to raise awareness and strengthen coordination within the United Nations system and beyond on the ongoing efforts to promote the role of youth;

8. *Decides* to include in the provisional agenda of its seventy-eighth session, under the item entitled "General and complete disarmament", the sub-item entitled "Youth, disarmament and non-proliferation".

Action by the General Assembly

Date: 6 December 2021   Meeting: 45th plenary meeting
Vote: Adopted without a vote   Report: A/76/444
172-0-4, p.p. 10

Sponsors

Austria, Belgium, Bulgaria, Canada, Chile, Colombia, Costa Rica, Croatia, Czechia, Denmark, Estonia, Finland, France, Georgia, Germany, Greece, Hungary, Iceland, India, Ireland, Italy, Japan, Jordan, Latvia, Lithuania, Luxembourg, Malaysia, Mexico, Netherlands, North Macedonia, Norway, Philippines, Poland, Portugal, **Republic of Korea**, Republic of Moldova, Slovakia, Spain, Sweden, Thailand, Turkey, United States, Uzbekistan, Viet Nam

Co-sponsors

Albania, Andorra, Australia, Bangladesh, Cyprus, Dominican Republic, Ecuador, El Salvador, Guatemala, Honduras, Indonesia, Kenya, Kyrgyzstan, Lebanon, Liechtenstein, Maldives, Malta, Marshall Islands, Monaco, Mongolia, Montenegro, Morocco, Myanmar, Namibia, Nepal, Papua New Guinea, Qatar, Romania, Samoa, San Marino, Singapore, Slovenia, Sri Lanka, Switzerland, Timor-Leste, Tunisia, Ukraine, United Arab Emirates, United Kingdom

Tenth preambular paragraph*

In favour

Afghanistan, Albania, Algeria, Andorra, Angola, Antigua and Barbuda, Argentina, Armenia, Australia, Austria, Azerbaijan, Bahamas, Bahrain, Bangladesh, Barbados, Belarus, Belgium, Belize, Bhutan, Bolivia (Plurinational State of), Bosnia and Herzegovina, Botswana, Brazil, Brunei Darussalam, Bulgaria, Burkina Faso, Burundi, Cabo Verde, Cambodia, Canada, Chad, Chile, China, Colombia, Comoros, Costa Rica, Côte d'Ivoire, Croatia, Cuba, Cyprus, Czechia, Denmark, Djibouti, Dominica, Dominican Republic, Ecuador, Egypt, El Salvador, Eritrea, Estonia, Eswatini, Ethiopia, Fiji, Finland, France, Gambia, Georgia, Germany,

---

* Subsequently, the delegation of Gabon informed the Secretariat that it had not intended to participate.

Ghana, Greece, Grenada, Guatemala, Guinea, Guinea-Bissau, Guyana, Haiti, Honduras, Hungary, Iceland, India, Indonesia, Iraq, Ireland, Israel, Italy, Jamaica, Japan, Jordan, Kazakhstan, Kenya, Kiribati, Kuwait, Kyrgyzstan, Lao People's Democratic Republic, Latvia, Lebanon, Lesotho, Liberia, Libya, Liechtenstein, Lithuania, Luxembourg, Madagascar, Malawi, Malaysia, Maldives, Mali, Malta, Marshall Islands, Mauritania, Mauritius, Mexico, Monaco, Mongolia, Montenegro, Morocco, Mozambique, Myanmar, Namibia, Nepal, Netherlands, New Zealand, Nicaragua, Niger, Nigeria, North Macedonia, Norway, Oman, Pakistan, Panama, Papua New Guinea, Paraguay, Peru, Philippines, Poland, Portugal, Qatar, Republic of Korea, Republic of Moldova, Romania, Saint Lucia, Saint Vincent and the Grenadines, Samoa, San Marino, Sao Tome and Principe, Saudi Arabia, Senegal, Serbia, Seychelles, Sierra Leone, Singapore, Slovakia, Slovenia, South Africa, Spain, Sri Lanka, Sudan, Suriname, Sweden, Switzerland, Tajikistan, Thailand, Timor-Leste, Togo, Trinidad and Tobago, Tunisia, Turkey, Turkmenistan, Uganda, Ukraine, United Arab Emirates, United Kingdom, United Republic of Tanzania, United States, Uruguay, Uzbekistan, Vanuatu, Venezuela (Bolivarian Republic of), Viet Nam, Yemen, Zambia, Zimbabwe

Against

None

Abstaining

Gabon, Iran (Islamic Republic of), Russian Federation, Syrian Arab Republic

Action by the First Committee

Date:	3 November 2021	Meeting:	17th meeting
Vote:	Adopted without a vote 168-0-4, p.p. 10	Draft resolution:	A/C.1/76/L.36

Agenda item 100 (b)

76/46   Nuclear disarmament

Text

The General Assembly,

Recalling its resolution 49/75 E of 15 December 1994 on a step-by-step reduction of the nuclear threat, and its resolutions 50/70 P of 12 December 1995, 51/45 O of 10 December 1996, 52/38 L of 9 December 1997, 53/77 X of 4 December 1998, 54/54 P of 1 December 1999, 55/33 T of 20 November 2000, 56/24 R of 29 November 2001, 57/79 of 22 November 2002, 58/56 of 8 December 2003, 59/77 of 3 December 2004, 60/70 of 8 December 2005, 61/78 of 6 December 2006, 62/42 of 5 December 2007, 63/46 of 2 December 2008, 64/53 of 2 December 2009, 65/56 of 8 December 2010, 66/51 of 2 December 2011, 67/60 of 3 December 2012, 68/47 of 5 December 2013, 69/48 of 2 December 2014, 70/52 of 7 December 2015, 71/63 of 5 December 2016, 72/38 of 4 December 2017, 73/50 of 5 December 2018, 74/45 of 12 December 2019 and 75/63 of 7 December 2020 on nuclear disarmament,

Reaffirming the commitment of the international community to the goal of the total elimination of nuclear weapons and the establishment of a nuclear-weapon-free world,

Bearing in mind that the Convention on the Prohibition of the Development, Production and Stockpiling of Bacteriological (Biological) and Toxin Weapons and on Their Destruction of 1972[1] and the Convention on the Prohibition of the Development, Production, Stockpiling and Use of Chemical Weapons and on Their Destruction of 1993[2] have already established legal regimes on the complete prohibition of biological and chemical weapons, respectively, and determined to achieve a comprehensive nuclear weapons convention on the prohibition of the development, testing, production, stockpiling, loan, transfer, use and threat of use of nuclear weapons and on their destruction, and to conclude such an international convention at an early date,

Recognizing the urgent need to take concrete practical steps towards achieving the establishment of a world free of nuclear weapons,

Bearing in mind paragraph 50 of the Final Document of the Tenth Special Session of the General Assembly, the first special session devoted to disarmament,[3] calling for the urgent negotiation of agreements for the cessation of the qualitative improvement and development of nuclear-weapon systems and for a comprehensive and phased programme with agreed time

---

[1] United Nations, *Treaty Series*, vol. 1015, No. 14860.
[2] Ibid., vol. 1974, No. 33757.
[3] Resolution S-10/2.

frames, wherever feasible, for the progressive and balanced reduction of nuclear weapons and their means of delivery, leading to their ultimate and complete elimination at the earliest possible time,

Reaffirming the conviction of the States parties to the Treaty on the Non-Proliferation of Nuclear Weapons[4] that the Treaty is a cornerstone of nuclear non-proliferation and nuclear disarmament, and the importance of the decision on strengthening the review process for the Treaty, the decision on principles and objectives for nuclear non-proliferation and disarmament, the decision on the extension of the Treaty and the resolution on the Middle East, adopted by the 1995 Review and Extension Conference of the Parties to the Treaty on the Non-Proliferation of Nuclear Weapons,[5]

Stressing the importance of the 13 steps for the systematic and progressive efforts to achieve the objective of nuclear disarmament leading to the total elimination of nuclear weapons, as agreed to by the States parties in the Final Document of the 2000 Review Conference of the Parties to the Treaty on the Non-Proliferation of Nuclear Weapons,[6]

Recognizing the important work done at the 2010 Review Conference of the Parties to the Treaty on the Non-Proliferation of Nuclear Weapons,[7] and affirming its 22-point action plan on nuclear disarmament as an impetus to intensify work aimed at beginning negotiations for a nuclear weapons convention,

Expressing deep concern that the 2015 Review Conference of the Parties to the Treaty on the Non-Proliferation of Nuclear Weapons, held from 27 April to 22 May 2015, did not reach agreement on a substantive final document,

Reaffirming the continued validity of agreements reached at the 1995 Review and Extension Conference and the 2000 and 2010 Review Conferences until all their objectives are achieved, and calling for their full and immediate fulfilment, including the action plan on nuclear disarmament adopted at the 2010 Review Conference,

Reiterating the highest priority accorded to nuclear disarmament in the Final Document of the Tenth Special Session of the General Assembly and by the international community,

---

[4] United Nations, *Treaty Series*, vol. 729, No. 10485.
[5] See *1995 Review and Extension Conference of the Parties to the Treaty on the Non-Proliferation of Nuclear Weapons, Final Document, Part I* (NPT/CONF.1995/32 (Part I) and NPT/CONF.1995/32 (Part I)/Corr.2), annex.
[6] *2000 Review Conference of the Parties to the Treaty on the Non-Proliferation of Nuclear Weapons, Final Document*, vol. I (NPT/CONF.2000/28 (Parts I and II)), part I, section entitled "Article VI and eighth to twelfth preambular paragraphs", para. 15.
[7] *2010 Review Conference of the Parties to the Treaty on the Non-Proliferation of Nuclear Weapons, Final Document*, vols. I–III (NPT/CONF.2010/50 (Vol. I), NPT/CONF.2010/50 (Vol. II) and NPT/CONF.2010/50 (Vol. III)).

Reiterating its call for an early entry into force of the Comprehensive Nuclear-Test-Ban Treaty,[8]

Noting the new strategic arms reduction treaty between the Russian Federation and the United States of America, in order to achieve further cuts in their deployed and non-deployed strategic nuclear weapons, and stressing that such cuts should be irreversible, verifiable and transparent,

Noting also the statements by nuclear-weapon States of their intention to pursue actions in achieving a world free of nuclear weapons, as well as the steps taken to reduce the role and number of nuclear weapons, and urging nuclear-weapon States to take further measures for progress on nuclear disarmament within a specified framework of time,

Recognizing the complementarity of bilateral, plurilateral and multilateral negotiations on nuclear disarmament, and that bilateral negotiations can never replace multilateral negotiations in this respect,

Noting the support expressed in the Conference on Disarmament and in the General Assembly for the elaboration of an international convention to assure non-nuclear-weapon States, without exception or discrimination, against the use or threat of use of nuclear weapons under any circumstances, and the multilateral efforts in the Conference to reach agreement on such an international convention at an early date,

Recalling the advisory opinion of the International Court of Justice on the legality of the threat or use of nuclear weapons, issued on 8 July 1996,[9] and welcoming the unanimous reaffirmation by all judges of the Court that there exists an obligation for all States to pursue in good faith and bring to a conclusion negotiations leading to nuclear disarmament in all its aspects under strict and effective international control,

Recalling also paragraph 176 of the Final Document of the Seventeenth Conference of Heads of State or Government of Non-Aligned Countries, held on Margarita Island, Bolivarian Republic of Venezuela, from 13 to 18 September 2016, in which the Conference on Disarmament was called upon to agree on a balanced and comprehensive programme of work by, inter alia, establishing an ad hoc committee on nuclear disarmament as soon as possible and as the highest priority, while the necessity was emphasized of starting negotiations in the Conference on Disarmament, without further delay, on a comprehensive nuclear weapons convention that sets, inter alia, a phased programme for the complete elimination of nuclear weapons within a specified framework of time,

---

[8] See resolution 50/245 and A/50/1027.

[9] A/51/218, annex.

Noting the adoption of the programme of work for the 2009 session by the Conference on Disarmament on 29 May 2009,[10] after years of stalemate, and regretting that the Conference did not succeed in reaching consensus on a programme of work for its 2021 session,

Reaffirming the proposals submitted by the States members of the Conference on Disarmament that are members of the Group of 21 on the follow-up to the 2013 high-level meeting of the General Assembly on nuclear disarmament, pursuant to Assembly resolution 68/32 of 5 December 2013, as contained in documents of the Conference,[11]

Reaffirming also the importance and validity of the Conference on Disarmament as the sole multilateral disarmament negotiating forum, and expressing the need to adopt and implement a balanced and comprehensive programme of work on the basis of its agenda and dealing with, inter alia, four core issues, in accordance with the rules of procedure,[12] and by taking into consideration the security concerns of all States,

Reaffirming further the specific mandate conferred upon the Disarmament Commission by the General Assembly, in its decision 52/492 of 8 September 1998, to discuss the subject of nuclear disarmament as one of its main substantive agenda items,

Recalling the United Nations Millennium Declaration,[13] in which Heads of State and Government resolved to strive for the elimination of weapons of mass destruction, in particular nuclear weapons, and to keep all options open for achieving that aim, including the possibility of convening an international conference to identify ways of eliminating nuclear dangers,

Underlining the importance of convening, as a priority, a United Nations high-level international conference on nuclear disarmament to review the progress made in this regard,

Recalling the high-level meeting of the General Assembly on nuclear disarmament held on 26 September 2013, and the strong support for nuclear disarmament expressed therein,

Welcoming the commemoration of 26 September as the International Day for the Total Elimination of Nuclear Weapons, devoted to furthering this objective, as declared by the General Assembly in its resolution 68/32 and subsequently welcomed in its resolutions 69/58 of 2 December 2014, 70/34 of 7 December 2015, 71/71 of 5 December 2016, 72/251 of 24 December 2017, 73/40 of 5 December 2018, 74/54 of 12 December 2019 and 75/45 of 7 December 2020,

---

[10] See *Official Records of the General Assembly, Sixty-fourth Session, Supplement No. 27* (A/64/27), para. 18.
[11] See CD/1999 and CD/2067.
[12] CD/8/Rev.9.
[13] Resolution 55/2.

Recalling the declaration of the States members of the Agency for the Prohibition of Nuclear Weapons in Latin America and the Caribbean on the International Day for the Total Elimination of Nuclear Weapons, in Mexico City on 26 September 2019,

Expressing deep concern about the catastrophic humanitarian consequences of any use of nuclear weapons,

Recalling the successful convening of the first, second and third Conferences on the Humanitarian Impact of Nuclear Weapons, in Oslo on 4 and 5 March 2013, in Nayarit, Mexico, on 13 and 14 February 2014, and in Vienna on 8 and 9 December 2014, and recalling also that 127 nations have formally endorsed the Humanitarian Pledge issued following the third Conference,[14]

Recalling also the signing by the nuclear-weapon States, namely, China, France, the Russian Federation, the United Kingdom of Great Britain and Northern Ireland and the United States of America, of the Protocol to the Treaty on a Nuclear-Weapon-Free Zone in Central Asia,[15] in New York on 6 May 2014,

Recalling further the proclamation of Latin America and the Caribbean as a Zone of Peace on 29 January 2014 during the Second Summit of the Community of Latin American and Caribbean States, held in Havana on 28 and 29 January 2014,

Welcoming the entry into force of the Treaty on the Prohibition of Nuclear Weapons[16] on 22 January 2021,

Reaffirming that, in accordance with the Charter of the United Nations, States should refrain from the use or threat of use of nuclear weapons in settling their disputes in international relations,

Seized of the danger of the use of weapons of mass destruction, particularly nuclear weapons, in terrorist acts and the urgent need for concerted international efforts to control and overcome it,

1. *Urges* all nuclear-weapon States to take effective disarmament measures to achieve the total elimination of all nuclear weapons at the earliest possible time;

2. *Reaffirms* that nuclear disarmament and nuclear non-proliferation are substantively interrelated and mutually reinforcing, that the two processes must go hand in hand and that there is a genuine need for a systematic and progressive process of nuclear disarmament;

---

[14] See CD/2039.

[15] United Nations, *Treaty Series*, vol. 2970, No. 51633.

[16] A/CONF.229/2017/8.

3.   *Welcomes and encourages* the efforts to establish new nuclear-weapon-free zones in different parts of the world, including the establishment of a Middle East zone free of nuclear weapons, on the basis of agreements or arrangements freely arrived at among the States of the regions concerned, which is an effective measure for limiting the further spread of nuclear weapons geographically and contributes to the cause of nuclear disarmament;

4.   *Encourages* States parties to the Treaty on the South-East Asia Nuclear-Weapon-Free Zone[17] and the nuclear-weapon States to intensify ongoing efforts to resolve all outstanding issues, in accordance with the objectives and principles of the Treaty;

5.   *Recognizes* that there is a genuine need to diminish the role of nuclear weapons in strategic doctrines and security policies to minimize the risk that these weapons will ever be used and to facilitate the process of their total elimination;

6.   *Urges* the nuclear-weapon States to stop immediately the qualitative improvement, development, production and stockpiling of nuclear warheads and their delivery systems;

7.   *Also urges* the nuclear-weapon States, as an interim measure, to de-alert and deactivate immediately their nuclear weapons and to take other concrete measures to reduce further the operational status of their nuclear-weapon systems, while stressing that reductions in deployments and in operational status cannot substitute for irreversible cuts in and the total elimination of nuclear weapons;

8.   *Reiterates its call upon* the nuclear-weapon States to carry out effective nuclear disarmament measures with a view to achieving the total elimination of nuclear weapons within a specified framework of time;

9.   *Calls upon* the nuclear-weapon States, pending the achievement of the total elimination of nuclear weapons, to agree on an internationally and legally binding instrument on a joint undertaking not to be the first to use nuclear weapons;

10.   *Urges* the nuclear-weapon States to commence plurilateral negotiations among themselves at an appropriate stage on further deep reductions of their nuclear weapons, in an irreversible, verifiable and transparent manner, as an effective measure of nuclear disarmament;

11.   *Underlines* the importance of applying the principles of transparency, irreversibility and verifiability to the process of nuclear disarmament;

12.   *Also underlines* the importance of the unequivocal undertaking by the nuclear-weapon States, in the Final Document of the 2000 Review

---

[17]   United Nations, *Treaty Series*, vol. 1981, No. 33873.

Conference of the Parties to the Treaty on the Non-Proliferation of Nuclear Weapons, to accomplish the total elimination of their nuclear arsenals leading to nuclear disarmament, to which all States parties are committed under article VI of the Treaty, and the reaffirmation by the States parties that the total elimination of nuclear weapons is the only absolute guarantee against the use or threat of use of nuclear weapons;[18]

13. *Calls for* the full and effective implementation of the 13 practical steps for nuclear disarmament contained in the Final Document of the 2000 Review Conference;

14. *Also calls for* the full implementation of the action plan as set out in the conclusions and recommendations for follow-on actions of the Final Document of the 2010 Review Conference of the Parties to the Treaty on the Non-Proliferation of Nuclear Weapons, particularly the 22-point action plan on nuclear disarmament;

15. *Urges* the nuclear-weapon States to carry out further reductions of non-strategic nuclear weapons, including on unilateral initiatives and as an integral part of the nuclear arms reduction and disarmament process;

16. *Calls for* the immediate commencement of negotiations in the Conference on Disarmament, in the context of an agreed, comprehensive and balanced programme of work, on a non-discriminatory, multilateral and internationally and effectively verifiable treaty banning the production of fissile material for nuclear weapons or other nuclear explosive devices on the basis of the report of the Special Coordinator[19] and the mandate contained therein;

17. *Urges* the Conference on Disarmament to commence as early as possible its substantive work during its 2022 session, on the basis of a comprehensive and balanced programme of work that takes into consideration all the real and existing priorities in the field of disarmament and arms control, including the immediate commencement of negotiations on a comprehensive nuclear weapons convention;

18. *Calls for* the conclusion of an international legal instrument on unconditional security assurances to non-nuclear-weapon States against the threat or use of nuclear weapons under any circumstances;

19. *Also calls for* the early entry into force, universalization and strict observance of the Comprehensive Nuclear-Test-Ban Treaty as a contribution to nuclear disarmament, while welcoming the latest ratification of the Treaty by Cuba, on 4 February 2021, and by the Comoros, on 19 February 2021;

---

[18] *2000 Review Conference of the Parties to the Treaty on the Non-Proliferation of Nuclear Weapons, Final Document*, vol. I (NPT/CONF.2000/28 (Parts I and II)), part I, section entitled "Article VII and the security of non-nuclear-weapon States", para. 2.

[19] CD/1299.

20. *Reiterates its call upon* the Conference on Disarmament to establish, as soon as possible and as the highest priority, an ad hoc committee on nuclear disarmament in 2022 and to commence negotiations on a phased programme of nuclear disarmament leading to the total elimination of nuclear weapons within a specified framework of time;

21. *Calls for* the convening, as soon as possible, of a United Nations high-level international conference on nuclear disarmament to review the progress made in this regard;

22. *Requests* the Secretary-General to submit to the General Assembly at its seventy-seventh session a report on the implementation of the present resolution;

23. *Decides* to include in the provisional agenda of its seventy-seventh session, under the item entitled "General and complete disarmament", the sub-item entitled "Nuclear disarmament".

Action by the General Assembly

Date: 6 December 2021   Meeting: 45th plenary meeting
Vote: 124-41-22   Report: A/76/444
      117-39-16, p.p. 32
      169-1-9, o.p. 16

Sponsors

Algeria, Eritrea, **Myanmar**, Nicaragua, Nigeria

Co-sponsors

Angola, Brunei Darussalam, Burkina Faso, Cuba, Indonesia, Kazakhstan, Lao People's Democratic Republic, Mongolia, Nepal, Philippines, Venezuela (Bolivarian Republic of), Viet Nam

Recorded vote

As a whole

In favour

Afghanistan, Algeria, Angola, Antigua and Barbuda, Argentina, Azerbaijan, Bahamas, Bahrain, Bangladesh, Barbados, Belize, Bolivia (Plurinational State of), Botswana, Brazil, Brunei Darussalam, Burkina Faso, Burundi, Cabo Verde, Cambodia, Cameroon, Central African Republic, Chad, Chile, China, Colombia, Comoros, Costa Rica, Côte d'Ivoire, Cuba, Djibouti, Dominica, Dominican Republic, Ecuador, Egypt, El Salvador, Equatorial Guinea, Eritrea, Eswatini, Ethiopia, Fiji, Gabon, Gambia, Ghana, Grenada, Guatemala, Guinea, Guinea-Bissau, Guyana, Haiti, Honduras, Indonesia, Iran (Islamic Republic of), Iraq, Jamaica, Jordan, Kazakhstan, Kenya, Kiribati, Kuwait, Kyrgyzstan, Lao People's Democratic Republic,

Lebanon, Lesotho, Liberia, Libya, Madagascar, Malawi, Malaysia, Maldives, Mali, Mauritania, Mauritius, Mexico, Mongolia, Morocco, Mozambique, Myanmar, Namibia, Nepal, Nicaragua, Niger, Nigeria, Oman, Palau, Panama, Papua New Guinea, Paraguay, Peru, Philippines, Qatar, Rwanda, Saint Kitts and Nevis, Saint Lucia, Saint Vincent and the Grenadines, Samoa, Sao Tome and Principe, Saudi Arabia, Senegal, Seychelles, Sierra Leone, Singapore, Solomon Islands, South Sudan, Sri Lanka, Sudan, Suriname, Syrian Arab Republic, Tajikistan, Thailand, Timor-Leste, Togo, Tonga, Trinidad and Tobago, Tunisia, Tuvalu, Uganda, United Arab Emirates, United Republic of Tanzania, Uruguay, Vanuatu, Venezuela (Bolivarian Republic of), Viet Nam, Yemen, Zambia

Against

Albania, Australia, Belgium, Bosnia and Herzegovina, Bulgaria, Canada, Croatia, Czechia, Denmark, Estonia, Finland, France, Georgia, Germany, Greece, Hungary, Iceland, Israel, Italy, Latvia, Lithuania, Luxembourg, Micronesia (Federated States of), Monaco, Montenegro, Netherlands, North Macedonia, Norway, Poland, Portugal, Republic of Korea, Romania, Russian Federation, Slovakia, Slovenia, Spain, Switzerland, Turkey, Ukraine, United Kingdom, United States

Abstaining

Andorra, Armenia, Austria, Belarus, Bhutan, Cyprus, Democratic People's Republic of Korea, India, Ireland, Japan, Liechtenstein, Malta, Marshall Islands, New Zealand, Pakistan, Republic of Moldova, San Marino, Serbia, South Africa, Sweden, Uzbekistan, Zimbabwe

Thirty-second preambular paragraph*

In favour

Afghanistan, Algeria, Andorra, Angola, Antigua and Barbuda, Argentina, Austria, Azerbaijan, Bahamas, Bahrain, Bangladesh, Barbados, Belize, Bolivia (Plurinational State of), Botswana, Brazil, Brunei Darussalam, Burkina Faso, Burundi, Cabo Verde, Cambodia, Chad, Chile, Colombia, Costa Rica, Côte d'Ivoire, Cuba, Cyprus, Djibouti, Dominica, Dominican Republic, Ecuador, Egypt, El Salvador, Eritrea, Eswatini, Ethiopia, Fiji, Gambia, Ghana, Grenada, Guatemala, Guinea, Guinea-Bissau, Guyana, Honduras, Indonesia, Iran (Islamic Republic of), Iraq, Ireland, Jamaica, Jordan, Kazakhstan, Kenya, Kiribati, Kuwait, Lao People's Democratic Republic, Lebanon, Lesotho, Libya, Liechtenstein, Malawi, Malaysia, Maldives, Mali, Malta, Mauritania, Mauritius, Mexico, Mongolia, Morocco, Mozambique, Myanmar, Namibia, Nepal, New Zealand, Nicaragua, Niger, Nigeria, Oman, Panama, Papua New Guinea, Paraguay, Peru, Philippines, Qatar, Republic of Moldova, Saint Lucia, Saint Vincent

---

* Subsequently, the delegation of Gabon informed the Secretariat that it had not intended to participate.

and the Grenadines, Samoa, San Marino, Sao Tome and Principe, Saudi Arabia, Senegal, Seychelles, Singapore, South Africa, South Sudan, Sri Lanka, Sudan, Suriname, Thailand, Timor-Leste, Togo, Trinidad and Tobago, Tunisia, Tuvalu, Uganda, United Arab Emirates, United Republic of Tanzania, Uruguay, Vanuatu, Venezuela (Bolivarian Republic of), Viet Nam, Yemen, Zambia, Zimbabwe

Against

Albania, Australia, Belgium, Bosnia and Herzegovina, Bulgaria, Canada, China, Croatia, Czechia, Denmark, Estonia, France, Georgia, Germany, Greece, Hungary, Iceland, Israel, Italy, Latvia, Lithuania, Luxembourg, Monaco, Montenegro, Netherlands, North Macedonia, Norway, Poland, Portugal, Republic of Korea, Romania, Russian Federation, Slovakia, Slovenia, Spain, Turkey, Ukraine, United Kingdom, United States

Abstaining

Armenia, Belarus, Bhutan, Finland, Gabon, Haiti, India, Japan, Madagascar, Marshall Islands, Pakistan, Serbia, Sierra Leone, Sweden, Switzerland, Uzbekistan

Operative paragraph 16*

In favour

Afghanistan, Albania, Algeria, Andorra, Angola, Antigua and Barbuda, Argentina, Armenia, Australia, Austria, Azerbaijan, Bahamas, Bahrain, Bangladesh, Barbados, Belarus, Belgium, Belize, Bhutan, Bolivia (Plurinational State of), Bosnia and Herzegovina, Botswana, Brazil, Brunei Darussalam, Bulgaria, Burkina Faso, Burundi, Cabo Verde, Cambodia, Canada, Chad, Chile, China, Colombia, Comoros, Costa Rica, Côte d'Ivoire, Croatia, Cuba, Cyprus, Czechia, Denmark, Djibouti, Dominica, Dominican Republic, Ecuador, Egypt, El Salvador, Eritrea, Estonia, Eswatini, Ethiopia, Fiji, Finland, Gambia, Georgia, Germany, Ghana, Greece, Grenada, Guatemala, Guinea, Guinea-Bissau, Guyana, Haiti, Honduras, Hungary, Iceland, India, Indonesia, Iraq, Ireland, Italy, Jamaica, Japan, Jordan, Kazakhstan, Kenya, Kiribati, Kuwait, Kyrgyzstan, Lao People's Democratic Republic, Latvia, Lebanon, Lesotho, Liberia, Libya, Liechtenstein, Lithuania, Luxembourg, Malawi, Malaysia, Maldives, Mali, Malta, Marshall Islands, Mauritania, Mauritius, Mexico, Micronesia (Federated States of), Monaco, Mongolia, Montenegro, Morocco, Mozambique, Myanmar, Namibia, Nepal, Netherlands, New Zealand, Nicaragua, Niger, Nigeria, North Macedonia, Norway, Oman, Palau, Panama, Papua New Guinea, Paraguay, Peru, Philippines, Poland,

---

* Subsequently, the delegation of Gabon informed the Secretariat that it had not intended to participate; the delegation of Madagascar informed the Secretariat that it had intended to vote in favour; the delegation of Monaco informed the Secretariat that it had intended to abstain.

Portugal, Qatar, Republic of Korea, Republic of Moldova, Romania, Russian Federation, Saint Lucia, Saint Vincent and the Grenadines, Samoa, San Marino, Sao Tome and Principe, Saudi Arabia, Senegal, Serbia, Seychelles, Singapore, Slovakia, Slovenia, South Africa, South Sudan, Spain, Sri Lanka, Sudan, Suriname, Sweden, Switzerland, Syrian Arab Republic, Thailand, Timor-Leste, Togo, Trinidad and Tobago, Tunisia, Turkey, Tuvalu, Uganda, Ukraine, United Arab Emirates, United Republic of Tanzania, Uruguay, Uzbekistan, Vanuatu, Venezuela (Bolivarian Republic of), Viet Nam, Yemen, Zambia, Zimbabwe

Against
Pakistan

Abstaining
Democratic People's Republic of Korea, France, Gabon, Iran (Islamic Republic of), Israel, Madagascar, Sierra Leone, United Kingdom, United States

Action by the First Committee

Date:	27 October 2021	Meeting:	13th meeting
Vote:	119-41-23	Draft resolution:	A/C.1/76/L.39
	110-39-17, p.p. 32		
	162-1-9, o.p. 16		

Agenda item 100 (ff)

76/47   Implementation of the Convention on Cluster Munitions

Text

The General Assembly,

Recalling its resolutions 63/71 of 2 December 2008 on the Convention on Cluster Munitions and 70/54 of 7 December 2015, 71/45 of 5 December 2016, 72/54 of 4 December 2017, 73/54 of 5 December 2018, 74/62 of 12 December 2019 and 75/62 of 7 December 2020 on the implementation of the Convention,

Reaffirming its determination to put an end for all time to the suffering and casualties caused by cluster munitions at the time of their use, when they fail to function as intended or when they are abandoned,

Deploring the recent cases of cluster munitions use and related civilian casualties, and calling upon those who continue to use cluster munitions to cease any such activity immediately,

Conscious that cluster munition remnants kill or maim civilians, including women and children, obstruct economic and social development, including through the loss of livelihood, impede post-conflict rehabilitation and reconstruction, delay or prevent the return of refugees and internally displaced persons, can have a negative impact on national and international peacebuilding and humanitarian assistance efforts, and have other severe consequences for many years after use,

Concerned about the dangers presented by the large national stockpiles of cluster munitions retained for operational use, and determined to ensure their rapid destruction,

Recognizing the impact of cluster munitions on women, men, girls and boys and the importance of relevant States providing adequate, gender- and age-sensitive assistance to victims of cluster munitions,

Believing it necessary to contribute effectively in an efficient, coordinated manner to resolving the challenge of removing cluster munition remnants located throughout the world, and to ensure their destruction,

Mindful of the need to adequately coordinate efforts undertaken in various forums, including through the Convention on the Rights of Persons with Disabilities,[1] to address the rights and needs of victims of various types of weapons, and resolved to avoid discrimination among victims of various types of weapons,

---

[1]   United Nations, *Treaty Series*, vol. 2515, No. 44910.

Reaffirming that in cases not covered by the Convention on Cluster Munitions[2] or by other international agreements, civilians and combatants remain under the protection and authority of the principles of international law, derived from established custom, from the principles of humanity and from the dictates of public conscience,

Welcoming the steps taken nationally, regionally and globally in recent years aimed at prohibiting, restricting or suspending the use, stockpiling, production and transfer of cluster munitions, and welcoming also in this regard that, since 2014, all Central American States have joined the Convention, thus fulfilling their aspiration to become the first cluster munitions-free region in the world,

Stressing the role of public conscience in furthering the principles of humanity, as evidenced by the global call for an end to civilian suffering caused by cluster munitions, and recognizing the efforts to that end undertaken by the United Nations, the International Committee of the Red Cross, the Cluster Munition Coalition and numerous other non-governmental organizations around the world,

Noting that a total of 123 States have joined the Convention, 110 as States parties and 13 as signatories,

Emphasizing the need to make further efforts in accelerating the universalization process,

Noting the outcome of the second Review Conference of States Parties to the Convention on Cluster Munitions, held in Geneva from 25 to 27 November 2020 and on 20 and 21 September 2021, and in particular the adoption of the Lausanne Declaration entitled "Protecting lives, empowering victims, enabling development" and the Lausanne Action Plan 2021–2026 to support the full and effective implementation of the Convention,

Recognizing the importance of full involvement and equal opportunities for the meaningful participation of women and men in disarmament processes, policy and programming decisions related to the Convention,

1. *Urges* all States not parties to the Convention on Cluster Munitions to ratify or accede to it as soon as possible, and all States parties that are in a position to do so to promote adherence to the Convention through bilateral, subregional and multilateral contacts, outreach and other means;

2. *Stresses* the importance of the full and effective implementation of and compliance with the Convention, including through the implementation of the Lausanne Action Plan, as appropriate;

3. *Expresses strong concern* regarding the number of allegations, reports or documented evidence of the use of cluster munitions in different

---

[2] Ibid., vol. 2688, No. 47713.

parts of the world, related civilian casualties and other consequences that impede the achievement of sustainable development;

4. *Urges* all States parties to provide the Secretary-General with complete and timely information as required under article 7 of the Convention in order to promote transparency and compliance with the Convention;

5. *Invites* all States that have not ratified the Convention or acceded to it to provide, on a voluntary basis, information that could make the clearance and destruction of cluster munition remnants and related activities more effective;

6. *Reiterates* the invitation to States not parties to participate in a continued dialogue on issues relevant to the Convention in order to enhance its humanitarian impact and to promote its universalization, as well as to engage in a military-to-military dialogue in order to address specific security issues related to cluster munitions;

7. *Reiterates its invitation and encouragement* to all States parties, interested States, the United Nations, other relevant international organizations or institutions, regional organizations, the International Committee of the Red Cross, the Cluster Munition Coalition and other relevant non-governmental organizations to participate in the upcoming formal meetings under the Convention;

8. *Invites and encourages* all interested States, the United Nations, other relevant international organizations or institutions, regional organizations, the International Committee of the Red Cross and relevant non-governmental organizations to attend the tenth Meeting of States Parties to the Convention on Cluster Munitions, to be held in Geneva from 30 August to 2 September 2022, and to participate in the future programme of meetings of the States parties to the Convention;

9. *Requests* the Secretary-General to continue to convene the Meetings of States Parties to the Convention and to continue to render the necessary assistance and to provide such services as may be necessary to fulfil the tasks entrusted to him under the Convention and in the relevant decisions of the Meetings of States Parties and the second Review Conference;

10. *Calls upon* States parties and participating States to address issues arising from outstanding dues, including options to ensure sustainable financing for all formal meetings and prompt payment of respective shares of the estimated costs;

11. *Decides* to include in the provisional agenda of its seventy-seventh session, under the item entitled "General and complete disarmament", the sub-item entitled "Implementation of the Convention on Cluster Munitions".

Action by the General Assembly

Date: 6 December 2021   Meeting: 45th plenary meeting
Vote: 146-1-37   Report: A/76/444

Sponsors

Australia, Bulgaria, Chile, France, Germany, Guyana, Iraq, Mexico, Montenegro, Namibia, New Zealand, Philippines, Spain, Sweden, Switzerland, **United Kingdom**

Recorded vote*

In favour

Afghanistan, Albania, Algeria, Andorra, Angola, Antigua and Barbuda, Armenia, Australia, Austria, Azerbaijan, Bahamas, Bangladesh, Barbados, Belgium, Belize, Bhutan, Bolivia (Plurinational State of), Bosnia and Herzegovina, Botswana, Brunei Darussalam, Bulgaria, Burkina Faso, Burundi, Cabo Verde, Cameroon, Canada, Chad, Chile, China, Colombia, Comoros, Congo, Costa Rica, Côte d'Ivoire, Croatia, Cuba, Czechia, Denmark, Djibouti, Dominica, Dominican Republic, Ecuador, El Salvador, Equatorial Guinea, Eritrea, Eswatini, Ethiopia, Fiji, France, Gabon, Gambia, Germany, Ghana, Grenada, Guatemala, Guinea, Guinea-Bissau, Guyana, Haiti, Honduras, Hungary, Iceland, Indonesia, Iraq, Ireland, Italy, Jamaica, Japan, Jordan, Kazakhstan, Kenya, Kiribati, Kuwait, Kyrgyzstan, Lao People's Democratic Republic, Lebanon, Lesotho, Liberia, Libya, Liechtenstein, Lithuania, Luxembourg, Madagascar, Malawi, Malaysia, Maldives, Mali, Malta, Marshall Islands, Mauritania, Mauritius, Mexico, Micronesia (Federated States of), Monaco, Mongolia, Montenegro, Mozambique, Namibia, Netherlands, New Zealand, Nicaragua, Niger, Nigeria, North Macedonia, Norway, Palau, Panama, Papua New Guinea, Paraguay, Peru, Philippines, Portugal, Republic of Moldova, Rwanda, Saint Lucia, Saint Vincent and the Grenadines, Samoa, San Marino, Sao Tome and Principe, Senegal, Seychelles, Sierra Leone, Singapore, Slovakia, Slovenia, Solomon Islands, South Africa, South Sudan, Spain, Sri Lanka, Sudan, Suriname, Sweden, Switzerland, Thailand, Timor-Leste, Togo, Tonga, Trinidad and Tobago, Tunisia, Tuvalu, United Kingdom, United Republic of Tanzania, Uruguay, Vanuatu, Yemen

Against

Russian Federation

Abstaining

Argentina, Bahrain, Belarus, Brazil, Cyprus, Egypt, Estonia, Finland, Georgia, Greece, India, Iran (Islamic Republic of), Israel, Latvia, Morocco,

---

* Subsequently, the delegation of Kuwait informed the Secretariat that it had intended to abstain.

Myanmar, Nepal, Oman, Pakistan, Poland, Qatar, Republic of Korea, Romania, Saudi Arabia, Serbia, Syrian Arab Republic, Tajikistan, Turkey, Uganda, Ukraine, United Arab Emirates, United States, Uzbekistan, Venezuela (Bolivarian Republic of), Viet Nam, Zambia, Zimbabwe

Action by the First Committee

Date: 2 November 2021	Meeting:	16th meeting
Vote: 140-1-39	Draft resolution:	A/C.1/76/L.41

Agenda item 100 (gg)

76/48   Universal Declaration on the Achievement of a Nuclear-Weapon-Free World

Text

The General Assembly,

Recalling its long-standing support for the total elimination of all nuclear weapons, its resolution 70/57 of 7 December 2015, by which it adopted the Universal Declaration on the Achievement of a Nuclear-Weapon-Free World, and its resolution 73/57 of 5 December 2018,

Recognizing the need to achieve a world without nuclear weapons,

Emphasizing, in this regard, the fundamental role of the agreement on the Final Document of the Tenth Special Session of the General Assembly of 30 June 1978,[1] in which it is stated, inter alia, that "effective measures of nuclear disarmament and the prevention of nuclear war have the highest priority",

Emphasizing also the crucial role of the Treaty on the Non-Proliferation of Nuclear Weapons[2] in achieving nuclear disarmament and nuclear non-proliferation, and recalling in particular the unequivocal undertaking by the nuclear-weapon States to accomplish the total elimination of their nuclear arsenals, leading to nuclear disarmament, in accordance with commitments made under article VI of the Treaty, agreed to at the 2000 Review Conference of the Parties to the Treaty on the Non-Proliferation of Nuclear Weapons and reaffirmed by the 2010 Review Conference,

Bearing in mind the advisory opinion of the International Court of Justice on the legality of the threat or use of nuclear weapons, issued on 8 July 1996,[3] in which the Court concluded unanimously that there exists an obligation to pursue in good faith and bring to a conclusion negotiations leading to nuclear disarmament in all its aspects under strict and effective international control,

Acknowledging the significant contribution made towards realizing the objectives of nuclear disarmament and non-proliferation, pending the total elimination of nuclear weapons, through the establishment of nuclear-weapon-free zones, although they are not an end in themselves, and reaffirming the political decision of 115 States parties to the treaties that establish nuclear-weapon-free zones and Mongolia to reject nuclear weapons,

---

[1] Resolution S-10/2.

[2] United Nations, *Treaty Series*, vol. 729, No. 10485.

[3] A/51/218, annex.

Marking the fifteenth anniversary of the signing of the Treaty on a Nuclear-Weapon-Free Zone in Central Asia[4] and the thirtieth anniversary of the closure of the Semipalatinsk nuclear test site,

Noting the entry into force, on 22 January 2021, of the Treaty on the Prohibition of Nuclear Weapons,[5] which has become a legally binding instrument to prohibit nuclear weapons, leading towards their total elimination,

Recalling the relevant principles and agreements of international humanitarian law and the laws of war, and recalling also the expression of deep concern by the 2010 Review Conference at the catastrophic humanitarian consequences of any use of nuclear weapons,[6]

Taking into account, in this context, the Secretary-General's disarmament agenda, *Securing Our Common Future: An Agenda for Disarmament*, announced in May 2018,

1. *Recalls* the adoption of the Universal Declaration on the Achievement of a Nuclear-Weapon-Free World, annexed to resolution 70/57;

2. *Invites* States, agencies and organizations of the United Nations system and intergovernmental and non-governmental organizations to disseminate the Declaration and to promote its implementation;

3. *Requests* the Secretary-General to seek the views of Member States on the efforts that they have made and the measures that they have taken with respect to the implementation of the Declaration, and also requests the Secretary-General to submit to the General Assembly at its seventy-ninth session a report on the implementation of the Declaration;

4. *Decides* to include in the provisional agenda of its seventy-ninth session, under the item entitled "General and complete disarmament", the sub-item entitled "Universal Declaration on the Achievement of a Nuclear-Weapon-Free World".

Action by the General Assembly

Date: 6 December 2021   Meeting: 45th plenary meeting
Vote: 141-22-24   Report: A/76/444
       122-27-23, p.p. 8
       141-3-30, p.p. 10

---

[4] United Nations, *Treaty Series*, vol. 2970, No. 51633.

[5] A/CONF.229/2017/8.

[6] See *2010 Review Conference of the Parties to the Treaty on the Non-Proliferation of Nuclear Weapons, Final Document*, vol. I (NPT/CONF.2010/50 (Vol. I)), part I, *Conclusions and recommendations for follow-on actions*.

Sponsors

Algeria, Azerbaijan, Bahrain, Belarus, Bolivia (Plurinational State of), Egypt, Ethiopia, **Kazakhstan**, Kiribati, Kyrgyzstan, Mauritania, Nicaragua, Saudi Arabia, Tajikistan, Turkmenistan, Uzbekistan

Co-sponsors

Afghanistan, Angola, Bangladesh, Botswana, Dominican Republic, Eritrea, Guatemala, Indonesia, Iran (Islamic Republic of), Lesotho, Morocco, Myanmar, Nepal, Paraguay, Qatar, Tuvalu, Venezuela (Bolivarian Republic of), Zambia

Recorded vote

As a whole

In favour

Afghanistan, Algeria, Andorra, Angola, Antigua and Barbuda, Argentina, Austria, Azerbaijan, Bahamas, Bahrain, Bangladesh, Barbados, Belarus, Belize, Bhutan, Bolivia (Plurinational State of), Botswana, Brazil, Brunei Darussalam, Burkina Faso, Burundi, Cabo Verde, Cambodia, Cameroon, Central African Republic, Chad, Chile, Colombia, Comoros, Congo, Costa Rica, Côte d'Ivoire, Cuba, Cyprus, Democratic People's Republic of Korea, Djibouti, Dominica, Dominican Republic, Ecuador, Egypt, El Salvador, Equatorial Guinea, Eritrea, Eswatini, Ethiopia, Fiji, Gabon, Gambia, Ghana, Grenada, Guatemala, Guinea, Guinea-Bissau, Guyana, Haiti, Honduras, India, Indonesia, Iran (Islamic Republic of), Iraq, Ireland, Jamaica, Jordan, Kazakhstan, Kenya, Kiribati, Kuwait, Kyrgyzstan, Lao People's Democratic Republic, Lebanon, Lesotho, Liberia, Libya, Liechtenstein, Madagascar, Malawi, Malaysia, Maldives, Mali, Malta, Marshall Islands, Mauritania, Mauritius, Mexico, Mongolia, Morocco, Mozambique, Myanmar, Namibia, Nepal, Nicaragua, Niger, Nigeria, Oman, Palau, Panama, Papua New Guinea, Paraguay, Peru, Philippines, Qatar, Republic of Moldova, Rwanda, Saint Kitts and Nevis, Saint Lucia, Saint Vincent and the Grenadines, Samoa, San Marino, Sao Tome and Principe, Saudi Arabia, Senegal, Serbia, Seychelles, Sierra Leone, Singapore, South Africa, South Sudan, Sri Lanka, Sudan, Suriname, Syrian Arab Republic, Tajikistan, Thailand, Timor-Leste, Togo, Tonga, Trinidad and Tobago, Tunisia, Turkmenistan, Tuvalu, Uganda, United Arab Emirates, United Republic of Tanzania, Uruguay, Uzbekistan, Vanuatu, Venezuela (Bolivarian Republic of), Viet Nam, Yemen, Zambia, Zimbabwe

Against

Albania, Australia, Belgium, Czechia, Denmark, Estonia, France, Israel, Italy, Latvia, Lithuania, Luxembourg, Monaco, Montenegro, Netherlands, North Macedonia, Poland, Republic of Korea, Slovakia, Slovenia, United Kingdom, United States

Abstaining

Armenia, Bosnia and Herzegovina, Bulgaria, Canada, China, Croatia, Finland, Georgia, Germany, Greece, Hungary, Iceland, Japan, New Zealand, Norway, Pakistan, Portugal, Romania, Russian Federation, Spain, Sweden, Switzerland, Turkey, Ukraine

Eighth preambular paragraph*

In favour

Algeria, Andorra, Angola, Antigua and Barbuda, Argentina, Austria, Azerbaijan, Bahamas, Bahrain, Bangladesh, Barbados, Belarus, Belize, Bolivia (Plurinational State of), Botswana, Brazil, Brunei Darussalam, Burkina Faso, Burundi, Cabo Verde, Cambodia, Chad, Chile, Colombia, Costa Rica, Côte d'Ivoire, Cuba, Cyprus, Djibouti, Dominica, Dominican Republic, Ecuador, Egypt, El Salvador, Eritrea, Eswatini, Ethiopia, Fiji, Gambia, Ghana, Grenada, Guatemala, Guinea, Guinea-Bissau, Guyana, Haiti, Honduras, Indonesia, Iran (Islamic Republic of), Iraq, Ireland, Jamaica, Jordan, Kazakhstan, Kenya, Kiribati, Kuwait, Lao People's Democratic Republic, Lebanon, Lesotho, Libya, Liechtenstein, Malawi, Malaysia, Maldives, Mali, Malta, Mauritania, Mauritius, Mexico, Mongolia, Morocco, Mozambique, Myanmar, Namibia, Nepal, New Zealand, Nicaragua, Niger, Nigeria, Oman, Panama, Papua New Guinea, Paraguay, Peru, Philippines, Qatar, Republic of Moldova, Saint Lucia, Saint Vincent and the Grenadines, Samoa, San Marino, Sao Tome and Principe, Saudi Arabia, Senegal, Seychelles, Singapore, South Africa, South Sudan, Sri Lanka, Sudan, Suriname, Sweden, Switzerland, Tajikistan, Thailand, Timor-Leste, Togo, Trinidad and Tobago, Tunisia, Turkmenistan, Tuvalu, Uganda, United Arab Emirates, United Republic of Tanzania, Uruguay, Uzbekistan, Vanuatu, Venezuela (Bolivarian Republic of), Viet Nam, Yemen, Zambia

Against

Albania, Australia, China, Croatia, Czechia, Denmark, Estonia, France, Germany, Israel, Italy, Latvia, Lithuania, Luxembourg, Monaco, Montenegro, Netherlands, North Macedonia, Poland, Republic of Korea, Romania, Russian Federation, Slovakia, Slovenia, Turkey, United Kingdom, United States

Abstaining

Armenia, Belgium, Bhutan, Bosnia and Herzegovina, Bulgaria, Canada, Finland, Gabon, Georgia, Greece, Hungary, Iceland, India, Japan, Madagascar, Marshall Islands, Norway, Pakistan, Portugal, Serbia, Spain, Ukraine, Zimbabwe

---

* Subsequently, the delegation of Gabon informed the Secretariat that it had not intended to participate; the delegation of Madagascar informed the Secretariat that it had intended to vote in favour.

*Tenth preambular paragraph**

In favour

Afghanistan, Algeria, Andorra, Angola, Antigua and Barbuda, Argentina, Australia, Austria, Azerbaijan, Bahamas, Bahrain, Bangladesh, Barbados, Belarus, Belgium, Belize, Bhutan, Bolivia (Plurinational State of), Botswana, Brazil, Brunei Darussalam, Burkina Faso, Burundi, Cabo Verde, Cambodia, Canada, Chad, Chile, China, Colombia, Costa Rica, Côte d'Ivoire, Cuba, Cyprus, Democratic People's Republic of Korea, Djibouti, Dominica, Dominican Republic, Ecuador, Egypt, El Salvador, Eritrea, Eswatini, Ethiopia, Fiji, Finland, Gambia, Germany, Ghana, Grenada, Guatemala, Guinea, Guinea-Bissau, Guyana, Haiti, Honduras, Iceland, India, Indonesia, Iran (Islamic Republic of), Iraq, Ireland, Jamaica, Japan, Jordan, Kazakhstan, Kenya, Kiribati, Kuwait, Kyrgyzstan, Lao People's Democratic Republic, Lebanon, Lesotho, Liberia, Libya, Liechtenstein, Madagascar, Malawi, Malaysia, Maldives, Mali, Malta, Mauritania, Mauritius, Mexico, Mongolia, Morocco, Mozambique, Myanmar, Namibia, Nepal, New Zealand, Nicaragua, Niger, Nigeria, Norway, Oman, Pakistan, Panama, Papua New Guinea, Paraguay, Peru, Philippines, Qatar, Republic of Korea, Republic of Moldova, Saint Lucia, Saint Vincent and the Grenadines, San Marino, Sao Tome and Principe, Saudi Arabia, Senegal, Serbia, Seychelles, Singapore, South Africa, South Sudan, Spain, Sri Lanka, Sudan, Suriname, Sweden, Switzerland, Tajikistan, Thailand, Timor-Leste, Togo, Trinidad and Tobago, Tunisia, Turkmenistan, Tuvalu, Uganda, United Arab Emirates, United Republic of Tanzania, Uruguay, Uzbekistan, Vanuatu, Venezuela (Bolivarian Republic of), Viet Nam, Yemen, Zambia

Against

France, Russian Federation, United States

Abstaining

Albania, Armenia, Bosnia and Herzegovina, Bulgaria, Croatia, Czechia, Denmark, Estonia, Gabon, Georgia, Greece, Hungary, Israel, Italy, Latvia, Lithuania, Luxembourg, Monaco, Montenegro, Netherlands, North Macedonia, Poland, Portugal, Romania, Slovakia, Slovenia, Syrian Arab Republic, Turkey, Ukraine, United Kingdom

Action by the First Committee

Date: 27 October 2021 Meeting: 13th meeting
Vote: 133-24-25 Draft resolution: A/C.1/76/L.42
118-27-24, p.p. 8
135-2-32, p.p. 10

---

* Subsequently, the delegation of Gabon informed the Secretariat that it had not intended to participate.

Agenda item 100 (q)

76/49   Towards a nuclear-weapon-free world: accelerating the implementation of nuclear disarmament commitments

Text

The General Assembly,

Recalling its resolutions 1 (I) of 24 January 1946, 71/54 of 5 December 2016, 72/39 of 4 December 2017, 73/70 of 5 December 2018, 74/46 of 12 December 2019 and 75/65 of 7 December 2020,

Noting the twenty-third anniversary of the launch of the New Agenda Coalition and the joint declaration outlining a new agenda for disarmament, adopted in Dublin on 9 June 1998,[1]

Welcoming the Secretary-General's disarmament agenda, *Securing Our Common Future: An Agenda for Disarmament*, and emphasizing the importance of its implementation,

Reiterating its grave concern at the danger to humanity posed by nuclear weapons, which should inform all deliberations, decisions and actions relating to nuclear disarmament and nuclear non-proliferation,

Recalling the expression of deep concern by the 2010 Review Conference of the Parties to the Treaty on the Non-Proliferation of Nuclear Weapons at the catastrophic humanitarian consequences of any use of nuclear weapons, and its resolve to seek a safer world for all and to achieve the peace and security of a world without nuclear weapons,[2]

Noting with satisfaction the renewed attention to the catastrophic humanitarian consequences and risks associated with nuclear weapons that has been generated by the international community since 2010 and the growing awareness that these concerns should underpin the need for nuclear disarmament and the urgency of achieving and maintaining a nuclear-weapon-free world, and noting with satisfaction also the prominence accorded to the humanitarian impact of nuclear weapons in multilateral disarmament forums,

Recalling the discussions held at the Conferences on the Humanitarian Impact of Nuclear Weapons, hosted by Norway, on 4 and 5 March 2013, Mexico, on 13 and 14 February 2014, and Austria, on 8 and 9 December 2014, aimed at understanding and developing a greater awareness of the catastrophic consequences of nuclear weapon detonations which further reinforce the urgency of nuclear disarmament,

---

[1] A/53/138, annex.

[2] See *2010 Review Conference of the Parties to the Treaty on the Non-Proliferation of Nuclear Weapons, Final Document*, vol. I (NPT/CONF.2010/50 (Vol. I)), part I, *Conclusions and recommendations for follow-on actions*.

Emphasizing the compelling evidence, including that presented at the Conferences on the Humanitarian Impact of Nuclear Weapons, that has detailed the catastrophic consequences that would result from any nuclear weapon detonation, reaching well beyond national borders and also imperilling the achievement of the Sustainable Development Goals,[3] the lack of capacity of States and international organizations to deal with the aftermath and the risk of an occurrence, including an occurrence due to an accident, systems failure or human error,

Noting the strongly disproportionate and gendered impact of exposure to ionizing radiation for women and girls,

Welcoming the entry into force on 22 January 2021 of the Treaty on the Prohibition of Nuclear Weapons, negotiated and adopted by the United Nations conference to negotiate a legally binding instrument to prohibit nuclear weapons, leading towards their total elimination, pursuant to resolution 71/258 of 23 December 2016,[4]

Welcoming also the commemoration and promotion of 26 September as the International Day for the Total Elimination of Nuclear Weapons, as established by resolution 68/32 of 5 December 2013,

Underlining the importance of nuclear disarmament and non-proliferation education,

Reaffirming that nuclear disarmament and nuclear non-proliferation are mutually reinforcing processes requiring urgent irreversible progress on both fronts,

Recalling the decisions and the resolution adopted at the 1995 Review and Extension Conference of the Parties to the Treaty on the Non-Proliferation of Nuclear Weapons,[5] the basis upon which the Treaty was indefinitely extended, and the Final Documents of the 2000[6] and the 2010[7] Review Conferences of the Parties to the Treaty on the Non-Proliferation of Nuclear Weapons, and in particular the unequivocal undertaking by the nuclear-weapon States to accomplish the total elimination of their nuclear arsenals, leading to nuclear disarmament, in accordance with commitments made under article VI of the Treaty,

---

[3] See resolution 70/1.

[4] A/CONF.229/2017/8.

[5] See *1995 Review and Extension Conference of the Parties to the Treaty on the Non-Proliferation of Nuclear Weapons, Final Document, Part I* (NPT/CONF.1995/32 (Part I) and NPT/CONF.1995/32 (Part I)/Corr.2), annex.

[6] *2000 Review Conference of the Parties to the Treaty on the Non-Proliferation of Nuclear Weapons, Final Document*, vols. I–III (NPT/CONF.2000/28 (Parts I and II), NPT/CONF.2000/28 (Part III) and NPT/CONF.2000/28 (Part IV)).

[7] *2010 Review Conference of the Parties to the Treaty on the Non-Proliferation of Nuclear Weapons, Final Document*, vols. I–III (NPT/CONF.2010/50 (Vol. I), NPT/CONF.2010/50 (Vol. II) and NPT/CONF.2010/50 (Vol. III)).

Reaffirming that transparency, verifiability and irreversibility are cardinal principles applying to nuclear disarmament and nuclear non-proliferation, and reaffirming also the commitment of all States parties to the Treaty on the Non-Proliferation of Nuclear Weapons[8] to applying these principles in relation to the implementation of their treaty obligations,

Recalling the twenty-fifth anniversary of the opening for signature of the Comprehensive Nuclear-Test-Ban Treaty[9] and the continued vital importance of its entry into force to the advancement of nuclear disarmament and nuclear Non-Proliferation objectives,

Recalling also that the total elimination of nuclear weapons is the only absolute guarantee against the use or threat of use of nuclear weapons and the legitimate interest of non-nuclear-weapon States in receiving unequivocal and legally binding negative security assurances from nuclear-weapon States pending the total elimination of nuclear weapons,

Reaffirming the conviction that, pending the total elimination of nuclear weapons, the establishment and maintenance of nuclear-weapon-free zones enhances global and regional peace and security, strengthens the nuclear non-proliferation regime and contributes towards realizing the objectives of nuclear disarmament, and welcoming the Conferences of States Parties and Signatories to Treaties that Establish Nuclear-Weapon-Free Zones and Mongolia,

Urging States to continue to make real progress towards strengthening all existing nuclear-weapon-free zones, inter alia, through the ratification of existing treaties and relevant protocols and the withdrawal or revision of any reservations or interpretative declarations contrary to the object and purpose of the treaties establishing such zones,

Recalling the encouragement expressed at the 2010 Review Conference for the establishment of further nuclear-weapon-free zones, on the basis of arrangements freely arrived at among the States of the region concerned, reaffirming the expectation that this will be followed by concerted international efforts to create such zones in areas where they do not currently exist, especially in the Middle East, in this context noting with deep disappointment the non-fulfilment of the agreement at the 2010 Review Conference on practical steps to fully implement the 1995 resolution on the Middle East, and disappointed that no agreement could be reached at the 2015 Review Conference of the Parties to the Treaty on the Non-Proliferation of Nuclear Weapons on this issue,

Recalling also its decision 73/546 of 22 December 2018, in which it decided to entrust to the Secretary-General the convening of a conference

---

[8] United Nations, *Treaty Series*, vol. 729, No. 10485.
[9] See resolution 50/245 and A/50/1027.

aimed at elaborating a treaty on the establishment of a Middle East zone free of nuclear weapons and all other weapons of mass destruction, on the basis of arrangements freely arrived at by the States of the region, and encouraged by the outcomes of the first session of the conference, which was successfully convened in 2019,

Deeply disappointed at the continued absence of progress towards multilateral nuclear disarmament at the Conference on Disarmament, which has been unable for the past 25 years to agree upon and implement a programme of work, and disappointed that the Disarmament Commission has not produced a substantive outcome on nuclear disarmament since 1999,

Deeply regretting the lack of any substantive outcome of the 2015 Review Conference, as it missed an opportunity to strengthen the Treaty on the Non-Proliferation of Nuclear Weapons, enhance progress towards its full implementation and universality and monitor the implementation of commitments made and actions agreed upon at the 1995, 2000 and 2010 Review Conferences, and deeply concerned about the impact of this failure on the Treaty and the balance between its three pillars,

Noting with serious concern the rising tensions in international relations and the increased prominence being given by some States to nuclear weapons in their security doctrines, as well as the extensive modernization programmes under way, all of which contribute to the erosion of the disarmament and non-proliferation regime,

Noting with regret that, owing to the coronavirus disease (COVID-19) pandemic, the 2020 Review Conference of the Parties to the Treaty on the Non-Proliferation of Nuclear Weapons had to be postponed, emphasizing the importance of holding a constructive, comprehensive and successful meeting that results in a substantive outcome at the 2020 Review Conference, urging all Member States to step up their efforts in this regard, and emphasizing also the vital importance of ensuring that the 2020 Review Conference contributes to the strengthening of the Treaty on the Non-Proliferation of Nuclear Weapons and making progress towards achieving its full implementation and universality, and monitors the implementation of commitments made and actions agreed upon at the 1995, 2000 and 2010 Review Conferences,

Welcoming that the Russian Federation and the United States of America have agreed on a five-year extension, to 4 February 2026, of the Treaty on Measures for the Further Reduction and Limitation of Strategic Offensive Arms, while re-emphasizing the encouragement of the 2000 and 2010 Review Conferences to both States to continue discussions on follow-on measures in order to achieve deeper reductions in their nuclear arsenals, and urging in this regard both States to conclude negotiations on a successor agreement as soon as possible,

Welcoming also the recent reaffirmations of the historic principle that "a nuclear war cannot be won and must never be fought",

Underlining the importance of multilateralism in relation to nuclear disarmament, while recognizing the value of unilateral, bilateral and regional initiatives and the importance of compliance with the terms of these initiatives,

1. *Reiterates* that each article of the Treaty on the Non-Proliferation of Nuclear Weapons is binding on the States parties at all times and in all circumstances and that all States parties should be held fully accountable with respect to strict compliance with their obligations under the Treaty, and calls upon all States parties to comply fully with all decisions, resolutions and commitments made at the 1995, 2000 and 2010 Review Conferences;

2. *Also reiterates* the deep concern expressed by the 2010 Review Conference of the Parties to the Treaty on the Non-Proliferation of Nuclear Weapons at the catastrophic humanitarian consequences of any use of nuclear weapons, and the need for all States at all times to comply with applicable international law, including international humanitarian law;

3. *Acknowledges* the evidence presented at the Conferences on the Humanitarian Impact of Nuclear Weapons, and calls upon Member States, in their relevant decisions and actions, to give due prominence to the humanitarian imperatives that underpin nuclear disarmament and to the urgency of achieving this goal;

4. *Recalls* the reaffirmation of the continued validity of the practical steps agreed to in the Final Document of the 2000 Review Conference of the Parties to the Treaty on the Non-Proliferation of Nuclear Weapons,[10] including the specific reaffirmation of the unequivocal undertaking of the nuclear-weapon States to accomplish the total elimination of their nuclear arsenals leading to nuclear disarmament, to which all States parties are committed under article VI of the Treaty, recalls the commitment of the nuclear-weapon States to accelerating concrete progress on the steps leading to nuclear disarmament, and calls upon the nuclear-weapon States to take all steps necessary to accelerate the fulfilment of their commitments;

5. *Calls upon* the nuclear-weapon States to fulfil their commitment to undertaking further efforts to reduce and ultimately eliminate all types of nuclear weapons, deployed and non-deployed, including through unilateral, bilateral, regional and multilateral measures;

6. *Urges* all States possessing nuclear weapons to decrease the operational readiness of nuclear-weapon systems in a verifiable and

---

[10] *2000 Review Conference of the Parties to the Treaty on the Non-Proliferation of Nuclear Weapons, Final Document*, vol. I (NPT/CONF.2000/28 (Parts I and II)), part I, section entitled "Article VI and eighth to twelfth preambular paragraphs", para. 15.

transparent manner with a view to ensuring that all nuclear weapons are removed from high alert status;

7.   *Encourages* the nuclear-weapon States to make concrete reductions in the role and significance of nuclear weapons in all military and security concepts, doctrines and policies, pending their total elimination;

8.   *Encourages* all States that are part of regional alliances that include nuclear-weapon States to diminish the role of nuclear weapons in their collective security doctrines, pending their total elimination;

9.   *Underlines* the recognition by States parties to the Treaty on the Non-Proliferation of Nuclear Weapons of the legitimate interest of non-nuclear-weapon States in the constraining by the nuclear-weapon States of the development and qualitative improvement of nuclear weapons and their ending the development of advanced new types of nuclear weapons, and calls upon the nuclear-weapon States to take steps in this regard;

10.   *Notes with concern* recent policy statements by nuclear-weapon States relating to the modernization of their nuclear weapon programmes, which undermine their commitments to nuclear disarmament and increase the risk of the use of nuclear weapons and the potential for a new arms race;

11.   *Encourages* further steps by all nuclear-weapon States, in accordance with the previous obligations and commitments on nuclear disarmament, to ensure the irreversible removal of all fissile material designated by each nuclear-weapon State as no longer required for military purposes, and calls upon all States to support, within the context of the International Atomic Energy Agency, the development of appropriate nuclear disarmament verification capabilities and legally binding verification arrangements, thereby ensuring that such material remains permanently outside military programmes in a verifiable manner;

12.   *Calls upon* all States parties to the Treaty on the Non-Proliferation of Nuclear Weapons to work towards the full implementation of the resolution on the Middle East adopted at the 1995 Review and Extension Conference of the Parties to the Treaty on the Non-Proliferation of Nuclear Weapons,[11] which is inextricably linked to the indefinite extension of the Treaty, and expresses disappointment and deep concern at the lack of a substantive outcome of the 2015 Review Conference of the Parties to the Treaty on the Non-Proliferation of Nuclear Weapons, including on the process to establish a Middle East zone free of nuclear weapons and all other weapons of mass destruction as contained in the 1995 resolution on the Middle East, which remains valid until fully implemented;

---

[11] See *1995 Review and Extension Conference of the Parties to the Treaty on the Non-Proliferation of Nuclear Weapons, Final Document, Part I* (NPT/CONF.1995/32 (Part I) and NPT/CONF.1995/32 (Part I)/Corr.2), annex.

13. *Urges* the co-sponsors of the 1995 resolution on the Middle East to exert their utmost efforts with a view to ensuring the early establishment of a Middle East zone free of nuclear weapons and all other weapons of mass destruction as contained in the 1995 resolution on the Middle East, including through support for the convening of the conference on the establishment of such a zone;

14. *Stresses* the fundamental role of the Treaty on the Non-Proliferation of Nuclear Weapons in achieving nuclear disarmament and nuclear non-proliferation, and looks forward to the Review Conference of the Parties to the Treaty on the Non-Proliferation of Nuclear Weapons once it has been rescheduled;

15. *Calls upon* all States parties to spare no effort to achieve the universality of the Treaty on the Non-Proliferation of Nuclear Weapons, and in this regard urges India, Israel and Pakistan to accede to the Treaty as non-nuclear-weapon States promptly and without conditions, and to place all their nuclear facilities under International Atomic Energy Agency safeguards;

16. *Urges* the Democratic People's Republic of Korea to fulfil its commitments, to abandon all nuclear weapons and existing nuclear programmes, to return, at an early date, to the Treaty on the Non-Proliferation of Nuclear Weapons and to adhere to its International Atomic Energy Agency safeguards agreement,[12] with a view to achieving the denuclearization of the Korean Peninsula in a peaceful, complete, verifiable and irreversible manner, welcomes diplomatic efforts, including through the holding of summits with all parties involved in the process, and encourages a continued dialogue to this end;

17. *Urges* all States to work together to overcome obstacles within the international disarmament machinery that are inhibiting efforts to advance the cause of nuclear disarmament in a multilateral context, and once again urges the Conference on Disarmament to commence immediately substantive work that advances the agenda of nuclear disarmament, particularly through multilateral negotiations;

18. *Urges* all States parties to the Treaty on the Non-Proliferation of Nuclear Weapons to fully implement without delay their obligations and commitments under the Treaty and as agreed to at the 1995, 2000 and 2010 Review Conferences;

19. *Also urges* all State parties to the Treaty on the Non-Proliferation of Nuclear Weapons to move forward with urgency in implementing their article VI obligations in order to ensure the good standing of the Treaty and its review process;

20. *Urges* the nuclear-weapon States to implement their nuclear disarmament obligations and commitments, both qualitative and quantitative,

---

[12] United Nations, *Treaty Series*, vol. 1677, No. 28986.

in a manner that enables all States parties to regularly monitor progress, including through a standard detailed reporting format, thereby enhancing confidence and trust not only among the nuclear-weapon States but also between the nuclear-weapon States and the non-nuclear-weapon States and contributing to nuclear disarmament;

21. *Also urges* the nuclear-weapon States to include in their reports to be submitted during the 2020 review cycle of the Treaty on the Non-Proliferation of Nuclear Weapons concrete and detailed information concerning the implementation of their obligations and commitments on nuclear disarmament;

22. *Encourages* States parties to the Treaty on the Non-Proliferation of Nuclear Weapons to improve the measurability of the implementation of nuclear disarmament obligations and commitments, including through tools such as a set of benchmarks, timelines and/or similar criteria, in order to ensure and facilitate the objective evaluation of progress;[13]

23. *Urges* Member States to pursue multilateral negotiations without delay in good faith on effective measures for the achievement and maintenance of a nuclear-weapon-free world, in keeping with the spirit and purpose of General Assembly resolution 1 (I) and article VI of the Treaty on the Non-Proliferation of Nuclear Weapons;

24. *Calls upon* Member States to continue to support efforts to identify, elaborate, negotiate and implement further effective legally binding measures for nuclear disarmament, and welcomes in this regard the entry into force on 22 January 2021 of the Treaty on the Prohibition of Nuclear Weapons;

25. *Recommends* that measures be taken to increase awareness among civil society of the risks and catastrophic impact of any nuclear detonation, including through disarmament education;

26. *Calls upon* all Member States to reflect on the vast amount of resources dedicated to the maintenance, development and modernization of nuclear arsenals and to consider whether these resources could be better utilized in pursuit of a better future as envisaged in the Sustainable Development Goals;

27. *Decides* to include in the provisional agenda of its seventy-seventh session, under the item entitled "General and complete disarmament", the sub-item entitled "Towards a nuclear-weapon-free world: accelerating the implementation of nuclear disarmament commitments" and to review the implementation of the present resolution at that session.

---

[13] See NPT/CONF.2020/PC.I/WP.13.

Action by the General Assembly

Date: 6 December 2021   Meeting: 45th plenary meeting
Vote: 140-34-15   Report: A/76/444
        146-2-28, p.p. 3
        115-37-19, p.p. 10
        161-4-10, p.p. 25
        164-4-9, o.p. 15
        118-37-19, o.p. 24

Sponsors

Austria, Brazil, Costa Rica, Egypt, Ireland, Kiribati, Lesotho, Mexico, New Zealand, Philippines, **South Africa**

Co-sponsors

Equatorial Guinea, Eswatini, Ghana, Liechtenstein, Namibia, Nigeria, Palau, Thailand, Zambia

Recorded vote

As a whole

In favour

Afghanistan, Algeria, Andorra, Angola, Antigua and Barbuda, Argentina, Austria, Azerbaijan, Bahamas, Bahrain, Bangladesh, Barbados, Belarus, Belize, Bhutan, Bolivia (Plurinational State of), Botswana, Brazil, Brunei Darussalam, Burkina Faso, Cabo Verde, Cambodia, Cameroon, Central African Republic, Chad, Chile, Colombia, Congo, Costa Rica, Côte d'Ivoire, Cuba, Cyprus, Djibouti, Dominica, Dominican Republic, Ecuador, Egypt, El Salvador, Equatorial Guinea, Eritrea, Eswatini, Ethiopia, Fiji, Gabon, Gambia, Ghana, Grenada, Guatemala, Guinea, Guinea-Bissau, Guyana, Haiti, Honduras, Indonesia, Iran (Islamic Republic of), Iraq, Ireland, Jamaica, Jordan, Kazakhstan, Kenya, Kiribati, Kuwait, Kyrgyzstan, Lao People's Democratic Republic, Lebanon, Lesotho, Liberia, Libya, Liechtenstein, Madagascar, Malawi, Malaysia, Maldives, Mali, Malta, Mauritania, Mauritius, Mexico, Mongolia, Morocco, Mozambique, Myanmar, Namibia, Nauru, Nepal, New Zealand, Nicaragua, Niger, Nigeria, Oman, Palau, Panama, Papua New Guinea, Paraguay, Peru, Philippines, Qatar, Republic of Moldova, Rwanda, Saint Kitts and Nevis, Saint Lucia, Saint Vincent and the Grenadines, Samoa, San Marino, Sao Tome and Principe, Saudi Arabia, Senegal, Seychelles, Sierra Leone, Singapore, Solomon Islands, South Africa, South Sudan, Sri Lanka, Sudan, Suriname, Sweden, Switzerland, Syrian Arab Republic, Tajikistan, Thailand, Timor-Leste, Togo, Tonga, Trinidad and Tobago, Tunisia, Turkmenistan, Tuvalu, Uganda, United Arab Emirates, United Republic of Tanzania, Uruguay, Uzbekistan, Vanuatu, Venezuela (Bolivarian Republic of), Viet Nam, Yemen, Zambia, Zimbabwe

Against

Albania, Belgium, Bulgaria, China, Croatia, Czechia, Democratic People's Republic of Korea, Denmark, Estonia, France, Germany, Greece, Hungary, India, Israel, Italy, Latvia, Lithuania, Luxembourg, Monaco, Montenegro, Netherlands, North Macedonia, Norway, Poland, Portugal, Romania, Russian Federation, Slovakia, Slovenia, Spain, Turkey, United Kingdom, United States

Abstaining

Armenia, Australia, Bosnia and Herzegovina, Burundi, Canada, Finland, Georgia, Iceland, Japan, Marshall Islands, Micronesia (Federated States of), Pakistan, Republic of Korea, Serbia, Ukraine

*Third preambular paragraph**

In favour

Afghanistan, Algeria, Andorra, Angola, Antigua and Barbuda, Argentina, Australia, Austria, Azerbaijan, Bahamas, Bahrain, Bangladesh, Barbados, Belarus, Belgium, Belize, Bhutan, Bolivia (Plurinational State of), Botswana, Brazil, Brunei Darussalam, Burkina Faso, Burundi, Cabo Verde, Cambodia, Canada, Chad, Chile, China, Colombia, Costa Rica, Côte d'Ivoire, Cuba, Cyprus, Democratic People's Republic of Korea, Denmark, Djibouti, Dominica, Dominican Republic, Ecuador, Egypt, El Salvador, Eritrea, Eswatini, Ethiopia, Fiji, Finland, Gambia, Germany, Ghana, Greece, Grenada, Guatemala, Guinea, Guinea-Bissau, Guyana, Haiti, Honduras, Iceland, India, Indonesia, Iran (Islamic Republic of), Iraq, Ireland, Jamaica, Japan, Jordan, Kazakhstan, Kenya, Kiribati, Kuwait, Kyrgyzstan, Lao People's Democratic Republic, Lebanon, Lesotho, Liberia, Libya, Liechtenstein, Madagascar, Malawi, Malaysia, Maldives, Mali, Malta, Mauritania, Mauritius, Mexico, Mongolia, Morocco, Mozambique, Myanmar, Namibia, Nepal, Netherlands, New Zealand, Nicaragua, Niger, Nigeria, Norway, Oman, Pakistan, Panama, Papua New Guinea, Paraguay, Peru, Philippines, Qatar, Republic of Korea, Republic of Moldova, Saint Lucia, Saint Vincent and the Grenadines, Samoa, San Marino, Sao Tome and Principe, Saudi Arabia, Senegal, Serbia, Seychelles, Sierra Leone, Singapore, South Africa, South Sudan, Spain, Sri Lanka, Sudan, Suriname, Sweden, Switzerland, Tajikistan, Thailand, Timor-Leste, Togo, Trinidad and Tobago, Tunisia, Turkmenistan, Tuvalu, Uganda, United Arab Emirates, United Republic of Tanzania, Uruguay, Uzbekistan, Vanuatu, Venezuela (Bolivarian Republic of), Viet Nam, Yemen, Zambia

Against

Russian Federation, United States

---

* Subsequently, the delegation of Gabon informed the Secretariat that it had not intended to participate.

Abstaining

Albania, Armenia, Bosnia and Herzegovina, Bulgaria, Croatia, Czechia, Estonia, France, Gabon, Georgia, Hungary, Israel, Italy, Latvia, Lithuania, Luxembourg, Monaco, Montenegro, North Macedonia, Poland, Portugal, Romania, Slovakia, Slovenia, Syrian Arab Republic, Turkey, Ukraine, United Kingdom

Tenth preambular paragraph*

In favour

Algeria, Andorra, Angola, Antigua and Barbuda, Argentina, Austria, Azerbaijan, Bahamas, Bahrain, Bangladesh, Barbados, Belize, Bhutan, Bolivia (Plurinational State of), Botswana, Brazil, Brunei Darussalam, Burkina Faso, Cabo Verde, Cambodia, Chad, Chile, Colombia, Costa Rica, Côte d'Ivoire, Cuba, Cyprus, Dominica, Dominican Republic, Ecuador, Egypt, El Salvador, Eritrea, Eswatini, Ethiopia, Fiji, Gambia, Ghana, Grenada, Guatemala, Guinea-Bissau, Guyana, Haiti, Honduras, Indonesia, Iran (Islamic Republic of), Iraq, Ireland, Jamaica, Jordan, Kazakhstan, Kenya, Kuwait, Lao People's Democratic Republic, Lebanon, Lesotho, Liberia, Libya, Liechtenstein, Madagascar, Malawi, Malaysia, Maldives, Mali, Malta, Mauritania, Mauritius, Mexico, Mongolia, Morocco, Mozambique, Myanmar, Namibia, Nepal, New Zealand, Nicaragua, Niger, Nigeria, Oman, Panama, Papua New Guinea, Paraguay, Peru, Philippines, Qatar, Republic of Moldova, Saint Lucia, Saint Vincent and the Grenadines, Samoa, San Marino, Sao Tome and Principe, Senegal, Seychelles, Singapore, South Africa, South Sudan, Sri Lanka, Sudan, Suriname, Thailand, Timor-Leste, Togo, Trinidad and Tobago, Tunisia, Turkmenistan, Tuvalu, Uganda, United Arab Emirates, United Republic of Tanzania, Uruguay, Vanuatu, Venezuela (Bolivarian Republic of), Viet Nam, Yemen, Zambia

Against

Albania, Australia, Belgium, Bulgaria, Canada, China, Croatia, Czechia, Denmark, Estonia, France, Germany, Greece, Hungary, Iceland, Israel, Italy, Latvia, Lithuania, Luxembourg, Monaco, Montenegro, Netherlands, North Macedonia, Norway, Poland, Portugal, Republic of Korea, Romania, Russian Federation, Sierra Leone, Slovakia, Slovenia, Spain, Turkey, United Kingdom, United States

Abstaining

Armenia, Belarus, Bosnia and Herzegovina, Burundi, Djibouti, Finland, Gabon, Georgia, Guinea, India, Japan, Kyrgyzstan, Marshall Islands, Pakistan, Saudi Arabia, Serbia, Sweden, Switzerland, Ukraine

---

* Subsequently, the delegation of Gabon informed the Secretariat that it had not intended to participate.

Twenty-fifth preambular paragraph*

In favour
> Afghanistan, Albania, Algeria, Andorra, Angola, Antigua and Barbuda, Argentina, Armenia, Australia, Austria, Azerbaijan, Bahamas, Bahrain, Bangladesh, Barbados, Belarus, Belgium, Belize, Bhutan, Bolivia (Plurinational State of), Bosnia and Herzegovina, Botswana, Brazil, Brunei Darussalam, Bulgaria, Burkina Faso, Burundi, Cabo Verde, Cambodia, Canada, Chad, Chile, China, Colombia, Costa Rica, Côte d'Ivoire, Croatia, Cuba, Cyprus, Czechia, Denmark, Dominica, Dominican Republic, Ecuador, Egypt, El Salvador, Eritrea, Estonia, Eswatini, Ethiopia, Fiji, Finland, Gambia, Germany, Ghana, Grenada, Guatemala, Guinea, Guinea-Bissau, Guyana, Haiti, Honduras, Hungary, Iceland, Indonesia, Iran (Islamic Republic of), Iraq, Ireland, Italy, Jamaica, Japan, Jordan, Kazakhstan, Kenya, Kiribati, Kuwait, Lao People's Democratic Republic, Latvia, Lebanon, Lesotho, Liberia, Libya, Liechtenstein, Lithuania, Luxembourg, Malawi, Malaysia, Maldives, Mali, Malta, Marshall Islands, Mauritania, Mauritius, Mexico, Monaco, Mongolia, Montenegro, Morocco, Mozambique, Myanmar, Namibia, Nepal, New Zealand, Nicaragua, Niger, Nigeria, North Macedonia, Norway, Oman, Panama, Papua New Guinea, Paraguay, Peru, Philippines, Portugal, Qatar, Republic of Korea, Republic of Moldova, Romania, Saint Lucia, Saint Vincent and the Grenadines, Samoa, San Marino, Sao Tome and Principe, Saudi Arabia, Senegal, Serbia, Seychelles, Sierra Leone, Singapore, Slovakia, Slovenia, South Africa, South Sudan, Spain, Sri Lanka, Sudan, Suriname, Sweden, Switzerland, Syrian Arab Republic, Tajikistan, Thailand, Timor-Leste, Togo, Trinidad and Tobago, Tunisia, Turkey, Turkmenistan, Tuvalu, Uganda, Ukraine, United Arab Emirates, United Republic of Tanzania, Uruguay, Uzbekistan, Vanuatu, Venezuela (Bolivarian Republic of), Viet Nam, Yemen, Zambia

Against
> India, Israel, Pakistan, United States

Abstaining
> Djibouti, France, Gabon, Georgia, Greece, Madagascar, Netherlands, Poland, Russian Federation, United Kingdom

Operative paragraph 15**

In favour
> Afghanistan, Albania, Algeria, Andorra, Angola, Antigua and Barbuda, Argentina, Armenia, Australia, Austria, Azerbaijan, Bahamas, Bahrain,

---

* Subsequently, the delegation of Gabon informed the Secretariat that it had not intended to participate; the delegation of Madagascar informed the Secretariat that it had intended to vote in favour; the delegation of Monaco informed the Secretariat that it had intended to abstain.

** Subsequently, the delegation of Gabon informed the Secretariat that it had not intended to participate; the delegation of Madagascar informed the Secretariat that it had intended to vote in favour.

Bangladesh, Barbados, Belarus, Belgium, Belize, Bhutan, Bolivia (Plurinational State of), Bosnia and Herzegovina, Botswana, Brazil, Brunei Darussalam, Bulgaria, Burkina Faso, Burundi, Cabo Verde, Cambodia, Canada, Chad, Chile, China, Colombia, Costa Rica, Côte d'Ivoire, Croatia, Cuba, Cyprus, Czechia, Denmark, Dominica, Dominican Republic, Ecuador, Egypt, El Salvador, Eritrea, Estonia, Eswatini, Ethiopia, Fiji, Finland, Gambia, Ghana, Greece, Grenada, Guatemala, Guinea, Guinea-Bissau, Guyana, Haiti, Honduras, Iceland, Indonesia, Iran (Islamic Republic of), Iraq, Ireland, Italy, Jamaica, Japan, Jordan, Kazakhstan, Kenya, Kiribati, Kuwait, Kyrgyzstan, Lao People's Democratic Republic, Latvia, Lebanon, Lesotho, Liberia, Libya, Liechtenstein, Lithuania, Luxembourg, Malawi, Malaysia, Maldives, Mali, Malta, Marshall Islands, Mauritania, Mauritius, Mexico, Mongolia, Montenegro, Morocco, Mozambique, Myanmar, Namibia, Nepal, Netherlands, New Zealand, Nicaragua, Niger, Nigeria, North Macedonia, Norway, Oman, Panama, Papua New Guinea, Paraguay, Peru, Philippines, Poland, Portugal, Qatar, Republic of Korea, Republic of Moldova, Romania, Russian Federation, Saint Lucia, Saint Vincent and the Grenadines, Samoa, San Marino, Sao Tome and Principe, Saudi Arabia, Senegal, Serbia, Seychelles, Sierra Leone, Singapore, Slovakia, Slovenia, South Africa, South Sudan, Spain, Sri Lanka, Sudan, Suriname, Sweden, Switzerland, Syrian Arab Republic, Tajikistan, Thailand, Timor-Leste, Togo, Trinidad and Tobago, Tunisia, Turkey, Turkmenistan, Tuvalu, Uganda, Ukraine, United Arab Emirates, United Republic of Tanzania, Uruguay, Uzbekistan, Vanuatu, Venezuela (Bolivarian Republic of), Viet Nam, Yemen, Zambia, Zimbabwe

Against

India, Israel, Pakistan, United States

Abstaining

Djibouti, France, Gabon, Georgia, Germany, Hungary, Madagascar, Monaco, United Kingdom

Operative paragraph 24*

In favour

Afghanistan, Algeria, Andorra, Angola, Antigua and Barbuda, Argentina, Austria, Azerbaijan, Bahamas, Bahrain, Bangladesh, Barbados, Belize, Bhutan, Bolivia (Plurinational State of), Botswana, Brazil, Brunei Darussalam, Burkina Faso, Cabo Verde, Cambodia, Chad, Chile, Colombia, Costa Rica, Côte d'Ivoire, Cuba, Cyprus, Dominica, Dominican Republic, Ecuador, Egypt, El Salvador, Eritrea, Eswatini, Ethiopia, Fiji, Gambia, Ghana, Grenada, Guatemala, Guinea, Guinea-Bissau, Guyana,

---

* Subsequently, the delegation of Gabon informed the Secretariat that it had not intended to participate; the delegation of Madagascar informed the Secretariat that it had intended to vote in favour.

Haiti, Honduras, Indonesia, Iran (Islamic Republic of), Iraq, Ireland, Jamaica, Jordan, Kazakhstan, Kenya, Kiribati, Kuwait, Lao People's Democratic Republic, Lebanon, Lesotho, Libya, Liechtenstein, Malawi, Malaysia, Maldives, Mali, Malta, Mauritania, Mauritius, Mexico, Mongolia, Morocco, Mozambique, Myanmar, Namibia, Nepal, New Zealand, Nicaragua, Niger, Nigeria, Oman, Palau, Panama, Papua New Guinea, Paraguay, Peru, Philippines, Qatar, Republic of Moldova, Saint Lucia, Saint Vincent and the Grenadines, Samoa, San Marino, Sao Tome and Principe, Senegal, Seychelles, Singapore, South Africa, South Sudan, Sri Lanka, Sudan, Suriname, Thailand, Timor-Leste, Togo, Trinidad and Tobago, Tunisia, Turkmenistan, Tuvalu, Uganda, United Arab Emirates, United Republic of Tanzania, Uruguay, Vanuatu, Venezuela (Bolivarian Republic of), Viet Nam, Yemen, Zambia, Zimbabwe

Against

Albania, Australia, Belgium, Bosnia and Herzegovina, Bulgaria, Canada, China, Croatia, Czechia, Denmark, Estonia, Germany, Greece, Hungary, Iceland, Israel, Italy, Latvia, Lithuania, Luxembourg, Monaco, Montenegro, Netherlands, North Macedonia, Norway, Poland, Portugal, Republic of Korea, Romania, Russian Federation, Sierra Leone, Slovakia, Slovenia, Spain, Turkey, United Kingdom, United States

Abstaining

Armenia, Belarus, Burundi, Djibouti, Finland, France, Gabon, Georgia, India, Japan, Kyrgyzstan, Madagascar, Marshall Islands, Pakistan, Saudi Arabia, Serbia, Sweden, Switzerland, Ukraine

Action by the First Committee

Date:	27 October 2021	Meeting:	13th meeting
Vote:	135-34-15	Draft resolution:	A/C.1/76/L.44
	138-2-31, p.p. 3		
	111-36-18, p.p. 10		
	152-4-13, p.p. 25		
	160-4-8, o.p. 15		
	114-36-17, o.p. 24		

Agenda item 100 (x)

76/50   The Arms Trade Treaty

Text

The General Assembly,

Recalling its resolutions 61/89 of 6 December 2006, 63/240 of 24 December 2008, 64/48 of 2 December 2009, 67/234 A of 24 December 2012, 67/234 B of 2 April 2013, 68/31 of 5 December 2013, 69/49 of 2 December 2014, 70/58 of 7 December 2015, 71/50 of 5 December 2016, 72/44 of 4 December 2017, 73/36 of 5 December 2018, 74/49 of 12 December 2019 and 75/64 of 7 December 2020 and its decision 66/518 of 2 December 2011,

Recognizing that disarmament, arms control and non-proliferation are essential for the maintenance of international peace and security,

Recognizing also the security, social, economic and humanitarian consequences of the illicit and unregulated trade in conventional arms,

Recognizing further the legitimate political, security, economic and commercial interests of States in the international trade in conventional arms,

Underlining the urgent need to prevent and eradicate the illicit trade in conventional arms, including small arms and light weapons, and to prevent their diversion to the illicit market, or for unauthorized end use or end users, including through improvements to stockpile management, thereby preventing the exacerbation of armed violence, the commission of terrorist acts and the violation of international humanitarian law and international human rights law,

Emphasizing the responsibility of all States, in accordance with their respective international and regional obligations and commitments, to effectively regulate the international trade in conventional arms,

Recalling the contribution made by the Programme of Action to Prevent, Combat and Eradicate the Illicit Trade in Small Arms and Light Weapons in All Its Aspects,[1] as well as the Protocol against the Illicit Manufacturing of and Trafficking in Firearms, Their Parts and Components and Ammunition, supplementing the United Nations Convention against Transnational Organized Crime,[2] and the International Instrument to Enable States to Identify and Trace, in a Timely and Reliable Manner, Illicit Small Arms and Light Weapons,[3]

---

[1] *Report of the United Nations Conference on the Illicit Trade in Small Arms and Light Weapons in All Its Aspects, New York, 9–20 July 2001* (A/CONF.192/15), chap. IV, para. 24.

[2] United Nations, *Treaty Series*, vol. 2326, No. 39574.

[3] See decision 60/519 and A/60/88 and A/60/88/Corr.2, annex.

Highlighting the relevance of the Arms Trade Treaty,[4] including its links and synergies with other relevant instruments on conventional arms, to efforts to meet Sustainable Development Goal 16 of the 2030 Agenda for Sustainable Development,[5] and specifically target 16.4, which aims at significantly reducing illicit arms flows by 2030,

Recalling the Secretary-General's disarmament agenda, *Securing Our Common Future: An Agenda for Disarmament*, in particular the section of the agenda entitled "Disarmament that saves lives",

Recognizing the negative impact of the illicit and unregulated trade in conventional arms and related ammunition on the lives of women, men, girls and boys, and that the Arms Trade Treaty was the first international agreement to identify and call upon States to address the link between conventional arms transfers and the risk of serious acts of gender-based violence and serious acts of violence against women and children,

Recognizing also the important role that civil society organizations, including non-governmental organizations, and industry play, by raising awareness, in efforts to prevent and eradicate the illicit and unregulated trade in conventional arms, including in preventing their diversion, and in supporting the implementation of the Treaty,

Recalling the adoption by the General Assembly and the entry into force of the Treaty on 2 April 2013 and 24 December 2014, respectively, and noting that the Treaty remains open for accession by any State that has not signed it, bearing in mind that the universalization of the Treaty is essential to achieving its object and purpose,

Noting the efforts by the States parties to the Treaty to continue to explore ways and means to enhance national implementation of the Treaty through the working group on effective treaty implementation and the voluntary trust fund for the implementation of the Treaty,

Noting with concern the persisting global effect of the coronavirus disease (COVID-19) pandemic, including on the full and effective implementation of the Treaty,

1.   *Welcomes* the decisions taken by the Seventh Conference of States Parties to the Arms Trade Treaty, held in hybrid format from 30 August to 2 September 2021, with a thematic focus of the Presidency on strengthening efforts to eradicate the illicit trade in small arms and light weapons and ensuring efficient stockpile management, and notes that the Eighth Conference of States Parties will be held in Geneva from 22 to 26 August 2022;

2.   *Also welcomes* the continuing progress by the standing working groups on effective treaty implementation, including the important work

---

[4]   United Nations, *Treaty Series*, vol. 3013, No. 52373.
[5]   Resolution 70/1.

undertaken in the context of its sub-working groups on articles 6 and 7, article 9 and article 11, on transparency and reporting, and on universalization in advancing the object and purpose of the Arms Trade Treaty;

3.   *Recognizes* that the consolidation of the institutional structure of the Treaty provides a framework for supporting further work under the Treaty, in particular its effective implementation, in this regard expresses concern about the unpaid assessed contributions of States and the potential adverse implications that this has for the Treaty processes, and calls upon States that have not yet done so to address their financial obligations under the Treaty in a prompt and timely manner;

4.   *Welcomes* the announcement by the Gambia that it would accede to the Treaty, and calls upon all States that have not yet done so to ratify, accept, approve or accede to the Treaty, in accordance with their respective constitutional processes, in order to achieve its universalization;

5.   *Calls upon* all States parties to submit and encourages them to make available, in a timely manner, and to update, as appropriate, their initial reports, as well as their annual reports for the preceding calendar year, as required under article 13 of the Treaty, thereby enhancing confidence, transparency, trust and accountability, and welcomes the ongoing efforts of the working group on transparency and reporting to facilitate compliance by States parties with their reporting obligations;

6.   *Calls upon* those States parties in a position to do so to provide assistance, including legal or legislative assistance, institutional capacity-building and technical, material or financial assistance, to requesting States in order to promote the implementation and universalization of the Treaty;

7.   *Stresses* the vital importance of the full and effective implementation of and compliance with all provisions of the Treaty by States parties, and urges States parties to meet their obligations under the Treaty, thereby contributing to international and regional peace, security and stability, to the reduction of human suffering and to the promotion of cooperation, transparency and responsible action;

8.   *Recognizes* the complementarity among all relevant international instruments on conventional arms and the Treaty, and to this end urges all States to implement effective national measures to prevent, combat and eradicate the illicit and unregulated trade in conventional arms and ammunition in fulfilment of their respective international obligations and commitments and to prevent their diversion;

9.   *Also recognizes* the outcome of the Seventh Biennial Meeting of States to Consider the Implementation of the Programme of Action to Prevent, Combat and Eradicate the Illicit Trade in Small Arms and Light Weapons in

All Its Aspects,[6] adopted in July 2021, and the potential synergies with the Treaty;

10.   *Encourages* further steps to enable States to increasingly prevent and tackle the diversion of conventional arms and ammunition to unauthorized end uses or end users during the entire life cycle of the items, and recognizes that enhancing reporting rates, transparency and information-sharing, in line with Treaty obligations, is fundamental to achieving this goal;

11.   *Encourages* States parties and signatory States to actively use the Diversion Information Exchange Forum and, on a voluntary basis, to share concrete and operational information about cases of suspected or detected diversion, and acknowledges that this is a step towards tackling diversion by enhancing information-sharing and a tool to improve practical implementation of the Treaty;

12.   *Recalls* the adoption of action-oriented decisions on gender and gender-based violence by the Fifth Conference of States Parties and the fact that States parties agreed to review progress on these two aspects on an ongoing basis, and in that respect encourages States parties and signatory States to ensure the full and equal participation of women and men in pursuing the object and purpose of the Treaty;

13.   *Welcomes* the continued support through the voluntary trust fund for the implementation of the Treaty, encourages eligible States to make best use of the voluntary trust fund, and encourages all States parties in a position to do so to contribute to the voluntary trust fund;

14.   *Encourages* States parties and signatory States in a position to do so to provide funding to the Treaty sponsorship programme to support participation in meetings under the Treaty for those States that would otherwise be unable to attend;

15.   *Encourages* States parties to strengthen their cooperation with civil society, including non-governmental organizations, industry and relevant international organizations and to work with other States parties at the national and regional levels, and invites those stakeholders, in particular those that are underrepresented in Treaty processes, to engage further with States parties with the aim of ensuring the effective implementation and universalization of the Treaty;

16.   *Decides* to include in the provisional agenda of its seventy-seventh session, under the item entitled "General and complete disarmament", the sub-item entitled "The Arms Trade Treaty", and to review the implementation of the present resolution at that session.

---

[6]   A/CONF.192/BMS/2021/1, annex.

Action by the General Assembly

Date: 6 December 2021   Meeting: 45th plenary meeting
Vote: 162-0-24   Report: A/76/444
      159-1-14, p.p. 9
      149-1-21, p.p. 10

Sponsors

Australia, Austria, Belgium, Bosnia and Herzegovina, Bulgaria, Canada, Chile, Costa Rica, Croatia, Czechia, Denmark, Estonia, Finland, **Germany**, Greece, Hungary, Iceland, Ireland, Italy, Japan, Latvia, Lesotho, Lithuania, Luxembourg, Mexico, Montenegro, Netherlands, New Zealand, Nigeria, North Macedonia, Norway, Philippines, Portugal, Republic of Korea, Republic of Moldova, Slovakia, South Africa, Spain, Sweden, Switzerland, United Kingdom

Co-sponsors

Albania, Andorra, Argentina, Bahamas, Barbados, Botswana, Burkina Faso, Cabo Verde, China, Cyprus, Dominican Republic, France, Georgia, Ghana, Guyana, Honduras, Jamaica, Kazakhstan, Liechtenstein, Malaysia, Maldives, Malta, Monaco, Mongolia, Namibia, Palau, Panama, Paraguay, Peru, Romania, Saint Kitts and Nevis, Saint Lucia, Samoa, San Marino, Serbia, Slovenia, Suriname, Thailand, Trinidad and Tobago, Tuvalu

Recorded vote

As a whole

In favour

Afghanistan, Albania, Algeria, Andorra, Angola, Antigua and Barbuda, Argentina, Australia, Austria, Bahamas, Bahrain, Bangladesh, Barbados, Belgium, Belize, Bhutan, Bosnia and Herzegovina, Botswana, Brazil, Brunei Darussalam, Bulgaria, Burkina Faso, Burundi, Cabo Verde, Cambodia, Cameroon, Canada, Central African Republic, Chad, Chile, China, Colombia, Comoros, Congo, Costa Rica, Côte d'Ivoire, Croatia, Cyprus, Czechia, Denmark, Djibouti, Dominica, Dominican Republic, El Salvador, Estonia, Eswatini, Ethiopia, Fiji, Finland, France, Gabon, Gambia, Georgia, Germany, Ghana, Greece, Grenada, Guatemala, Guinea, Guinea-Bissau, Guyana, Haiti, Honduras, Hungary, Iceland, Iraq, Ireland, Israel, Italy, Jamaica, Japan, Jordan, Kazakhstan, Kenya, Kiribati, Kuwait, Latvia, Lebanon, Lesotho, Liberia, Libya, Liechtenstein, Lithuania, Luxembourg, Madagascar, Malawi, Malaysia, Maldives, Mali, Malta, Marshall Islands, Mauritania, Mauritius, Mexico, Micronesia (Federated States of), Monaco, Mongolia, Montenegro, Morocco, Mozambique, Myanmar, Namibia, Nepal, Netherlands, New Zealand, Niger, Nigeria, North Macedonia, Norway, Pakistan, Palau, Panama, Papua New Guinea,

Paraguay, Peru, Philippines, Poland, Portugal, Republic of Korea, Republic of Moldova, Romania, Rwanda, Saint Kitts and Nevis, Saint Lucia, Saint Vincent and the Grenadines, Samoa, San Marino, Sao Tome and Principe, Senegal, Serbia, Seychelles, Sierra Leone, Singapore, Slovakia, Slovenia, Solomon Islands, Somalia, South Africa, South Sudan, Spain, Sudan, Suriname, Sweden, Switzerland, Thailand, Timor-Leste, Togo, Tonga, Trinidad and Tobago, Tunisia, Turkey, Turkmenistan, Tuvalu, Ukraine, United Arab Emirates, United Kingdom, United Republic of Tanzania, United States, Uruguay, Vanuatu, Zambia, Zimbabwe

Against

None

Abstaining

Armenia, Belarus, Bolivia (Plurinational State of), Cuba, Democratic People's Republic of Korea, Ecuador, Egypt, Equatorial Guinea, Eritrea, India, Indonesia, Iran (Islamic Republic of), Lao People's Democratic Republic, Nicaragua, Oman, Qatar, Russian Federation, Saudi Arabia, Sri Lanka, Syrian Arab Republic, Tajikistan, Uganda, Venezuela (Bolivarian Republic of), Yemen

Ninth preambular paragraph*

In favour

Afghanistan, Albania, Algeria, Andorra, Angola, Antigua and Barbuda, Argentina, Australia, Austria, Bahamas, Bahrain, Bangladesh, Barbados, Belarus, Belgium, Belize, Bhutan, Bolivia (Plurinational State of), Bosnia and Herzegovina, Botswana, Brazil, Brunei Darussalam, Bulgaria, Burkina Faso, Burundi, Cabo Verde, Cambodia, Canada, Chad, Chile, China, Colombia, Comoros, Costa Rica, Côte d'Ivoire, Croatia, Cuba, Cyprus, Czechia, Democratic People's Republic of Korea, Denmark, Djibouti, Dominica, Dominican Republic, Ecuador, El Salvador, Estonia, Eswatini, Ethiopia, Fiji, Finland, France, Gambia, Georgia, Germany, Ghana, Greece, Grenada, Guatemala, Guinea, Guinea-Bissau, Guyana, Haiti, Honduras, Hungary, Iceland, India, Indonesia, Iraq, Ireland, Italy, Jamaica, Japan, Jordan, Kazakhstan, Kenya, Kiribati, Lao People's Democratic Republic, Latvia, Lebanon, Lesotho, Liberia, Libya, Liechtenstein, Lithuania, Luxembourg, Madagascar, Malawi, Malaysia, Maldives, Mali, Malta, Marshall Islands, Mauritania, Mauritius, Mexico, Micronesia (Federated States of), Monaco, Mongolia, Montenegro, Morocco, Myanmar, Namibia, Nepal, Netherlands, New Zealand, Niger, Nigeria, North Macedonia, Norway, Oman, Pakistan, Panama, Papua New Guinea, Paraguay, Peru, Philippines, Poland, Portugal, Republic of Korea, Republic of Moldova, Romania, Rwanda, Saint Kitts and Nevis, Saint Lucia, Saint Vincent and

---

* Subsequently, the delegation of Gabon informed the Secretariat that it had not intended to participate.

the Grenadines, Samoa, San Marino, Sao Tome and Principe, Senegal, Serbia, Seychelles, Sierra Leone, Singapore, Slovakia, Slovenia, South Africa, South Sudan, Spain, Sudan, Suriname, Sweden, Switzerland, Thailand, Timor-Leste, Togo, Trinidad and Tobago, Tunisia, Turkey, Turkmenistan, Tuvalu, Ukraine, United Arab Emirates, United Kingdom, United Republic of Tanzania, Uruguay, Vanuatu, Zambia, Zimbabwe

Against
Russian Federation

Abstaining
Armenia, Egypt, Eritrea, Gabon, Iran (Islamic Republic of), Israel, Kuwait, Qatar, Saudi Arabia, Sri Lanka, Syrian Arab Republic, United States, Venezuela (Bolivarian Republic of), Yemen

Tenth preambular paragraph*

In favour
Afghanistan, Albania, Andorra, Angola, Antigua and Barbuda, Argentina, Australia, Austria, Bahamas, Bahrain, Bangladesh, Barbados, Belgium, Belize, Bhutan, Bosnia and Herzegovina, Botswana, Brazil, Brunei Darussalam, Bulgaria, Burkina Faso, Burundi, Cabo Verde, Cambodia, Canada, Chad, Chile, China, Colombia, Costa Rica, Côte d'Ivoire, Croatia, Cyprus, Czechia, Denmark, Djibouti, Dominica, Dominican Republic, Ecuador, El Salvador, Estonia, Eswatini, Ethiopia, Fiji, Finland, France, Gambia, Georgia, Germany, Ghana, Greece, Grenada, Guatemala, Guinea, Guinea-Bissau, Guyana, Haiti, Honduras, Hungary, Iceland, Iraq, Ireland, Italy, Jamaica, Japan, Jordan, Kazakhstan, Kenya, Kiribati, Latvia, Lebanon, Lesotho, Liberia, Libya, Liechtenstein, Lithuania, Luxembourg, Madagascar, Malawi, Malaysia, Maldives, Mali, Malta, Marshall Islands, Mauritius, Mexico, Micronesia (Federated States of), Monaco, Mongolia, Montenegro, Morocco, Myanmar, Namibia, Nepal, Netherlands, New Zealand, Niger, Nigeria, North Macedonia, Norway, Oman, Pakistan, Panama, Papua New Guinea, Paraguay, Peru, Philippines, Poland, Portugal, Republic of Korea, Republic of Moldova, Romania, Rwanda, Saint Kitts and Nevis, Saint Lucia, Saint Vincent and the Grenadines, Samoa, San Marino, Sao Tome and Principe, Senegal, Serbia, Seychelles, Sierra Leone, Singapore, Slovakia, Slovenia, South Africa, South Sudan, Spain, Sudan, Suriname, Sweden, Switzerland, Thailand, Timor-Leste, Togo, Trinidad and Tobago, Tunisia, Turkey, Turkmenistan, Tuvalu, Ukraine, United Arab Emirates, United Kingdom, United States, Uruguay, Vanuatu, Zambia, Zimbabwe

---

* Subsequently, the delegation of Israel informed the Secretariat that it had intended to vote in favour.

Against
> Israel

Abstaining
> Algeria, Armenia, Belarus, Bolivia (Plurinational State of), Cuba, Democratic People's Republic of Korea, Egypt, Eritrea, India, Indonesia, Iran (Islamic Republic of), Kuwait, Mauritania, Nicaragua, Qatar, Russian Federation, Saudi Arabia, Sri Lanka, Syrian Arab Republic, Venezuela (Bolivarian Republic of), Yemen

Action by the First Committee

Date:	2 November 2021	Meeting:	16th meeting
Vote:	151-0-27	Draft resolution:	A/C.1/76/L.46
	149-1-17, p.p. 9		
	143-0-23, p.p. 10		

Agenda item 100 (a)

76/51 Treaty banning the production of fissile material for nuclear weapons or other nuclear explosive devices

Text

The General Assembly,

Recalling its resolutions 48/75 L of 16 December 1993, 53/77 I of 4 December 1998, 55/33 Y of 20 November 2000, 56/24 J of 29 November 2001, 57/80 of 22 November 2002, 58/57 of 8 December 2003, 59/81 of 3 December 2004, 64/29 of 2 December 2009, 65/65 of 8 December 2010, 66/44 of 2 December 2011 and 67/53 of 3 December 2012, its decisions 68/518 of 5 December 2013 and 69/516 of 2 December 2014, its resolutions 70/39 of 7 December 2015 and 71/259 of 23 December 2016, its decision 72/513 of 4 December 2017, its resolution 73/65 of 5 December 2018 and its decisions 74/509 of 12 December 2019 and 75/515 of 7 December 2020, on the subject of a treaty banning the production of fissile material for nuclear weapons or other nuclear explosive devices,

Mindful of the continuing importance and relevance of the Conference on Disarmament, and recalling the past achievements of that body in successfully negotiating non-proliferation and disarmament agreements,

Expressing concern at the years of stalemate in the Conference on Disarmament, regretting that negotiations have not been pursued on this issue, and looking forward to the Conference again fulfilling its mandate as the world's single multilateral disarmament negotiating forum,

Convinced that a non-discriminatory, multilateral and effectively verifiable treaty banning the production of fissile material for nuclear weapons or other nuclear explosive devices would represent a significant practical contribution to nuclear disarmament and non-proliferation efforts,

Recognizing the essential role of fissile material in the manufacture of nuclear weapons or other nuclear explosive devices and the long-standing efforts of the international community to negotiate a treaty that would ban its production for such purposes,

Recognizing also that a future treaty should not prohibit the production of fissile material for non-proscribed military purposes or civilian use, consistent with the obligations of States parties, or interfere in any other way with a State's right to peaceful uses of nuclear energy,

Recalling action 15 of the conclusions and recommendations for follow-on actions agreed by consensus at the 2010 Review Conference of the Parties to the Treaty on the Non-Proliferation of Nuclear Weapons[1] that, inter alia, the Conference on Disarmament should, within the context of an agreed, comprehensive and balanced programme of work, immediately begin negotiation of a treaty banning the production of fissile material for use in nuclear weapons or other nuclear explosive devices in accordance with the report of the Special Coordinator of 1995 (CD/1299) and the mandate contained therein,

Noting with appreciation the consensus report of the Group of Governmental Experts, mandated in resolution 67/53, as contained in document A/70/81,

Noting with appreciation also the work accomplished in 2017 and 2018 by the high-level fissile material cut-off treaty expert preparatory group convened by the Secretary-General following resolution 71/259, on the basis of equitable geographic distribution, to consider and make recommendations on substantial elements of a future non-discriminatory, multilateral and effectively verifiable treaty banning the production of fissile material for nuclear weapons or other nuclear explosive devices, on the basis of document CD/1299 and the mandate contained therein,

Reaffirming the need to ensure the equal, full and meaningful participation of women in the negotiation process of a future treaty,

Reaffirming also its desire to achieve substantive progress in nuclear Non-Proliferation and disarmament, and in particular on a non-discriminatory, multilateral and effectively verifiable treaty banning the production of fissile material for nuclear weapons or other nuclear explosive devices,

1.   *Urges* the Conference on Disarmament to agree on and implement at its earliest opportunity a programme of work that includes the immediate commencement of negotiations on a treaty banning the production of fissile material for nuclear weapons or other nuclear explosive devices on the basis of document CD/1299 and the mandate contained therein;

2.   *Calls upon* Member States to make innovative contributions in all appropriate formal and informal forums, including the tenth Review Conference of the Parties to the Treaty on the Non-Proliferation of Nuclear Weapons, for facilitating negotiations in the Conference on Disarmament on a treaty banning the production of fissile material for nuclear weapons or other nuclear explosive devices;

3.   *Decides* to include in the provisional agenda of its seventy-seventh session, under the item entitled "General and complete disarmament", the sub-item entitled "Treaty banning the production of fissile material for nuclear weapons or other nuclear explosive devices".

---

[1] See *2010 Review Conference of the Parties to the Treaty on the Non-Proliferation of Nuclear Weapons, Final Document*, vol. I (NPT/CONF.2010/50 (Vol. I)), part I, *Conclusions and recommendations for follow-on actions.*

Action by the General Assembly

Date: 6 December 2021   Meeting: 45th plenary meeting
Vote: 182-1-5   Report: A/76/444
      166-1-11, p.p. 3

Sponsors

Canada, Germany, Netherlands

Recorded vote

As a whole

In favour

Afghanistan, Albania, Algeria, Andorra, Angola, Antigua and Barbuda, Argentina, Armenia, Australia, Austria, Azerbaijan, Bahamas, Bahrain, Bangladesh, Barbados, Belarus, Belgium, Belize, Bhutan, Bolivia (Plurinational State of), Bosnia and Herzegovina, Botswana, Brazil, Brunei Darussalam, Bulgaria, Burkina Faso, Burundi, Cabo Verde, Cambodia, Cameroon, Canada, Chad, Chile, China, Colombia, Comoros, Congo, Costa Rica, Côte d'Ivoire, Croatia, Cuba, Cyprus, Czechia, Denmark, Djibouti, Dominica, Dominican Republic, Ecuador, Equatorial Guinea, Eritrea, Estonia, Eswatini, Ethiopia, Fiji, Finland, France, Gabon, Gambia, Georgia, Germany, Ghana, Greece, Grenada, Guatemala, Guinea, Guinea-Bissau, Guyana, Haiti, Honduras, Hungary, Iceland, India, Indonesia, Iraq, Ireland, Italy, Jamaica, Japan, Jordan, Kazakhstan, Kenya, Kiribati, Kuwait, Kyrgyzstan, Lao People's Democratic Republic, Latvia, Lebanon, Lesotho, Liberia, Libya, Liechtenstein, Lithuania, Luxembourg, Madagascar, Malawi, Malaysia, Maldives, Mali, Malta, Marshall Islands, Mauritania, Mauritius, Mexico, Micronesia (Federated States of), Monaco, Mongolia, Montenegro, Morocco, Mozambique, Myanmar, Namibia, Nepal, Netherlands, New Zealand, Nicaragua, Niger, Nigeria, North Macedonia, Norway, Oman, Palau, Panama, Papua New Guinea, Paraguay, Peru, Philippines, Poland, Portugal, Qatar, Republic of Korea, Republic of Moldova, Romania, Russian Federation, Rwanda, Saint Kitts and Nevis, Saint Lucia, Saint Vincent and the Grenadines, Samoa, San Marino, Sao Tome and Principe, Saudi Arabia, Senegal, Serbia, Seychelles, Sierra Leone, Singapore, Slovakia, Slovenia, Solomon Islands, Somalia, South Africa, South Sudan, Spain, Sri Lanka, Sudan, Suriname, Sweden, Switzerland, Tajikistan, Thailand, Timor-Leste, Togo, Tonga, Trinidad and Tobago, Tunisia, Turkey, Turkmenistan, Tuvalu, Uganda, Ukraine, United Arab Emirates, United Kingdom, United Republic of Tanzania, United States, Uruguay, Uzbekistan, Vanuatu, Venezuela (Bolivarian Republic of), Viet Nam, Yemen, Zambia, Zimbabwe

Against

Pakistan

Abstaining
> Democratic People's Republic of Korea, Egypt, Iran (Islamic Republic of), Israel, Syrian Arab Republic

Third preambular paragraph*

In favour
> Afghanistan, Albania, Algeria, Andorra, Angola, Antigua and Barbuda, Argentina, Armenia, Australia, Austria, Azerbaijan, Bahamas, Bahrain, Bangladesh, Barbados, Belarus, Belgium, Belize, Bhutan, Bolivia (Plurinational State of), Bosnia and Herzegovina, Botswana, Brazil, Brunei Darussalam, Bulgaria, Burkina Faso, Burundi, Cabo Verde, Cambodia, Canada, Chad, Chile, Colombia, Costa Rica, Côte d'Ivoire, Croatia, Cuba, Cyprus, Czechia, Denmark, Djibouti, Dominica, Dominican Republic, Ecuador, El Salvador, Estonia, Eswatini, Ethiopia, Fiji, Finland, France, Gambia, Georgia, Germany, Ghana, Greece, Grenada, Guatemala, Guinea, Guinea-Bissau, Guyana, Haiti, Honduras, Hungary, Iceland, India, Indonesia, Iraq, Ireland, Italy, Jamaica, Japan, Jordan, Kazakhstan, Kenya, Kiribati, Kuwait, Lao People's Democratic Republic, Latvia, Lebanon, Lesotho, Liberia, Libya, Liechtenstein, Lithuania, Luxembourg, Malawi, Malaysia, Maldives, Mali, Malta, Marshall Islands, Mauritania, Mauritius, Mexico, Micronesia (Federated States of), Monaco, Mongolia, Montenegro, Morocco, Mozambique, Myanmar, Namibia, Nepal, Netherlands, New Zealand, Nicaragua, Niger, Nigeria, North Macedonia, Norway, Oman, Panama, Papua New Guinea, Paraguay, Peru, Philippines, Poland, Portugal, Qatar, Republic of Korea, Republic of Moldova, Romania, Rwanda, Saint Lucia, Saint Vincent and the Grenadines, Samoa, San Marino, Sao Tome and Principe, Saudi Arabia, Senegal, Seychelles, Sierra Leone, Singapore, Slovakia, Slovenia, Solomon Islands, South Africa, South Sudan, Spain, Sudan, Suriname, Sweden, Switzerland, Tajikistan, Thailand, Timor-Leste, Togo, Trinidad and Tobago, Tunisia, Turkey, Turkmenistan, Uganda, Ukraine, United Arab Emirates, United Kingdom, United Republic of Tanzania, United States, Uruguay, Uzbekistan, Vanuatu, Venezuela (Bolivarian Republic of), Viet Nam, Yemen, Zambia, Zimbabwe

Against
> Pakistan

Abstaining
> China, Democratic People's Republic of Korea, Egypt, Eritrea, Iran (Islamic Republic of), Israel, Madagascar, Russian Federation, Serbia, Sri Lanka, Syrian Arab Republic

---

* Subsequently, the delegation of Madagascar informed the Secretariat that it had intended to vote in favour.

Action by the First Committee

Date: 27 October 2021   Meeting: 13th meeting
Vote: 177-1-6   Draft resolution: A/C.1/76/L.51
      162-1-11, p.p. 3

Agenda item 100

76/52   Brazilian-Argentine Agency for Accounting and Control of Nuclear Materials

Text

The General Assembly,

Recalling the principles of the Agreement between the Republic of Argentina and the Federative Republic of Brazil for the Exclusively Peaceful Use of Nuclear Energy,[1] which was signed on 18 July 1991 and by which the Common System of Accounting and Control of Nuclear Materials and the Brazilian-Argentine Agency for Accounting and Control of Nuclear Materials were established,

Recalling also the provisions of the Agreement of 13 December 1991 between the Republic of Argentina, the Federative Republic of Brazil, the Brazilian-Argentine Agency for Accounting and Control of Nuclear Materials and the International Atomic Energy Agency for the Application of Safeguards,[2]

Reaffirming the conviction of the States parties to the Treaty on the Non-Proliferation of Nuclear Weapons[3] that the Treaty is the cornerstone of the nuclear non-proliferation and disarmament regime while ensuring the benefits of the peaceful uses of nuclear energy,

Recognizing the principles of the Treaty for the Prohibition of Nuclear Weapons in Latin America and the Caribbean (Treaty of Tlatelolco),[4] and welcoming its important contribution to the achievement of the objectives of nuclear disarmament and nuclear non-proliferation,

Mindful of the role played by the International Atomic Energy Agency with respect to nuclear safeguards and verification pursuant to article III of the Treaty on the Non-Proliferation of Nuclear Weapons, with a view to preventing the diversion of nuclear energy from peaceful uses to nuclear weapons or other nuclear explosive devices,

Considering that, in accordance with the aforementioned article, non-nuclear-weapon States parties to the Treaty on the Non-Proliferation of Nuclear Weapons may enter into agreements with the International Atomic Energy Agency either individually or together with other States, in accordance with the Agency's statute,

---

[1] CD/1117.
[2] International Atomic Energy Agency, document INFCIRC/435.
[3] United Nations, *Treaty Series*, vol. 729, No. 10485.
[4] Ibid., vol. 634, No. 9068.

Considering also that bilateral and regional safeguards agreements involving the International Atomic Energy Agency play an important role in the further promotion of transparency and mutual confidence between States and also provide assurances concerning nuclear non-proliferation,

Considering further the contribution by the Brazilian-Argentine Agency for Accounting and Control of Nuclear Materials in researching and developing innovative verification methods for improving efficiency in safeguards implementation,

1.   *Notes with satisfaction* that the year 2021 marks the thirtieth anniversary of the entry into force of the Agreement between the Republic of Argentina and the Federative Republic of Brazil for the Exclusively Peaceful Use of Nuclear Energy, on 12 December 1991, and of the establishment of the Common System of Accounting and Control of Nuclear Materials and the Brazilian-Argentine Agency for Accounting and Control of Nuclear Materials;

2.   *Welcomes* the continued cooperation between the Brazilian-Argentine Agency for Accounting and Control of Nuclear Materials and the International Atomic Energy Agency, and encourages them to increase their cooperation, taking into account their respective responsibilities and competencies;

3.   *Notes* that the Brazilian-Argentine Agency for Accounting and Control of Nuclear Materials has proved itself as an innovative and effective bilateral confidence-building mechanism, with positive effects for peace and security at the subregional and regional levels, and as a reference of best practice in nuclear safeguards and non-proliferation verification;

4.   *Decides* to include in the provisional agenda of its seventy-seventh session an item entitled "Brazilian-Argentine Agency for Accounting and Control of Nuclear Materials".

Action by the General Assembly

Date: 6 December 2021   Meeting: 45th plenary meeting
Vote: Adopted without a vote   Report: A/76/444

Sponsors

Argentina, **Brazil**

Action by the First Committee

Date: 27 October 2021   Meeting: 13th meeting
Vote: Adopted without a vote   Draft resolution: A/C.1/76/L.56

Agenda item 100 (k)

76/53 Follow-up to the advisory opinion of the International Court of Justice on the legality of the threat or use of nuclear weapons

Text

The General Assembly,

Recalling its resolutions 49/75 K of 15 December 1994, 51/45 M of 10 December 1996, 52/38 O of 9 December 1997, 53/77 W of 4 December 1998, 54/54 Q of 1 December 1999, 55/33 X of 20 November 2000, 56/24 S of 29 November 2001, 57/85 of 22 November 2002, 58/46 of 8 December 2003, 59/83 of 3 December 2004, 60/76 of 8 December 2005, 61/83 of 6 December 2006, 62/39 of 5 December 2007, 63/49 of 2 December 2008, 64/55 of 2 December 2009, 65/76 of 8 December 2010, 66/46 of 2 December 2011, 67/33 of 3 December 2012, 68/42 of 5 December 2013, 69/43 of 2 December 2014, 70/56 of 7 December 2015, 71/58 of 5 December 2016, 72/58 of 4 December 2017, 73/64 of 5 December 2018, 74/59 of 12 December 2019 and 75/66 of 7 December 2020,

Convinced that the continuing existence of nuclear weapons poses a threat to humanity and all life on Earth, and recognizing that the only defence against a nuclear catastrophe is the total elimination of nuclear weapons and the certainty that they will never be produced again,

Reaffirming the commitment of the international community to the realization of the goal of a nuclear-weapon-free world through the total elimination of nuclear weapons,

Mindful of the solemn obligations of States parties, in particular the obligations undertaken in article VI of the Treaty on the Non-Proliferation of Nuclear Weapons,[1] to pursue negotiations in good faith on effective measures relating to cessation of the nuclear arms race at an early date and to nuclear disarmament,

Recalling the principles and objectives for nuclear non-proliferation and disarmament adopted at the 1995 Review and Extension Conference of the Parties to the Treaty on the Non-Proliferation of Nuclear Weapons,[2] the unequivocal commitment of nuclear-weapon States to accomplish the total elimination of their nuclear arsenals leading to nuclear disarmament, agreed at the 2000 Review Conference of the Parties to the Treaty on the

---

[1] United Nations, *Treaty Series*, vol. 729, No. 10485.
[2] *1995 Review and Extension Conference of the Parties to the Treaty on the Non-Proliferation of Nuclear Weapons, Final Document, Part I* (NPT/CONF.1995/32 (Part I) and NPT/CONF.1995/32 (Part I)/Corr.2), annex, decision 2.

Non-Proliferation of Nuclear Weapons,[3] and the action points agreed at the 2010 Review Conference of the Parties to the Treaty on the Non-Proliferation of Nuclear Weapons as part of the conclusions and recommendations for follow-on actions on nuclear disarmament,[4]

Sharing the deep concern at the catastrophic humanitarian consequences of any use of nuclear weapons, and in this context reaffirming the need for all States at all times to comply with applicable international law, including international humanitarian law,

Calling upon all nuclear-weapon States to undertake concrete disarmament efforts, and stressing that all States need to make special efforts to achieve and maintain a world without nuclear weapons,

Recalling the five-point proposal for nuclear disarmament of the Secretary-General, in which he proposes, inter alia, the consideration of negotiations on a nuclear weapons convention or agreement on a framework of separate mutually reinforcing instruments, backed by a strong system of verification,

Noting continued efforts towards realizing nuclear disarmament, including through the Secretary-General's disarmament agenda, *Securing Our Common Future: An Agenda for Disarmament*,

Recalling the adoption of the Comprehensive Nuclear-Test-Ban Treaty in its resolution 50/245 of 10 September 1996, and expressing its satisfaction at the increasing number of States that have signed and ratified the Treaty,

Recognizing with satisfaction that the Antarctic Treaty,[5] the treaties of Tlatelolco,[6] Rarotonga,[7] Bangkok[8] and Pelindaba[9] and the Treaty on a Nuclear-Weapon-Free Zone in Central Asia,[10] as well as Mongolia's nuclear-weapon-free status, are gradually freeing the entire southern hemisphere and adjacent areas covered by those treaties from nuclear weapons,

Recognizing the need for a multilaterally negotiated and legally binding instrument to assure non-nuclear-weapon States against the threat or use of nuclear weapons pending the total elimination of nuclear weapons,

---

[3] See *2000 Review Conference of the Parties to the Treaty on the Non-Proliferation of Nuclear Weapons, Final Document*, vol. I (NPT/CONF.2000/28 (Parts I and II)), part I, section entitled "Article VI and eighth to twelfth preambular paragraphs", para. 15.

[4] See *2010 Review Conference of the Parties to the Treaty on the Non-Proliferation of Nuclear Weapons, Final Document*, vol. I (NPT/CONF.2010/50 (Vol. I)), part I.

[5] United Nations, *Treaty Series*, vol. 402, No. 5778.

[6] Ibid., vol. 634, No. 9068.

[7] *The United Nations Disarmament Yearbook*, vol. 10: 1985 (United Nations publication, Sales No. E.86.IX.7), appendix VII.

[8] United Nations, *Treaty Series*, vol. 1981, No. 33873.

[9] A/50/426, annex.

[10] United Nations, *Treaty Series*, vol. 2970, No. 51633.

Reaffirming the central role of the Conference on Disarmament as the sole multilateral disarmament negotiating forum,

Emphasizing the need for the Conference on Disarmament to commence negotiations on a phased programme for the complete elimination of nuclear weapons with a specified framework of time,

Stressing the urgent need for the nuclear-weapon States to accelerate concrete progress on the 13 practical steps to implement article VI of the Treaty on the Non-Proliferation of Nuclear Weapons leading to nuclear disarmament, contained in the Final Document of the 2000 Review Conference,

Recalling the Model Nuclear Weapons Convention submitted to the Secretary-General by Costa Rica and Malaysia in 2007 and circulated by the Secretary-General,[11]

Recalling also the adoption on 7 July 2017 of the Treaty on the Prohibition of Nuclear Weapons[12] and welcoming the entry into force of the Treaty on 22 January 2021, which have contributed to achieving the objective of a legally binding prohibition of the development, production, testing, deployment, stockpiling, threat or use of nuclear weapons and their destruction under effective international control,

Recalling further the advisory opinion of the International Court of Justice on the legality of the threat or use of nuclear weapons, issued on 8 July 1996,[13]

1. *Underlines once again* the unanimous conclusion of the International Court of Justice that there exists an obligation to pursue in good faith and bring to a conclusion negotiations leading to nuclear disarmament in all its aspects under strict and effective international control;

2. *Calls once again upon* all States to immediately engage in multilateral negotiations leading to nuclear disarmament in all its aspects under strict and effective international control, including under the Treaty on the Prohibition of Nuclear Weapons;

3. *Requests* all States to inform the Secretary-General of the efforts and measures which they have taken with respect to the implementation of the present resolution and nuclear disarmament, and requests the Secretary-General to apprise the General Assembly of that information at its seventy-seventh session;

4. *Decides* to include in the provisional agenda of its seventy-seventh session, under the item entitled "General and complete disarmament", the

---

[11] A/62/650, annex.
[12] A/CONF.229/2017/8.
[13] A/51/218, annex.

sub-item entitled "Follow-up to the advisory opinion of the International Court of Justice on the legality of the threat or use of nuclear weapons".

Action by the General Assembly

Date: 6 December 2021   Meeting: 45th plenary meeting
Vote: 143-33-14   Report: A/76/444
     144-2-29, p.p. 9
     116-36-18, p.p. 17
     121-36-15, o.p. 2

Sponsors

Algeria, Brunei Darussalam, Cuba, Egypt, Lao People's Democratic Republic, Libya, **Malaysia**, Mexico, Nepal, Nicaragua, Philippines, Viet Nam

Co-sponsors

Angola, Bahamas, Bangladesh, Bolivia (Plurinational State of), Brazil, Burkina Faso, Cambodia, Chile, Costa Rica, Côte d'Ivoire, Ecuador, Eritrea, Ghana, Guatemala, Guyana, Honduras, Indonesia, Iran (Islamic Republic of), Iraq, Jamaica, Lebanon, Madagascar, Maldives, Morocco, Myanmar, Palau, Peru, Samoa, Sierra Leone, Sri Lanka, Sudan, Thailand, Timor-Leste, Tunisia, Tuvalu, Uruguay, Venezuela (Bolivarian Republic of), Zimbabwe

Recorded vote

As a whole

In favour

Afghanistan, Algeria, Andorra, Angola, Antigua and Barbuda, Argentina, Austria, Azerbaijan, Bahamas, Bahrain, Bangladesh, Barbados, Belize, Bhutan, Bolivia (Plurinational State of), Botswana, Brazil, Brunei Darussalam, Burkina Faso, Burundi, Cabo Verde, Cambodia, Cameroon, Central African Republic, Chad, Chile, China, Colombia, Comoros, Congo, Costa Rica, Côte d'Ivoire, Cuba, Cyprus, Djibouti, Dominica, Dominican Republic, Ecuador, Egypt, El Salvador, Equatorial Guinea, Eritrea, Eswatini, Ethiopia, Fiji, Gabon, Gambia, Ghana, Grenada, Guatemala, Guinea, Guinea-Bissau, Guyana, Haiti, Honduras, Indonesia, Iran (Islamic Republic of), Iraq, Ireland, Jamaica, Jordan, Kazakhstan, Kenya, Kiribati, Kuwait, Kyrgyzstan, Lao People's Democratic Republic, Lebanon, Lesotho, Liberia, Libya, Liechtenstein, Madagascar, Malawi, Malaysia, Maldives, Mali, Malta, Mauritania, Mauritius, Mexico, Mongolia, Morocco, Mozambique, Myanmar, Namibia, Nepal, New Zealand, Nicaragua, Niger, Nigeria, Oman, Pakistan, Palau, Panama, Papua New Guinea, Paraguay, Peru, Philippines, Qatar, Republic of Moldova, Rwanda, Saint Kitts and Nevis, Saint Lucia, Saint Vincent and the Grenadines,

Samoa, San Marino, Sao Tome and Principe, Saudi Arabia, Senegal, Seychelles, Sierra Leone, Singapore, Solomon Islands, Somalia, South Africa, South Sudan, Sri Lanka, Sudan, Suriname, Sweden, Switzerland, Syrian Arab Republic, Tajikistan, Thailand, Timor-Leste, Togo, Tonga, Trinidad and Tobago, Tunisia, Turkmenistan, Tuvalu, Uganda, United Arab Emirates, United Republic of Tanzania, Uruguay, Uzbekistan, Vanuatu, Venezuela (Bolivarian Republic of), Viet Nam, Yemen, Zambia, Zimbabwe

Against

Albania, Australia, Belgium, Bulgaria, Croatia, Czechia, Denmark, Estonia, France, Germany, Greece, Hungary, Israel, Italy, Latvia, Lithuania, Luxembourg, Monaco, Montenegro, Netherlands, North Macedonia, Norway, Poland, Portugal, Republic of Korea, Romania, Russian Federation, Slovakia, Slovenia, Spain, Turkey, United Kingdom, United States

Abstaining

Armenia, Belarus, Bosnia and Herzegovina, Canada, Democratic People's Republic of Korea, Finland, Georgia, Iceland, India, Japan, Marshall Islands, Micronesia (Federated States of), Serbia, Ukraine

Ninth preambular paragraph*

In favour

Afghanistan, Algeria, Andorra, Angola, Antigua and Barbuda, Argentina, Australia, Austria, Azerbaijan, Bahamas, Bahrain, Bangladesh, Barbados, Belarus, Belgium, Belize, Bhutan, Bolivia (Plurinational State of), Botswana, Brazil, Brunei Darussalam, Burkina Faso, Burundi, Cabo Verde, Cambodia, Canada, Chad, Chile, China, Colombia, Costa Rica, Côte d'Ivoire, Cuba, Cyprus, Democratic People's Republic of Korea, Dominica, Dominican Republic, Ecuador, Egypt, El Salvador, Eritrea, Eswatini, Ethiopia, Fiji, Finland, Gambia, Germany, Ghana, Greece, Grenada, Guatemala, Guinea, Guinea-Bissau, Guyana, Haiti, Honduras, Iceland, India, Indonesia, Iran (Islamic Republic of), Iraq, Ireland, Italy, Jamaica, Japan, Jordan, Kazakhstan, Kenya, Kiribati, Kuwait, Kyrgyzstan, Lao People's Democratic Republic, Lebanon, Lesotho, Liberia, Libya, Liechtenstein, Madagascar, Malawi, Malaysia, Maldives, Mali, Malta, Mauritania, Mauritius, Mexico, Mongolia, Morocco, Mozambique, Myanmar, Namibia, Nepal, Netherlands, New Zealand, Nicaragua, Niger, Nigeria, Norway, Oman, Pakistan, Papua New Guinea, Paraguay, Peru, Philippines, Qatar, Republic of Korea, Republic of Moldova, Saint Lucia, Saint Vincent and the Grenadines, Samoa, San Marino, Sao Tome and Principe, Saudi Arabia, Senegal, Serbia, Seychelles, Singapore,

---

* Subsequently, the delegation of Gabon informed the Secretariat that it had not intended to participate; the delegation of Panama informed the Secretariat that it had intended to vote in favour.

South Africa, South Sudan, Spain, Sri Lanka, Sudan, Suriname, Sweden, Switzerland, Tajikistan, Thailand, Timor-Leste, Togo, Trinidad and Tobago, Tunisia, Turkmenistan, Tuvalu, Uganda, United Arab Emirates, United Republic of Tanzania, Uruguay, Uzbekistan, Vanuatu, Venezuela (Bolivarian Republic of), Viet Nam, Yemen, Zambia, Zimbabwe

Against

Russian Federation, United States

Abstaining

Albania, Armenia, Bosnia and Herzegovina, Bulgaria, Croatia, Czechia, Denmark, Djibouti, Estonia, France, Gabon, Georgia, Hungary, Israel, Latvia, Lithuania, Luxembourg, Monaco, Montenegro, North Macedonia, Poland, Portugal, Romania, Slovakia, Slovenia, Syrian Arab Republic, Turkey, Ukraine, United Kingdom

Seventeenth preambular paragraph*

In favour

Afghanistan, Algeria, Andorra, Angola, Antigua and Barbuda, Argentina, Austria, Azerbaijan, Bahamas, Bahrain, Bangladesh, Barbados, Belize, Bhutan, Bolivia (Plurinational State of), Botswana, Brazil, Brunei Darussalam, Burkina Faso, Burundi, Cabo Verde, Cambodia, Chad, Colombia, Costa Rica, Côte d'Ivoire, Cuba, Cyprus, Dominica, Dominican Republic, Ecuador, Egypt, El Salvador, Eritrea, Eswatini, Ethiopia, Fiji, Gambia, Ghana, Grenada, Guatemala, Guinea-Bissau, Guyana, Haiti, Honduras, Indonesia, Iran (Islamic Republic of), Iraq, Ireland, Jamaica, Jordan, Kazakhstan, Kenya, Kiribati, Kuwait, Lao People's Democratic Republic, Lebanon, Lesotho, Libya, Liechtenstein, Madagascar, Malawi, Malaysia, Maldives, Mali, Malta, Mauritania, Mauritius, Mexico, Mongolia, Morocco, Mozambique, Myanmar, Namibia, Nepal, New Zealand, Nicaragua, Niger, Nigeria, Oman, Panama, Papua New Guinea, Paraguay, Peru, Philippines, Qatar, Republic of Moldova, Saint Lucia, Saint Vincent and the Grenadines, Samoa, San Marino, Sao Tome and Principe, Senegal, Seychelles, Singapore, South Africa, South Sudan, Sri Lanka, Sudan, Suriname, Thailand, Timor-Leste, Togo, Trinidad and Tobago, Tunisia, Turkmenistan, Tuvalu, Uganda, United Arab Emirates, Uruguay, Vanuatu, Venezuela (Bolivarian Republic of), Viet Nam, Yemen, Zambia, Zimbabwe

Against

Albania, Australia, Belgium, Bulgaria, Canada, China, Croatia, Czechia, Denmark, Estonia, France, Germany, Greece, Hungary, Iceland, Israel, Italy, Latvia, Lithuania, Luxembourg, Monaco, Montenegro, Netherlands,

---

* Subsequently, the delegation of Gabon informed the Secretariat that it had not intended to participate.

North Macedonia, Norway, Poland, Portugal, Republic of Korea, Romania, Russian Federation, Slovakia, Slovenia, Spain, Turkey, United Kingdom, United States

Abstaining

Armenia, Belarus, Bosnia and Herzegovina, Djibouti, Finland, Gabon, Georgia, Guinea, India, Japan, Kyrgyzstan, Marshall Islands, Pakistan, Saudi Arabia, Serbia, Sweden, Switzerland, Ukraine

Operative paragraph 2*

In favour

Afghanistan, Algeria, Andorra, Angola, Antigua and Barbuda, Argentina, Austria, Azerbaijan, Bahamas, Bahrain, Bangladesh, Barbados, Belize, Bhutan, Bolivia (Plurinational State of), Botswana, Brazil, Brunei Darussalam, Burkina Faso, Burundi, Cabo Verde, Cambodia, Chad, Chile, Colombia, Costa Rica, Côte d'Ivoire, Cuba, Cyprus, Dominica, Dominican Republic, Ecuador, Egypt, El Salvador, Eritrea, Eswatini, Ethiopia, Fiji, Gambia, Ghana, Grenada, Guatemala, Guinea, Guinea-Bissau, Guyana, Haiti, Honduras, Indonesia, Iran (Islamic Republic of), Iraq, Ireland, Jamaica, Jordan, Kazakhstan, Kenya, Kiribati, Kuwait, Lao People's Democratic Republic, Lebanon, Lesotho, Libya, Liechtenstein, Madagascar, Malawi, Malaysia, Maldives, Mali, Malta, Mauritania, Mauritius, Mexico, Mongolia, Morocco, Mozambique, Myanmar, Namibia, Nepal, New Zealand, Nicaragua, Niger, Nigeria, Oman, Panama, Papua New Guinea, Paraguay, Peru, Philippines, Qatar, Republic of Moldova, Saint Lucia, Saint Vincent and the Grenadines, Samoa, San Marino, Sao Tome and Principe, Saudi Arabia, Senegal, Seychelles, Singapore, South Africa, South Sudan, Sri Lanka, Sudan, Suriname, Syrian Arab Republic, Thailand, Timor-Leste, Togo, Trinidad and Tobago, Tunisia, Turkmenistan, Tuvalu, Uganda, United Arab Emirates, United Republic of Tanzania, Uruguay, Vanuatu, Venezuela (Bolivarian Republic of), Viet Nam, Yemen, Zambia, Zimbabwe

Against

Albania, Australia, Belgium, Bulgaria, Canada, China, Croatia, Czechia, Denmark, Estonia, France, Germany, Greece, Hungary, Iceland, Israel, Italy, Latvia, Lithuania, Luxembourg, Monaco, Montenegro, Netherlands, North Macedonia, Norway, Poland, Portugal, Republic of Korea, Romania, Russian Federation, Slovakia, Slovenia, Spain, Turkey, United Kingdom, United States

---

* Subsequently, the delegation of Gabon informed the Secretariat that it had not intended to participate.

Abstaining

Armenia, Belarus, Bosnia and Herzegovina, Djibouti, Finland, Gabon, Georgia, India, Japan, Kyrgyzstan, Pakistan, Serbia, Sweden, Switzerland, Ukraine

Action by the First Committee

Date: 3 November 2021   Meeting: 17th meeting
Vote: 131-33-17   Draft resolution: A/C.1/76/L.58
      138-2-30, p.p. 9
      110-36-19, p.p. 17
      111-36-17, o.p. 2

Agenda item 100 (z)

76/54 Joint courses of action and future-oriented dialogue towards a world without nuclear weapons

Text

The General Assembly,

Reaffirming that achieving a world without nuclear weapons is a common goal for the international community,

Reaffirming also that the Treaty on the Non-Proliferation of Nuclear Weapons[1] is the cornerstone of the international nuclear non-proliferation regime and an essential foundation for the pursuit of nuclear disarmament, nuclear non-proliferation and the peaceful uses of nuclear energy, which are mutually reinforcing, and reaffirming its determination to further enhance the universality of the Treaty,

Noting the postponement of the tenth Review Conference of the Parties to the Treaty on the Non-Proliferation of Nuclear Weapons, underscoring the importance of its successful outcome, commemorating that the year 2020 was the fiftieth anniversary of the entry into force of the Treaty and recalling that it has been 76 years since the use of nuclear weapons in Hiroshima and Nagasaki, stressing that since that time no nuclear weapons have been used,

Emphasizing the necessity for all States parties to comply with all of their obligations regarding nuclear disarmament and non-proliferation under the Treaty on the Non-Proliferation of Nuclear Weapons, and reaffirming the importance of implementing commitments contained in the Final Documents of the 1995[2] Review and Extension Conference of the Parties to the Treaty on the Non-Proliferation of Nuclear Weapons and of the 2000[3] and 2010[4] Review Conferences of the Parties to the Treaty on the Non-Proliferation of Nuclear Weapons,

Bearing in mind that various approaches exist towards the realization of a world without nuclear weapons and that confidence-building among all States is essential to this end,

---

[1] United Nations, *Treaty Series*, vol. 729, No. 10485.

[2] *1995 Review and Extension Conference of the Parties to the Treaty on the Non-Proliferation of Nuclear Weapons, Final Document, Part I* (NPT/CONF.1995/32 (Part I) and NPT/CONF.1995/32 (Part I)/Corr.2).

[3] *2000 Review Conference of the Parties to the Treaty on the Non-Proliferation of Nuclear Weapons, Final Document*, vols. I–III (NPT/CONF.2000/28 (Parts I and II), NPT/CONF.2000/28 (Part III) and NPT/CONF.2000/28 (Part IV)).

[4] *2010 Review Conference of the Parties to the Treaty on the Non-Proliferation of Nuclear Weapons, Final Document*, vols. I–III (NPT/CONF.2010/50 (Vol. I), NPT/CONF.2010/50 (Vol. II) and NPT/CONF.2010/50 (Vol. III)).

Emphasizing the importance for all States of taking further practical steps and effective measures towards the total elimination of nuclear weapons, in a way that promotes international stability, peace and security, and based on the principle of undiminished and increased security for all,

Stressing that effective nuclear disarmament and the enhancement of international security should be pursued in a mutually reinforcing manner,

Reaffirming that further strengthening of the international regime for nuclear non-proliferation is essential to international peace and security,

Encouraging the establishment of further nuclear-weapon-free zones, where appropriate, on the basis of arrangements freely arrived at among States of the region concerned, and in accordance with the 1999 guidelines of the Disarmament Commission,[5] adopted by consensus,

Recognizing the importance of the decisions and the resolution on the Middle East of the 1995 Review and Extension Conference of the Parties to the Treaty on the Non-Proliferation of Nuclear Weapons[6] and the Final Documents of the 2000 and 2010 Review Conferences of the Parties to the Treaty on the Non-Proliferation of Nuclear Weapons, and reaffirming its support for the establishment of a Middle East zone free of nuclear weapons and all other weapons of mass destruction and their delivery systems on the basis of arrangements freely arrived at by the States of the region and in accordance with the 1995 resolution on the Middle East,

Stressing the importance of the immediate commencement and early conclusion of negotiations on a treaty banning the production of fissile material for use in nuclear weapons or other nuclear explosive devices in the Conference on Disarmament, and supporting the commencement of such negotiations in accordance with document CD/1299 and the mandate contained therein, and voluntarily ceasing such production pending the entry into force of such a treaty, which not all nuclear-weapon States parties to the Treaty on the Non-Proliferation of Nuclear Weapons have declared to date,

Recalling that it has been 25 years since the opening for signature of the Comprehensive Nuclear-Test-Ban Treaty,[7]

Recognizing the importance of reducing the risk of nuclear weapons being used either by miscalculation or by misunderstanding,

Recalling the indispensable role of effective and credible nuclear disarmament verification in assuring compliance, in the course of achieving

---

[5] *Official Records of the General Assembly, Fifty-fourth Session, Supplement No. 42* (A/54/42), annex I, sect. C.

[6] See *1995 Review and Extension Conference of the Parties to the Treaty on the Non-Proliferation of Nuclear Weapons, Final Document, Part I* (NPT/CONF.1995/32 (Part I) and NPT/CONF.1995/32 (Part I)/Corr.2), annex.

[7] See resolution 50/245 and A/50/1027.

and then maintaining the elimination of nuclear weapons, and welcoming the establishment of the Group of Governmental Experts to further consider nuclear disarmament verification issues, including, inter alia, the concept of a Group of Scientific and Technical Experts pursuant to resolution 74/50 of 12 December 2019,

Welcoming the extension of the Treaty between the United States of America and the Russian Federation on Measures for the Further Reduction and Limitation of Strategic Offensive Arms (New START Treaty), welcoming demonstrations of transparency, but stressing specifically the importance of concrete actions for more transparency between and among nuclear-weapon States, and reaffirming their special responsibility to initiate and actively engage in arms control dialogues in good faith on effective measures to prevent nuclear arms racing and help to prepare the way for the eventual elimination of nuclear weapons,

Recognizing the value of cooperative work across the existing multilateral disarmament machinery to support work towards disarmament objectives,

Recalling relevant Security Council resolutions deciding that the Democratic People's Republic of Korea shall abandon all nuclear weapons and existing nuclear programmes, and all other weapons of mass destruction and its ballistic missile programmes, in a complete, verifiable and irreversible manner, and welcoming diplomatic efforts towards that goal,

Noting that efforts to encompass different generations, areas of the world and genders in disarmament and non-proliferation education underscore efforts and create momentum towards achieving a world without nuclear weapons,

Recognizing the catastrophic humanitarian consequences that would result from the use of nuclear weapons,

Welcoming the visits of leaders, youth and others to Hiroshima and Nagasaki,

Reaffirming that the equal, full and effective participation of both women and men is one of the essential factors for the promotion and attainment of sustainable peace and security,

Reaffirming also that the international community needs to take immediate actions together and to conduct future-oriented dialogues in order to further facilitate the implementation of concrete nuclear disarmament measures through confidence-building,

1. *Reaffirms* that all States parties to the Treaty on the Non-Proliferation of Nuclear Weapons are committed to the ultimate goal of eliminating nuclear weapons, including through the easing of international tension, as well as the strengthening of trust between States and of the

international regime for nuclear non-proliferation, and to the full and steady implementation of the Treaty in all its aspects, including article VI of the Treaty, towards the realization of a world without nuclear weapons;

2.   *Calls upon* all States parties to the Treaty on the Non-Proliferation of Nuclear Weapons to identify concrete measures to put the commitments into practice towards and beyond the tenth Review Conference;

3.   *Encourages* the following, inter alia, as joint courses of action:

(a)   All States, in particular the nuclear-weapon States, to immediately take concrete measures to enhance transparency and mutual confidence, including, inter alia, by providing frequent and detailed reporting on the implementation of the Treaty on the Non-Proliferation of Nuclear Weapons and opportunities for discussion of these reports;

(b)   All States possessing nuclear weapons to take actions to reduce the risks of nuclear detonation occurring, inter alia, by miscalculation or by misunderstanding, and to make further efforts to this end, including transparency and dialogue on nuclear doctrines and postures, military-to-military dialogues, hotlines or information and data exchanges;

(c)   All States to immediately make every effort, including declaring and maintaining voluntary moratoriums on the production of fissile material for use in nuclear weapons or other nuclear explosive devices, as well as deepening substantive discussions in the Conference on Disarmament, to immediately commence negotiations on a treaty banning the production of fissile material for use in nuclear weapons or other nuclear explosive devices in the Conference on Disarmament in accordance with document CD/1299 and the mandate contained therein;

(d)   All States, including the eight remaining States listed in annex 2 to the Comprehensive Nuclear-Test-Ban Treaty that have not yet signed and/or ratified the Treaty, to do so without waiting for any other State, to work to achieve entry into force of the Treaty, and to declare or maintain existing moratoriums on nuclear-weapon test explosions or any other nuclear explosions pending the entry into force of the Treaty, as well as to continue support for the Preparatory Commission for the Comprehensive Nuclear-Test-Ban Treaty Organization and its work in preparing for entry into force;

(e)   All States to continue to make practical contributions to nuclear disarmament verification, including through concrete exercises, at the United Nations and the Conference on Disarmament, and in initiatives such as the International Partnership for Nuclear Disarmament Verification;

(f)   All States to facilitate efforts on nuclear disarmament and Non-Proliferation education, inter alia, efforts in which the young generation can actively engage, including through dialogue platforms, mentoring, internships, fellowships, scholarships, model events and youth group activities, as well as to raise awareness of the realities of the use of nuclear weapons, including through, among others, visits by leaders, youth and others to and interactions with communities and people, including the hibakusha (those who have suffered the use of nuclear weapons) who pass on their experiences to the future generations;

4.   *Also encourages*, for the purpose of facilitating future-oriented dialogues in order to advance nuclear disarmament, the following:

(a)   Nuclear-weapon States to clearly set out their nuclear policies and doctrines at international forums, including the Review Conference and Preparatory Committees of the Treaty on the Non-Proliferation of Nuclear Weapons, the Conference on Disarmament, the First Committee of the General Assembly and the Disarmament Commission, and all States to conduct interactive discussions, based on such nuclear policies and doctrines;

(b)   All States to conduct dialogue regarding the possible impacts of developments in science and technology on arms control, disarmament and Non-Proliferation;

(c)   All States to conduct candid dialogue on the relationship between nuclear disarmament and security;

5.   *Reaffirms* the commitment to strengthening the international regime for nuclear non-proliferation, including through adherence to International Atomic Energy Agency safeguards, including comprehensive safeguards agreements and additional protocols, and compliance with non-proliferation obligations, including through the implementation of relevant resolutions of the Security Council, including resolution 1540 (2004) of 28 April 2004;

6.   *Also reaffirms* the commitment to achieving the complete, verifiable and irreversible abandonment of all nuclear weapons and existing nuclear programmes, as well as all other existing weapons of mass destruction and ballistic missiles of all ranges, of the Democratic People's Republic of Korea in accordance with relevant Security Council resolutions, and the obligation of all Member States for the full implementation of all relevant Security Council resolutions, and urges the Democratic People's Republic of Korea to return at an early date to and fully comply with the Treaty on the Non-Proliferation of Nuclear Weapons and International Atomic Energy Agency safeguards;

7.   *Decides* to include in the provisional agenda of its seventy-seventh session, under the item entitled "General and complete disarmament", the sub-item entitled "Joint courses of action and future-oriented dialogue towards a world without nuclear weapons".

Action by the General Assembly

Date: 6 December 2021   Meeting: 45th plenary meeting
Vote: 158-4-27   Report: A/76/444
     155-2-16, p.p. 2
     143-0-28, p.p. 7
     160-0-12, p.p. 8
     163-1-7, p.p. 10
     154-3-16, p.p. 11
     168-0-5, p.p. 16
     156-1-14, p.p. 17
     161-2-6, p.p. 18
     156-1-16, p.p. 19
     163-2-9, p.p. 20
     133-10-24, o.p. 1
     129-0-39, o.p. 3 (b)
     152-2-17, o.p. 3 (c)
     138-2-29, o.p. 3 (d)
     147-1-23, o.p. 3 (e)
     162-2-9, o.p. 3 (f)
     154-0-19, o.p. 5
     151-3-19, o.p. 6

Sponsors

Japan, Nepal, Nicaragua, United Kingdom, United States

Co-sponsors

Afghanistan, Albania, Australia, Belgium, Belize, Bosnia and Herzegovina, Bulgaria, Canada, Comoros, Croatia, Czechia, Denmark, Dominican Republic, Eswatini, Finland, Gambia, Georgia, Germany, Guinea-Bissau, Iceland, Italy, Kiribati, Lebanon, Lesotho, Lithuania, Madagascar, Malawi, Marshall Islands, Micronesia (Federated States of), Netherlands, Niger, Norway, Palau, Papua New Guinea, Paraguay, Poland, Romania, Samoa, Sao Tome and Principe, Singapore, Slovakia, Slovenia, Spain, Sri Lanka, Sweden, Turkey, Turkmenistan, Tuvalu, Uganda, United Arab Emirates, Uzbekistan, Zambia

Recorded vote

As a whole

In favour

Afghanistan, Albania, Andorra, Angola, Antigua and Barbuda, Argentina, Armenia, Australia, Azerbaijan, Bahamas, Bahrain, Bangladesh, Barbados, Belarus, Belgium, Belize, Bhutan, Bolivia (Plurinational State of), Bosnia and Herzegovina, Botswana, Brunei Darussalam, Bulgaria, Burkina Faso,

Cabo Verde, Cambodia, Cameroon, Canada, Central African Republic, Chad, Colombia, Congo, Côte d'Ivoire, Croatia, Cyprus, Czechia, Denmark, Djibouti, Dominica, Dominican Republic, El Salvador, Equatorial Guinea, Eritrea, Estonia, Eswatini, Ethiopia, Fiji, Finland, France, Gabon, Gambia, Georgia, Germany, Ghana, Greece, Grenada, Guatemala, Guinea, Guinea-Bissau, Guyana, Haiti, Honduras, Iceland, Iraq, Italy, Jamaica, Japan, Jordan, Kazakhstan, Kenya, Kiribati, Kuwait, Kyrgyzstan, Lao People's Democratic Republic, Latvia, Lebanon, Lesotho, Liberia, Libya, Lithuania, Luxembourg, Madagascar, Malawi, Maldives, Mali, Malta, Marshall Islands, Mauritania, Mauritius, Micronesia (Federated States of), Monaco, Mongolia, Montenegro, Morocco, Mozambique, Namibia, Nauru, Nepal, Netherlands, Nicaragua, Niger, North Macedonia, Norway, Oman, Palau, Panama, Papua New Guinea, Paraguay, Peru, Philippines, Poland, Portugal, Qatar, Republic of Moldova, Romania, Rwanda, Saint Kitts and Nevis, Saint Lucia, Saint Vincent and the Grenadines, Samoa, San Marino, Sao Tome and Principe, Saudi Arabia, Senegal, Serbia, Seychelles, Sierra Leone, Singapore, Slovakia, Slovenia, Solomon Islands, South Sudan, Spain, Sri Lanka, Sudan, Suriname, Sweden, Switzerland, Tajikistan, Thailand, Timor-Leste, Togo, Tonga, Tunisia, Turkey, Turkmenistan, Tuvalu, Uganda, Ukraine, United Arab Emirates, United Kingdom, United Republic of Tanzania, United States, Uruguay, Uzbekistan, Vanuatu, Viet Nam, Yemen, Zambia

Against

China, Democratic People's Republic of Korea, Russian Federation, Syrian Arab Republic

Abstaining

Algeria, Austria, Brazil, Burundi, Chile, Costa Rica, Cuba, Ecuador, Egypt, Hungary, India, Indonesia, Iran (Islamic Republic of), Ireland, Israel, Liechtenstein, Malaysia, Mexico, Myanmar, New Zealand, Nigeria, Pakistan, Republic of Korea, South Africa, Trinidad and Tobago, Venezuela (Bolivarian Republic of), Zimbabwe

*Second preambular paragraph**

In favour

Afghanistan, Albania, Algeria, Andorra, Angola, Antigua and Barbuda, Argentina, Armenia, Australia, Azerbaijan, Bahrain, Bangladesh, Barbados, Belarus, Belgium, Belize, Bolivia (Plurinational State of), Bosnia and Herzegovina, Botswana, Brazil, Brunei Darussalam, Bulgaria, Burkina Faso, Burundi, Cabo Verde, Cambodia, Canada, Chad, Chile, China, Colombia, Côte d'Ivoire, Croatia, Cuba, Cyprus, Czechia, Denmark, Djibouti, Dominican Republic, Ecuador, El Salvador,

---

* Subsequently, the delegation of Gabon informed the Secretariat that it had not intended to participate.

Eritrea, Estonia, Eswatini, Ethiopia, Fiji, Finland, France, Gambia, Georgia, Germany, Ghana, Greece, Guatemala, Guinea, Guinea-Bissau, Guyana, Haiti, Honduras, Hungary, Iceland, Indonesia, Iran (Islamic Republic of), Iraq, Italy, Jamaica, Japan, Jordan, Kazakhstan, Kenya, Kiribati, Kuwait, Kyrgyzstan, Lao People's Democratic Republic, Latvia, Lebanon, Lesotho, Liberia, Libya, Lithuania, Luxembourg, Madagascar, Malawi, Maldives, Mali, Malta, Marshall Islands, Mauritania, Mauritius, Micronesia (Federated States of), Monaco, Mongolia, Montenegro, Morocco, Myanmar, Nepal, Netherlands, New Zealand, Nicaragua, Niger, North Macedonia, Norway, Oman, Panama, Papua New Guinea, Paraguay, Peru, Philippines, Poland, Portugal, Qatar, Republic of Korea, Republic of Moldova, Romania, Russian Federation, Rwanda, Saint Lucia, Saint Vincent and the Grenadines, Samoa, San Marino, Sao Tome and Principe, Saudi Arabia, Senegal, Serbia, Seychelles, Singapore, Slovakia, Slovenia, Spain, Sri Lanka, Sudan, Suriname, Sweden, Switzerland, Tajikistan, Thailand, Timor-Leste, Togo, Tunisia, Turkey, Turkmenistan, Tuvalu, Uganda, Ukraine, United Arab Emirates, United Kingdom, United Republic of Tanzania, United States, Uruguay, Uzbekistan, Vanuatu, Venezuela (Bolivarian Republic of), Viet Nam, Yemen, Zambia

Against

India, Pakistan

Abstaining

Austria, Bahamas, Bhutan, Costa Rica, Egypt, Gabon, Ireland, Israel, Liechtenstein, Malaysia, Mexico, Mozambique, Namibia, Nigeria, South Africa, Trinidad and Tobago

Seventh preambular paragraph*

In favour

Afghanistan, Albania, Andorra, Angola, Antigua and Barbuda, Argentina, Armenia, Australia, Azerbaijan, Bahrain, Bangladesh, Barbados, Belarus, Belgium, Belize, Bhutan, Bosnia and Herzegovina, Botswana, Brunei Darussalam, Bulgaria, Burkina Faso, Burundi, Cabo Verde, Cambodia, Canada, Chad, China, Colombia, Côte d'Ivoire, Croatia, Cyprus, Czechia, Denmark, Djibouti, Dominican Republic, El Salvador, Eritrea, Estonia, Eswatini, Ethiopia, Fiji, Finland, France, Gambia, Georgia, Germany, Greece, Guatemala, Guinea, Guinea-Bissau, Guyana, Haiti, Hungary, Iceland, India, Iraq, Italy, Japan, Jordan, Kazakhstan, Kenya, Kiribati, Kuwait, Kyrgyzstan, Lao People's Democratic Republic, Latvia, Lebanon, Lesotho, Liberia, Libya, Lithuania, Luxembourg, Madagascar, Malawi, Malaysia, Maldives, Mali, Malta, Marshall Islands, Mauritania, Mauritius, Micronesia (Federated States of), Monaco, Mongolia, Montenegro,

---

* Subsequently, the delegation of Gabon informed the Secretariat that it had not intended to participate.

Morocco, Myanmar, Namibia, Nepal, Netherlands, Nicaragua, Niger, North Macedonia, Norway, Oman, Pakistan, Panama, Papua New Guinea, Paraguay, Peru, Poland, Portugal, Qatar, Republic of Korea, Republic of Moldova, Romania, Russian Federation, Rwanda, Saint Lucia, Saint Vincent and the Grenadines, Samoa, Sao Tome and Principe, Saudi Arabia, Senegal, Serbia, Seychelles, Singapore, Slovakia, Slovenia, Spain, Sri Lanka, Sudan, Suriname, Sweden, Tajikistan, Timor-Leste, Togo, Tunisia, Turkey, Turkmenistan, Tuvalu, Uganda, Ukraine, United Arab Emirates, United Kingdom, United Republic of Tanzania, United States, Uruguay, Uzbekistan, Vanuatu, Viet Nam, Yemen, Zambia

Against

None

Abstaining

Algeria, Austria, Bahamas, Bolivia (Plurinational State of), Brazil, Chile, Costa Rica, Cuba, Ecuador, Egypt, Gabon, Ghana, Indonesia, Iran (Islamic Republic of), Ireland, Israel, Liechtenstein, Mexico, Mozambique, New Zealand, Nigeria, Philippines, San Marino, South Africa, Switzerland, Thailand, Trinidad and Tobago, Venezuela (Bolivarian Republic of)

Eighth preambular paragraph*

In favour

Afghanistan, Albania, Algeria, Andorra, Angola, Antigua and Barbuda, Argentina, Armenia, Australia, Austria, Azerbaijan, Bahrain, Bangladesh, Barbados, Belarus, Belgium, Belize, Bhutan, Bosnia and Herzegovina, Botswana, Brazil, Brunei Darussalam, Bulgaria, Burkina Faso, Burundi, Cabo Verde, Cambodia, Canada, Chad, Chile, China, Colombia, Côte d'Ivoire, Croatia, Cyprus, Czechia, Denmark, Djibouti, Dominican Republic, Ecuador, El Salvador, Eritrea, Estonia, Eswatini, Ethiopia, Fiji, Finland, France, Gambia, Georgia, Germany, Ghana, Greece, Guatemala, Guinea, Guinea-Bissau, Guyana, Haiti, Honduras, Hungary, Iceland, Indonesia, Iraq, Ireland, Italy, Japan, Jordan, Kazakhstan, Kenya, Kiribati, Kuwait, Kyrgyzstan, Lao People's Democratic Republic, Latvia, Lebanon, Lesotho, Liberia, Libya, Liechtenstein, Lithuania, Luxembourg, Madagascar, Malawi, Malaysia, Maldives, Mali, Malta, Marshall Islands, Mauritania, Mauritius, Micronesia (Federated States of), Monaco, Mongolia, Montenegro, Morocco, Myanmar, Namibia, Nepal, Netherlands, New Zealand, Nicaragua, Niger, Nigeria, North Macedonia, Norway, Oman, Pakistan, Panama, Papua New Guinea, Paraguay, Peru, Philippines, Poland, Portugal, Qatar, Republic of Korea, Republic of Moldova, Romania, Russian Federation, Rwanda, Saint Lucia, Saint Vincent and the Grenadines, Samoa, San Marino, Sao Tome and Principe, Saudi Arabia,

---

* Subsequently, the delegation of Gabon informed the Secretariat that it had not intended to participate.

Senegal, Serbia, Seychelles, Sierra Leone, Singapore, Slovakia, Slovenia, South Africa, Spain, Sri Lanka, Sudan, Suriname, Sweden, Switzerland, Tajikistan, Thailand, Timor-Leste, Togo, Tunisia, Turkey, Turkmenistan, Tuvalu, Uganda, Ukraine, United Arab Emirates, United Kingdom, United Republic of Tanzania, United States, Uruguay, Uzbekistan, Vanuatu, Viet Nam, Yemen, Zambia

Against
None

Abstaining
Bahamas, Bolivia (Plurinational State of), Costa Rica, Cuba, Egypt, Gabon, India, Iran (Islamic Republic of), Israel, Mozambique, Trinidad and Tobago, Venezuela (Bolivarian Republic of)

Tenth preambular paragraph*

In favour
Afghanistan, Albania, Andorra, Angola, Antigua and Barbuda, Argentina, Armenia, Australia, Austria, Azerbaijan, Bahrain, Bangladesh, Barbados, Belarus, Belgium, Belize, Bhutan, Bolivia (Plurinational State of), Bosnia and Herzegovina, Botswana, Brazil, Brunei Darussalam, Bulgaria, Burkina Faso, Burundi, Cabo Verde, Cambodia, Canada, Chad, Chile, China, Colombia, Costa Rica, Côte d'Ivoire, Croatia, Cuba, Cyprus, Czechia, Denmark, Djibouti, Dominican Republic, Ecuador, Egypt, El Salvador, Eritrea, Estonia, Eswatini, Ethiopia, Fiji, Finland, France, Gambia, Georgia, Germany, Ghana, Greece, Guatemala, Guinea, Guinea-Bissau, Guyana, Haiti, Honduras, Hungary, Iceland, Indonesia, Iraq, Ireland, Italy, Japan, Jordan, Kazakhstan, Kenya, Kiribati, Kuwait, Kyrgyzstan, Lao People's Democratic Republic, Latvia, Lebanon, Lesotho, Liberia, Libya, Liechtenstein, Lithuania, Luxembourg, Madagascar, Malawi, Malaysia, Maldives, Mali, Malta, Marshall Islands, Mauritania, Mauritius, Mexico, Micronesia (Federated States of), Monaco, Mongolia, Montenegro, Morocco, Myanmar, Namibia, Nepal, Netherlands, New Zealand, Nicaragua, Niger, Nigeria, North Macedonia, Norway, Oman, Pakistan, Panama, Papua New Guinea, Paraguay, Peru, Philippines, Poland, Portugal, Qatar, Republic of Korea, Romania, Russian Federation, Rwanda, Saint Lucia, Saint Vincent and the Grenadines, Samoa, San Marino, Sao Tome and Principe, Saudi Arabia, Senegal, Serbia, Seychelles, Sierra Leone, Singapore, Slovakia, Slovenia, South Africa, Spain, Sri Lanka, Sudan, Suriname, Sweden, Switzerland, Tajikistan, Thailand, Timor-Leste, Togo, Tunisia, Turkey, Turkmenistan, Tuvalu, Uganda, Ukraine, United Arab Emirates, United Kingdom, United Republic of Tanzania, United States, Uruguay, Uzbekistan, Vanuatu, Viet Nam, Yemen, Zambia

---

* Subsequently, the delegation of Gabon informed the Secretariat that it had not intended to participate.

Against
    Israel

Abstaining
    Algeria, Gabon, India, Iran (Islamic Republic of), Mozambique, Trinidad and Tobago, Venezuela (Bolivarian Republic of)

Eleventh preambular paragraph*

In favour
    Afghanistan, Albania, Andorra, Angola, Antigua and Barbuda, Argentina, Armenia, Australia, Austria, Azerbaijan, Bahrain, Bangladesh, Barbados, Belarus, Belgium, Belize, Bhutan, Bosnia and Herzegovina, Botswana, Brazil, Brunei Darussalam, Bulgaria, Burkina Faso, Cabo Verde, Cambodia, Canada, Chad, Chile, Colombia, Côte d'Ivoire, Croatia, Cyprus, Czechia, Denmark, Dominican Republic, Ecuador, El Salvador, Eritrea, Estonia, Eswatini, Ethiopia, Fiji, Finland, France, Gambia, Georgia, Germany, Ghana, Greece, Guatemala, Guinea, Guinea-Bissau, Guyana, Haiti, Honduras, Hungary, Iceland, Indonesia, Iraq, Ireland, Italy, Jamaica, Japan, Jordan, Kazakhstan, Kenya, Kiribati, Kuwait, Kyrgyzstan, Lao People's Democratic Republic, Latvia, Lebanon, Lesotho, Liberia, Libya, Liechtenstein, Lithuania, Luxembourg, Madagascar, Malawi, Malaysia, Maldives, Mali, Marshall Islands, Mauritius, Mexico, Micronesia (Federated States of), Monaco, Mongolia, Montenegro, Morocco, Myanmar, Namibia, Nepal, Netherlands, New Zealand, Nicaragua, Niger, Nigeria, North Macedonia, Norway, Oman, Panama, Papua New Guinea, Paraguay, Peru, Philippines, Poland, Portugal, Qatar, Republic of Korea, Republic of Moldova, Romania, Rwanda, Saint Lucia, Saint Vincent and the Grenadines, Samoa, San Marino, Sao Tome and Principe, Saudi Arabia, Senegal, Serbia, Seychelles, Sierra Leone, Singapore, Slovakia, Slovenia, South Africa, Spain, Sri Lanka, Sudan, Suriname, Sweden, Switzerland, Tajikistan, Thailand, Timor-Leste, Togo, Tunisia, Turkey, Turkmenistan, Tuvalu, Uganda, Ukraine, United Arab Emirates, United Kingdom, United Republic of Tanzania, United States, Uruguay, Uzbekistan, Vanuatu, Viet Nam, Yemen, Zambia

Against
    China, Israel, Pakistan

Abstaining
    Algeria, Bahamas, Bolivia (Plurinational State of), Burundi, Costa Rica, Cuba, Djibouti, Egypt, India, Iran (Islamic Republic of), Malta, Mauritania, Mozambique, Russian Federation, Trinidad and Tobago, Venezuela (Bolivarian Republic of)

---

* Subsequently, the delegation of Gabon informed the Secretariat that it had not intended to participate; the delegation of Israel informed the Secretariat that it had intended to abstain.

Sixteenth preambular paragraph*

In favour

Afghanistan, Albania, Algeria, Andorra, Angola, Antigua and Barbuda, Argentina, Armenia, Australia, Austria, Azerbaijan, Bahrain, Bangladesh, Barbados, Belarus, Belgium, Belize, Bhutan, Bolivia (Plurinational State of), Bosnia and Herzegovina, Botswana, Brazil, Brunei Darussalam, Bulgaria, Burkina Faso, Burundi, Cabo Verde, Cambodia, Canada, Chad, Chile, China, Colombia, Costa Rica, Côte d'Ivoire, Croatia, Cuba, Cyprus, Czechia, Denmark, Djibouti, Dominican Republic, Ecuador, Egypt, El Salvador, Eritrea, Estonia, Eswatini, Ethiopia, Fiji, Finland, France, Gambia, Georgia, Germany, Ghana, Greece, Guatemala, Guinea, Guinea-Bissau, Guyana, Haiti, Honduras, Hungary, Iceland, India, Indonesia, Iraq, Ireland, Italy, Jamaica, Japan, Jordan, Kazakhstan, Kenya, Kiribati, Kuwait, Kyrgyzstan, Lao People's Democratic Republic, Latvia, Lebanon, Lesotho, Liberia, Libya, Liechtenstein, Lithuania, Luxembourg, Madagascar, Malawi, Malaysia, Maldives, Mali, Malta, Marshall Islands, Mauritania, Mauritius, Mexico, Micronesia (Federated States of), Monaco, Mongolia, Montenegro, Morocco, Myanmar, Namibia, Nepal, Netherlands, New Zealand, Nicaragua, Niger, Nigeria, North Macedonia, Norway, Oman, Pakistan, Panama, Papua New Guinea, Paraguay, Peru, Philippines, Poland, Portugal, Qatar, Republic of Korea, Republic of Moldova, Romania, Russian Federation, Rwanda, Saint Lucia, Saint Vincent and the Grenadines, Samoa, San Marino, Sao Tome and Principe, Saudi Arabia, Senegal, Serbia, Seychelles, Sierra Leone, Singapore, Slovakia, Slovenia, Solomon Islands, South Africa, Spain, Sri Lanka, Sudan, Suriname, Sweden, Switzerland, Thailand, Timor-Leste, Togo, Tunisia, Turkey, Turkmenistan, Tuvalu, Uganda, Ukraine, United Arab Emirates, United Kingdom, United Republic of Tanzania, United States, Uruguay, Uzbekistan, Vanuatu, Venezuela (Bolivarian Republic of), Viet Nam, Yemen, Zambia

Against

None

Abstaining

Gabon, Iran (Islamic Republic of), Israel, Mozambique, Trinidad and Tobago

Seventeenth preambular paragraph**

In favour

Afghanistan, Albania, Andorra, Angola, Antigua and Barbuda, Argentina, Armenia, Australia, Austria, Azerbaijan, Bahrain, Bangladesh, Barbados,

---

* Subsequently, the delegation of Gabon informed the Secretariat that it had not intended to participate.

** Subsequently, the delegation of Gabon informed the Secretariat that it had not intended to participate.

Belarus, Belgium, Belize, Bhutan, Bolivia (Plurinational State of), Bosnia and Herzegovina, Botswana, Brazil, Brunei Darussalam, Bulgaria, Burkina Faso, Cambodia, Canada, Chad, Chile, Colombia, Costa Rica, Côte d'Ivoire, Croatia, Cyprus, Czechia, Denmark, Djibouti, Ecuador, El Salvador, Eritrea, Estonia, Eswatini, Ethiopia, Fiji, Finland, France, Gambia, Georgia, Germany, Ghana, Greece, Guatemala, Guinea, Guinea-Bissau, Guyana, Haiti, Honduras, Hungary, Iceland, India, Iraq, Ireland, Israel, Italy, Jamaica, Japan, Jordan, Kazakhstan, Kenya, Kiribati, Kuwait, Kyrgyzstan, Lao People's Democratic Republic, Latvia, Lebanon, Lesotho, Liberia, Libya, Liechtenstein, Lithuania, Luxembourg, Madagascar, Malawi, Malaysia, Maldives, Mali, Malta, Marshall Islands, Mauritius, Mexico, Micronesia (Federated States of), Monaco, Mongolia, Montenegro, Morocco, Myanmar, Namibia, Nepal, Netherlands, Nicaragua, Niger, Nigeria, North Macedonia, Norway, Oman, Pakistan, Panama, Papua New Guinea, Paraguay, Peru, Philippines, Poland, Portugal, Qatar, Republic of Korea, Republic of Moldova, Romania, Rwanda, Saint Lucia, Saint Vincent and the Grenadines, Samoa, San Marino, Sao Tome and Principe, Senegal, Serbia, Seychelles, Sierra Leone, Singapore, Slovakia, Slovenia, South Africa, Spain, Sri Lanka, Sudan, Suriname, Sweden, Switzerland, Tajikistan, Thailand, Timor-Leste, Togo, Tunisia, Turkey, Turkmenistan, Tuvalu, Uganda, Ukraine, United Arab Emirates, United Kingdom, United Republic of Tanzania, United States, Uruguay, Uzbekistan, Vanuatu, Viet Nam, Yemen, Zambia

Against

Democratic People's Republic of Korea

Abstaining

Algeria, Bahamas, Burundi, China, Cuba, Egypt, Indonesia, Iran (Islamic Republic of), Mauritania, Mozambique, Russian Federation, Saudi Arabia, Trinidad and Tobago, Venezuela (Bolivarian Republic of)

Eighteenth preambular paragraph*

In favour

Afghanistan, Albania, Andorra, Angola, Antigua and Barbuda, Argentina, Armenia, Australia, Austria, Azerbaijan, Bahrain, Bangladesh, Barbados, Belarus, Belgium, Belize, Bhutan, Bolivia (Plurinational State of), Bosnia and Herzegovina, Botswana, Brazil, Brunei Darussalam, Bulgaria, Burkina Faso, Cabo Verde, Cambodia, Canada, Chad, Chile, Colombia, Costa Rica, Côte d'Ivoire, Croatia, Cuba, Cyprus, Czechia, Denmark, Djibouti, Dominican Republic, Ecuador, Egypt, El Salvador, Eritrea, Estonia, Eswatini, Ethiopia, Fiji, Finland, France, Gambia, Georgia, Germany, Ghana, Greece, Guatemala, Guinea-Bissau, Guyana, Haiti,

---

* Subsequently, the delegation of Gabon informed the Secretariat that it had not intended to participate.

Honduras, Iceland, India, Indonesia, Iraq, Ireland, Israel, Italy, Jamaica, Japan, Jordan, Kazakhstan, Kenya, Kiribati, Kuwait, Kyrgyzstan, Lao People's Democratic Republic, Latvia, Lebanon, Lesotho, Liberia, Libya, Liechtenstein, Lithuania, Luxembourg, Madagascar, Malawi, Malaysia, Maldives, Mali, Malta, Marshall Islands, Mauritania, Mauritius, Mexico, Micronesia (Federated States of), Monaco, Mongolia, Montenegro, Morocco, Myanmar, Namibia, Nepal, Netherlands, Nicaragua, Niger, Nigeria, North Macedonia, Norway, Oman, Pakistan, Panama, Papua New Guinea, Paraguay, Peru, Philippines, Poland, Portugal, Qatar, Republic of Korea, Republic of Moldova, Romania, Rwanda, Saint Lucia, Saint Vincent and the Grenadines, Samoa, San Marino, Sao Tome and Principe, Saudi Arabia, Senegal, Serbia, Seychelles, Sierra Leone, Singapore, Slovakia, Slovenia, South Africa, Spain, Sri Lanka, Sudan, Suriname, Sweden, Switzerland, Tajikistan, Thailand, Timor-Leste, Togo, Tunisia, Turkey, Turkmenistan, Tuvalu, Uganda, Ukraine, United Arab Emirates, United Kingdom, United States, Uruguay, Uzbekistan, Vanuatu, Venezuela (Bolivarian Republic of), Viet Nam, Yemen, Zambia

Against

Hungary, Russian Federation

Abstaining

Algeria, Bahamas, China, Iran (Islamic Republic of), Mozambique, Trinidad and Tobago

Nineteenth preambular paragraph*

In favour

Afghanistan, Albania, Algeria, Andorra, Angola, Antigua and Barbuda, Argentina, Armenia, Australia, Austria, Azerbaijan, Bahrain, Bangladesh, Barbados, Belarus, Belgium, Belize, Bhutan, Bolivia (Plurinational State of), Bosnia and Herzegovina, Botswana, Brazil, Brunei Darussalam, Bulgaria, Burkina Faso, Burundi, Cabo Verde, Cambodia, Canada, Chad, Chile, Colombia, Côte d'Ivoire, Croatia, Cuba, Cyprus, Czechia, Denmark, Djibouti, Dominican Republic, Ecuador, El Salvador, Eritrea, Estonia, Eswatini, Ethiopia, Fiji, Finland, Gambia, Georgia, Germany, Ghana, Greece, Guatemala, Guinea, Guinea-Bissau, Guyana, Haiti, Hungary, Iceland, India, Indonesia, Iran (Islamic Republic of), Iraq, Italy, Jamaica, Japan, Jordan, Kazakhstan, Kenya, Kiribati, Kuwait, Kyrgyzstan, Lao People's Democratic Republic, Latvia, Lebanon, Lesotho, Liberia, Libya, Liechtenstein, Lithuania, Luxembourg, Madagascar, Malawi, Malaysia, Maldives, Mali, Malta, Marshall Islands, Mauritania, Mauritius, Mexico, Micronesia (Federated States of), Monaco, Mongolia, Montenegro,

---

* Subsequently, the delegation of France informed the Secretariat that it had intended to abstain; the delegation of Gabon informed the Secretariat that it had not intended to participate.

Morocco, Nepal, Netherlands, New Zealand, Nicaragua, Niger, North Macedonia, Norway, Oman, Panama, Papua New Guinea, Paraguay, Peru, Philippines, Poland, Portugal, Qatar, Republic of Korea, Republic of Moldova, Romania, Rwanda, Saint Lucia, Saint Vincent and the Grenadines, Samoa, San Marino, Sao Tome and Principe, Saudi Arabia, Senegal, Serbia, Seychelles, Sierra Leone, Singapore, Slovakia, Slovenia, Spain, Sri Lanka, Sudan, Suriname, Sweden, Switzerland, Tajikistan, Timor-Leste, Togo, Tunisia, Turkey, Turkmenistan, Tuvalu, Uganda, Ukraine, United Arab Emirates, United Kingdom, United Republic of Tanzania, United States, Uruguay, Uzbekistan, Vanuatu, Venezuela (Bolivarian Republic of), Viet Nam, Yemen, Zambia

Against

France

Abstaining

Bahamas, China, Costa Rica, Egypt, Gabon, Ireland, Israel, Mozambique, Myanmar, Namibia, Nigeria, Pakistan, Russian Federation, South Africa, Thailand, Trinidad and Tobago

Twentieth preambular paragraph*

In favour

Afghanistan, Albania, Algeria, Andorra, Angola, Antigua and Barbuda, Argentina, Armenia, Australia, Austria, Azerbaijan, Bahrain, Bangladesh, Barbados, Belarus, Belgium, Belize, Bhutan, Bolivia (Plurinational State of), Bosnia and Herzegovina, Botswana, Brazil, Brunei Darussalam, Bulgaria, Burkina Faso, Cabo Verde, Cambodia, Canada, Chad, Chile, Colombia, Costa Rica, Côte d'Ivoire, Croatia, Cyprus, Czechia, Denmark, Djibouti, Dominican Republic, Ecuador, Egypt, El Salvador, Eritrea, Estonia, Eswatini, Ethiopia, Fiji, Finland, France, Gambia, Georgia, Germany, Ghana, Greece, Guatemala, Guinea, Guinea-Bissau, Guyana, Haiti, Honduras, Hungary, Iceland, India, Indonesia, Iran (Islamic Republic of), Iraq, Ireland, Italy, Jamaica, Japan, Jordan, Kazakhstan, Kenya, Kiribati, Kuwait, Kyrgyzstan, Lao People's Democratic Republic, Latvia, Lebanon, Lesotho, Liberia, Libya, Liechtenstein, Lithuania, Luxembourg, Madagascar, Malawi, Malaysia, Maldives, Mali, Malta, Marshall Islands, Mauritania, Mauritius, Mexico, Micronesia (Federated States of), Monaco, Mongolia, Montenegro, Morocco, Myanmar, Namibia, Nepal, Netherlands, New Zealand, Nicaragua, Niger, Nigeria, North Macedonia, Norway, Oman, Pakistan, Panama, Papua New Guinea, Paraguay, Peru, Philippines, Poland, Portugal, Qatar, Republic of Moldova, Romania, Rwanda, Saint Lucia, Saint Vincent and the Grenadines, Samoa, San Marino, Sao Tome and Principe, Saudi Arabia, Senegal, Serbia, Seychelles, Sierra Leone,

---

* Subsequently, the delegation of Gabon informed the Secretariat that it had not intended to participate.

Singapore, Slovakia, Slovenia, South Africa, Spain, Sri Lanka, Sudan, Suriname, Sweden, Switzerland, Tajikistan, Thailand, Timor-Leste, Togo, Tunisia, Turkey, Turkmenistan, Tuvalu, Uganda, Ukraine, United Arab Emirates, United Kingdom, United Republic of Tanzania, United States, Uruguay, Uzbekistan, Vanuatu, Viet Nam, Yemen, Zambia

Against

China, Russian Federation

Abstaining

Bahamas, Burundi, Gabon, Israel, Mozambique, Republic of Korea, Trinidad and Tobago, Venezuela (Bolivarian Republic of), Zimbabwe

Operative paragraph 1*

In favour

Albania, Andorra, Angola, Antigua and Barbuda, Argentina, Armenia, Australia, Azerbaijan, Bahrain, Bangladesh, Barbados, Belarus, Belgium, Belize, Bhutan, Bosnia and Herzegovina, Botswana, Brunei Darussalam, Bulgaria, Burkina Faso, Burundi, Cambodia, Canada, Chad, China, Colombia, Côte d'Ivoire, Croatia, Cyprus, Czechia, Denmark, Djibouti, Dominican Republic, El Salvador, Eritrea, Estonia, Eswatini, Ethiopia, Fiji, Finland, France, Gambia, Georgia, Germany, Greece, Guatemala, Guinea, Guinea-Bissau, Guyana, Haiti, Hungary, Iceland, Iraq, Italy, Japan, Jordan, Kazakhstan, Kenya, Kiribati, Kuwait, Kyrgyzstan, Lao People's Democratic Republic, Latvia, Lebanon, Lesotho, Libya, Luxembourg, Madagascar, Malawi, Maldives, Mali, Malta, Marshall Islands, Mauritius, Micronesia (Federated States of), Monaco, Mongolia, Montenegro, Morocco, Myanmar, Nepal, Netherlands, Nicaragua, Niger, North Macedonia, Norway, Oman, Panama, Papua New Guinea, Paraguay, Poland, Portugal, Qatar, Republic of Korea, Republic of Moldova, Romania, Russian Federation, Rwanda, Saint Lucia, Saint Vincent and the Grenadines, Samoa, Sao Tome and Principe, Saudi Arabia, Senegal, Serbia, Seychelles, Sierra Leone, Singapore, Slovakia, Slovenia, Spain, Sri Lanka, Sudan, Suriname, Sweden, Tajikistan, Timor-Leste, Togo, Tunisia, Turkey, Turkmenistan, Uganda, Ukraine, United Arab Emirates, United Kingdom, United Republic of Tanzania, United States, Uruguay, Uzbekistan, Vanuatu, Viet Nam, Yemen, Zambia

Against

Austria, Brazil, Costa Rica, Egypt, Ireland, Liechtenstein, Mexico, New Zealand, Nigeria, South Africa

---

* Subsequently, the delegation of Gabon informed the Secretariat that it had not intended to participate; the delegation of Lithuania informed the Secretariat that it had intended to vote in favour.

Abstaining

Algeria, Bahamas, Bolivia (Plurinational State of), Chile, Cuba, Ecuador, Gabon, Ghana, India, Indonesia, Iran (Islamic Republic of), Israel, Malaysia, Mauritania, Mozambique, Namibia, Pakistan, Peru, Philippines, San Marino, Switzerland, Thailand, Trinidad and Tobago, Venezuela (Bolivarian Republic of)

Operative paragraph 3 (b)*

In favour

Albania, Andorra, Angola, Antigua and Barbuda, Argentina, Armenia, Australia, Azerbaijan, Bangladesh, Barbados, Belarus, Belgium, Belize, Bhutan, Bosnia and Herzegovina, Botswana, Brunei Darussalam, Bulgaria, Burkina Faso, Burundi, Cambodia, Canada, Colombia, Côte d'Ivoire, Croatia, Cyprus, Czechia, Denmark, Djibouti, Dominican Republic, Ecuador, El Salvador, Eritrea, Estonia, Eswatini, Ethiopia, Fiji, Finland, France, Gambia, Georgia, Germany, Greece, Guatemala, Guinea, Guinea-Bissau, Guyana, Haiti, Hungary, Iceland, India, Indonesia, Italy, Japan, Kazakhstan, Kenya, Kiribati, Kuwait, Kyrgyzstan, Lao People's Democratic Republic, Latvia, Lesotho, Liberia, Luxembourg, Madagascar, Malawi, Maldives, Mali, Malta, Marshall Islands, Mauritius, Micronesia (Federated States of), Monaco, Mongolia, Montenegro, Myanmar, Nepal, Netherlands, Nicaragua, Niger, North Macedonia, Norway, Panama, Papua New Guinea, Paraguay, Peru, Philippines, Poland, Portugal, Republic of Korea, Republic of Moldova, Romania, Russian Federation, Rwanda, Saint Lucia, Saint Vincent and the Grenadines, Samoa, San Marino, Sao Tome and Principe, Senegal, Serbia, Seychelles, Sierra Leone, Singapore, Slovakia, Slovenia, Spain, Suriname, Sweden, Switzerland, Tajikistan, Thailand, Timor-Leste, Togo, Tunisia, Turkey, Turkmenistan, Tuvalu, Uganda, Ukraine, United Arab Emirates, United Kingdom, United Republic of Tanzania, United States, Uruguay, Uzbekistan, Vanuatu, Viet Nam, Zambia

Against

None

Abstaining

Algeria, Austria, Bahamas, Bahrain, Bolivia (Plurinational State of), Brazil, Chile, China, Costa Rica, Cuba, Egypt, Gabon, Ghana, Iran (Islamic Republic of), Iraq, Ireland, Israel, Jordan, Lebanon, Liechtenstein, Malaysia, Mauritania, Mexico, Morocco, Mozambique, Namibia, New Zealand, Nigeria, Oman, Pakistan, Qatar, Saudi Arabia, South Africa, Sri

---

* Subsequently, the delegation of Gabon informed the Secretariat that it had not intended to participate; the delegation of Lithuania informed the Secretariat that it had intended to vote in favour.

Lanka, Sudan, Trinidad and Tobago, Venezuela (Bolivarian Republic of), Yemen, Zimbabwe

Operative paragraph 3 (c)*

In favour

Afghanistan, Albania, Andorra, Angola, Antigua and Barbuda, Argentina, Armenia, Australia, Austria, Azerbaijan, Bahrain, Bangladesh, Barbados, Belarus, Belgium, Belize, Bhutan, Bosnia and Herzegovina, Botswana, Brazil, Brunei Darussalam, Bulgaria, Burkina Faso, Cabo Verde, Cambodia, Canada, Chad, Chile, Colombia, Côte d'Ivoire, Croatia, Cyprus, Czechia, Denmark, Djibouti, Dominican Republic, Ecuador, El Salvador, Eritrea, Estonia, Eswatini, Ethiopia, Fiji, Finland, Gambia, Georgia, Germany, Ghana, Greece, Guatemala, Guinea, Guinea-Bissau, Guyana, Haiti, Honduras, Hungary, Iceland, India, Indonesia, Iraq, Ireland, Italy, Japan, Jordan, Kazakhstan, Kenya, Kiribati, Kuwait, Kyrgyzstan, Lao People's Democratic Republic, Latvia, Lebanon, Lesotho, Liberia, Libya, Liechtenstein, Luxembourg, Madagascar, Malawi, Malaysia, Maldives, Mali, Malta, Marshall Islands, Mauritius, Mexico, Micronesia (Federated States of), Monaco, Mongolia, Montenegro, Morocco, Myanmar, Namibia, Nepal, Netherlands, New Zealand, Nicaragua, Niger, Nigeria, North Macedonia, Norway, Oman, Panama, Papua New Guinea, Paraguay, Peru, Philippines, Poland, Portugal, Qatar, Republic of Korea, Republic of Moldova, Romania, Rwanda, Saint Lucia, Saint Vincent and the Grenadines, Samoa, San Marino, Sao Tome and Principe, Saudi Arabia, Senegal, Serbia, Seychelles, Sierra Leone, Singapore, Slovakia, Slovenia, South Africa, Spain, Suriname, Sweden, Switzerland, Tajikistan, Thailand, Timor-Leste, Togo, Tunisia, Turkey, Turkmenistan, Tuvalu, Uganda, Ukraine, United Arab Emirates, United Kingdom, United Republic of Tanzania, United States, Uruguay, Uzbekistan, Vanuatu, Viet Nam, Yemen, Zambia

Against

China, Pakistan

Abstaining

Algeria, Bahamas, Bolivia (Plurinational State of), Costa Rica, Cuba, Egypt, France, Gabon, Iran (Islamic Republic of), Israel, Mauritania, Mozambique, Russian Federation, Sri Lanka, Sudan, Trinidad and Tobago, Venezuela (Bolivarian Republic of)

---

* Subsequently, the delegation of Gabon informed the Secretariat that it had not intended to participate; the delegation of Lithuania informed the Secretariat that it had intended to vote in favour.

Operative paragraph 3 (d)*

In favour

Afghanistan, Albania, Andorra, Angola, Antigua and Barbuda, Argentina, Armenia, Australia, Azerbaijan, Bahrain, Bangladesh, Barbados, Belarus, Belgium, Belize, Bhutan, Bolivia (Plurinational State of), Bosnia and Herzegovina, Botswana, Brunei Darussalam, Bulgaria, Burkina Faso, Burundi, Cambodia, Canada, Chad, Colombia, Côte d'Ivoire, Croatia, Cuba, Cyprus, Czechia, Denmark, Djibouti, Dominican Republic, Ecuador, El Salvador, Eritrea, Estonia, Eswatini, Ethiopia, Fiji, Finland, Gambia, Georgia, Germany, Greece, Guatemala, Guinea, Guinea-Bissau, Guyana, Haiti, Hungary, Iceland, Iraq, Italy, Japan, Jordan, Kazakhstan, Kenya, Kiribati, Kuwait, Kyrgyzstan, Lao People's Democratic Republic, Latvia, Lebanon, Lesotho, Liberia, Libya, Luxembourg, Madagascar, Malawi, Maldives, Mali, Marshall Islands, Micronesia (Federated States of), Monaco, Mongolia, Montenegro, Morocco, Namibia, Nepal, Netherlands, Nicaragua, Niger, North Macedonia, Norway, Oman, Pakistan, Panama, Papua New Guinea, Paraguay, Peru, Philippines, Poland, Portugal, Qatar, Republic of Korea, Romania, Rwanda, Saint Lucia, Saint Vincent and the Grenadines, Samoa, San Marino, Sao Tome and Principe, Saudi Arabia, Senegal, Serbia, Seychelles, Sierra Leone, Singapore, Slovakia, Slovenia, South Africa, Spain, Sri Lanka, Suriname, Sweden, Switzerland, Tajikistan, Timor-Leste, Togo, Tunisia, Turkey, Turkmenistan, Tuvalu, Uganda, Ukraine, United Arab Emirates, United Kingdom, United Republic of Tanzania, United States, Uruguay, Uzbekistan, Vanuatu, Viet Nam, Yemen, Zambia

Against

India, Nigeria

Abstaining

Algeria, Austria, Bahamas, Brazil, Chile, China, Costa Rica, Egypt, France, Gabon, Ghana, Indonesia, Iran (Islamic Republic of), Ireland, Israel, Liechtenstein, Malaysia, Malta, Mauritania, Mexico, Mozambique, Myanmar, New Zealand, Republic of Moldova, Russian Federation, Sudan, Thailand, Trinidad and Tobago, Venezuela (Bolivarian Republic of)

---

* Subsequently, the delegation of Gabon informed the Secretariat that it had not intended to participate; the delegation of Lithuania informed the Secretariat that it had intended to vote in favour.

Operative paragraph 3 (e)*

In favour

> Afghanistan, Albania, Andorra, Angola, Antigua and Barbuda, Argentina, Armenia, Australia, Austria, Azerbaijan, Bahrain, Bangladesh, Barbados, Belarus, Belgium, Belize, Bhutan, Bolivia (Plurinational State of), Bosnia and Herzegovina, Botswana, Brazil, Brunei Darussalam, Bulgaria, Burkina Faso, Cabo Verde, Cambodia, Canada, Chad, Chile, Colombia, Côte d'Ivoire, Croatia, Cyprus, Czechia, Denmark, Djibouti, Dominican Republic, Ecuador, El Salvador, Eritrea, Estonia, Eswatini, Ethiopia, Fiji, Finland, France, Gambia, Georgia, Germany, Greece, Guatemala, Guinea, Guinea-Bissau, Guyana, Haiti, Honduras, Hungary, Iceland, India, Iraq, Italy, Japan, Jordan, Kazakhstan, Kenya, Kiribati, Kuwait, Kyrgyzstan, Lao People's Democratic Republic, Latvia, Lebanon, Lesotho, Liberia, Libya, Liechtenstein, Luxembourg, Madagascar, Malawi, Malaysia, Maldives, Mali, Malta, Marshall Islands, Mauritius, Mexico, Micronesia (Federated States of), Monaco, Mongolia, Montenegro, Morocco, Myanmar, Nepal, Netherlands, Nicaragua, Niger, North Macedonia, Norway, Oman, Panama, Papua New Guinea, Paraguay, Peru, Philippines, Poland, Portugal, Qatar, Republic of Korea, Republic of Moldova, Romania, Rwanda, Saint Lucia, Saint Vincent and the Grenadines, Samoa, San Marino, Sao Tome and Principe, Saudi Arabia, Senegal, Serbia, Seychelles, Sierra Leone, Singapore, Slovakia, Slovenia, Spain, Sri Lanka, Suriname, Sweden, Switzerland, Tajikistan, Thailand, Timor-Leste, Togo, Tunisia, Turkey, Turkmenistan, Tuvalu, Uganda, Ukraine, United Arab Emirates, United Kingdom, United Republic of Tanzania, United States, Uruguay, Uzbekistan, Vanuatu, Viet Nam, Yemen

Against

Russian Federation

Abstaining

> Algeria, Bahamas, Burundi, China, Costa Rica, Cuba, Egypt, Gabon, Ghana, Indonesia, Iran (Islamic Republic of), Ireland, Israel, Mauritania, Mozambique, Namibia, New Zealand, Nigeria, Pakistan, South Africa, Sudan, Trinidad and Tobago, Venezuela (Bolivarian Republic of)

Operative paragraph 3 (f)**

In favour

> Afghanistan, Albania, Andorra, Angola, Antigua and Barbuda, Argentina, Armenia, Australia, Austria, Azerbaijan, Bahrain, Bangladesh, Barbados,

---

* Subsequently, the delegation of Gabon informed the Secretariat that it had not intended to participate; the delegation of Lithuania informed the Secretariat that it had intended to vote in favour.

** Subsequently, the delegation of Gabon informed the Secretariat that it had not intended to participate.

Belarus, Belgium, Belize, Bhutan, Bolivia (Plurinational State of), Bosnia and Herzegovina, Botswana, Brazil, Brunei Darussalam, Bulgaria, Burkina Faso, Cabo Verde, Cambodia, Canada, Chad, Chile, Colombia, Costa Rica, Côte d'Ivoire, Croatia, Cyprus, Czechia, Denmark, Djibouti, Dominican Republic, Ecuador, Egypt, El Salvador, Eritrea, Estonia, Eswatini, Ethiopia, Fiji, Finland, France, Gambia, Georgia, Germany, Ghana, Greece, Guatemala, Guinea, Guinea-Bissau, Guyana, Haiti, Honduras, Hungary, Iceland, India, Indonesia, Iran (Islamic Republic of), Iraq, Ireland, Israel, Italy, Jamaica, Japan, Jordan, Kazakhstan, Kenya, Kiribati, Kuwait, Kyrgyzstan, Lao People's Democratic Republic, Latvia, Lebanon, Lesotho, Liberia, Libya, Liechtenstein, Lithuania, Luxembourg, Madagascar, Malawi, Malaysia, Maldives, Mali, Malta, Marshall Islands, Mauritania, Mauritius, Mexico, Micronesia (Federated States of), Monaco, Mongolia, Montenegro, Morocco, Myanmar, Namibia, Nepal, Netherlands, New Zealand, Nicaragua, Niger, Nigeria, North Macedonia, Norway, Oman, Panama, Papua New Guinea, Paraguay, Peru, Philippines, Poland, Portugal, Qatar, Republic of Moldova, Romania, Rwanda, Saint Lucia, Saint Vincent and the Grenadines, Samoa, San Marino, Sao Tome and Principe, Saudi Arabia, Senegal, Serbia, Seychelles, Sierra Leone, Singapore, Slovakia, Slovenia, South Africa, Spain, Sri Lanka, Sudan, Suriname, Sweden, Switzerland, Tajikistan, Thailand, Timor-Leste, Togo, Tunisia, Turkey, Turkmenistan, Tuvalu, Uganda, Ukraine, United Arab Emirates, United Kingdom, United Republic of Tanzania, United States, Uruguay, Uzbekistan, Vanuatu, Viet Nam, Yemen, Zambia

Against

China, Russian Federation

Abstaining

Algeria, Bahamas, Burundi, Gabon, Mozambique, Pakistan, Republic of Korea, Trinidad and Tobago, Venezuela (Bolivarian Republic of)

Operative paragraph 5*

In favour

Afghanistan, Albania, Andorra, Angola, Antigua and Barbuda, Armenia, Australia, Austria, Azerbaijan, Bahrain, Bangladesh, Barbados, Belarus, Belgium, Belize, Bhutan, Bolivia (Plurinational State of), Bosnia and Herzegovina, Botswana, Brunei Darussalam, Bulgaria, Burkina Faso, Burundi, Cambodia, Canada, Chad, Chile, China, Colombia, Costa Rica, Côte d'Ivoire, Croatia, Cyprus, Czechia, Denmark, Djibouti, Dominican Republic, Ecuador, El Salvador, Eritrea, Estonia, Eswatini, Ethiopia, Fiji, Finland, Gambia, Georgia, Germany, Ghana, Greece, Guatemala, Guinea, Guinea-Bissau, Guyana, Haiti, Honduras, Hungary, Iceland, Iraq, Ireland,

---

* Subsequently, the delegation of Gabon informed the Secretariat that it had not intended to participate.

Italy, Jamaica, Japan, Jordan, Kazakhstan, Kenya, Kiribati, Kuwait, Kyrgyzstan, Lao People's Democratic Republic, Latvia, Lebanon, Lesotho, Liberia, Libya, Liechtenstein, Lithuania, Luxembourg, Madagascar, Malawi, Malaysia, Maldives, Mali, Malta, Marshall Islands, Mauritania, Mauritius, Mexico, Micronesia (Federated States of), Monaco, Mongolia, Montenegro, Morocco, Myanmar, Nepal, Netherlands, New Zealand, Nicaragua, Niger, Nigeria, North Macedonia, Norway, Oman, Panama, Papua New Guinea, Paraguay, Peru, Philippines, Poland, Portugal, Qatar, Republic of Korea, Republic of Moldova, Romania, Russian Federation, Rwanda, Saint Lucia, Saint Vincent and the Grenadines, Samoa, San Marino, Sao Tome and Principe, Senegal, Serbia, Seychelles, Sierra Leone, Singapore, Slovakia, Slovenia, Spain, Sri Lanka, Sudan, Suriname, Sweden, Switzerland, Tajikistan, Thailand, Timor-Leste, Togo, Tunisia, Turkey, Turkmenistan, Tuvalu, Uganda, Ukraine, United Arab Emirates, United Kingdom, United Republic of Tanzania, United States, Uruguay, Uzbekistan, Vanuatu, Viet Nam, Yemen, Zambia

Against

None

Abstaining

Algeria, Argentina, Bahamas, Brazil, Cuba, Egypt, France, Gabon, India, Indonesia, Iran (Islamic Republic of), Israel, Mozambique, Namibia, Pakistan, Saudi Arabia, South Africa, Trinidad and Tobago, Venezuela (Bolivarian Republic of)

Operative paragraph 6*

In favour

Afghanistan, Albania, Andorra, Angola, Antigua and Barbuda, Argentina, Armenia, Australia, Austria, Azerbaijan, Bahrain, Bangladesh, Barbados, Belarus, Belgium, Belize, Bhutan, Bolivia (Plurinational State of), Bosnia and Herzegovina, Botswana, Brazil, Brunei Darussalam, Bulgaria, Burkina Faso, Cambodia, Canada, Chad, Chile, Colombia, Costa Rica, Côte d'Ivoire, Croatia, Cyprus, Czechia, Denmark, Djibouti, Dominican Republic, Ecuador, El Salvador, Estonia, Eswatini, Ethiopia, Fiji, Finland, France, Gambia, Georgia, Germany, Ghana, Greece, Guatemala, Guinea, Guinea-Bissau, Guyana, Haiti, Honduras, Hungary, Iceland, Iraq, Ireland, Israel, Italy, Jamaica, Japan, Jordan, Kazakhstan, Kenya, Kiribati, Kuwait, Kyrgyzstan, Lao People's Democratic Republic, Latvia, Lebanon, Lesotho, Liberia, Libya, Liechtenstein, Lithuania, Luxembourg, Madagascar, Malawi, Malaysia, Maldives, Mali, Malta, Marshall Islands, Mauritania, Mauritius, Mexico, Micronesia (Federated States of), Monaco, Mongolia, Montenegro, Morocco, Nepal, Netherlands, New Zealand, Nicaragua,

---

* Subsequently, the delegation of Gabon informed the Secretariat that it had not intended to participate.

Niger, North Macedonia, Norway, Oman, Pakistan, Panama, Papua New Guinea, Paraguay, Peru, Philippines, Poland, Portugal, Qatar, Republic of Korea, Republic of Moldova, Romania, Rwanda, Saint Lucia, Saint Vincent and the Grenadines, Samoa, San Marino, Sao Tome and Principe, Senegal, Serbia, Seychelles, Sierra Leone, Singapore, Slovakia, Slovenia, Spain, Sri Lanka, Suriname, Sweden, Switzerland, Tajikistan, Thailand, Timor-Leste, Togo, Tunisia, Turkey, Turkmenistan, Tuvalu, Ukraine, United Arab Emirates, United Kingdom, United Republic of Tanzania, United States, Uruguay, Uzbekistan, Vanuatu, Viet Nam, Yemen, Zambia

Against

China, Democratic People's Republic of Korea, Russian Federation

Abstaining

Algeria, Bahamas, Burundi, Cuba, Egypt, Eritrea, Gabon, India, Indonesia, Iran (Islamic Republic of), Mozambique, Myanmar, Namibia, Nigeria, Saudi Arabia, South Africa, Sudan, Trinidad and Tobago, Venezuela (Bolivarian Republic of)

Action by the First Committee

Date:	27 October 2021	Meeting:	13th meeting
Vote:	152-4-30	Draft resolution:	A/C.1/76/L.59
	150-2-15, p.p. 2		
	141-0-28, p.p. 7		
	153-1-15, p.p. 8		
	163-1-7, p.p. 10		
	154-2-16, p.p. 11		
	164-0-6, p.p. 16		
	155-1-14, p.p. 17		
	159-2-8, p.p. 18		
	157-0-14, p.p. 19		
	160-2-9, p.p. 20		
	135-10-26, o.p. 1		
	130-0-39, o.p. 3 (b)		
	155-2-17, o.p. 3 (c)		
	138-1-29, o.p. 3 (d)		
	150-1-22, o.p. 3 (e)		
	158-2-10, o.p. 3 (f)		
	154-0-19, o.p. 5		
	147-3-19, o.p. 6		

Agenda item 100 (v)

76/55 Transparency and confidence-building measures in outer space activities

Text

The General Assembly,

Recalling its resolutions 60/66 of 8 December 2005, 61/75 of 6 December 2006, 62/43 of 5 December 2007, 63/68 of 2 December 2008, 64/49 of 2 December 2009, 65/68 of 8 December 2010, 68/50 of 5 December 2013, 69/38 of 2 December 2014, 70/53 of 7 December 2015, 71/42 of 5 December 2016, 71/90 of 6 December 2016, 72/56 of 4 December 2017, 73/72 of 5 December 2018, 74/67 of 12 December 2019 and 75/69 of 7 December 2020, as well as its decision 66/517 of 2 December 2011,

Recalling also the report of the Secretary-General of 15 October 1993 to the General Assembly at its forty-eighth session, the annex to which contains the study by governmental experts on the application of confidence-building measures in outer space,[1]

Reaffirming the right of all countries to explore and use outer space in accordance with international law,

Reaffirming also that preventing an arms race in outer space is in the interest of maintaining international peace and security and is an essential condition for the promotion and strengthening of international cooperation in the exploration and use of outer space for peaceful purposes,

Recalling, in this context, its resolutions 45/55 B of 4 December 1990 and 48/74 B of 16 December 1993, in which, inter alia, it recognized the need for increased transparency and confirmed the importance of confidence-building measures as a means of reinforcing the objective of preventing an arms race in outer space,

Noting the constructive debates that the Conference on Disarmament has held on this subject and the views expressed by Member States,

Recalling the introduction by China and the Russian Federation at the Conference on Disarmament of the draft treaty on prevention of the placement of weapons in outer space and of the threat or use of force against outer space objects,[2] and the submission of its updated version[3] in 2014,

---

[1] A/48/305 and A/48/305/Corr.1.
[2] See CD/1839.
[3] See CD/1985.

Noting that, since 2004, several States[4] have introduced a policy of not being the first State to place weapons in outer space,

Expressing regret that, owing to the coronavirus disease (COVID-19) pandemic and unresolved organizational problems within the Disarmament Commission, its working group tasked with preparing recommendations relating to the practical implementation of transparency and confidence-building measures in outer space activities with the goal of preventing an arms race in outer space was not in a position to conduct its work, and stressing the importance of resuming its deliberations,

Recognizing that the work within the Committee on the Peaceful Uses of Outer Space, its Scientific and Technical Subcommittee and its Legal Subcommittee, including the promotion of the long-term sustainability of outer space activities, has a fundamental role to play in enhancing transparency and confidence-building among States and in ensuring that outer space is maintained for peaceful purposes,

Noting the contribution of Member States that have submitted to the Secretary-General concrete proposals on international outer space transparency and confidence-building measures pursuant to paragraph 1 of resolution 61/75, paragraph 2 of resolution 62/43, paragraph 2 of resolution 63/68 and paragraph 2 of resolution 64/49,

Recalling the work done in 2012 and 2013 by the Group of Governmental Experts on Transparency and Confidence-building Measures in Outer Space Activities, which was convened by the Secretary-General, on the basis of equitable geographical distribution, to conduct a study on outer space transparency and confidence-building measures,

Recalling also the consideration of the report of the Group of Governmental Experts,[5] as well as views on the modalities of making practical use of the recommendations contained therein, as set out in the report of the Committee on the Peaceful Uses of Outer Space on its fifty-eighth session, held in 2015,[6] at which it found that the Committee had a fundamental role to play in enhancing transparency and confidence-building among States, as well as in ensuring that outer space is maintained for peaceful purposes,

Noting that, in its report, the Group of Governmental Experts had recognized the value of the work of the Committee on the Peaceful Uses of Outer Space in developing a set of voluntary, non-legally binding guidelines

---

[4] Argentina, Armenia, Belarus, Bolivia (Plurinational State of), Brazil, Burundi, Cambodia, Congo, Cuba, Ecuador, Guatemala, Indonesia, Kazakhstan, Kyrgyzstan, Myanmar, Nicaragua, Pakistan, Russian Federation, Seychelles, Sierra Leone, Sri Lanka, Suriname, Syrian Arab Republic, Tajikistan, Togo, Turkmenistan, Uruguay, Uzbekistan, Venezuela (Bolivarian Republic of) and Viet Nam.

[5] A/68/189.

[6] *Official Records of the General Assembly, Seventieth Session, Supplement No. 20* (A/70/20).

for the long-term sustainability of outer space activities, some of which could be considered as potential transparency and confidence-building measures, while others could enhance the safety of outer space activities and thereby provide the technical basis for the further implementation of additional transparency and confidence-building measures,

Welcoming the adoption in 2019 by the Committee on the Peaceful Uses of Outer Space at its sixty-second session of the preamble and 21 Guidelines for the Long-term Sustainability of Outer Space Activities, as contained in annex II to the report of the Committee,[7] the implementation of which may have a positive effect on international peace and security, as well as the continuation of efforts both to identify and study challenges and to consider possible new guidelines for the long-term sustainability of outer space activities,

Recalling the special report by the Inter-Agency Meeting on Outer Space Activities (UN-Space) on the implementation of the report of the Group of Governmental Experts, and the recommendations contained therein, as submitted to the Committee on the Peaceful Uses of Outer Space at its fifty-ninth session, in 2016,[8]

Welcoming the revised International Telecommunication Union resolution 186 on strengthening the role of the Union with regard to transparency and confidence-building measures in outer space activities, adopted by the 2018 Plenipotentiary Conference of the Union, held in Dubai, United Arab Emirates, from 29 October to 16 November 2018,

1.   *Stresses* the importance of the report of the Group of Governmental Experts on Transparency and Confidence-building Measures in Outer Space Activities, considered by the General Assembly on 5 December 2013;

2.   *Encourages* Member States to continue to review and implement, to the greatest extent practicable, the proposed transparency and confidence-building measures contained in the report, through the relevant national mechanisms, on a voluntary basis and in a manner consistent with the national interests of Member States;

3.   *Also encourages* Member States, in accordance with the recommendations contained in the report, with a view to promoting the practical implementation of transparency and confidence-building measures, to hold regular discussions in the Committee on the Peaceful Uses of Outer Space, the Disarmament Commission and the Conference on Disarmament on the prospects for their implementation;

4.   *Requests* the relevant entities and organizations of the United Nations system, to which, in accordance with its resolution 68/50, the report

---

[7] Ibid., *Seventy-fourth Session, Supplement No. 20* (A/74/20).
[8] A/AC.105/1116.

was circulated, to assist in effectively implementing the conclusions and recommendations contained therein, as appropriate;

5. *Encourages* the relevant entities and organizations of the United Nations system to coordinate, as appropriate, on matters related to the recommendations contained in the report;

6. *Emphasizes* the importance of undertaking further work at the Disarmament Commission on preparing recommendations relating to the practical implementation of transparency and confidence-building measures in outer space activities with the goal of preventing an arms race in outer space;

7. *Welcomes* the joint ad hoc meetings of the First and Fourth Committees, held on 22 October 2015, 12 October 2017 and 31 October 2019, on possible challenges to space security and sustainability, convened in accordance with the report and its resolutions 69/38, 71/90, 73/72 and 73/91, and the substantive exchanges of opinions on various aspects of security in outer space that took place during the meetings;

8. *Decides* to convene, within existing resources, a joint half-day panel discussion of the Disarmament and International Security Committee (First Committee) and the Special Political and Decolonization Committee (Fourth Committee) to address possible challenges to space security and sustainability, and to include in the provisional agenda of its seventy-seventh session, under the item entitled "General and complete disarmament", the sub-item entitled "Joint panel discussion of the First and Fourth Committees on possible challenges to space security and sustainability";

9. *Calls upon* Member States and the relevant entities and organizations of the United Nations system to support the implementation of the full range of conclusions and recommendations contained in the report;

10. *Recalls* the report of the Secretary-General on transparency and confidence-building measures in outer space activities in the United Nations system, which contains summaries of the submissions received from Member States giving their views on transparency and confidence-building measures in outer space activities;[9]

11. *Invites* Member States to continue to submit, within the relevant forums, information on the specific unilateral, bilateral, regional and multilateral transparency and confidence-building measures in outer space activities implemented in accordance with the recommendations contained in the report of the Group of Governmental Experts;

12. *Decides* to include in the provisional agenda of its seventy-seventh session, under the item entitled "General and complete disarmament", the

---

[9] A/72/65 and A/72/65/Add.1.

sub-item entitled "Transparency and confidence-building measures in outer space activities".

Action by the General Assembly

    Date: 6 December 2021   Meeting: 45th plenary meeting

    Vote: Adopted without a vote   Report: A/76/444

Sponsors

China, **Russian Federation**, United States

Co-sponsors

Armenia, Belarus, Bolivia (Plurinational State of), Brazil, Cambodia, Comoros, Cuba, Dominica, Eritrea, Eswatini, Ethiopia, Kazakhstan, Kyrgyzstan, Lesotho, Madagascar, Morocco, Myanmar, Namibia, Nicaragua, Nigeria, Singapore, South Africa, Suriname, Syrian Arab Republic, Tajikistan, Thailand, Turkmenistan, Uzbekistan, Venezuela (Bolivarian Republic of), Zambia, Zimbabwe

Action by the First Committee

    Date: 1 November 2021   Meeting: 15th meeting

    Vote: Adopted without a vote   Draft resolution: A/C.1/76/L.60

Agenda item 101 (a)

76/56   Convention on the Prohibition of the Use of Nuclear Weapons

Text

The General Assembly,

Convinced that the use of nuclear weapons poses the most serious threat to the survival of humankind,

Bearing in mind the advisory opinion of the International Court of Justice of 8 July 1996 on the legality of the threat or use of nuclear weapons,[1]

Convinced that a multilateral, universal and binding agreement prohibiting the use or threat of use of nuclear weapons would contribute to the elimination of the nuclear threat and to the climate for negotiations leading to the ultimate elimination of nuclear weapons, thereby strengthening international peace and security,

Conscious that some steps have been taken by the Russian Federation and the United States of America towards a reduction of their nuclear weapons and that further steps – in all relevant formats – on nuclear arms control and disarmament can contribute to the improvement of the international climate and the goal of the complete elimination of nuclear weapons,

Recalling that, in paragraph 58 of the Final Document of the Tenth Special Session of the General Assembly,[2] it is stated that all States should actively participate in efforts to bring about conditions in international relations among States in which a code of peaceful conduct of nations in international affairs could be agreed upon and which would preclude the use or threat of use of nuclear weapons,

Reaffirming that any use of nuclear weapons would be a violation of the Charter of the United Nations and a crime against humanity, as declared in its resolutions 1653 (XVI) of 24 November 1961, 33/71 B of 14 December 1978, 34/83 G of 11 December 1979, 35/152 D of 12 December 1980 and 36/92 I of 9 December 1981,

Recognizing that a legally binding prohibition of the use of nuclear weapons is not contrary to but in fact contributes to international efforts for the achievement and maintenance of a world free of nuclear weapons,

Stressing that an international convention on the prohibition of the use of nuclear weapons would be an important step in a phased programme towards the complete elimination of nuclear weapons, with a specified framework of time,

---

[1]   A/51/218, annex.
[2]   Resolution S-10/2.

Noting with regret that the Conference on Disarmament, during its 2021 session, was unable to undertake negotiations on this subject as called for in General Assembly resolution 75/75 of 7 December 2020,

1. *Reiterates its request* to the Conference on Disarmament to commence negotiations in order to reach agreement on an international convention prohibiting the use or threat of use of nuclear weapons under any circumstances;

2. *Requests* the Conference on Disarmament to report to the General Assembly on the results of those negotiations.

Action by the General Assembly

Date: 6 December 2021   Meeting: 45th plenary meeting
Vote: 125-50-13   Report: A/76/445

Sponsors

Bangladesh, Bhutan, Cuba, **India**, Lao People's Democratic Republic, Nepal, Vanuatu, Viet Nam

Co-sponsors

Afghanistan, Indonesia, Iran (Islamic Republic of), Kazakhstan, Kiribati, Maldives, Mauritius, Myanmar, Palau, Sri Lanka, Venezuela (Bolivarian Republic of), Zambia

Recorded vote

In favour

Afghanistan, Algeria, Angola, Antigua and Barbuda, Argentina, Azerbaijan, Bahamas, Bahrain, Bangladesh, Barbados, Belize, Bhutan, Bolivia (Plurinational State of), Botswana, Brunei Darussalam, Burkina Faso, Burundi, Cabo Verde, Cambodia, Cameroon, Central African Republic, Chad, Chile, China, Colombia, Comoros, Congo, Costa Rica, Côte d'Ivoire, Cuba, Djibouti, Dominica, Dominican Republic, Egypt, El Salvador, Equatorial Guinea, Eritrea, Eswatini, Ethiopia, Fiji, Gabon, Gambia, Ghana, Grenada, Guatemala, Guinea, Guinea-Bissau, Haiti, Honduras, India, Indonesia, Iran (Islamic Republic of), Iraq, Jamaica, Jordan, Kazakhstan, Kenya, Kiribati, Kuwait, Lao People's Democratic Republic, Lebanon, Lesotho, Libya, Madagascar, Malawi, Malaysia, Maldives, Mali, Mauritania, Mauritius, Mexico, Mongolia, Morocco, Mozambique, Myanmar, Namibia, Nauru, Nepal, Nicaragua, Niger, Nigeria, Oman, Palau, Panama, Papua New Guinea, Paraguay, Peru, Qatar, Rwanda, Saint Kitts and Nevis, Saint Lucia, Saint Vincent and the Grenadines, Samoa, Sao Tome and Principe, Saudi Arabia, Senegal, Seychelles, Singapore, Solomon Islands, Somalia, South Africa, South Sudan, Sri Lanka, Sudan, Suriname, Syrian Arab Republic, Tajikistan, Timor-Leste, Togo, Tonga,

Trinidad and Tobago, Tunisia, Turkmenistan, Tuvalu, Uganda, United Arab Emirates, United Republic of Tanzania, Uruguay, Uzbekistan, Vanuatu, Venezuela (Bolivarian Republic of), Viet Nam, Yemen, Zambia, Zimbabwe

Against

Albania, Andorra, Australia, Austria, Belgium, Bosnia and Herzegovina, Bulgaria, Canada, Croatia, Cyprus, Czechia, Denmark, Estonia, Finland, France, Georgia, Germany, Greece, Hungary, Iceland, Ireland, Israel, Italy, Latvia, Liechtenstein, Lithuania, Luxembourg, Malta, Micronesia (Federated States of), Monaco, Montenegro, Netherlands, New Zealand, North Macedonia, Norway, Poland, Portugal, Republic of Korea, Republic of Moldova, Romania, San Marino, Slovakia, Slovenia, Spain, Sweden, Switzerland, Turkey, Ukraine, United Kingdom, United States

Abstaining

Armenia, Belarus, Brazil, Democratic People's Republic of Korea, Ecuador, Guyana, Japan, Marshall Islands, Pakistan, Philippines, Russian Federation, Serbia, Thailand

Action by the First Committee

Date:	27 October 2021	Meeting:	13th meeting
Vote:	115-50-16	Draft resolution:	A/C.1/76/L.9

Agenda item 101 (b)

76/57 United Nations Regional Centre for Peace and Disarmament in Africa

Text

The General Assembly,

Mindful of the provisions of Article 11, paragraph 1, of the Charter of the United Nations, in which it is stipulated that a function of the General Assembly is to consider the general principles of cooperation in the maintenance of international peace and security, including the principles governing disarmament and arms limitation,

Recalling its resolutions 40/151 G of 16 December 1985, 41/60 D of 3 December 1986, 42/39 J of 30 November 1987 and 43/76 D of 7 December 1988 on the United Nations Regional Centre for Peace and Disarmament in Africa and its resolutions 46/36 F of 6 December 1991 and 47/52 G of 9 December 1992 on regional disarmament, including confidence-building measures,

Recalling also its subsequent resolutions on the Regional Centre, the most recent of which is resolution 75/76 of 7 December 2020,

Recalling further its resolution 73/46 of 5 December 2018, in which it recognized the role of women in disarmament, non-proliferation and arms control,

Reaffirming the role of the Regional Centre in promoting disarmament, peace and security at the regional level,

Welcoming the continuing and deepening cooperation between the Regional Centre, the African Union and African subregional organizations in the context of the adoption of Agenda 2063 by the Assembly of Heads of State and Government of the African Union, and in particular the objective of silencing the guns in Africa,

Welcoming also the work of the Regional Centre in support of the achievement of the Sustainable Development Goals,[1] in particular Goal 16 on peace, justice and strong institutions, and target 16.4, which addresses the reduction of illicit arms flows,

Recalling the decision taken by the Executive Council of the African Union at its eighth ordinary session, held in Khartoum from 16 to 21 January 2006,[2] in which the Council called upon member States to make voluntary contributions to the Regional Centre to maintain its operations,

---

[1] See resolution 70/1.
[2] A/60/693, annex II, decision EX.CL/Dec.263 (VIII).

Recalling also the call by the Secretary-General for continued financial and in-kind support from Member States, which would enable the Regional Centre to discharge its mandate in full and to respond more effectively to requests for assistance from African States,

1.   *Takes note* of the report of the Secretary-General;[3]

2.   *Commends* the United Nations Regional Centre for Peace and Disarmament in Africa for its sustained support to Member States in implementing disarmament, arms control and non-proliferation activities through seminars and conferences, capacity-building and training, policy and technical expertise, and information and advocacy at the regional and national levels;

3.   *Welcomes* the continental dimension of the activities of the Regional Centre in response to the evolving needs of African Member States and the region's new and emerging challenges in the areas of disarmament, peace and security, including maritime security;

4.   *Recalls* the undertaking by the Regional Centre to deepen its partnership with the African Union Commission in the context of the Joint United Nations-African Union Framework for Enhanced Partnership in Peace and Security, signed on 19 April 2017, as well as with African subregional organizations, and requests the Secretary-General to continue to facilitate close cooperation between the Regional Centre and the African Union, in particular in the areas of disarmament, peace and security;

5.   *Welcomes* the contribution of the Regional Centre to continental disarmament, peace and security, in particular its contribution to the implementation of Agenda 2063 adopted by the Assembly of Heads of State and Government of the African Union, the objective of silencing the guns in Africa and its master road map of practical steps to silence the guns in Africa, as well as its assistance to the African Commission on Nuclear Energy in its implementation of the African Nuclear-Weapon-Free Zone Treaty (Treaty of Pelindaba);[4]

6.   *Also welcomes* efforts by the Regional Centre to promote the role and representation of women in disarmament, non-proliferation and arms control activities;

7.   *Calls upon* Member States and other bilateral and multilateral stakeholders to further enable the Regional Centre to provide adequate assistance to African Member States on arms control and disarmament from a human security perspective, notably in the following areas of arms control: prevention of violent extremism, youth and peace and security, and women and peace and security;

---

[3]   A/76/96.
[4]   A/50/426, annex.

8.   *Notes with appreciation* the tangible achievements of the Regional Centre and the impact of the assistance that it provides to African States to control small arms and light weapons through capacity-building for national commissions on small arms and light weapons, defence and security forces, and United Nations peacekeeping mission personnel, as well as the support that the Centre provided to States in preventing the diversion of such weapons, in particular to non-State armed groups and terrorist groups,[5] and also notes with appreciation the assistance provided by the Centre in the implementation of the Central African Convention for the Control of Small Arms and Light Weapons, Their Ammunition and All Parts and Components That Can Be Used for Their Manufacture, Repair and Assembly (Kinshasa Convention),[6] which entered into force on 8 March 2017, and its substantive support to the United Nations Standing Advisory Committee on Security Questions in Central Africa, in the implementation of the Economic Community of West African States Convention on Small Arms and Light Weapons, Their Ammunition and Other Related Materials and on security sector reform initiatives, and to East Africa on programmes to control brokering of small arms and light weapons, including the additional assistance provided by the Centre to African Member States in the implementation of Security Council resolution 1540 (2004) of 28 April 2004;

9.   *Commends* the Regional Centre for the support and assistance that it provided to African States, upon request, on the Arms Trade Treaty,[7] including through the organization of subregional and regional seminars and workshops;

10.   *Urges* all States, as well as international, governmental and non-governmental organizations and foundations, to make voluntary contributions to enable the Regional Centre to carry out its programmes and activities and meet the needs of African States;

11.   *Urges*, in particular, States members of the African Union to make voluntary contributions to the trust fund for the United Nations Regional Centre for Peace and Disarmament in Africa, in conformity with the decision taken by the Executive Council of the African Union in Khartoum in January 2006;

12.   *Requests* the Secretary-General to continue to provide the Regional Centre with the support necessary for greater achievements and results;

13.   *Also requests* the Secretary-General to report to the General Assembly at its seventy-seventh session on the implementation of the present resolution;

---

[5]   Security Council resolution 2370 (2017).
[6]   See A/65/517-S/2010/534, annex.
[7]   United Nations, *Treaty Series*, vol. 3013, No. 52373.

14. *Decides* to include in the provisional agenda of its seventy-seventh session, under the item entitled "Review and implementation of the Concluding Document of the Twelfth Special Session of the General Assembly", the sub-item entitled "United Nations Regional Centre for Peace and Disarmament in Africa".

Action by the General Assembly

Date:	6 December 2021	Meeting:	45th plenary meeting
Vote:	Adopted without a vote	Report:	A/76/445

Sponsors

Austria, Nicaragua, **Nigeria** (on behalf of the States Members of the United Nations that are members of the Group of African States)

Co-sponsors

Italy, Kazakhstan, Portugal

Action by the First Committee

Date:	3 November 2021	Meeting:	17th meeting
Vote:	Adopted without a vote	Draft resolution:	A/C.1/76/L.21

Agenda item 101 (c)

76/58 United Nations Regional Centre for Peace, Disarmament and Development in Latin America and the Caribbean

Text

The General Assembly,

Recalling its resolutions 41/60 J of 3 December 1986, 42/39 K of 30 November 1987 and 43/76 H of 7 December 1988 on the United Nations Regional Centre for Peace, Disarmament and Development in Latin America and the Caribbean, with headquarters in Lima,

Recalling also its resolution 75/77 of 7 December 2020 and all previous resolutions on the Regional Centre,

Recognizing that the Regional Centre has continued to provide substantive support for the implementation of regional and subregional initiatives and has intensified its contribution to the coordination of United Nations efforts towards peace and disarmament and for the promotion of economic and social development, and emphasizing the role of the Centre in providing support for the realization of the 2030 Agenda for Sustainable Development,[1]

Reaffirming the mandate of the Regional Centre to provide, on request, substantive support for the initiatives and other activities of the Member States of the region for the implementation of measures for peace and disarmament and for the promotion of economic and social development,

Taking note of the report of the Secretary-General,[2] and expressing its appreciation for the important assistance provided, upon request, by the Regional Centre to several countries in the region, including through capacity-building and technical assistance activities for the implementation of disarmament, non-proliferation and arms control instruments,

Welcoming the support provided by the Regional Centre to Member States in the implementation of disarmament and non-proliferation instruments,

Emphasizing the need for the Regional Centre to develop and strengthen its activities and programmes in a comprehensive and balanced manner, in accordance with its mandate and in line with the requests for assistance by Member States,

---

[1] Resolution 70/1.

[2] A/76/98.

Welcoming the ongoing support provided by the Regional Centre to Member States in the implementation of the Programme of Action to Prevent, Combat and Eradicate the Illicit Trade in Small Arms and Light Weapons in All Its Aspects,[3]

Welcoming also the assistance provided by the Regional Centre to some States, upon request, in the management and securing of national weapons stockpiles and in the identification and destruction of surplus, obsolete or seized weapons and ammunition, as declared by competent national authorities, in particular the implementation of a Caribbean firearms road map to prevent and combat the illicit trafficking in arms and ammunition,

Welcoming further the initiative of the Regional Centre to continue to conduct activities in line with efforts to promote the equitable representation of women in all decision-making processes with regard to matters related to disarmament, Non-Proliferation and arms control, as encouraged in its resolution 65/69 of 8 December 2010 and subsequent resolutions, including resolution 73/46 of 5 December 2018,

Recalling the report of the Group of Governmental Experts on the relationship between disarmament and development,[4] referred to in General Assembly resolution 59/78 of 3 December 2004, which is of utmost interest with regard to the role that the Regional Centre plays in promoting the issue in the region in pursuit of its mandate to promote economic and social development related to peace and disarmament,

Noting that security, disarmament and development issues have always been recognized as significant topics in Latin America and the Caribbean, the first inhabited region in the world to be declared a nuclear-weapon-free zone,

Recognizing the cooperation between the Regional Centre and the Agency for the Prohibition of Nuclear Weapons in Latin America and the Caribbean on strengthening the nuclear-weapon-free zone established by the Treaty for the Prohibition of Nuclear Weapons in Latin America and the Caribbean (Treaty of Tlatelolco),[5] as well as its efforts in promoting peace and disarmament education, especially among youth,

Bearing in mind the important role of the Regional Centre in promoting confidence-building measures, arms control and limitation, disarmament and development at the regional level,

Recognizing the importance of information, research, education and training for peace, disarmament and development in order to achieve understanding and cooperation among States,

---

[3] *Report of the United Nations Conference on the Illicit Trade in Small Arms and Light Weapons in All Its Aspects, New York, 9–20 July 2001* (A/CONF.192/15), chap. IV, para. 24.

[4] See A/59/119.

[5] United Nations, *Treaty Series*, vol. 634, No. 9068.

1.   *Reiterates its strong support* for the role of the United Nations Regional Centre for Peace, Disarmament and Development in Latin America and the Caribbean in the promotion of activities of the United Nations at the regional and subregional levels to strengthen peace, disarmament, stability, security and development among its Member States;

2.   *Welcomes* the activities carried out in the past year by the Regional Centre, and requests the Centre to continue to take into account the proposals to be submitted by the countries of the region for the implementation of the mandate of the Centre in the areas of peace, disarmament and development and for the promotion of, inter alia, the prevention, combating and eradication of the illicit trade in small arms and light weapons, ammunition and explosives, the non-proliferation of weapons of mass destruction and the reduction and prevention of armed violence at the regional and subregional levels;

3.   *Expresses its appreciation* for the political support provided by Member States, as well as for the financial contributions made by Member States and international governmental and non-governmental organizations, to strengthen the Regional Centre, its programme of activities and the implementation thereof, and encourages them to continue to make and to increase voluntary contributions;

4.   *Invites* all States of the region to continue to take part in the activities of the Regional Centre, proposing items for inclusion in its programme of activities and maximizing the potential of the Centre to meet the current challenges facing the international community with a view to fulfilling the aims of the Charter of the United Nations in the areas of peace, disarmament and development;

5.   *Recognizes* that the Regional Centre has an important role in the promotion and development of regional and subregional initiatives agreed upon by the countries of Latin America and the Caribbean in the field of weapons of mass destruction, in particular nuclear weapons, and conventional arms, including small arms and light weapons, in the relationship between disarmament and development, including the implementation of the Sustainable Development Goals,[6] in the promotion of the participation of women in this field and in strengthening voluntary confidence-building measures among the countries of the region;

6.   *Encourages* the Regional Centre to further develop activities in all countries of the region in the important areas of peace, disarmament and development and to provide, upon request and in accordance with its mandate, support to Member States of the region in the national implementation of relevant instruments, inter alia, the Programme of Action to Prevent, Combat and Eradicate the Illicit Trade in Small Arms and Light Weapons in All Its

---

[6] See resolution 70/1.

Aspects and the Arms Trade Treaty,[7] as well as in the implementation of the 1540 programme on the non-proliferation of weapons of mass destruction;

7.   *Requests* the Secretary-General to report to the General Assembly at its seventy-seventh session on the implementation of the present resolution;

8.   *Decides* to include in the provisional agenda of its seventy-seventh session, under the item entitled "Review and implementation of the Concluding Document of the Twelfth Special Session of the General Assembly", the sub-item entitled "United Nations Regional Centre for Peace, Disarmament and Development in Latin America and the Caribbean".

Action by the General Assembly

Date: 6 December 2021   Meeting: 45th plenary meeting
Vote: Adopted without a vote   Report: A/76/445

Sponsors

Peru (on behalf of the States Members of the United Nations that are members of the Group of Latin American and Caribbean States)

Action by the First Committee

Date: 3 November 2021   Meeting: 17th meeting
Vote: Adopted without a vote   Draft resolution: A/C.1/76/L.38

---

[7] United Nations, *Treaty Series*, vol. 3013, No. 52373.

Agenda item 101 (d)

76/59   United Nations Regional Centre for Peace and Disarmament in Asia and the Pacific

Text

The General Assembly,

Recalling its resolutions 42/39 D of 30 November 1987 and 44/117 F of 15 December 1989, by which it established the United Nations Regional Centre for Peace and Disarmament in Asia and renamed it the United Nations Regional Centre for Peace and Disarmament in Asia and the Pacific, with headquarters in Kathmandu,

Recalling also the mandate of the Regional Centre to provide, on request, substantive support for the initiatives and other activities mutually agreed upon by the Member States of the Asia-Pacific region for the implementation of measures for peace and disarmament, through appropriate utilization of available resources,

Taking note of the report of the Secretary-General,[1] and expressing its appreciation to the Regional Centre for its important work in promoting dialogue and confidence-building measures through the organization of meetings, conferences and workshops in the region, including national and subregional workshops on the implementation of Security Council resolution 1540 (2004) of 28 April 2004 in South Asia and Mongolia; capacity-building training for States of Asia and the Pacific on preparing and submitting online national reports on the implementation of the Programme of Action to Prevent, Combat and Eradicate the Illicit Trade in Small Arms and Light Weapons in All Its Aspects[2] and the Arms Trade Treaty;[3] and a capacity-building project for States of Asia and the Pacific on gun violence and illicit small arms trafficking from a gender perspective,

Expressing appreciation for the timely execution by Nepal of its host country commitments for the physical operation of the Regional Centre,

Welcoming the work by the Regional Centre in support of the achievement of Sustainable Development Goals 5 and 16,[4] in particular target 5.2 to eliminate all forms of violence against all women and girls, target 5.5 to ensure women's full and effective participation and equal

---

[1] A/76/97.

[2] *Report of the United Nations Conference on the Illicit Trade in Small Arms and Light Weapons in All Its Aspects, New York, 9–20 July 2001* (A/CONF.192/15), chap. IV, para. 24.

[3] United Nations, *Treaty Series*, vol. 3013, No. 52373.

[4] See resolution 70/1.

opportunities for leadership and target 16.4 to significantly reduce illicit financial and arms flows,

Welcoming also the efforts by the Regional Centre to promote the role and representation of women in disarmament, non-proliferation and arms control activities,

Welcoming further the youth-focused outreach activities undertaken by the Regional Centre,

1. *Expresses its satisfaction* at the activities carried out over the past year by the United Nations Regional Centre for Peace and Disarmament in Asia and the Pacific, and invites all States of the region to continue to support the activities of the Regional Centre, including by continuing to take part in them, where possible, and by proposing items for inclusion in the programme of activities of the Centre, in order to contribute to the implementation of measures for peace and disarmament;

2. *Expresses its gratitude* to the Government of Nepal for its cooperation and financial support, which has enabled the Regional Centre to operate from Kathmandu;

3. *Expresses its appreciation* to the Secretary-General and the Office for Disarmament Affairs of the Secretariat for providing the necessary support with a view to ensuring the smooth operation of the Regional Centre and to enabling the Centre to function effectively;

4. *Appeals* to Member States, in particular those within the Asia-Pacific region, as well as to international governmental and non-governmental organizations and foundations, to make voluntary contributions, the only resources of the Regional Centre, to strengthen its programme of activities and the implementation thereof;

5. *Reaffirms its strong support* for the role of the Regional Centre in the promotion of activities of the United Nations at the regional level to strengthen peace, stability and security among its Member States;

6. *Underlines* the importance of the Kathmandu process for the development of the practice of region-wide security and disarmament dialogues;

7. *Requests* the Secretary-General to report to the General Assembly at its seventy-seventh session on the implementation of the present resolution;

8. *Decides* to include in the provisional agenda of its seventy-seventh session, under the item entitled "Review and implementation of the Concluding Document of the Twelfth Special Session of the General Assembly", the sub-item entitled "United Nations Regional Centre for Peace and Disarmament in Asia and the Pacific".

Action by the General Assembly

Date: 6 December 2021   Meeting: 45th plenary meeting
Vote: Adopted without a vote   Report: A/76/445

Sponsors

Australia, Austria, Bangladesh, Bhutan, China, Japan, Malaysia, Micronesia (Federated States of), Mongolia, Myanmar, **Nepal**, New Zealand, Nicaragua, Nigeria, Philippines, Republic of Korea, Singapore, Thailand, Viet Nam, Zambia

Co-sponsors

India, Kazakhstan, Maldives, Papua New Guinea, Portugal, Sri Lanka, Timor-Leste

Action by the First Committee

Date: 3 November 2021   Meeting: 17th meeting
Vote: Adopted without a vote   Draft resolution: A/C.1/76/L.18/Rev.1

Agenda item 101 (e)

**76/60   Regional confidence-building measures: activities
of the United Nations Standing Advisory
Committee on Security Questions in Central Africa**

Text

The General Assembly,

Recalling its previous relevant resolutions, in particular its resolution 75/79 of 7 December 2020,

Recalling also the guidelines for general and complete disarmament adopted at its tenth special session, the first special session devoted to disarmament,

Bearing in mind the establishment by the Secretary-General on 28 May 1992 of the United Nations Standing Advisory Committee on Security Questions in Central Africa, the purpose of which is to encourage arms limitation, disarmament, Non-Proliferation and development in the Central Africa subregion,

Recalling that the purpose of the Standing Advisory Committee is to conduct reconstruction and confidence-building activities in Central Africa among its member States, including through confidence-building and arms limitation measures,

Reaffirming the importance and relevance of the Standing Advisory Committee as an instrument of preventive diplomacy in the subregional architecture for the promotion of peace and security in Central Africa,

Bearing in mind the revitalization of the activities of the Standing Advisory Committee decided upon at the forty-fourth ministerial meeting of the Committee, held in Yaoundé from 29 May to 2 June 2017, with a view to enhancing its contribution to the achievement of the objectives of peace, security and development in Central Africa,

Recalling the entry into force of the Central African Convention for the Control of Small Arms and Light Weapons, Their Ammunition and All Parts and Components That Can Be Used for Their Manufacture, Repair and Assembly (Kinshasa Convention) on 8 March 2017[1] and the third Conference of States Parties to the Arms Trade Treaty, held in Geneva from 11 to 15 September 2017,

Convinced that the resources released by disarmament, including regional disarmament, can be devoted to economic and social development

---

[1] See A/65/517-S/2010/534, annex.

and to the protection of the environment for the benefit of all peoples, in particular those of developing countries,

Reaffirming the Libreville Declaration on the Adoption and Implementation of the Regional Strategy and Plan of Action for Combating Terrorism and the Trafficking in Small Arms and Light Weapons in Central Africa, adopted by the States members of the Standing Advisory Committee on 26 November 2015 at their forty-first ministerial meeting, held in Libreville from 23 to 27 November 2015,[2]

Considering the importance and effectiveness of confidence-building measures taken on the initiative and with the participation of all States concerned and taking into account the specific characteristics of each region, since such measures can contribute to regional stability and to international peace and security,

Convinced that development can be achieved only in a climate of peace, security and mutual confidence both within and among States,

Recalling the communiqués of the forty-eighth[3] and forty-ninth ministerial meetings of the Standing Advisory Committee, held from 27 to 31 May and from 25 to 29 November 2019 in Kinshasa and Luanda, respectively, the Brazzaville Declaration on Cooperation for Peace and Security in Central Africa,[4] the Bata Declaration for the Promotion of Lasting Democracy, Peace and Development in Central Africa[5] and the Yaoundé Declaration on Peace, Security and Stability in Central Africa,[6]

Bearing in mind resolutions 1196 (1998) and 1197 (1998), adopted by the Security Council on 16 and 18 September 1998, respectively, following its consideration of the report of the Secretary-General on the causes of conflict and the promotion of durable peace and sustainable development in Africa,[7]

Recalling the successful conclusion of the Summit of Heads of State and Government on Maritime Safety and Security in the Gulf of Guinea, held in Yaoundé on 24 and 25 June 2013, the inauguration in Yaoundé, on 11 September 2014, of the Interregional Coordination Centre for Maritime Security in the Gulf of Guinea, the effective commencement of its activities with the installation of its statutory officials in Yaoundé on 22 February 2017, the inauguration of new offices of the Regional Centre for Maritime Security in Central Africa in Pointe Noire, Congo, on 20 October 2014, and the launch of the Multinational Maritime Coordination Centre in Cotonou, Benin, in March 2015, and also the conclusion of the African Union Extraordinary

---

[2] See A/70/682-S/2016/39, annex 3.
[3] A/73/967-S/2019/613, annex, enclosure I.
[4] A/50/474, annex I.
[5] A/53/258-S/1998/763, annex II, appendix I.
[6] A/53/868-S/1999/303, annex II.
[7] A/52/871-S/1998/318.

Summit of Heads of State and Government on Maritime Security and Safety and Development in Africa, held in Lomé on 15 October 2016,

Recalling also its resolution 69/314 of 30 July 2015, the first such resolution on tackling illicit trafficking in wildlife, and also its resolutions 70/301 of 9 September 2016, 71/326 of 11 September 2017, 73/343 of 16 September 2019 and 75/311 of 23 July 2021, and reaffirming the outcome of the high-level meetings on poaching and illicit wildlife trafficking, hosted by Gabon and Germany and held on the margins of the high-level segments of the sixty-eighth and sixty-ninth sessions of the General Assembly,

Emphasizing the need to strengthen the capacity for early warning, conflict prevention and peacekeeping in Africa, and recalling in this regard the concrete conflict prevention initiatives facilitated by the Department of Political and Peacebuilding Affairs of the Secretariat,

Welcoming the establishment of the Commission of the Economic Community of Central African States and the close cooperation established between the United Nations Regional Office for Central Africa and the Economic Community, as well as the signing of the framework of cooperation agreement between the two entities on 14 June 2016,

Taking note of the decisions adopted by the Conference of Heads of State and Government of the Economic Community of Central African States at its eighteenth ordinary session, held in Libreville on 27 November 2020, and at its nineteenth ordinary session, held virtually on 30 July 2021,

Bearing in mind the increased focus of the Standing Advisory Committee on human security questions, such as trafficking in persons, especially women and children, as an important consideration for subregional peace, stability and conflict prevention, and recalling the adoption by the General Assembly at its seventy-second session of the political declaration on the implementation of the United Nations Global Plan of Action to Combat Trafficking in Persons[8] following the high-level meeting of the Assembly on the appraisal of the Global Plan of Action,

Expressing continued concern about the fragile situation in the Central African Republic and in the neighbouring countries affected, and noting the importance of promoting the political process through the reactivation of the joint bilateral commissions between the Central African Republic and its neighbours and the implementation of the Political Agreement for Peace and Reconciliation in the Central African Republic[9] between the Government and armed groups for lasting peace, in particular with regard to the protection of civilians, disarmament, demobilization and reintegration of former combatants, and strengthening the authority of the State,

---

[8] Resolution 72/1.
[9] S/2019/145, annex.

Welcoming the adoption of the joint road map for peace in the Central African Republic at the third mini-summit of the International Conference on the Great Lakes Region, held in Luanda on 16 September 2021,

Highlighting the regional security implications of the situation in the Central African Republic, and reiterating the commitment of the region and the international community to supporting the parties in the effective implementation of the Political Agreement, including through the provision of political, security, technical and financial support,

Recalling the Brazzaville Declaration on Confidence-Building Measures,[10] and expressing concern that the issue of mercenaries has become a major security concern, undermining trust and creating tensions among States members of the Standing Advisory Committee,

Welcoming the adoption of the declaration on democratic and peaceful elections as a means of strengthening stability and achieving the Sustainable Development Goals in Central Africa at the fiftieth ministerial meeting of the Standing Advisory Committee, held in Malabo from 2 to 4 December 2020,[11]

Recalling the conclusions of the fifty-first meeting of the Standing Advisory Committee, held in Bujumbura from 24 to 28 May 2021,

Welcoming the call by States members of the Economic Community of Central African States during the forty-ninth ministerial meeting of the Standing Advisory Committee, in Luanda, on the need to strengthen partnership with the United Nations to address the impact of climate change on peace and security in the subregion,

Expressing concern about the impact of cross-border criminality, in particular the activities of the Lord's Resistance Army, the terrorist attacks by groups affiliated with Boko Haram in the Lake Chad basin region and incidents of piracy in the Gulf of Guinea, the illegal exploitation of natural resources, and the issue of transhumance and its cross-border security implications for peace, security and development in Central Africa,

Welcoming the progress made by the States members of the Lake Chad Basin Commission and Benin in making the Multinational Joint Task Force operational in order to combat effectively the threat posed by the Boko Haram terrorist group to the Lake Chad basin region,

Recalling the adoption by the Lake Chad Basin Commission, with the support of the African Union, of the Regional Stabilization, Recovery and Resilience Strategy for Areas Affected by Boko Haram in the Lake Chad Basin Region in Abuja on 30 August 2018,

---

[10] A/73/224, annex IV.
[11] A/76/274, annex I.

Bearing in mind Security Council resolution 2349 (2017) of 31 March 2017, in which the Council called for, inter alia, increased assistance to the countries of the region,

Considering the urgent need to prevent the possible movement of illicit weapons, mercenaries and combatants involved in conflicts in the Sahel and in neighbouring countries in the Central African subregion,

1.   *Reaffirms its support* for efforts aimed at promoting confidence-building measures at the regional and subregional levels in order to ease tensions and conflicts in Central Africa and to further sustainable peace, stability and development in the subregion;

2.   *Welcomes and encourages* the initiative of the States members of the United Nations Standing Advisory Committee on Security Questions in Central Africa to further develop collaboration and synergies with the Economic Community of Central African States;

3.   *Invites* the Standing Advisory Committee and the Economic Community of Central African States to initiate discussions on the relationship between the two entities in the light of the institutional reform of the Economic Community;

4.   *Welcomes* efforts under way by the Standing Advisory Committee and its secretariat to implement the communication strategy adopted at the forty-fifth ministerial meeting of the Committee, held in Kigali from 4 to 8 December 2017, and encourages Member States and other partners to support initiatives aimed at increasing the visibility of the Committee, including among the populations of the subregion, in cooperation with civil society;

5.   *Reaffirms* the importance of disarmament and arms control programmes in Central Africa carried out by the States of the subregion with the support of the United Nations, the African Union and other international partners;

6.   *Encourages* Member States to provide assistance to those States members of the Standing Advisory Committee that have ratified the Arms Trade Treaty,[12] and encourages those that have not yet done so to ratify the Treaty;

7.   *Encourages* States members of the Standing Advisory Committee and other interested States to provide financial support for the implementation of the Central African Convention for the Control of Small Arms and Light Weapons, Their Ammunition and All Parts and Components That Can Be Used for Their Manufacture, Repair and Assembly (Kinshasa Convention), and encourages signatories that have not yet done so to ratify the Convention;

---

[12]   United Nations, *Treaty Series*, vol. 3013, No. 52373.

8. *Welcomes* the holding of the first Conference of States Parties to the Central African Convention for the Control of Small Arms and Light Weapons, Their Ammunition and All Parts and Components That Can Be Used for Their Manufacture, Repair and Assembly, in Yaoundé from 11 to 13 June 2018, in accordance with article 34, paragraph 3, of the Kinshasa Convention;

9. *Encourages* Member States to assist States parties to the Kinshasa Convention with coordination activities for the control of small arms and light weapons at the regional and national levels, including funding thereof, as expeditiously as possible;

10. *Reaffirms its support* for the United Nations Global Counter-Terrorism Strategy[13] and its four pillars, which constitute an ongoing effort, and calls upon Member States, the United Nations and other appropriate international, regional and subregional organizations to step up their efforts to implement the Strategy in an integrated and balanced manner and in all aspects;

11. *Welcomes* the adoption, by the Conference of Heads of State and Government of the Economic Community of Central African States at its seventeenth ordinary session, on 30 July 2020, of the strategy on preventing and combating terrorism in Central Africa, and requests United Nations, regional and international partners to support its implementation;

12. *Welcomes* the joint summit of the Heads of State and Government of the Economic Community of West African States and the Economic Community of Central African States, in coordination with the African Union Commission, on peace, security, stability and the fight against terrorism and violent extremism, held in Lomé on 30 July 2018, and recalls the Lomé Declaration on Peace, Security, Stability and the Fight against Terrorism and Violent Extremism adopted at that summit;

13. *Encourages* the Economic Community of Central African States and the Economic Community of West African States to work together towards the implementation of the Lomé Declaration;

14. *Encourages* the States members of the Standing Advisory Committee to carry out the programmes of activities adopted at their ministerial meetings, and requests the United Nations Regional Office for Central Africa to continue to provide support;

15. *Appeals* to the international community to support the efforts undertaken by the States concerned to implement disarmament, demobilization and reintegration programmes, and urges the States concerned to ensure that such programmes take into consideration the needs of women and children associated with former combatants;

---

[13] Resolution 60/288.

16.   *Welcomes* the efforts of Cameroon and the Congo in providing assistance to the Interregional Coordination Centre for Maritime Security in the Gulf of Guinea and the Regional Centre for Maritime Security in Central Africa, respectively, and urges other member States to honour their financial commitments in order to ensure the predictable and sustainable operation of the two Centres;

17.   *Encourages* Member States to continue to implement the outcomes of the Summit of Heads of State and Government on Maritime Safety and Security in the Gulf of Guinea by operationalizing the Interregional Coordination Centre for Maritime Security in the Gulf of Guinea and activities of the Regional Centre for Maritime Security in Central Africa, and also encourages the implementation of the Charter on Maritime Security and Safety and Development in Africa adopted at the African Union Extraordinary Summit of Heads of State and Government on Maritime Security and Safety and Development in Africa;

18.   *Calls upon* Member States and subregional bodies to take immediate concerted action to counter the phenomenon of poaching and trafficking in wildlife and natural resources, including through the implementation of the provisions of its resolutions 69/314, 70/301, 71/326, 73/343 and 75/311;

19.   *Welcomes* the progress made by the Economic Community of Central African States and the Economic Community of West African States in initiating common policies and joint programmes on the management of pastoralism and cross-border transhumance, and encourages the Economic Community of Central African States to adopt the protocol on pastoralism and cross-border transhumance in Central Africa;

20.   *Encourages* the development of mechanisms for regulation by the Economic Community of Central African States, and calls for the holding of a high-level conference to discuss issues relating to pastoralism and cross-border transhumance with a view to ensuring joint and integrated management thereof;

21.   *Requests* the United Nations Regional Office for Central Africa, in collaboration with the United Nations Regional Centre for Peace and Disarmament in Africa, to facilitate the efforts undertaken by the States members of the Standing Advisory Committee, in particular for their execution of the Implementation Plan for the Kinshasa Convention;[14]

22.   *Requests* the Secretary-General and the Office of the United Nations High Commissioner for Refugees, with the support of the international community, to continue to assist the countries of Central Africa in tackling the issues of refugees and displaced persons in their territories;

---

[14]   See A/65/717-S/2011/53, annex.

23. *Requests* the Secretary-General and the Office of the United Nations High Commissioner for Human Rights to continue to provide their full assistance to the Subregional Centre for Human Rights and Democracy in Central Africa;

24. *Welcomes* the increased contributions made by several Member States to the trust fund of the United Nations Standing Advisory Committee on Security Questions in Central Africa, reminds the States members of the Standing Advisory Committee of the commitments that they undertook on the adoption of the Declaration on the Trust Fund of the United Nations Standing Advisory Committee on Security Questions in Central Africa on 8 May 2009[15] and the Bangui Declaration on 10 June 2016,[16] and invites those States members of the Committee that have not already done so to contribute to the trust fund;

25. *Urges* other Member States and intergovernmental and non-governmental organizations to support the activities of the Standing Advisory Committee effectively through voluntary contributions to the trust fund;

26. *Urges* the States members of the Standing Advisory Committee, in accordance with Security Council resolution 1325 (2000) of 31 October 2000, to strengthen the gender component of the various meetings of the Committee relating to disarmament and international security, in line with the Sao Tome Declaration on the Participation of Women in the Statutory Meetings of the United Nations Standing Advisory Committee on Security Questions in Central Africa, adopted on 1 December 2016,[17] in which member States were invited to increase the representation of women in delegations participating in the statutory meetings of the Committee, and strongly encourages the States members of the Committee to ensure that gender-related considerations are taken into account in the activities of the Committee;

27. *Expresses its satisfaction* to the Secretary-General for his support to the Standing Advisory Committee, expresses appreciation for the role played by the United Nations Regional Office for Central Africa, welcomes the outcome of the strategic review of the Office, and strongly encourages the States members of the Standing Advisory Committee and international partners to support the work of the Office;

28. *Welcomes* the efforts of the Standing Advisory Committee towards addressing cross-border security threats in Central Africa, including activities of groups affiliated with Boko Haram and the Lord's Resistance Army, and acts of piracy and armed robbery at sea in the Gulf of Guinea, the issue of transhumance and its cross-border security implications, as well as the fallout

---

[15] A/64/85-S/2009/288, annex I.
[16] A/71/293, annex I.
[17] A/72/363, annex II.

from the situation in the Central African Republic, and also welcomes the role of the United Nations Regional Office for Central Africa in coordinating those efforts, working closely with the Economic Community of Central African States, the African Union and all relevant regional and international partners;

29. *Expresses its satisfaction* to the Secretary-General for his support for the revitalization of the activities of the Standing Advisory Committee, and requests him to continue to provide the assistance needed to ensure the success of its regular meetings;

30. *Calls upon* the Secretary-General to submit to the General Assembly at its seventy-seventh session a report on the implementation of the present resolution;

31. *Decides* to include in the provisional agenda of its seventy-seventh session, under the item entitled "Review and implementation of the Concluding Document of the Twelfth Special Session of the General Assembly", the sub-item entitled "Regional confidence-building measures: activities of the United Nations Standing Advisory Committee on Security Questions in Central Africa".

Action by the General Assembly

Date:	6 December 2021	Meeting:	45th plenary meeting
Vote:	Adopted without a vote	Report:	A/76/445

Sponsors

Burundi (on behalf of the States Members of the United Nations that are members of the Economic Community of Central African States)

Action by the First Committee

Date:	3 November 2021	Meeting:	17th meeting
Vote:	Adopted without a vote	Draft resolution:	A/C.1/76/L.61

Agenda item 101 (f)

76/61 United Nations regional centres for peace and disarmament

Text

The General Assembly,

Recalling its resolutions 60/83 of 8 December 2005, 61/90 of 6 December 2006, 62/50 of 5 December 2007, 63/76 of 2 December 2008, 64/58 of 2 December 2009, 65/78 of 8 December 2010, 66/53 of 2 December 2011, 67/63 of 3 December 2012, 68/57 of 5 December 2013, 69/70 of 2 December 2014, 70/61 of 7 December 2015, 71/80 of 5 December 2016, 72/64 of 4 December 2017, 73/80 of 5 December 2018, 74/70 of 12 December 2019 and 75/81 of 7 December 2020 regarding the maintenance and revitalization of the three United Nations regional centres for peace and disarmament,

Recalling also the reports of the Secretary-General on the United Nations Regional Centre for Peace and Disarmament in Africa,[1] the United Nations Regional Centre for Peace and Disarmament in Asia and the Pacific[2] and the United Nations Regional Centre for Peace, Disarmament and Development in Latin America and the Caribbean,[3]

Reaffirming its decision, taken in 1982 at its twelfth special session, to establish the United Nations Disarmament Information Programme, the purpose of which is to inform, educate and generate public understanding and support for the objectives of the United Nations in the field of arms control and disarmament,

Bearing in mind its resolutions 40/151 G of 16 December 1985, 41/60 J of 3 December 1986, 42/39 D of 30 November 1987 and 44/117 F of 15 December 1989 on the regional centres for peace and disarmament in Nepal, Peru and Togo,

Recalling that the thirtieth anniversary of the establishment by the General Assembly of the United Nations Regional Centre for Peace and Disarmament in Africa, the United Nations Regional Centre for Peace and Disarmament in Asia and the Pacific and the United Nations Regional Centre for Peace, Disarmament and Development in Latin America and the Caribbean was celebrated in 2016 and in 2017,

Recognizing that the changes that have taken place in the world have created new opportunities and posed new challenges for the pursuit of disarmament, and bearing in mind in this regard that the regional centres for

---

[1] A/76/96.
[2] A/76/97.
[3] A/76/98.

peace and disarmament can contribute substantially to understanding and cooperation among States in each particular region in the areas of peace, disarmament and development,

Noting that, in paragraph 279 of the Final Document of the Eighteenth Summit of Heads of State or Government of Non-Aligned Countries, held in Baku on 25 and 26 October 2019,[4] the Heads of State or Government emphasized the importance of United Nations activities at the regional level to increase the stability and security of its Member States, which could be promoted in a substantive manner by the maintenance and revitalization of the three regional centres for peace and disarmament,

1. *Reiterates* the importance of United Nations activities at the regional level to advance disarmament and to increase the stability and security of its Member States, which could be promoted in a substantive manner by the maintenance and further strengthening of the three regional centres for peace and disarmament;

2. *Commends* the three regional centres for peace and disarmament for their sustained support provided to Member States for over 30 years in implementing disarmament, arms control and non-proliferation activities through seminars and conferences, capacity-building and training, policy and technical expertise, and information and advocacy at the global, regional and national levels;

3. *Reaffirms* that, in order to achieve positive results, it is useful for the three regional centres to carry out dissemination and educational programmes that promote regional peace and security and that are aimed at changing basic attitudes with respect to peace and security and disarmament so as to support the achievement of the purposes and principles of the United Nations;

4. *Appeals* to Member States in each region that are able to do so, as well as to international governmental and non-governmental organizations and foundations, to make voluntary contributions to the regional centres in their respective regions in order to strengthen their activities and initiatives;

5. *Emphasizes* the importance of the activities of the Regional Disarmament Branch of the Office for Disarmament Affairs of the Secretariat;

6. *Requests* the Secretary-General to provide all support necessary, within existing resources, to the regional centres in carrying out their programmes of activities;

7. *Decides* to include in the provisional agenda of its seventy-seventh session, under the item entitled "Review and implementation of the Concluding Document of the Twelfth Special Session of the General

---

[4] A/74/548, annex.

Assembly", the sub-item entitled "United Nations regional centres for peace and disarmament".

Action by the General Assembly

Date: 6 December 2021 Meeting: 45th plenary meeting
Vote: Adopted without a vote Report: A/76/445

Sponsors

Indonesia (on behalf of the States Members of the United Nations that are members of the Movement of Non-Aligned Countries)

Action by the First Committee

Date: 3 November 2021 Meeting: 17th meeting
Vote: Adopted without a vote Draft resolution: A/C.1/76/L.28

Agenda item 102 (a)

76/62   Report of the Conference on Disarmament

Text

The General Assembly,

Having considered the report of the Conference on Disarmament,[1]

Recalling its resolution 75/83 of 7 December 2020,

Convinced that the Conference on Disarmament, as the single multilateral disarmament negotiating forum of the international community, has the primary role in substantive negotiations on priority questions of disarmament,

Recognizing the addresses of the Ministers for Foreign Affairs and other high-level officials in the Conference on Disarmament, and referring to their various expressions of support for and concern about the endeavours of the Conference and calls for the Conference to commence negotiations without delay to advance disarmament goals through the adoption of a balanced and comprehensive programme of work,

Recognizing also the need to conduct multilateral negotiations with the aim of reaching agreement on concrete issues, and emphasizing the importance of effective multilateralism in the context of the changing international climate,

Noting with renewed concern that, despite the intensive efforts by States members and Presidents of the Conference on Disarmament at its 2021 session to reach consensus on a programme of work on the basis of relevant proposals and suggestions, the Conference did not succeed in commencing its substantive work by means of negotiations or agree to a programme of work,

Recalling, in this respect, that the Conference on Disarmament has a number of priority issues for negotiation to achieve disarmament goals,

Welcoming the overwhelming call for greater flexibility with respect to implementing the substantive work of the Conference on Disarmament on the basis of a balanced and comprehensive programme of work,

Underlining the need for continued cooperation among the States members of the Conference on Disarmament as well as among the successive Presidents of the Conference,

Noting with appreciation the contributions made at the 2021 session to promote substantive discussions on issues on the agenda,

---

[1] *Official Records of the General Assembly, Seventy-sixth Session, Supplement No. 27* (A/76/27).

Acknowledging the United Nations Institute for Disarmament Research, as a stand-alone, autonomous institution, and the contribution that its research makes,

Recognizing the importance of engagement between civil society and the Conference on Disarmament according to decisions taken by the Conference,

1.   *Reaffirms* the role of the Conference on Disarmament as the single multilateral disarmament negotiating forum of the international community;

2.   *Appreciates* the strong support expressed for the Conference on Disarmament at its 2021 session by Ministers for Foreign Affairs and other high-level officials, while also acknowledging their concern about its ongoing impasse, and takes into account their calls for greater flexibility with respect to commencing the substantive work of the Conference without further delay;

3.   *Calls upon* the Conference on Disarmament to further intensify consultations and to explore possibilities for overcoming its ongoing deadlock of two decades by adopting and implementing a balanced and comprehensive programme of work at the earliest possible date during its 2022 session, bearing in mind the decision on the programme of work adopted by the Conference on 29 May 2009,[2] as well as other relevant present, past and future proposals;

4.   *Encourages* the current President and the incoming President of the Conference on Disarmament to conduct consultations during the intersessional period and, if possible, to make recommendations, taking into account all relevant proposals, past, present and future, including those submitted as documents of the Conference, views presented and discussions held, and to endeavour to keep the membership of the Conference informed, as appropriate, of their consultations;

5.   *Requests* the current President and successive Presidents of the Conference on Disarmament to cooperate with the States members of the Conference in the effort to guide the Conference to the early commencement of its substantive work, including negotiations, at its 2022 session;

6.   *Recognizes* the importance of continuing consultations in 2022 on the question of the expansion of the membership of the Conference on Disarmament;

7.   *Requests* the Secretary-General to continue to ensure and to strengthen, if needed, the provision to the Conference on Disarmament of all necessary administrative, substantive and conference support services;

8.   *Requests* the Conference on Disarmament to submit to the General Assembly at its seventy-seventh session a report on its work;

---

[2]   Ibid., *Sixty-fourth Session, Supplement No. 27* (A/64/27), para. 18.

9.   *Decides* to include in the provisional agenda of its seventy-seventh session, under the item entitled "Review of the implementation of the recommendations and decisions adopted by the General Assembly at its tenth special session", the sub-item entitled "Report of the Conference on Disarmament".

Action by the General Assembly

Date: 6 December 2021   Meeting: 45th plenary meeting
Vote: Adopted without a vote   Report: A/76/446

Sponsors

Chile

Action by the First Committee

Date: 3 November 2021   Meeting: 17th meeting
Vote: Adopted without a vote   Draft resolution: A/C.1/76/L.48

Agenda item 103

76/63   The risk of nuclear proliferation in the Middle East

Text

The General Assembly,

Bearing in mind its relevant resolutions, the latest of which is resolution 75/84 of 7 December 2020,

Taking note of the relevant resolutions adopted by the General Conference of the International Atomic Energy Agency, the latest of which is resolution GC(65)/RES/14, adopted on 23 September 2021,

Cognizant that the proliferation of nuclear weapons in the region of the Middle East would pose a serious threat to international peace and security,

Mindful of the immediate need for placing all nuclear facilities in the region of the Middle East under full-scope safeguards of the Agency,

Recalling the decision on principles and objectives for nuclear non-proliferation and disarmament adopted by the 1995 Review and Extension Conference of the Parties to the Treaty on the Non-Proliferation of Nuclear Weapons on 11 May 1995,[1] in which the Conference urged universal adherence to the Treaty on the Non-Proliferation of Nuclear Weapons[2] as an urgent priority and called upon all States not yet parties to the Treaty to accede to it at the earliest date, particularly those States that operate unsafeguarded nuclear facilities,

Recognizing with satisfaction that, in the Final Document of the 2000 Review Conference of the Parties to the Treaty on the Non-Proliferation of Nuclear Weapons,[3] the Conference undertook to make determined efforts towards the achievement of the goal of universality of the Treaty, called upon those remaining States not parties to the Treaty to accede to it, thereby accepting an international legally binding commitment not to acquire nuclear weapons or nuclear explosive devices and to accept Agency safeguards on all their nuclear activities, and underlined the necessity of universal adherence to the Treaty and of strict compliance by all parties with their obligations under the Treaty,

Recalling the resolution on the Middle East adopted by the 1995 Review and Extension Conference of the Parties to the Treaty on 11 May 1995, in

---

[1] See *1995 Review and Extension Conference of the Parties to the Treaty on the Non-Proliferation of Nuclear Weapons, Final Document, Part I* (NPT/CONF.1995/32 (Part I) and NPT/CONF.1995/32 (Part I)/Corr.2), annex.

[2] United Nations, *Treaty Series*, vol. 729, No. 10485.

[3] *2000 Review Conference of the Parties to the Treaty on the Non-Proliferation of Nuclear Weapons, Final Document*, vols. I–III (NPT/CONF.2000/28 (Parts I and II), NPT/CONF.2000/28 (Part III) and NPT/CONF.2000/28 (Part IV)).

which the Conference noted with concern the continued existence in the Middle East of unsafeguarded nuclear facilities, reaffirmed the importance of the early realization of universal adherence to the Treaty, and called upon all States in the Middle East that had not yet done so, without exception, to accede to the Treaty as soon as possible and to place all their nuclear facilities under full-scope Agency safeguards,

Acknowledging that, in the Final Document of the 2010 Review Conference of the Parties to the Treaty on the Non-Proliferation of Nuclear Weapons,[4] the Conference emphasized the importance of a process leading to full implementation of the 1995 resolution on the Middle East and decided, inter alia, that the Secretary-General of the United Nations and the co-sponsors of the 1995 resolution, in consultation with the States of the region, would convene a conference in 2012, to be attended by all States of the Middle East, on the establishment of a Middle East zone free of nuclear weapons and all other weapons of mass destruction, on the basis of arrangements freely arrived at by the States of the region, and with the full support and engagement of the nuclear-weapon States,

Expressing regret and concern that the conference was not convened in 2012 as mandated and that little progress has been achieved towards the implementation of the resolution on the Middle East adopted by the 1995 Review and Extension Conference of the Parties to the Treaty,

Noting, in this context, the relevant resolutions of the League of Arab States aiming at the establishment of a Middle East zone free of nuclear weapons and all other weapons of mass destruction,

Taking note with appreciation of the report of the Secretary-General,[5]

Recalling that Israel remains the only State in the Middle East that has not yet become a party to the Treaty,

Concerned about the threats posed by the proliferation of nuclear weapons to the security and stability of the Middle East region,

Stressing the importance of taking confidence-building measures, in particular the establishment of a nuclear-weapon-free zone in the Middle East, in order to enhance peace and security in the region and to consolidate the global Non-Proliferation regime,

Emphasizing the need for all parties directly concerned to seriously consider taking the practical and urgent steps required for the implementation of the proposal to establish a nuclear-weapon-free zone in the region of the Middle East in accordance with the relevant resolutions of the General

---

[4] *2010 Review Conference of the Parties to the Treaty on the Non-Proliferation of Nuclear Weapons, Final Document*, vols. I–III (NPT/CONF.2010/50 (Vol. I), NPT/CONF.2010/50 (Vol. II) and NPT/CONF.2010/50 (Vol. III)).

[5] A/76/190 (Part II).

Assembly and, as a means of promoting this objective, inviting the countries concerned to adhere to the Treaty and, pending the establishment of the zone, to agree to place all their nuclear activities under Agency safeguards,

Noting that 185 States have signed the Comprehensive Nuclear-Test-Ban Treaty,[6] including a number of States in the region,

1.   *Recalls* the conclusions on the Middle East of the 2010 Review Conference of the Parties to the Treaty on the Non-Proliferation of Nuclear Weapons,[7] and calls for the speedy and full implementation of the commitments contained therein;

2.   *Stresses* that the resolution on the Middle East adopted by the 1995 Review and Extension Conference of the Parties to the Treaty[8] is an essential element of the outcome of the 1995 Conference and of the basis on which the Treaty was indefinitely extended without a vote in 1995;

3.   *Reiterates* that the resolution on the Middle East adopted by the 1995 Review and Extension Conference of the Parties to the Treaty remains valid until its goals and objectives are achieved;

4.   *Calls for* immediate steps towards the full implementation of that resolution;

5.   *Reaffirms* the importance of Israel's accession to the Treaty on the Non-Proliferation of Nuclear Weapons and placement of all its nuclear facilities under comprehensive International Atomic Energy Agency safeguards, in realizing the goal of universal adherence to the Treaty in the Middle East;

6.   *Calls upon* that State to accede to the Treaty without further delay, not to develop, produce, test or otherwise acquire nuclear weapons, to renounce possession of nuclear weapons and to place all its unsafeguarded nuclear facilities under full-scope Agency safeguards as an important confidence-building measure among all States of the region and as a step towards enhancing peace and security;

7.   *Requests* the Secretary-General to report to the General Assembly at its seventy-seventh session on the implementation of the present resolution;

8.   *Decides* to include in the provisional agenda of its seventy-seventh session the item entitled "The risk of nuclear proliferation in the Middle East".

---

[6] See resolution 50/245 and A/50/1027.

[7] *2010 Review Conference of the Parties to the Treaty on the Non-Proliferation of Nuclear Weapons, Final Document*, vol. I (NPT/CONF.2010/50 (Vol. I)), part I, *Conclusions and recommendations for follow-on actions*, sect. IV.

[8] See *1995 Review and Extension Conference of the Parties to the Treaty on the Non-Proliferation of Nuclear Weapons, Final Document, Part I* (NPT/CONF.1995/32 (Part I) and NPT/CONF.1995/32 (Part I)/Corr.2), annex.

Action by the General Assembly

Date: 6 December 2021   Meeting: 45th plenary meeting
Vote: 157-6-24   Report: A/76/447
      164-3-7, p.p. 5
      165-3-7, p.p. 6

Sponsors

Algeria, Bahrain, Comoros, Djibouti, **Egypt** (on behalf of the States Members of the United Nations that are members of the League of Arab States), Iraq, Jordan, Kuwait, Lebanon, Libya, Mauritania, Morocco, Oman, Qatar, Saudi Arabia, Somalia, Sudan, Tunisia, United Arab Emirates, Yemen, State of Palestine

Recorded vote

As a whole

In favour

Afghanistan, Algeria, Andorra, Angola, Antigua and Barbuda, Argentina, Armenia, Austria, Azerbaijan, Bahamas, Bahrain, Bangladesh, Barbados, Belarus, Belize, Bhutan, Bolivia (Plurinational State of), Bosnia and Herzegovina, Botswana, Brazil, Brunei Darussalam, Bulgaria, Burkina Faso, Burundi, Cabo Verde, Cambodia, Chad, Chile, China, Colombia, Comoros, Congo, Costa Rica, Cuba, Cyprus, Democratic People's Republic of Korea, Djibouti, Dominica, Dominican Republic, Ecuador, Egypt, El Salvador, Equatorial Guinea, Eritrea, Ethiopia, Fiji, Finland, Gabon, Gambia, Ghana, Greece, Grenada, Guatemala, Guinea, Guinea-Bissau, Guyana, Haiti, Honduras, Iceland, Indonesia, Iran (Islamic Republic of), Iraq, Ireland, Jamaica, Japan, Jordan, Kazakhstan, Kenya, Kiribati, Kuwait, Kyrgyzstan, Lao People's Democratic Republic, Lebanon, Lesotho, Liberia, Libya, Liechtenstein, Madagascar, Malawi, Malaysia, Maldives, Mali, Malta, Mauritania, Mauritius, Mexico, Mongolia, Montenegro, Morocco, Mozambique, Myanmar, Namibia, Nauru, Nepal, New Zealand, Nicaragua, Niger, Nigeria, North Macedonia, Norway, Oman, Pakistan, Papua New Guinea, Paraguay, Peru, Philippines, Portugal, Qatar, Republic of Korea, Republic of Moldova, Russian Federation, Rwanda, Saint Kitts and Nevis, Saint Lucia, Saint Vincent and the Grenadines, Samoa, San Marino, Sao Tome and Principe, Saudi Arabia, Senegal, Serbia, Sierra Leone, Singapore, Slovakia, Slovenia, Solomon Islands, Somalia, South Africa, Spain, Sri Lanka, Sudan, Suriname, Sweden, Switzerland, Syrian Arab Republic, Tajikistan, Thailand, Timor-Leste, Togo, Tonga, Trinidad and Tobago, Tunisia, Turkey, Turkmenistan, Tuvalu, Uganda, Ukraine, United Arab Emirates, United Republic of Tanzania, Uruguay, Uzbekistan, Vanuatu, Venezuela (Bolivarian Republic of), Viet Nam, Yemen, Zambia, Zimbabwe

Against

Canada, Israel, Marshall Islands, Micronesia (Federated States of), Palau, United States

Abstaining

Albania, Australia, Belgium, Cameroon, Côte d'Ivoire, Croatia, Czechia, Denmark, Estonia, France, Georgia, Germany, Hungary, India, Italy, Latvia, Lithuania, Luxembourg, Monaco, Netherlands, Panama, Poland, Romania, United Kingdom

Fifth preambular paragraph*

In favour

Afghanistan, Albania, Algeria, Andorra, Angola, Antigua and Barbuda, Argentina, Armenia, Australia, Austria, Azerbaijan, Bahamas, Bahrain, Bangladesh, Barbados, Belarus, Belgium, Belize, Bolivia (Plurinational State of), Bosnia and Herzegovina, Botswana, Brazil, Brunei Darussalam, Bulgaria, Burkina Faso, Burundi, Cabo Verde, Cambodia, Canada, Chad, Chile, China, Colombia, Comoros, Costa Rica, Côte d'Ivoire, Croatia, Cuba, Cyprus, Czechia, Denmark, Djibouti, Dominica, Dominican Republic, Ecuador, Egypt, El Salvador, Eritrea, Estonia, Eswatini, Ethiopia, Fiji, Finland, Gambia, Germany, Ghana, Greece, Grenada, Guatemala, Guinea, Guinea-Bissau, Guyana, Haiti, Honduras, Hungary, Iceland, Indonesia, Iran (Islamic Republic of), Iraq, Ireland, Italy, Jamaica, Japan, Jordan, Kazakhstan, Kenya, Kiribati, Kuwait, Kyrgyzstan, Lao People's Democratic Republic, Latvia, Lebanon, Lesotho, Liberia, Libya, Liechtenstein, Lithuania, Luxembourg, Malawi, Malaysia, Maldives, Mali, Malta, Mauritania, Mauritius, Mexico, Monaco, Mongolia, Montenegro, Morocco, Mozambique, Myanmar, Namibia, Nepal, Netherlands, New Zealand, Nicaragua, Niger, North Macedonia, Norway, Oman, Papua New Guinea, Paraguay, Peru, Philippines, Poland, Portugal, Qatar, Republic of Korea, Republic of Moldova, Romania, Russian Federation, Rwanda, Saint Lucia, Saint Vincent and the Grenadines, Samoa, San Marino, Sao Tome and Principe, Saudi Arabia, Senegal, Serbia, Sierra Leone, Singapore, Slovakia, Slovenia, Somalia, South Africa, Spain, Sri Lanka, Sudan, Suriname, Sweden, Switzerland, Syrian Arab Republic, Tajikistan, Thailand, Timor-Leste, Togo, Trinidad and Tobago, Tunisia, Turkey, Turkmenistan, Uganda, Ukraine, United Arab Emirates, United Kingdom, United Republic of Tanzania, Uruguay, Uzbekistan, Vanuatu, Venezuela (Bolivarian Republic of), Viet Nam, Yemen, Zambia

Against

India, Israel, Pakistan

---

* Subsequently, the delegation of Gabon informed the Secretariat that it had not intended to participate; the delegation of Madagascar informed the Secretariat that it had intended to vote in favour.

Abstaining
> Bhutan, France, Gabon, Georgia, Madagascar, Panama, United States

Sixth preambular paragraph*

In favour
> Afghanistan, Albania, Algeria, Andorra, Angola, Antigua and Barbuda, Argentina, Armenia, Australia, Austria, Azerbaijan, Bahamas, Bahrain, Bangladesh, Barbados, Belarus, Belgium, Belize, Bolivia (Plurinational State of), Bosnia and Herzegovina, Botswana, Brazil, Brunei Darussalam, Bulgaria, Burkina Faso, Burundi, Cabo Verde, Cambodia, Canada, Chad, Chile, China, Colombia, Comoros, Costa Rica, Côte d'Ivoire, Croatia, Cuba, Cyprus, Czechia, Denmark, Djibouti, Dominica, Dominican Republic, Ecuador, Egypt, El Salvador, Eritrea, Estonia, Eswatini, Ethiopia, Fiji, Finland, Gambia, Germany, Ghana, Greece, Grenada, Guatemala, Guinea, Guinea-Bissau, Guyana, Haiti, Honduras, Hungary, Iceland, Indonesia, Iran (Islamic Republic of), Iraq, Ireland, Italy, Jamaica, Japan, Jordan, Kazakhstan, Kenya, Kiribati, Kuwait, Kyrgyzstan, Lao People's Democratic Republic, Latvia, Lebanon, Lesotho, Liberia, Libya, Liechtenstein, Lithuania, Luxembourg, Malawi, Malaysia, Maldives, Mali, Malta, Mauritania, Mauritius, Mexico, Monaco, Mongolia, Montenegro, Morocco, Mozambique, Myanmar, Namibia, Nepal, Netherlands, New Zealand, Nicaragua, Niger, North Macedonia, Norway, Oman, Papua New Guinea, Paraguay, Peru, Philippines, Poland, Portugal, Qatar, Republic of Korea, Republic of Moldova, Romania, Russian Federation, Rwanda, Saint Lucia, Saint Vincent and the Grenadines, Samoa, San Marino, Sao Tome and Principe, Saudi Arabia, Senegal, Serbia, Sierra Leone, Singapore, Slovakia, Slovenia, Somalia, South Africa, Spain, Sri Lanka, Sudan, Suriname, Sweden, Switzerland, Syrian Arab Republic, Tajikistan, Thailand, Timor-Leste, Togo, Trinidad and Tobago, Tunisia, Turkey, Turkmenistan, Uganda, Ukraine, United Arab Emirates, United Kingdom, United Republic of Tanzania, Uruguay, Uzbekistan, Vanuatu, Venezuela (Bolivarian Republic of), Viet Nam, Yemen, Zambia, Zimbabwe

Against
> India, Israel, Pakistan

Abstaining
> Bhutan, France, Gabon, Georgia, Madagascar, Panama, United States

---

* Subsequently, the delegation of Gabon informed the Secretariat that it had not intended to participate; the delegation of Madagascar informed the Secretariat that it had intended to vote in favour.

Action by the First Committee

Date:	27 October 2021	Meeting:	13th meeting
Vote:	148-6-27	Draft resolution:	A/C.1/76/L.2
	160-3-9, p.p. 5		
	159-3-6, p.p. 6		

Agenda item 104

76/64 Convention on Prohibitions or Restrictions on the Use of Certain Conventional Weapons Which May Be Deemed to Be Excessively Injurious or to Have Indiscriminate Effects

Text

The General Assembly,

Recalling its resolution 75/85 of 7 December 2020,

Recalling with satisfaction the adoption and entry into force of the Convention on Prohibitions or Restrictions on the Use of Certain Conventional Weapons Which May Be Deemed to Be Excessively Injurious or to Have Indiscriminate Effects[1] and its amended article 1,[2] the Protocol on Non-Detectable Fragments (Protocol I),[3] the Protocol on Prohibitions or Restrictions on the Use of Mines, Booby Traps and Other Devices (Protocol II)[4] and its amended version,[5] the Protocol on Prohibitions or Restrictions on the Use of Incendiary Weapons (Protocol III),[6] the Protocol on Blinding Laser Weapons (Protocol IV)[7] and the Protocol on Explosive Remnants of War (Protocol V),[8]

Recalling the results of the Fifth Review Conference of the High Contracting Parties to the Convention, held in Geneva from 12 to 16 December 2016,

Taking into account that, due to the extraordinary circumstances related to the COVID-19 pandemic, the 2020 Meeting of the High Contracting Parties did not take place, and technical decisions were adopted by silence procedure,

Taking note of the informal consultations of the High Contracting Parties and close cooperation with each other in 2020 on issues related to the operation of the Convention,

Welcoming the technical decisions by the High Contracting Parties to the Convention of 3 May 2021,

Welcoming also the technical decisions by the High Contracting Parties to Amended Protocol II of 14 April 2021,

---

[1] United Nations, *Treaty Series*, vol. 1342, No. 22495.
[2] Ibid., vol. 2260, No. 22495.
[3] Ibid., vol. 1342, No. 22495.
[4] Ibid., vol. 1342, No. 22495.
[5] Ibid., vol. 2048, No. 22495.
[6] Ibid., vol. 1342, No. 22495.
[7] Ibid., vol. 2024, No. 22495.
[8] Ibid., vol. 2399, No. 22495.

Welcoming further the technical decisions by the High Contracting Parties to Protocol V of 13 April 2021,

Noting with satisfaction that the Meeting of the Group of Experts of the High Contracting Parties to Amended Protocol II, the Meeting of Experts of the High Contracting Parties to Protocol V and two out of the three planned sessions of the Group of Governmental Experts related to emerging technologies in the area of lethal autonomous weapons systems of the High Contracting Parties to the Convention were already held in 2021,

Recalling the role played by the International Committee of the Red Cross in the elaboration of the Convention and the Protocols thereto, and welcoming the particular efforts of various international, non-governmental and other organizations in raising awareness of the humanitarian consequences of various categories of conventional weapons which may be deemed to be excessively injurious or to have indiscriminate effects,

Emphasizing the importance of the perspectives of women, men, boys and girls in considering the issues addressed by the Convention and its Protocols,

1. *Calls upon* all States that have not yet done so to take all measures to become parties, as soon as possible, to the Convention on Prohibitions or Restrictions on the Use of Certain Conventional Weapons Which May Be Deemed to Be Excessively Injurious or to Have Indiscriminate Effects and the Protocols thereto, as amended, with a view to achieving the widest possible adherence to these instruments at an early date and so as to ultimately achieve their universality;

2. *Calls upon* all High Contracting Parties to the Convention that have not yet done so to express their consent to be bound by the Protocols to the Convention and the amendment extending the scope of the Convention and the Protocols thereto to include armed conflicts of a non-international character;

3. *Emphasizes* the importance of the universalization of the Protocol on Explosive Remnants of War (Protocol V);

4. *Welcomes* additional ratifications and acceptances of or accessions to the Convention, as well as consents to be bound by the Protocols thereto;

5. *Acknowledges* the continued efforts of the Secretary-General, as depositary of the Convention and the Protocols thereto, and of the respective office holders of the conferences of the High Contracting Parties to the Convention, Protocol V and Amended Protocol II, on behalf of the High Contracting Parties, to achieve the goal of universality;

6. *Recalls* the following decisions by the Fifth Review Conference of the High Contracting Parties to the Convention:

(a) To establish an open-ended Group of Governmental Experts related to emerging technologies in the area of lethal autonomous weapons systems in the context of the objectives and purposes of the Convention, adhering to the agreed recommendations contained in document CCW/CONF.V/2, and to submit a report to the 2017 Meeting of the High Contracting Parties to the Convention consistent with those recommendations;

(b)   To add to the agenda of the next Meeting of the High Contracting Parties in 2017 the item "Protocol III";

(c)   To add to the agenda of the next Meeting of the High Contracting Parties in 2017 the item "Mines other than anti-personnel mines";[9]

(d)   To add to the agenda of the next Meeting of the High Contracting Parties in 2017 the item for informal discussion "Consideration of how developments in the field of science and technology relevant to the Convention may be addressed under the Convention";

(e)   To invite the Chair-elect to conduct consultations with a view to including on the agenda of the 2017 annual Meeting of the High Contracting Parties the item "Strengthening the respect for international humanitarian law and addressing, in the context and objectives of the Convention and its annexed Protocols, the challenges presented by the use of conventional weapons in armed conflicts and their impact on civilians, particularly in areas where there are concentrations of civilians";

(f)   To include on the agenda of the annual Meetings of the High Contracting Parties the item "Financial issues related to the Convention and its annexed Protocols" and to consider at the next such meeting efficiency and cost-saving measures and a report to be prepared by the Chair-elect;

(g)   To retain the practice of keeping summary records only for the final sessions of the future Review Conferences, the meetings of the High Contracting Parties to the Convention, and the Conferences of the High Contracting Parties to Amended Protocol II and Protocol V;

(h)   To continue the Sponsorship Programme;

7.   *Also recalls* the following technical decisions by the High Contracting Parties to the Convention of 3 May 2021:

(a)   To organize a total of 20 days of meetings, to be held in Geneva in 2021, of the Group of Governmental Experts related to emerging technologies in the area of lethal autonomous weapons systems;

(b)   To mandate the President-designate of the Sixth Review Conference of the High Contracting Parties to the Convention to undertake consultations during the intersessional period on possible measures to address all aspects of the financial situation of the Convention;

---

[9] Noting the update included in paragraph 34 of the final report of the 2018 Meeting of the High Contracting Parties to the Convention (CCW/MSP/2018/11).

8.   *Calls upon* all High Contracting Parties to ensure full and prompt compliance with their financial obligations under the Convention and its annexed Protocols;

9.   *Welcomes* the technical decisions by the High Contracting Parties to the Convention pertaining to the Group of Governmental Experts related to emerging technologies in the area of lethal autonomous weapons systems;

10.   *Also welcomes* the commitment by the High Contracting Parties to continue to contribute to the further development of international humanitarian law, and, in this context, to keep under review both the development of new weapons and uses of weapons, which may have indiscriminate effects or cause unnecessary suffering;

11.   *Further welcomes* the commitment of the High Contracting Parties to Protocol V to the effective and efficient implementation of the Protocol and the implementation of the decisions of the First and Second Conferences of the High Contracting Parties to the Protocol establishing a comprehensive framework for the exchange of information and cooperation;

12.   *Notes* that, in conformity with article 8 of the Convention, conferences may be convened to examine amendments to the Convention or to any of the Protocols thereto, to examine additional protocols concerning other categories of conventional weapons not covered by existing Protocols or to review the scope and application of the Convention and the Protocols thereto and to examine any proposed amendments or additional protocols;

13.   *Underlines* the vital role of the full and equal participation of women in decision-making and implementation of the Convention;

14.   *Notes* the work of the meeting of the Preparatory Committee for the Sixth Review Conference held from 6 to 8 September 2021 under the overall responsibility of the President-designate of the Sixth Review Conference;

15.   *Requests* the Secretary-General to render the assistance necessary and to provide such services as may be required for the Sixth Review Conference, to be held from 13 to 17 December 2021, and other annual conferences and expert meetings of the High Contracting Parties to the Convention and of the High Contracting Parties to Amended Protocol II and Protocol V, as well as for any continuation of the work after the meetings;

16.   *Also requests* the Secretary-General, in his capacity as depositary of the Convention and the Protocols thereto, to continue to inform the General Assembly periodically, by electronic means, of ratifications and acceptances of and accessions to the Convention, its amended article 1 and the Protocols;

17.   *Decides* to include in the provisional agenda of its seventy-seventh session the item entitled "Convention on Prohibitions or Restrictions on the Use of Certain Conventional Weapons Which May Be Deemed to Be Excessively Injurious or to Have Indiscriminate Effects".

Action by the General Assembly

  Date: 6 December 2021   Meeting: 45th plenary meeting

  Vote: Adopted without a vote Report: A/76/448

Sponsors

  Netherlands

Action by the First Committee

  Date: 2 November 2021   Meeting: 16th meeting

  Vote: Adopted without a vote Draft resolution: A/C.1/76/L.12

Agenda item 105

76/65   Strengthening of security and cooperation in the Mediterranean region

Text

The General Assembly,

Recalling its previous resolutions on the subject, including resolution 75/86 of 7 December 2020,

Reaffirming the primary role of the Mediterranean countries in strengthening and promoting peace, security and cooperation in the Mediterranean region,

Welcoming the efforts deployed by the Euro-Mediterranean countries to strengthen their cooperation in combating terrorism, in particular through the adoption of the Euro-Mediterranean Code of Conduct on Countering Terrorism by the Euro-Mediterranean Summit, held in Barcelona, Spain, on 27 and 28 November 2005,

Bearing in mind all the previous declarations and commitments, as well as all the initiatives taken by the riparian countries at the recent summits, ministerial meetings and various forums concerning the question of the Mediterranean region,

Recalling, in this regard, the adoption on 13 July 2008 of the Joint Declaration of the Paris Summit for the Mediterranean, which launched a reinforced partnership, named the "Barcelona Process: Union for the Mediterranean", and the common political will to revive efforts to transform the Mediterranean into an area of peace, democracy, cooperation and prosperity,

Welcoming the entry into force of the African Nuclear-Weapon-Free Zone Treaty (Treaty of Pelindaba)[1] as a contribution to the strengthening of peace and security both regionally and internationally,

Recognizing the indivisible character of security in the Mediterranean and that the enhancement of cooperation among Mediterranean countries with a view to promoting the economic and social development of all peoples of the region will contribute significantly to stability, peace and security in the region,

Recognizing also the efforts made so far and the determination of the Mediterranean countries to intensify the process of dialogue and consultations with a view to resolving the problems existing in the Mediterranean region and to eliminating the causes of tension and the consequent threat to peace

---

[1]   A/50/426, annex.

and security, as well as their growing awareness of the need for further joint efforts to strengthen economic, social, cultural and environmental cooperation in the region,

Recognizing further that prospects for closer Euro-Mediterranean cooperation in all spheres can be enhanced by positive developments worldwide, in particular in Europe, in the Maghreb and in the Middle East,

Reaffirming the responsibility of all States to contribute to the stability and prosperity of the Mediterranean region and their commitment to respecting the purposes and principles of the Charter of the United Nations as well as the provisions of the Declaration on Principles of International Law concerning Friendly Relations and Cooperation among States in accordance with the Charter of the United Nations,[2]

Noting the peace negotiations in the Middle East, which should be of a comprehensive nature and represent an appropriate framework for the peaceful settlement of contentious issues in the region,

Expressing concern at the persistent tension and continuing military activities in parts of the Mediterranean that hinder efforts to strengthen security and cooperation in the region,

Taking note of the report of the Secretary-General,[3]

1.　*Reaffirms* that security in the Mediterranean is closely linked to European security as well as to international peace and security;

2.　*Invites* Mediterranean countries to consolidate their efforts in order to contribute actively to the elimination of all causes of tension in the region and to the promotion of just and lasting solutions to the persistent problems of the region through peaceful means, thus ensuring the withdrawal of foreign forces of occupation and respecting the sovereignty, independence and territorial integrity of all countries of the Mediterranean and the right of peoples to self-determination, and therefore calls for full adherence to the principles of non-interference, non-intervention, non-use of force or threat of use of force and the inadmissibility of the acquisition of territory by force, in accordance with the Charter and the relevant resolutions of the United Nations;

3.　*Commends* the Mediterranean countries for their efforts in meeting common challenges through coordinated overall responses, based on a spirit of multilateral partnership, towards the general objective of turning the Mediterranean basin into an area of dialogue, exchanges and cooperation, guaranteeing peace, stability and prosperity, encourages them to strengthen such efforts through, inter alia, a lasting multilateral and action-oriented

---

[2] Resolution 2625 (XXV), annex.
[3] A/76/89.

cooperative dialogue among States of the region, and recognizes the role of the United Nations in promoting regional and international peace and security;

4.   *Recognizes* that the elimination of the economic and social disparities in levels of development and other obstacles, as well as respect and greater understanding among cultures in the Mediterranean area, will contribute to enhancing peace, security and cooperation among Mediterranean countries through the existing forums;

5.   *Highlights* the importance for all countries of the Mediterranean region to adhere to the relevant multilaterally negotiated legal instruments related to the field of disarmament and non-proliferation, thus creating the conditions necessary for strengthening peace and cooperation in the region;

6.   *Encourages* all States of the region to favour the conditions necessary for strengthening the confidence-building measures among them by promoting genuine openness and transparency on all military matters, by participating, inter alia, in the United Nations Report on Military Expenditures and by providing accurate data and information to the United Nations Register of Conventional Arms;

7.   *Encourages* the Mediterranean countries to strengthen further their cooperation in combating terrorism in all its forms and manifestations, including the possible resort by terrorists to weapons of mass destruction, taking into account the relevant resolutions of the United Nations, and in combating international crime and illicit arms transfers and illicit drug production, consumption and trafficking, which pose a serious threat to peace, security and stability in the region and therefore to the improvement of the current political, economic and social situation and which jeopardize friendly relations among States, hinder the development of international cooperation and result in the destruction of human rights, fundamental freedoms and the democratic basis of pluralistic society;

8.   *Requests* the Secretary-General to submit to the General Assembly at its seventy-seventh session a report on means to strengthen security and cooperation in the Mediterranean region;

9.   *Decides* to include in the provisional agenda of its seventy-seventh session the item entitled "Strengthening of security and cooperation in the Mediterranean region".

Action by the General Assembly

Date:	6 December 2021	Meeting:	45th plenary meeting
Vote:	182-1-1	Report:	A/76/449
	173-2-1, o.p. 2		
	170-2-2, o.p. 5		

Sponsors

Algeria, Egypt, Georgia, Iraq, Jordan, Kazakhstan, Libya, Mauritania, Netherlands, Saudi Arabia, Tunisia

Co-sponsors

Cyprus, Eritrea, Greece, Lebanon, Malta, Myanmar, Nigeria, Portugal, Slovenia, Turkey

Recorded vote

As a whole

In favour

Afghanistan, Albania, Algeria, Andorra, Angola, Antigua and Barbuda, Argentina, Armenia, Australia, Austria, Azerbaijan, Bahamas, Bahrain, Bangladesh, Barbados, Belarus, Belgium, Belize, Bhutan, Bolivia (Plurinational State of), Bosnia and Herzegovina, Botswana, Brazil, Brunei Darussalam, Bulgaria, Burkina Faso, Burundi, Cabo Verde, Cambodia, Cameroon, Canada, Central African Republic, Chad, Chile, China, Colombia, Comoros, Congo, Costa Rica, Côte d'Ivoire, Croatia, Cuba, Cyprus, Czechia, Democratic People's Republic of Korea, Denmark, Djibouti, Dominica, Dominican Republic, Ecuador, Egypt, El Salvador, Equatorial Guinea, Eritrea, Estonia, Eswatini, Ethiopia, Fiji, Finland, France, Gabon, Gambia, Georgia, Germany, Ghana, Greece, Grenada, Guatemala, Guinea, Guinea-Bissau, Guyana, Haiti, Honduras, Hungary, Iceland, India, Indonesia, Iraq, Ireland, Italy, Jamaica, Japan, Jordan, Kazakhstan, Kenya, Kiribati, Kuwait, Kyrgyzstan, Lao People's Democratic Republic, Latvia, Lebanon, Lesotho, Liberia, Libya, Liechtenstein, Lithuania, Luxembourg, Madagascar, Malawi, Malaysia, Maldives, Mali, Malta, Mauritania, Mauritius, Mexico, Monaco, Mongolia, Montenegro, Morocco, Mozambique, Myanmar, Namibia, Nepal, Netherlands, New Zealand, Nicaragua, Niger, Nigeria, North Macedonia, Norway, Oman, Pakistan, Panama, Papua New Guinea, Paraguay, Peru, Philippines, Poland, Portugal, Qatar, Republic of Korea, Republic of Moldova, Romania, Russian Federation, Rwanda, Saint Kitts and Nevis, Saint Lucia, Saint Vincent and the Grenadines, Samoa, San Marino, Sao Tome and Principe, Saudi Arabia, Senegal, Serbia, Sierra Leone, Singapore, Slovakia, Slovenia, Solomon Islands, Somalia, South Africa, South Sudan, Spain, Sri Lanka, Sudan, Suriname, Sweden, Switzerland, Syrian Arab Republic, Tajikistan, Thailand, Timor-Leste, Togo, Tonga, Trinidad and Tobago, Tunisia, Turkey, Turkmenistan, Tuvalu, Uganda, Ukraine, United Arab Emirates, United Kingdom, United Republic of Tanzania, Uruguay, Uzbekistan, Vanuatu, Venezuela (Bolivarian Republic of), Viet Nam, Yemen, Zambia

Against
United States

Abstaining
Israel

Operative paragraph 2*

In favour
Afghanistan, Albania, Algeria, Andorra, Angola, Antigua and Barbuda, Argentina, Armenia, Australia, Austria, Azerbaijan, Bahamas, Bahrain, Bangladesh, Barbados, Belarus, Belgium, Belize, Bhutan, Bolivia (Plurinational State of), Bosnia and Herzegovina, Botswana, Brazil, Brunei Darussalam, Bulgaria, Burkina Faso, Burundi, Cabo Verde, Cambodia, Canada, Chad, Chile, China, Colombia, Comoros, Costa Rica, Côte d'Ivoire, Croatia, Cuba, Cyprus, Czechia, Democratic People's Republic of Korea, Denmark, Djibouti, Dominica, Dominican Republic, Ecuador, Egypt, El Salvador, Eritrea, Estonia, Eswatini, Ethiopia, Fiji, Finland, France, Gambia, Georgia, Germany, Ghana, Greece, Grenada, Guatemala, Guinea, Guinea-Bissau, Guyana, Haiti, Honduras, Hungary, Iceland, India, Indonesia, Iran (Islamic Republic of), Iraq, Ireland, Italy, Jamaica, Japan, Jordan, Kazakhstan, Kenya, Kiribati, Kuwait, Kyrgyzstan, Lao People's Democratic Republic, Latvia, Lebanon, Lesotho, Liberia, Libya, Liechtenstein, Lithuania, Luxembourg, Madagascar, Malawi, Malaysia, Maldives, Mali, Malta, Mauritania, Mauritius, Mexico, Monaco, Mongolia, Montenegro, Mozambique, Myanmar, Namibia, Nepal, Netherlands, New Zealand, Nicaragua, Niger, Nigeria, North Macedonia, Norway, Oman, Pakistan, Panama, Papua New Guinea, Paraguay, Peru, Philippines, Poland, Portugal, Qatar, Republic of Korea, Republic of Moldova, Romania, Russian Federation, Rwanda, Saint Lucia, Saint Vincent and the Grenadines, Samoa, San Marino, Sao Tome and Principe, Saudi Arabia, Senegal, Serbia, Sierra Leone, Singapore, Slovakia, Slovenia, Somalia, South Africa, Spain, Sri Lanka, Sudan, Suriname, Sweden, Switzerland, Syrian Arab Republic, Tajikistan, Thailand, Timor-Leste, Togo, Trinidad and Tobago, Tunisia, Turkey, Turkmenistan, Uganda, Ukraine, United Arab Emirates, United Kingdom, United Republic of Tanzania, Uruguay, Uzbekistan, Vanuatu, Venezuela (Bolivarian Republic of), Viet Nam, Yemen, Zambia, Zimbabwe

Against
Israel, United States

Abstaining
Gabon

---

* Subsequently, the delegation of Gabon informed the Secretariat that it had not intended to participate.

Operative paragraph 5*

In favour

> Afghanistan, Albania, Algeria, Andorra, Angola, Antigua and Barbuda, Argentina, Armenia, Australia, Austria, Azerbaijan, Bahamas, Bahrain, Bangladesh, Barbados, Belarus, Belgium, Belize, Bhutan, Bolivia (Plurinational State of), Bosnia and Herzegovina, Botswana, Brazil, Brunei Darussalam, Bulgaria, Burkina Faso, Burundi, Cabo Verde, Cambodia, Canada, Chad, Chile, China, Colombia, Comoros, Costa Rica, Côte d'Ivoire, Croatia, Cuba, Cyprus, Czechia, Democratic People's Republic of Korea, Denmark, Djibouti, Dominica, Dominican Republic, Ecuador, Egypt, El Salvador, Eritrea, Estonia, Eswatini, Ethiopia, Fiji, Finland, France, Gambia, Georgia, Germany, Ghana, Greece, Grenada, Guatemala, Guinea, Guinea-Bissau, Guyana, Haiti, Honduras, Hungary, Iceland, India, Indonesia, Iran (Islamic Republic of), Iraq, Italy, Jamaica, Jordan, Kazakhstan, Kenya, Kiribati, Kuwait, Kyrgyzstan, Lao People's Democratic Republic, Latvia, Lebanon, Lesotho, Liberia, Libya, Liechtenstein, Lithuania, Luxembourg, Madagascar, Malawi, Malaysia, Maldives, Mali, Malta, Mauritania, Mauritius, Mexico, Monaco, Mongolia, Montenegro, Mozambique, Myanmar, Namibia, Nepal, Netherlands, New Zealand, Nicaragua, Niger, Nigeria, North Macedonia, Norway, Oman, Pakistan, Panama, Papua New Guinea, Paraguay, Peru, Philippines, Poland, Portugal, Qatar, Republic of Korea, Republic of Moldova, Romania, Russian Federation, Rwanda, Saint Lucia, Saint Vincent and the Grenadines, Samoa, San Marino, Sao Tome and Principe, Saudi Arabia, Senegal, Serbia, Sierra Leone, Singapore, Slovakia, Slovenia, South Africa, Spain, Sri Lanka, Sudan, Suriname, Sweden, Switzerland, Syrian Arab Republic, Tajikistan, Thailand, Timor-Leste, Togo, Trinidad and Tobago, Tunisia, Turkey, Turkmenistan, Uganda, Ukraine, United Arab Emirates, United Kingdom, United Republic of Tanzania, Uruguay, Uzbekistan, Vanuatu, Venezuela (Bolivarian Republic of), Viet Nam, Yemen, Zambia, Zimbabwe

Against

> Israel, United States

Abstaining

> Gabon, Ireland

Action by the First Committee

Date:	3 November 2021	Meeting:	17th meeting
Vote:	176-1-2	Draft resolution:	A/C.1/76/L.37
	169-2-0, o.p. 2		
	167-2-1, o.p. 5		

---

* Subsequently, the delegation of Gabon informed the Secretariat that it had not intended to participate.

Agenda item 106

76/66   Comprehensive Nuclear-Test-Ban Treaty

Text

The General Assembly,

Reiterating that the cessation of nuclear-weapon test explosions or any other nuclear explosions constitutes an effective nuclear disarmament and non-proliferation measure, and convinced that this is a meaningful step in the realization of a systematic process for achieving nuclear disarmament,

Recalling that the Comprehensive Nuclear-Test-Ban Treaty, adopted by the General Assembly by its resolution 50/245 of 10 September 1996, was opened for signature on 24 September 1996,

Stressing that a universal and effectively verifiable Treaty constitutes a fundamental instrument in the field of nuclear disarmament and non-proliferation and will be a major contribution to international peace and security,

Stressing also the vital importance and urgency of achieving the entry into force of the Treaty, and affirming its resolute determination, 25 years after the Treaty was opened for signature, to achieve its entry into force,

Encouraged by the signing of the Treaty by 185 States, including 41 of the 44 whose ratification is needed for its entry into force, and welcoming the ratification of the Treaty by 170 States, including 36 of the 44 whose ratification is needed for its entry into force, among which there are 3 nuclear-weapon States,

Recalling its resolution 75/87 of 7 December 2020,

Recalling also the adoption by consensus of the conclusions and recommendations for follow-on actions of the 2010 Review Conference of the Parties to the Treaty on the Non-Proliferation of Nuclear Weapons,[1] in which the Conference, inter alia, reaffirmed the vital importance of the entry into force of the Comprehensive Nuclear-Test-Ban Treaty as a core element of the international nuclear disarmament and non-proliferation regime and included specific actions to be taken in support of the entry into force of the Treaty,

Recalling further the Final Declaration adopted by the twelfth Conference on Facilitating the Entry into Force of the Comprehensive Nuclear-Test-Ban Treaty, held in New York on 23 and 24 September 2021, convened pursuant to article XIV of the Treaty, and recalling the message issued by the Friends of the Comprehensive Nuclear-Test-Ban Treaty on 1 October 2020,

---

[1] *2010 Review Conference of the Parties to the Treaty on the Non-Proliferation of Nuclear Weapons, Final Document*, vol. I (NPT/CONF.2010/50 (Vol. I)), part I, *Conclusions and recommendations for follow-on actions*.

Noting the contribution of diverse and inclusive participation in building and sustaining momentum for the universalization and entry into force of the Treaty, including through the Youth Group of the Preparatory Commission for the Comprehensive Nuclear-Test-Ban Treaty Organization,

Welcoming continuing progress in the development of the Treaty's verification regime, which advances the Treaty's primary non-proliferation and disarmament objective, and the establishment of 302 certified facilities of the International Monitoring System network,

Recognizing the civil and scientific benefits provided by the Treaty's global monitoring system,

Commending the Preparatory Commission for the Comprehensive Nuclear-Test-Ban Treaty Organization for maintaining its vital operations, including that of the International Monitoring System and the International Data Centre, during the coronavirus disease (COVID-19) pandemic,

1.   *Stresses* the vital importance and urgency of signature and ratification, without delay and without conditions, in order to achieve the earliest entry into force of the Comprehensive Nuclear-Test-Ban Treaty;[2]

2.   *Welcomes* the contributions by the signatory States to the work of the Preparatory Commission for the Comprehensive Nuclear-Test-Ban Treaty Organization, in particular its efforts to ensure that the verification regime of the Treaty will be capable of meeting the verification requirements of the Treaty upon its entry into force, in accordance with article IV of the Treaty, and encourages their continuation;

3.   *Underlines* the need to maintain momentum towards the completion of all elements of the verification regime;

4.   *Urges* all States not to carry out nuclear-weapon test explosions or any other nuclear explosions, to maintain their moratoriums in this regard and to refrain from acts that would defeat the object and purpose of the Treaty, while stressing that these measures do not have the same permanent and legally binding effect as the entry into force of the Treaty;

5.   *Reiterates its condemnation* of the six nuclear tests conducted by the Democratic People's Republic of Korea in violation of relevant Security Council resolutions,[3] urges full compliance with the obligations under those resolutions, including that the Democratic People's Republic of Korea abandon its nuclear weapons programme and not conduct any further nuclear tests, reaffirms its support for the complete, verifiable and irreversible denuclearization of the Korean Peninsula in a peaceful manner, including through the Six-Party Talks, welcomes all efforts and dialogue to this end,

---

[2] See resolution 50/245 and A/50/1027.
[3] Including Security Council resolutions 1718 (2006), 1874 (2009), 2094 (2013), 2270 (2016), 2321 (2016) and 2375 (2017).

including the inter-Korean summits and summits between the United States of America and the Democratic People's Republic of Korea, and encourages all parties to continue such efforts and dialogue;

6. *Urges* all States that have not yet signed or ratified, or that have signed but not yet ratified, the Treaty, in particular those whose ratification is needed for its entry into force, to sign and ratify it as soon as possible and to accelerate their ratification processes with a view to ensuring their earliest successful conclusion;

7. *Welcomes*, since the adoption of its previous resolution on the subject, the signature and ratification of the Treaty by Cuba and the ratification of the Treaty by the Comoros, since each signature or ratification is a significant step towards the entry into force and universalization of the Treaty;

8. *Encourages* further expressions from among the remaining States whose ratification is needed for the Treaty to enter into force of their intention to pursue and complete the ratification process;

9. *Welcomes* the election by States signatories to the Comprehensive Nuclear-Test-Ban Treaty of Robert Floyd as the Executive Secretary of the Preparatory Commission for the Comprehensive Nuclear-Test-Ban Treaty Organization;

10. *Urges* all States to remain seized of the issue at the highest political level and, where in a position to do so, to promote adherence to the Treaty through bilateral and joint outreach, seminars and other means;

11. *Decides* to include in the provisional agenda of its seventy-seventh session the item entitled "Comprehensive Nuclear-Test-Ban Treaty".

Action by the General Assembly

Date:	6 December 2021	Meeting:	45th plenary meeting
Vote:	182-1-3	Report:	A/76/450
	176-0-5, p.p. 7		

Sponsors

Australia, Austria, Belgium, Bosnia and Herzegovina, Bulgaria, Canada, Chile, Costa Rica, Croatia, Czechia, Denmark, Estonia, Finland, Germany, Hungary, Iceland, Iraq, Ireland, Italy, Japan, Kazakhstan, Kiribati, Lao People's Democratic Republic, Latvia, Lithuania, Luxembourg, Malaysia, **Mexico**, Netherlands, **New Zealand**, North Macedonia, Norway, Paraguay, Philippines, Poland, Portugal, Republic of Korea, Republic of Moldova, San Marino, Slovakia, Spain, Sweden, Switzerland, Turkey, United Kingdom

Co-sponsors

Albania, Andorra, Argentina, Armenia, Belize, Bolivia (Plurinational State of), Botswana, Côte d'Ivoire, Cyprus, Ecuador, Eswatini, Fiji, France, Georgia, Ghana, Greece, Honduras, Kenya, Kyrgyzstan, Lebanon, Lesotho, Liechtenstein, Maldives, Malta, Micronesia (Federated States of), Monaco, Mongolia, Montenegro, Morocco, Namibia, Nigeria, Palau, Papua New Guinea, Peru, Romania, Samoa, Senegal, Serbia, Singapore, Slovenia, South Africa, Sri Lanka, Thailand, Ukraine, United States, Zambia

Recorded vote

As a whole*

In favour

Afghanistan, Albania, Algeria, Andorra, Angola, Antigua and Barbuda, Argentina, Armenia, Australia, Austria, Azerbaijan, Bahamas, Bahrain, Bangladesh, Barbados, Belarus, Belgium, Belize, Bhutan, Bolivia (Plurinational State of), Bosnia and Herzegovina, Botswana, Brazil, Brunei Darussalam, Bulgaria, Burkina Faso, Burundi, Cabo Verde, Cambodia, Cameroon, Canada, Central African Republic, Chad, Chile, China, Colombia, Comoros, Congo, Costa Rica, Côte d'Ivoire, Croatia, Cuba, Cyprus, Czechia, Denmark, Djibouti, Dominica, Dominican Republic, Ecuador, Egypt, El Salvador, Equatorial Guinea, Eritrea, Estonia, Eswatini, Ethiopia, Fiji, Finland, Gabon, Gambia, Georgia, Germany, Ghana, Greece, Grenada, Guatemala, Guinea, Guinea-Bissau, Guyana, Haiti, Honduras, Hungary, Iceland, Indonesia, Iran (Islamic Republic of), Iraq, Ireland, Israel, Italy, Jamaica, Japan, Jordan, Kazakhstan, Kenya, Kiribati, Kuwait, Kyrgyzstan, Lao People's Democratic Republic, Latvia, Lebanon, Lesotho, Liberia, Libya, Liechtenstein, Lithuania, Luxembourg, Madagascar, Malawi, Malaysia, Maldives, Mali, Malta, Marshall Islands, Mauritania, Mexico, Micronesia (Federated States of), Monaco, Mongolia, Montenegro, Morocco, Mozambique, Myanmar, Namibia, Nauru, Nepal, Netherlands, New Zealand, Nicaragua, Niger, Nigeria, North Macedonia, Norway, Oman, Pakistan, Palau, Panama, Papua New Guinea, Paraguay, Peru, Philippines, Poland, Portugal, Qatar, Republic of Korea, Romania, Russian Federation, Rwanda, Saint Lucia, Saint Vincent and the Grenadines, Samoa, San Marino, Sao Tome and Principe, Saudi Arabia, Senegal, Serbia, Seychelles, Sierra Leone, Singapore, Slovakia, Slovenia, Solomon Islands, South Africa, Spain, Sri Lanka, Sudan, Suriname, Sweden, Switzerland, Tajikistan, Thailand, Timor-Leste, Togo, Tonga, Trinidad and Tobago, Tunisia, Turkey, Turkmenistan, Tuvalu, Uganda, Ukraine, United Arab Emirates, United Kingdom, United Republic of

---

* Subsequently, the delegation of France informed the Secretariat that it had intended to vote in favour.

Tanzania, United States, Uruguay, Uzbekistan, Vanuatu, Venezuela (Bolivarian Republic of), Viet Nam, Yemen, Zambia, Zimbabwe

Against

Democratic People's Republic of Korea

Abstaining

India, Mauritius, Syrian Arab Republic

Seventh preambular paragraph*

In favour

Afghanistan, Albania, Algeria, Andorra, Angola, Antigua and Barbuda, Argentina, Armenia, Australia, Austria, Azerbaijan, Bahamas, Bahrain, Bangladesh, Barbados, Belarus, Belgium, Belize, Bhutan, Bolivia (Plurinational State of), Bosnia and Herzegovina, Botswana, Brazil, Brunei Darussalam, Bulgaria, Burkina Faso, Burundi, Cabo Verde, Cambodia, Canada, Chad, Chile, China, Colombia, Comoros, Costa Rica, Côte d'Ivoire, Croatia, Cuba, Cyprus, Czechia, Denmark, Djibouti, Dominica, Dominican Republic, Ecuador, Egypt, El Salvador, Eritrea, Estonia, Eswatini, Ethiopia, Fiji, Finland, France, Gambia, Georgia, Germany, Ghana, Greece, Grenada, Guatemala, Guinea, Guinea-Bissau, Guyana, Haiti, Honduras, Hungary, Iceland, Indonesia, Iran (Islamic Republic of), Iraq, Ireland, Italy, Jamaica, Japan, Jordan, Kazakhstan, Kenya, Kiribati, Kuwait, Kyrgyzstan, Lao People's Democratic Republic, Latvia, Lebanon, Lesotho, Liberia, Libya, Liechtenstein, Lithuania, Luxembourg, Madagascar, Malawi, Malaysia, Maldives, Mali, Malta, Marshall Islands, Mauritania, Mexico, Micronesia (Federated States of), Monaco, Mongolia, Montenegro, Morocco, Mozambique, Myanmar, Namibia, Nepal, Netherlands, New Zealand, Nicaragua, Niger, Nigeria, North Macedonia, Norway, Oman, Palau, Panama, Papua New Guinea, Paraguay, Peru, Philippines, Poland, Portugal, Qatar, Republic of Korea, Republic of Moldova, Romania, Russian Federation, Rwanda, Saint Lucia, Saint Vincent and the Grenadines, Samoa, San Marino, Sao Tome and Principe, Saudi Arabia, Senegal, Serbia, Seychelles, Sierra Leone, Singapore, Slovakia, Slovenia, Solomon Islands, Somalia, South Africa, Spain, Sri Lanka, Sudan, Suriname, Sweden, Switzerland, Tajikistan, Thailand, Timor-Leste, Togo, Trinidad and Tobago, Tunisia, Turkey, Turkmenistan, Tuvalu, Uganda, Ukraine, United Arab Emirates, United Kingdom, United Republic of Tanzania, United States, Uruguay, Uzbekistan, Vanuatu, Venezuela (Bolivarian Republic of), Viet Nam, Yemen, Zambia, Zimbabwe

Against

None

---

* Subsequently, the delegation of Gabon informed the Secretariat that it had not intended to participate.

Abstaining
Gabon, India, Israel, Pakistan, Syrian Arab Republic

Action by the First Committee

Date:	27 October 2021	Meeting:	13th meeting
Vote:	Adopted without a vote* 170-0-6, p.p. 7	Draft resolution:	A/C.1/76/L.49

---

* Subsequent to adoption by the First Committee, a request was made for a vote on the resolution as a whole in the General Assembly.

Agenda item 107

76/67 Convention on the Prohibition of the Development, Production and Stockpiling of Bacteriological (Biological) and Toxin Weapons and on Their Destruction

Text

The General Assembly,

Recalling its previous resolutions relating to the complete and effective prohibition of bacteriological (biological) and toxin weapons and on their destruction,

Noting that there has been no increase in the number of ratifications of and accessions to the Convention on the Prohibition of the Development, Production and Stockpiling of Bacteriological (Biological) and Toxin Weapons and on Their Destruction,[1] and stressing at the same time that there is a continuing need to achieve its universalization,

Reaffirming its call upon all signatory States that have not yet ratified the Convention to do so without delay, and calling upon those States that have not signed the Convention to become parties thereto at the earliest possible date, thus contributing to the achievement of universal adherence to the Convention, which will facilitate its success,

Bearing in mind its call upon all States parties to the Convention to participate in the implementation of the recommendations of the review conferences of the parties to the Convention, including the exchange of information and data agreed to in the Final Declaration of the Third Review Conference of the Parties to the Convention on the Prohibition of the Development, Production and Stockpiling of Bacteriological (Biological) and Toxin Weapons and on Their Destruction, later amended by the Final Declaration of the Seventh Review Conference, and to provide such information and data in conformity with the standardized procedure to the Implementation Support Unit within the Office for Disarmament Affairs of the Secretariat on an annual basis and no later than 15 April,

Welcoming the reaffirmation made in the Final Declarations of the Fourth, Sixth, Seventh and Eighth Review Conferences that under all circumstances the use of bacteriological (biological) and toxin weapons and their development, production and stockpiling are effectively prohibited under article I of the Convention,

Recognizing the importance of ongoing efforts by States parties to enhance international cooperation, assistance and the fullest possible

---

[1] United Nations, *Treaty Series*, vol. 1015, No. 14860.

exchange of equipment, materials and scientific and technological information for the use of bacteriological (biological) agents and toxins for peaceful purposes, recognizing also that there still remain challenges to be overcome in order to enhance international cooperation, and recognizing further the value of building capacity through international cooperation as well as strengthening coordination and coherence of efforts of all relevant international organizations, in line with the Final Document of the Eighth Review Conference,[2]

Reaffirming the importance of national measures, in accordance with constitutional processes, in strengthening the implementation of the Convention by States parties, in line with the Final Document of the Eighth Review Conference,

Reaffirming also the importance of the review of developments in the field of science and technology related to the Convention,

Encouraging the equitable participation of women and men in the framework of the Convention,

Recalling previous intersessional processes carried out under the Convention,

Noting, in the decisions and recommendations of the Final Document, that the Eighth Review Conference decided that States parties would hold annual meetings and that the first such meeting would start on 4 December 2017, have a duration of up to five days and seek to make progress on issues of substance and process for the period before the next Review Conference, with a view to reaching consensus on an intersessional process,

Recalling the decision of the Eighth Review Conference that the Ninth Review Conference shall be held in Geneva not later than 2021,

1. *Notes* the consensus outcome of and the decisions on all provisions of the Convention on the Prohibition of the Development, Production and Stockpiling of Bacteriological (Biological) and Toxin Weapons and on Their Destruction reached at the Eighth Review Conference of the Parties to the Convention, and calls upon States parties to the Convention to participate and actively engage in their continued implementation;

2. *Notes with appreciation* that the meeting of States parties to the Convention, held in Geneva from 4 to 8 December 2017, was able to reach consensus on reaffirming previous intersessional programmes carried out during the period 2003–2015, on retaining the previous structure of annual meetings of States parties preceded by annual meetings of experts, and on reaffirming that the purpose of the intersessional programme was to discuss, and promote common understanding and effective action on, those issues

---

[2] BWC/CONF.VIII/4 and BWC/CONF.VIII/4/Corr.1.

identified for inclusion in the intersessional programme, and that the work of the intersessional period would be guided by the aim of strengthening the implementation of all articles of the Convention in order to better respond to current challenges;[3]

3.   *Also notes with appreciation* that, in the light of the need to balance an ambition to improve the intersessional programme within the financial and human resources constraints facing States parties, 12 days were allocated to the intersessional programme each year from 2018 to 2020, that the meetings of experts for eight days would be held back to back and at least three months before the annual meetings of States parties of four days each, and that the meetings of experts would be open-ended and would consider the following topics: cooperation and assistance, with a particular focus on strengthening cooperation and assistance under article X (two days); review of developments in the field of science and technology related to the Convention (two days); strengthening national implementation (one day); assistance, response and preparedness (two days); and institutional strengthening of the Convention (one day);

4.   *Appreciates* the information and data on confidence-building measures provided by States parties to the Convention to date, and calls upon all States parties to participate in the exchange of information and data on confidence-building measures called for in the relevant decisions of the review conferences, and invites them to make use of the new platform for electronic submission, on a voluntary basis, without prejudice to their choice of methods for submission;

5.   *Notes* the decision of the Eighth Review Conference to continue and improve the database established by the Seventh Review Conference to facilitate requests for and offers of exchange of assistance and cooperation, and urges States parties to submit to the Implementation Support Unit, on a voluntary basis, requests for and offers of cooperation and assistance, including in terms of equipment, materials and scientific and technological information regarding the use of biological and toxin agents for peaceful purposes;

6.   *Encourages* States parties to provide, at least biannually, appropriate information on their implementation of article X of the Convention and to collaborate to offer assistance or training, upon request, as contained in specific proposals, in support of the legislative and other implementation measures of States parties needed to ensure their compliance with the Convention;

7.   *Notes* the decision of the Eighth Review Conference to renew the sponsorship programme established by the Seventh Review Conference in order to support and increase the participation of developing States parties in

---

[3] See BWC/MSP/2017/6.

the annual meetings, welcomes the continued willingness among States parties to provide voluntary contributions, and calls upon States parties in a position to do so to offer voluntary contributions for the programme;

8.   *Also notes* the decision of the Eighth Review Conference to renew the mandate of the Implementation Support Unit agreed to at the Seventh Review Conference, mutatis mutandis, for the period from 2017 to 2021, and notes with appreciation the work of the Unit;

9.   *Notes with appreciation* the events organized by some States parties, regional organizations and the Office for Disarmament Affairs of the Secretariat for exchanges of views on the implementation of the Convention, and encourages States parties to continue to participate in such informal exchanges and discussions;

10.   *Requests* the Secretary-General to continue to render the necessary assistance to the depositary Governments of the Convention and to continue to provide such services as may be required for the conduct and the implementation of the decisions and recommendations of the review conferences;

11.   *Recalls* that the meeting of States parties in Geneva in December 2018 agreed that the financial difficulties of the Convention stemmed from three principal sources, namely the non-payment of contributions by some States parties, delays in the receipt of contributions from other States parties and the financial requirements of the United Nations with respect to activities not funded from its regular budget, and calls upon States parties to consider ways of addressing these serious issues as a matter of urgency;

12.   *Notes* that the meeting of States parties in Geneva in December 2019 welcomed the improvement of the financial situation for that year, following the measures endorsed by the meeting of States parties in 2018, including the establishment of the working capital fund, and stressed the need to continue monitoring the financial situation of the Convention and requested the Chair of the 2020 meeting of States parties, in close consultation with the States parties, the Implementation Support Unit, the Office for Disarmament Affairs and the United Nations Office at Geneva, to report on the overall financial situation of the Convention, implementation of the measures endorsed in 2018, and possible further measures, in a transparent way and taking into account outstanding credits for those States parties that paid their contribution in full, to bring about timely payment as required, for consideration by the 2020 meeting of States parties;[4]

13.   *Encourages* the meeting of States parties in 2021 to consider and to agree upon arrangements for the Ninth Review Conference, and its

---

[4] BWC/MSP/2019/7, para. 23.

Preparatory Committee, taking into account section VIII of the report of the 2019 meeting of States parties;[5]

14.   *Decides* to include in the provisional agenda of its seventy-seventh session the item entitled "Convention on the Prohibition of the Development, Production and Stockpiling of Bacteriological (Biological) and Toxin Weapons and on Their Destruction".

Action by the General Assembly

Date: 6 December 2021   Meeting: 45th plenary meeting
Vote: Adopted without a vote   Report: A/76/451

Sponsors

Hungary

Action by the First Committee

Date: 27 October 2021   Meeting: 14th meeting
Vote: Adopted without a vote   Draft resolution: A/C.1/76/L.35

---

[5] Ibid., paras. 31–32.

Agenda item 98 (c)

76/230 Further practical measures for the prevention of an arms race in outer space

Text

The General Assembly,

Recalling its resolutions 71/31 and 71/32 of 5 December 2016, 71/90 of 6 December 2016, 72/250 of 24 December 2017, 73/6 of 26 October 2018, 73/91 of 7 December 2018 and 74/34 of 12 December 2019 and its decisions 73/512 of 5 December 2018 and 75/514 of 7 December 2020, as well as its other resolutions and decisions on this subject,

Expressing grave alarm over the threat of an arms race in outer space, which would impair the prospects for limiting and reducing armaments in general and erect insurmountable barriers to international cooperation in the peaceful exploration of outer space,

Recognizing the catastrophic consequences of an arms race in outer space, which should be used exclusively for peaceful and creative purposes, or any military conflicts in outer space and that the prevention of an arms race in outer space would avert a grave danger for international peace and security,

Emphasizing the importance of article IV of the Treaty on Principles Governing the Activities of States in the Exploration and Use of Outer Space, including the Moon and Other Celestial Bodies,[1]

Bearing in mind that all States, in particular those with major space capabilities, should contribute actively to the prevention of an arms race in outer space with a view to promoting and strengthening international cooperation in the exploration and use of outer space for peaceful purposes, with the objective of shaping a community of shared future for humankind,

Recognizing that, while the existing international treaties related to outer space and the legal regime provided for therein play a positive role in regulating outer space activities, they are unable to fully prevent an arms race in outer space, the placement of weapons in outer space and the threat or use of force in outer space, from space against Earth and from Earth against objects in outer space, and preserve outer space for peaceful purposes, and that there is a need to consolidate and reinforce this regime,

Expressing serious concern over the plans declared by certain States that include placement of weapons, in particular strike combat systems, in outer space, the threat or use of force in outer space, from space against Earth and from Earth against objects in outer space and the use of outer space for combat operations,

---

[1] United Nations, *Treaty Series*, vol. 610, No. 8843.

Convinced that further measures should be examined in the search for effective and verifiable bilateral and multilateral agreements in order to prevent an arms race in outer space and preserve outer space for peaceful purposes,

Welcoming, in this regard, the draft treaty on the prevention of the placement of weapons in outer space and of the threat or use of force against outer space objects, introduced by China and the Russian Federation at the Conference on Disarmament in 2008,[2] and the submission of its updated version in 2014,[3]

Stressing the importance of the political statements made by a number of States[4] that they would not be the first to place weapons in outer space,

Recognizing the primary role and responsibility of the Conference on Disarmament in the negotiation of a multilateral agreement or agreements on the prevention of an arms race in outer space,

Taking into account the work done by the Group of Governmental Experts on Further Practical Measures for the Prevention of an Arms Race in Outer Space in 2018 and 2019 in the search for further practical measures for the prevention of an arms race in outer space, in particular in the course of future negotiations at the Conference on Disarmament on the international legally binding instrument in this regard,

1.   *Proclaims* it a historic responsibility of all States to ensure that the exploration of outer space is carried out exclusively for peaceful purposes for the benefit of mankind;

2.   *Declares* that the exclusion of outer space from the sphere of the arms race and the preservation of outer space for peaceful purposes should become a mandatory norm of State policy and a generally recognized international obligation;

3.   *Calls upon* all States, and above all those with major space capabilities, to this end:

(a)   To take urgent measures to prevent for all time the placement of weapons in outer space and the threat or use of force in outer space, from space against Earth and from Earth against objects in outer space;

(b)   To seek through negotiations the early elaboration of appropriate reliably verifiable legally binding multilateral agreements;

---

[2]   See CD/1839.

[3]   See CD/1985.

[4]   Argentina, Armenia, Belarus, Bolivia (Plurinational State of), Brazil, Burundi, Cambodia, Congo, Cuba, Ecuador, Guatemala, Indonesia, Kazakhstan, Kyrgyzstan, Myanmar, Nicaragua, Pakistan, Russian Federation, Seychelles, Sierra Leone, Sri Lanka, Suriname, Syrian Arab Republic, Tajikistan, Togo, Turkmenistan, Uruguay, Uzbekistan, Venezuela (Bolivarian Republic of) and Viet Nam.

4. *Expresses its deep regret* over the years of stalemate in the work of the Conference on Disarmament, and looks forward to the Conference again fulfilling its mandate as the single multilateral disarmament negotiating forum;

5. *Urges* the Conference on Disarmament to agree on and implement at its earliest opportunity a balanced and comprehensive programme of work that includes the immediate commencement of negotiations on an international legally binding instrument on the prevention of an arms race in outer space, including on the prevention of the placement of weapons in outer space and of the threat or use of force in outer space, from space against Earth and from Earth against objects in outer space;

6. *Acknowledges* that the guaranteed prevention of an arms race in outer space will provide an opportunity for the peaceful exploration of outer space and its use in solving acute major problems relating to economic, social and cultural development facing mankind today, as well as in consolidating the efforts of States of the world in this domain;

7. *Requests* the Secretary-General, within existing resources, to seek the views and proposals of Member States on the provision of guarantees for the prevention of an arms race in outer space and preserving outer space for peaceful purposes, and to submit a substantive report, with an annex containing those views, to the General Assembly at its seventy-seventh session, for further discussion by Member States;

8. *Decides* to include in the provisional agenda of its seventy-seventh session, under the item entitled "Prevention of an arms race in outer space", the sub-item entitled "Further practical measures for the prevention of an arms race in outer space".

Action by the General Assembly

Date: 24 December 2021   Meeting: 54th plenary meeting
Vote: 114-9-44   Report: A/76/442
       109-46-6, p.p. 5
       107-18-35, o.p. 7

Sponsors

Armenia, Cuba, Egypt, Kyrgyzstan, Lao People's Democratic Republic, Nicaragua, **Russian Federation**, Syrian Arab Republic, Uzbekistan, Zimbabwe

Co-sponsors

Belarus, Bolivia (Plurinational State of), China, Comoros, Dominica, Ecuador, Equatorial Guinea, Eritrea, Eswatini, Ethiopia, Iran (Islamic Republic of), Kazakhstan, Madagascar, Myanmar, Somalia, South Africa, Tajikistan, Turkmenistan, Venezuela (Bolivarian Republic of), Zambia

Recorded vote

As a whole

In favour

Algeria, Angola, Argentina, Armenia, Azerbaijan, Bahamas, Bahrain, Bangladesh, Barbados, Belarus, Bhutan, Bolivia (Plurinational State of), Botswana, Brunei Darussalam, Burkina Faso, Burundi, Cambodia, Cameroon, Central African Republic, Chad, Chile, China, Colombia, Comoros, Congo, Costa Rica, Côte d'Ivoire, Cuba, Democratic People's Republic of Korea, Djibouti, Dominica, Dominican Republic, Ecuador, Egypt, El Salvador, Equatorial Guinea, Eritrea, Ethiopia, Fiji, Gambia, Ghana, Grenada, Guatemala, Guinea, Guinea-Bissau, Guyana, Honduras, India, Indonesia, Iran (Islamic Republic of), Iraq, Jamaica, Jordan, Kazakhstan, Kenya, Kiribati, Kuwait, Kyrgyzstan, Lao People's Democratic Republic, Lebanon, Lesotho, Liberia, Libya, Madagascar, Malaysia, Maldives, Mali, Mauritania, Mauritius, Mexico, Mongolia, Morocco, Mozambique, Myanmar, Namibia, Nepal, Nicaragua, Nigeria, Oman, Pakistan, Panama, Paraguay, Peru, Philippines, Qatar, Russian Federation, Saint Lucia, Saint Vincent and the Grenadines, Saudi Arabia, Senegal, Serbia, Singapore, Somalia, South Africa, Sri Lanka, Sudan, Suriname, Syrian Arab Republic, Tajikistan, Thailand, Timor-Leste, Togo, Trinidad and Tobago, Tunisia, Turkmenistan, Uganda, United Arab Emirates, United Republic of Tanzania, Uruguay, Uzbekistan, Venezuela (Bolivarian Republic of), Viet Nam, Yemen, Zimbabwe

Against

Australia, Canada, France, Israel, Japan, Marshall Islands, Ukraine, United Kingdom, United States

Abstaining

Albania, Andorra, Austria, Belgium, Bosnia and Herzegovina, Brazil, Bulgaria, Croatia, Cyprus, Czechia, Denmark, Estonia, Finland, Georgia, Germany, Greece, Hungary, Iceland, Ireland, Italy, Latvia, Liechtenstein, Lithuania, Luxembourg, Malta, Monaco, Montenegro, Netherlands, New Zealand, North Macedonia, Norway, Papua New Guinea, Poland, Portugal, Republic of Korea, Republic of Moldova, Romania, San Marino, Slovakia, Slovenia, Spain, Sweden, Switzerland, Turkey

Fifth preambular paragraph*

In favour

Algeria, Angola, Argentina, Armenia, Bahamas, Bahrain, Bangladesh, Barbados, Belarus, Bhutan, Bolivia (Plurinational State of), Botswana, Brazil, Brunei Darussalam, Burkina Faso, Burundi, Cambodia, Cameroon,

---

* Subsequently, the delegation of Zambia informed the Secretariat that it had intended to abstain.

Central African Republic, Chad, Chile, China, Colombia, Comoros, Congo, Costa Rica, Côte d'Ivoire, Cuba, Democratic People's Republic of Korea, Djibouti, Dominica, Dominican Republic, Ecuador, Egypt, El Salvador, Equatorial Guinea, Eritrea, Ethiopia, Fiji, Ghana, Grenada, Guatemala, Guinea, Guinea-Bissau, Guyana, Haiti, Honduras, Indonesia, Iran (Islamic Republic of), Jamaica, Jordan, Kazakhstan, Kenya, Kiribati, Kuwait, Kyrgyzstan, Lao People's Democratic Republic, Lebanon, Lesotho, Libya, Madagascar, Malaysia, Maldives, Mali, Mauritania, Mexico, Mongolia, Morocco, Mozambique, Myanmar, Namibia, Nepal, Nicaragua, Nigeria, Oman, Pakistan, Panama, Paraguay, Peru, Philippines, Qatar, Russian Federation, Saint Lucia, Saint Vincent and the Grenadines, Saudi Arabia, Senegal, Singapore, Somalia, South Africa, Sri Lanka, Sudan, Suriname, Syrian Arab Republic, Tajikistan, Thailand, Timor-Leste, Togo, Trinidad and Tobago, Tunisia, Turkmenistan, Uganda, United Arab Emirates, United Republic of Tanzania, Uruguay, Uzbekistan, Venezuela (Bolivarian Republic of), Viet Nam, Yemen, Zimbabwe

Against

Albania, Andorra, Australia, Austria, Belgium, Bulgaria, Canada, Croatia, Cyprus, Czechia, Denmark, Estonia, Finland, France, Georgia, Germany, Greece, Hungary, Iceland, India, Ireland, Israel, Italy, Japan, Latvia, Liechtenstein, Lithuania, Luxembourg, Malta, Monaco, Montenegro, Netherlands, North Macedonia, Norway, Poland, Portugal, Republic of Korea, Romania, San Marino, Slovakia, Slovenia, Spain, Sweden, Ukraine, United Kingdom, United States

Abstaining

Bosnia and Herzegovina, New Zealand, Papua New Guinea, Republic of Moldova, Switzerland, Turkey

Operative paragraph 7*

In favour

Algeria, Angola, Argentina, Armenia, Bahrain, Bangladesh, Barbados, Belarus, Bolivia (Plurinational State of), Botswana, Brunei Darussalam, Burkina Faso, Burundi, Cambodia, Cameroon, Central African Republic, Chad, Chile, China, Colombia, Comoros, Congo, Costa Rica, Côte d'Ivoire, Cuba, Democratic People's Republic of Korea, Djibouti, Dominica, Dominican Republic, Ecuador, Egypt, El Salvador, Equatorial Guinea, Eritrea, Ethiopia, Fiji, Gambia, Ghana, Grenada, Guatemala, Guinea, Guinea-Bissau, Guyana, Honduras, Indonesia, Iran (Islamic Republic of), Jamaica, Jordan, Kazakhstan, Kenya, Kiribati, Kuwait, Kyrgyzstan, Lao People's Democratic Republic, Lebanon, Lesotho, Libya, Madagascar, Malaysia, Maldives, Mali, Mauritania, Mexico, Mongolia,

---

* Subsequently, the delegation of Iraq informed the Secretariat that it had intended to vote in favour; the delegation of Zambia informed the Secretariat that it had intended to abstain.

Morocco, Mozambique, Myanmar, Namibia, Nepal, Nicaragua, Nigeria, Oman, Pakistan, Panama, Paraguay, Peru, Philippines, Qatar, Russian Federation, Saint Lucia, Saint Vincent and the Grenadines, Saudi Arabia, Senegal, Singapore, Somalia, South Africa, Sri Lanka, Sudan, Suriname, Switzerland, Syrian Arab Republic, Tajikistan, Thailand, Timor-Leste, Togo, Trinidad and Tobago, Tunisia, Turkmenistan, Uganda, United Arab Emirates, United Republic of Tanzania, Uruguay, Uzbekistan, Venezuela (Bolivarian Republic of), Viet Nam, Yemen, Zimbabwe

Against

Albania, Andorra, Canada, Czechia, Denmark, Estonia, France, Germany, Israel, Japan, Latvia, Lithuania, Monaco, Poland, Spain, Ukraine, United Kingdom, United States

Abstaining

Australia, Austria, Belgium, Bhutan, Bosnia and Herzegovina, Brazil, Bulgaria, Croatia, Cyprus, Finland, Georgia, Greece, Hungary, Iceland, India, Ireland, Italy, Liechtenstein, Luxembourg, Malta, Montenegro, Netherlands, New Zealand, North Macedonia, Norway, Papua New Guinea, Portugal, Republic of Korea, Republic of Moldova, Romania, San Marino, Slovakia, Slovenia, Sweden, Turkey

Action by the First Committee

Date: 1 November 2021   Meeting: 15th meeting
Vote: 126-9-46   Draft resolution: A/C.1/76/L.53
      112-47-10, p.p. 5
      112-19-38, o.p. 7

Agenda item 98 (d)

76/231 Reducing space threats through norms, rules and principles of responsible behaviours

Text

The General Assembly,

Recalling its resolutions 68/50 of 5 December 2013 and 75/35 of 7 December 2020,

Recalling also its resolution 75/36 of 7 December 2020, in which it requested the Secretary-General to seek the views of Member States on the further development and implementation of norms, rules and principles of responsible behaviours and on the reduction of the risks of misunderstanding and miscalculations with respect to outer space, and to submit a substantive report, with an annex containing these views, to the General Assembly at its seventy-sixth session,

Reaffirming the applicability of international law, including the Charter of the United Nations, to activities in outer space and the right of all States to explore and use outer space without discrimination of any kind, on a basis of equality and in accordance with such law, and emphasizing the importance of full compliance with such law,

Reaffirming also the Treaty on Principles Governing the Activities of States in the Exploration and Use of Outer Space, including the Moon and Other Celestial Bodies,[1] and the obligations for States parties to the Treaty to explore and use outer space for the benefit and in the interests of all countries, and to be guided by the principle of cooperation and mutual assistance,

Welcoming the ongoing work by the Committee on the Peaceful Uses of Outer Space on the implementation of the 21 Guidelines for the Long-term Sustainability of Outer Space Activities,[2] which may have a positive effect on international peace and security,

Emphasizing the need to maintain outer space as a peaceful, safe, stable, secure and sustainable environment for the benefit of all and the significant contribution of outer space activities to social, economic, scientific and technological development, as well as to international peace and security,

Urging all States, when developing, planning and executing their space activities, to remain committed to the peaceful exploration and use of outer space and to refrain from conducting activities contrary to their obligations

---

[1] United Nations, *Treaty Series*, vol. 610, No. 8843.
[2] *Official Records of the General Assembly, Seventy-fourth Session, Supplement No. 20* (A/74/20), annex II.

under international law, including those that could threaten the ability of all States to freely use and explore outer space, now and in the future,

Stressing that the creation of long-lived orbital debris arising from the deliberate destruction of space systems increases the risk of in-orbit collisions and the potential for misunderstanding and miscalculations that could lead to conflict,

Seriously concerned about the possibility of an arms race in outer space, and reaffirming that the prevention of an arms race in outer space would avert a grave danger for international peace and security, as well as being an essential condition for the promotion and strengthening of international cooperation in the exploration and use of outer space for peaceful purposes,

Recalling paragraph 80 of the Final Document of the Tenth Special Session of the General Assembly,[3] in which it is stated that, in order to prevent an arms race in outer space, further measures should be taken and appropriate international negotiations held in accordance with the spirit of the Treaty on Principles Governing the Activities of States in the Exploration and Use of Outer Space, including the Moon and Other Celestial Bodies,

Convinced that possible solutions to outer space security can involve a combination of legally binding obligations and political commitments, and that work in both of these areas can be further pursued in a progressive, sustained and complementary manner, without undermining existing legal obligations,

Recalling the primary role of the Conference on Disarmament on questions relating to the prevention of an arms race in outer space in all its aspects, including the weaponization of outer space and threats from capabilities on Earth, and the relevant responsibilities of the First Committee of the General Assembly and the Disarmament Commission,

Noting the rapid advances of technologies in space systems, the use of which could have positive or negative effects on international security, and encouraging further discussion among States of the impact of these developments,

Recognizing that efforts to prevent an arms race and to prevent conflict from beginning in or extending into outer space must include consideration of the use of all potential technologies and means, whether on Earth or in outer space,

Stressing that uses of these technologies and means for purposes inconsistent with the objectives of maintaining international stability and security, including against signals for operators and users and the terrestrial infrastructure supporting space systems, can lead to the perception of threats

---

[3] Resolution S-10/2.

on Earth as well as in outer space and can have destabilizing effects on peace and security, and that such threats already exist in outer space and on Earth,

Recognizing the need for States to seek to avoid and mitigate the potential impact on peace and security arising from accidents, miscommunication or a lack of transparency, which could lead to miscalculations and the escalation of tensions and contribute to an arms race,

Reiterating the need for all States to work together to reduce threats to space systems through the further development and implementation of norms, rules and principles of responsible behaviours with the aim of maintaining a peaceful, safe, stable, secure and sustainable outer space environment, which might, as appropriate and without prejudice, contribute to further consideration of legally binding instruments on the prevention of an arms race in outer space,

Reaffirming that verification is one of the essential components of legally binding arms control instruments, and encouraging further consideration of effective verification regarding space systems,

Recognizing the importance of the full involvement and equal participation of women and men in discussions on reducing space threats through responsible behaviours and the need to assess the possible differentiated impacts of such threats,

1. *Affirms* that all States must conduct their activities in the exploration and use of outer space, including the Moon and other celestial bodies, in conformity with international law, including the Charter of the United Nations, and urges Member States to take this into account when formulating their space policies;

2. *Encourages* those States that have not yet become parties to the international treaties governing the exploration and use of outer space to give consideration to ratifying or acceding to those treaties in accordance with their national law, as well as incorporating them into their national legislation;

3. *Expresses the desire* that all Member States reach a common understanding of how best to act to reduce threats to space systems in order to maintain outer space as a peaceful, safe, stable and sustainable environment, free from an arms race and conflict, for the benefit of all, and consider establishing channels of direct communication, including for the management of perceptions of threat;

4. *Welcomes* the report of the Secretary-General to the General Assembly pursuant to its resolution 75/36,[4] and his recommendation that Member States study the ideas contained therein and decide on an inclusive

---

[4] A/76/77.

process to take these issues forward at the seventy-sixth session of the General Assembly;

5.   *Decides* to convene, beginning in 2022, an open-ended working group:

(a)   To take stock of the existing international legal and other normative frameworks concerning threats arising from State behaviours with respect to outer space;

(b)   To consider current and future threats by States to space systems, and actions, activities and omissions that could be considered irresponsible;

(c)   To make recommendations on possible norms, rules and principles of responsible behaviours relating to threats by States to space systems, including, as appropriate, how they would contribute to the negotiation of legally binding instruments, including on the prevention of an arms race in outer space;

(d)   To submit a report to the General Assembly at its seventy-eighth session;

6.   *Also decides* that the open-ended working group shall work on the basis of consensus, hold its organizational session in Geneva for two days, and meet in Geneva for two sessions of five days each in both 2022 and 2023, with the participation of intergovernmental organizations and other entities having received a standing invitation to participate as observers in the work of the General Assembly, as well as organizations and bodies of the United Nations, and with the attendance of other international organizations, commercial actors and civil society representatives, in accordance with established practice, and further decides that the Chair may also hold intersessional consultative meetings with interested parties to exchange views on the issues within the mandate of the open-ended working group;

7.   *Requests* the Secretary-General to provide all necessary assistance to the open-ended working group and its Chair and to transmit its report to the Conference on Disarmament and the Disarmament Commission;

8.   *Continues to invite* States members and observers of the Conference on Disarmament and the Disarmament Commission to inform those bodies of their national space security policies, strategies or doctrines, on a voluntary basis, in accordance with and in support of the mandates of those bodies;

9.   *Decides* to include in the provisional agenda of its seventy-seventh session, under the item entitled "Prevention of an arms race in outer space", the sub-item entitled "Reducing space threats through norms, rules and principles of responsible behaviours".

Action by the General Assembly

Date: 24 December 2021   Meeting: 54th plenary meeting
Vote: 150-8-7   Report: A/76/442
      143-4-13, o.p. 3
      143-9-6, o.p. 5 (a)
      140-9-7, o.p. 5 (b)
      139-9-7, o.p. 5 (c)

Sponsors

Australia, Belgium, Bulgaria, Canada, Chile, Croatia, Czechia, Denmark, Estonia, Finland, France, Germany, Greece, Hungary, Iceland, Italy, Japan, Latvia, Lithuania, Luxembourg, Montenegro, Netherlands, North Macedonia, Norway, Poland, Portugal, Republic of Korea, Republic of Moldova, Romania, Slovakia, Slovenia, Spain, Sweden, Switzerland, Ukraine, **United Kingdom**, United States

Co-sponsors

Albania, Cyprus, Georgia, New Zealand, Turkey

Recorded vote

As a whole*

In favour

Albania, Algeria, Andorra, Angola, Argentina, Australia, Austria, Azerbaijan, Bahamas, Bahrain, Bangladesh, Barbados, Belgium, Bhutan, Bolivia (Plurinational State of), Bosnia and Herzegovina, Botswana, Brunei Darussalam, Bulgaria, Burkina Faso, Burundi, Cameroon, Canada, Chad, Chile, Colombia, Comoros, Congo, Costa Rica, Côte d'Ivoire, Croatia, Cyprus, Czechia, Denmark, Djibouti, Dominican Republic, Ecuador, Egypt, El Salvador, Equatorial Guinea, Eritrea, Estonia, Ethiopia, Fiji, Finland, France, Gambia, Georgia, Germany, Ghana, Greece, Grenada, Guatemala, Guinea-Bissau, Guyana, Haiti, Honduras, Hungary, Iceland, Indonesia, Iraq, Ireland, Italy, Jamaica, Japan, Jordan, Kazakhstan, Kenya, Kiribati, Kuwait, Lao People's Democratic Republic, Latvia, Lebanon, Lesotho, Liberia, Libya, Liechtenstein, Lithuania, Luxembourg, Madagascar, Malaysia, Maldives, Mali, Malta, Marshall Islands, Mauritania, Mauritius, Mexico, Micronesia (Federated States of), Monaco, Mongolia, Montenegro, Morocco, Mozambique, Myanmar, Namibia, Nepal, Netherlands, New Zealand, Nigeria, North Macedonia, Norway, Oman, Palau, Panama, Papua New Guinea, Paraguay, Peru, Philippines, Poland, Portugal, Qatar, Republic of Korea, Republic of

---

* Subsequently, the delegation of South Africa informed the Secretariat that it had intended to vote against.

Moldova, Romania, Saint Lucia, Saint Vincent and the Grenadines, San Marino, Saudi Arabia, Senegal, Serbia, Singapore, Slovakia, Slovenia, Solomon Islands, Somalia, South Africa, Spain, Sri Lanka, Sudan, Suriname, Sweden, Switzerland, Thailand, Timor-Leste, Togo, Trinidad and Tobago, Tunisia, Turkey, Uganda, Ukraine, United Arab Emirates, United Kingdom, United Republic of Tanzania, United States, Uruguay, Uzbekistan, Viet Nam, Yemen, Zambia

Against

China, Cuba, Democratic People's Republic of Korea, Iran (Islamic Republic of), Nicaragua, Russian Federation, Syrian Arab Republic, Venezuela (Bolivarian Republic of)

Abstaining

Armenia, Belarus, Central African Republic, India, Israel, Pakistan, Tajikistan

Operative paragraph 3*

In favour

Albania, Algeria, Andorra, Angola, Argentina, Australia, Austria, Bahamas, Bahrain, Bangladesh, Barbados, Belgium, Bhutan, Bolivia (Plurinational State of), Bosnia and Herzegovina, Botswana, Brazil, Brunei Darussalam, Bulgaria, Burundi, Canada, Chad, Chile, Colombia, Comoros, Costa Rica, Côte d'Ivoire, Croatia, Cyprus, Czechia, Denmark, Djibouti, Dominica, Ecuador, Egypt, El Salvador, Eritrea, Estonia, Ethiopia, Fiji, Finland, France, Gambia, Georgia, Germany, Ghana, Greece, Grenada, Guatemala, Guinea, Guinea-Bissau, Guyana, Haiti, Honduras, Hungary, Iceland, Indonesia, Iraq, Ireland, Italy, Jamaica, Japan, Jordan, Kazakhstan, Kenya, Kiribati, Kuwait, Lao People's Democratic Republic, Latvia, Lebanon, Lesotho, Liberia, Libya, Liechtenstein, Lithuania, Luxembourg, Malaysia, Maldives, Mali, Malta, Marshall Islands, Mauritania, Mexico, Micronesia (Federated States of), Monaco, Mongolia, Montenegro, Morocco, Mozambique, Myanmar, Namibia, Nepal, Netherlands, New Zealand, Nigeria, North Macedonia, Norway, Oman, Panama, Papua New Guinea, Paraguay, Peru, Philippines, Poland, Portugal, Qatar, Republic of Korea, Republic of Moldova, Romania, Saint Lucia, Saint Vincent and the Grenadines, San Marino, Saudi Arabia, Senegal, Singapore, Slovakia, Slovenia, Somalia, South Africa, Spain, Sri Lanka, Sudan, Suriname, Sweden, Switzerland, Thailand, Timor-Leste, Togo, Trinidad and Tobago, Tunisia, Turkey, Uganda, Ukraine, United Arab Emirates, United Kingdom, United Republic of Tanzania, United States, Uruguay, Uzbekistan, Viet Nam, Yemen, Zambia, Zimbabwe

---

* Subsequently, the delegation of the Dominican Republic informed the Secretariat that it had intended to vote in favour.

Against

Central African Republic, India, Iran (Islamic Republic of), Syrian Arab Republic

Abstaining

Belarus, Burkina Faso, China, Cuba, Democratic People's Republic of Korea, Dominican Republic, Equatorial Guinea, Israel, Madagascar, Nicaragua, Pakistan, Russian Federation, Venezuela (Bolivarian Republic of)

Operative paragraph 5 (a)

In favour

Albania, Algeria, Andorra, Angola, Argentina, Australia, Austria, Bahamas, Bahrain, Bangladesh, Barbados, Belgium, Bhutan, Bolivia (Plurinational State of), Bosnia and Herzegovina, Botswana, Brazil, Brunei Darussalam, Bulgaria, Burundi, Canada, Chad, Chile, Colombia, Comoros, Costa Rica, Côte d'Ivoire, Croatia, Cyprus, Czechia, Denmark, Djibouti, Dominican Republic, Ecuador, Egypt, El Salvador, Eritrea, Estonia, Ethiopia, Fiji, Finland, France, Gambia, Georgia, Germany, Ghana, Greece, Grenada, Guatemala, Guinea, Guinea-Bissau, Guyana, Haiti, Honduras, Hungary, Iceland, Indonesia, Iraq, Ireland, Italy, Jamaica, Japan, Jordan, Kazakhstan, Kenya, Kiribati, Kuwait, Lao People's Democratic Republic, Latvia, Lebanon, Lesotho, Liberia, Libya, Liechtenstein, Lithuania, Luxembourg, Malaysia, Maldives, Mali, Malta, Marshall Islands, Mauritania, Mexico, Micronesia (Federated States of), Monaco, Mongolia, Montenegro, Morocco, Mozambique, Myanmar, Namibia, Nepal, Netherlands, New Zealand, Nigeria, North Macedonia, Norway, Oman, Panama, Papua New Guinea, Paraguay, Peru, Philippines, Poland, Portugal, Qatar, Republic of Korea, Republic of Moldova, Romania, Saint Lucia, Saint Vincent and the Grenadines, San Marino, Saudi Arabia, Senegal, Singapore, Slovakia, Slovenia, Somalia, South Africa, Spain, Sri Lanka, Sudan, Suriname, Sweden, Switzerland, Thailand, Timor-Leste, Togo, Trinidad and Tobago, Tunisia, Turkey, Uganda, Ukraine, United Arab Emirates, United Kingdom, United Republic of Tanzania, United States, Uruguay, Uzbekistan, Viet Nam, Yemen, Zambia, Zimbabwe

Against

China, Cuba, Democratic People's Republic of Korea, India, Iran (Islamic Republic of), Nicaragua, Russian Federation, Syrian Arab Republic, Venezuela (Bolivarian Republic of)

Abstaining

Belarus, Burkina Faso, Central African Republic, Israel, Madagascar, Pakistan

Operative paragraph 5 (b)*

In favour

Albania, Algeria, Andorra, Angola, Argentina, Australia, Austria, Bahamas, Bahrain, Bangladesh, Barbados, Belgium, Bhutan, Bolivia (Plurinational State of), Bosnia and Herzegovina, Botswana, Brazil, Brunei Darussalam, Bulgaria, Burundi, Canada, Chad, Chile, Colombia, Comoros, Costa Rica, Côte d'Ivoire, Croatia, Cyprus, Czechia, Denmark, Djibouti, Dominican Republic, Ecuador, Egypt, El Salvador, Eritrea, Estonia, Ethiopia, Fiji, Finland, France, Gambia, Georgia, Germany, Ghana, Greece, Grenada, Guatemala, Guinea-Bissau, Guyana, Honduras, Hungary, Iceland, Indonesia, Iraq, Ireland, Italy, Jamaica, Japan, Jordan, Kazakhstan, Kenya, Kiribati, Kuwait, Lao People's Democratic Republic, Latvia, Lebanon, Lesotho, Liberia, Libya, Liechtenstein, Lithuania, Luxembourg, Malaysia, Maldives, Mali, Malta, Marshall Islands, Mauritania, Mexico, Micronesia (Federated States of), Monaco, Mongolia, Montenegro, Morocco, Mozambique, Myanmar, Namibia, Nepal, Netherlands, New Zealand, Nigeria, North Macedonia, Norway, Oman, Panama, Papua New Guinea, Paraguay, Peru, Philippines, Poland, Portugal, Qatar, Republic of Korea, Republic of Moldova, Romania, Saint Lucia, Saint Vincent and the Grenadines, San Marino, Saudi Arabia, Senegal, Singapore, Slovakia, Slovenia, Somalia, South Africa, Spain, Sri Lanka, Sudan, Suriname, Sweden, Switzerland, Thailand, Timor-Leste, Togo, Trinidad and Tobago, Tunisia, Turkey, Uganda, Ukraine, United Arab Emirates, United Kingdom, United States, Uruguay, Uzbekistan, Viet Nam, Yemen, Zambia, Zimbabwe

Against

China, Cuba, Democratic People's Republic of Korea, India, Iran (Islamic Republic of), Nicaragua, Russian Federation, Syrian Arab Republic, Venezuela (Bolivarian Republic of)

Abstaining

Belarus, Burkina Faso, Central African Republic, Guinea, Israel, Madagascar, Pakistan

Operative paragraph 5 (c)**

In favour

Albania, Algeria, Andorra, Angola, Argentina, Australia, Austria, Bahamas, Bahrain, Bangladesh, Barbados, Belgium, Bhutan, Bolivia (Plurinational State of), Bosnia and Herzegovina, Botswana, Brazil, Brunei Darussalam, Bulgaria, Burundi, Canada, Chad, Chile, Colombia, Comoros, Costa Rica, Côte d'Ivoire, Croatia, Cyprus, Czechia, Denmark, Djibouti, Dominican

---

* Subsequently, the delegation of South Africa informed the Secretariat that it had intended to vote against.

** Subsequently, the delegation of South Africa informed the Secretariat that it had intended to vote against.

Republic, Ecuador, Egypt, El Salvador, Eritrea, Estonia, Ethiopia, Fiji, Finland, France, Gambia, Georgia, Germany, Ghana, Greece, Grenada, Guatemala, Guinea-Bissau, Guyana, Honduras, Hungary, Iceland, Indonesia, Iraq, Ireland, Italy, Jamaica, Japan, Jordan, Kazakhstan, Kenya, Kiribati, Kuwait, Lao People's Democratic Republic, Latvia, Lebanon, Lesotho, Liberia, Libya, Liechtenstein, Lithuania, Luxembourg, Malaysia, Maldives, Mali, Malta, Marshall Islands, Mauritania, Mexico, Micronesia (Federated States of), Monaco, Mongolia, Montenegro, Morocco, Mozambique, Myanmar, Namibia, Nepal, Netherlands, New Zealand, Nigeria, North Macedonia, Norway, Oman, Panama, Papua New Guinea, Peru, Philippines, Poland, Portugal, Qatar, Republic of Korea, Republic of Moldova, Romania, Saint Lucia, Saint Vincent and the Grenadines, San Marino, Saudi Arabia, Senegal, Singapore, Slovakia, Slovenia, Somalia, South Africa, Spain, Sri Lanka, Sudan, Suriname, Sweden, Switzerland, Thailand, Timor-Leste, Togo, Trinidad and Tobago, Tunisia, Turkey, Uganda, Ukraine, United Arab Emirates, United Kingdom, United States, Uruguay, Uzbekistan, Viet Nam, Yemen, Zambia, Zimbabwe

Against

China, Cuba, Democratic People's Republic of Korea, India, Iran (Islamic Republic of), Nicaragua, Russian Federation, Syrian Arab Republic, Venezuela (Bolivarian Republic of)

Abstaining

Belarus, Burkina Faso, Central African Republic, Guinea, Israel, Madagascar, Pakistan

Action by the First Committee

Date:	1 November 2021	Meeting:	15th meeting
Vote:	163-8-9	Draft resolution:	A/C.1/76/L.52
	148-3-15, o.p. 3		
	147-9-9, o.p. 5 (a)		
	147-9-9, o.p. 5 (b)		
	146-9-9, o.p. 5 (c)		

Agenda item 100 (p)

76/232 The illicit trade in small arms and light weapons in all its aspects

Text

The General Assembly,

Recalling its resolution 75/241 of 31 December 2020, as well as all previous resolutions on the illicit trade in small arms and light weapons in all its aspects, including resolution 56/24 V of 24 December 2001,

Emphasizing the importance of the continued and full implementation of the Programme of Action to Prevent, Combat and Eradicate the Illicit Trade in Small Arms and Light Weapons in All Its Aspects, adopted by the United Nations Conference on the Illicit Trade in Small Arms and Light Weapons in All Its Aspects,[1] and recognizing its important contribution to international efforts on this matter,

Emphasizing also the importance of the continued and full implementation of the International Instrument to Enable States to Identify and Trace, in a Timely and Reliable Manner, Illicit Small Arms and Light Weapons (the International Tracing Instrument),[2]

Recalling the commitment of States to the Programme of Action as the main framework for measures within the activities of the international community to prevent, combat and eradicate the illicit trade in small arms and light weapons in all its aspects,

Underlining the need for States to enhance their efforts to build national capacity for the effective implementation of the Programme of Action and the International Tracing Instrument,

Mindful of the implementation of the outcomes adopted by the follow-up meetings on the Programme of Action,

Welcoming the successful conclusion of the Seventh Biennial Meeting of States to Consider the Implementation of the Programme of Action to Prevent, Combat and Eradicate the Illicit Trade in Small Arms and Light Weapons in All Its Aspects, held in New York from 26 to 30 July 2021, to consider the full and effective implementation of the Programme of Action, and the outcome document adopted at the Meeting,[3]

---

[1] *Report of the United Nations Conference on the Illicit Trade in Small Arms and Light Weapons in All Its Aspects, New York, 9–20 July 2001* (A/CONF.192/15), chap. IV, para. 24.

[2] See decision 60/519 and A/60/88 and A/60/88/Corr.2, annex.

[3] A/CONF.192/BMS/2021/1, annex.

Recognizing the need for the strengthened participation of women in decision-making and implementation processes relating to the Programme of Action and the International Tracing Instrument, and reaffirming the need for States to mainstream gender dimensions into their implementation efforts,

Noting that web-based tools developed by the Secretariat, including its searchable database and the Modular Small-arms-control Implementation Compendium, and the tools developed by Member States could be used to assess progress made in the implementation of the Programme of Action,

Reaffirming the acknowledgement, by the third United Nations Conference to Review Progress Made in the Implementation of the Programme of Action to Prevent, Combat and Eradicate the Illicit Trade in Small Arms and Light Weapons in All Its Aspects (the third Review Conference) in its outcome document,[4] as welcomed by the Seventh Biennial Meeting of States, of the proposal on the establishment of a dedicated fellowship training programme on small arms and light weapons in order to strengthen technical knowledge and expertise in areas relating to the implementation of the Programme of Action and the International Tracing Instrument, in particular in developing countries,

Welcoming the series of open, informal consultations held by the Chair-designate of the Seventh Biennial Meeting of States during the first part of 2021,

Noting that voluntary national reports on the implementation of the Programme of Action can serve, inter alia, to provide a baseline for measuring progress in its implementation, build confidence and promote transparency, provide a basis for information exchange and action and serve to identify needs and opportunities for international assistance and cooperation, including the matching of needs with available resources and expertise,

Noting with satisfaction regional and subregional efforts being undertaken in support of the implementation of the Programme of Action, and commending the progress that has already been made in this regard, including the tackling of both supply and demand factors that are relevant to addressing the illicit trade in small arms and light weapons,

Recognizing that sharing and applying best practices, on a voluntary basis, at the regional, subregional and national levels support the full and effective implementation of the Programme of Action and the International Tracing Instrument and should therefore be an ongoing effort, in order to address ongoing challenges associated with the diversion of and illicit trade in small arms and light weapons,

---

[4] A/CONF.192/2018/RC/3, annex.

Reaffirming that international cooperation and assistance are an essential aspect of the full and effective implementation of the Programme of Action and the International Tracing Instrument,

Recognizing the efforts undertaken by civil society in the provision of assistance to States for the implementation of the Programme of Action,

Recalling that Governments bear the primary responsibility for preventing, combating and eradicating the illicit trade in small arms and light weapons in all its aspects, in accordance with the sovereignty of States and their relevant international obligations,

Reiterating that illicit brokering in small arms and light weapons is a serious problem that the international community should address urgently,

Highlighting new challenges and potential opportunities with regard to effective marking, record-keeping and tracing resulting from developments in the manufacturing, technology and design of small arms and light weapons, and bearing in mind the different situations, capacities and priorities of States and regions,

Recognizing that the opportunities and challenges associated with these developments in the manufacturing, technology and design of small arms and light weapons, including polymer and modular weapons, must be addressed in a timely manner,

Taking note of the report of the Secretary-General,[5] which includes an overview of recent developments in the illicit trade and efforts deployed by States and other partners in curbing the multifaceted aspects of the small arms problem and contains the main outcomes of the Seventh Biennial Meeting of States and information on the International Tracing Instrument,

Welcoming the inclusion of small arms and light weapons in the scope of the Arms Trade Treaty,[6]

Acknowledging that effective national control systems for the transfer of conventional arms contribute to the prevention and eradication of the illicit trade in small arms and light weapons in all its aspects,

Recognizing, in this regard, that it was acknowledged in the outcome document of the Seventh Biennial Meeting of States that States that apply provisions of the Programme of Action to small arms and light weapons ammunition can integrate applicable policies and practices into their small arms and light weapons control efforts with a view to strengthening the implementation of the Programme of Action,

1.   *Underlines* the fact that the issue of the illicit trade in small arms and light weapons in all its aspects requires concerted efforts at the national,

---

[5] A/76/284.

[6] United Nations, *Treaty Series*, vol. 3013, No. 52373.

regional and international levels to prevent, combat and eradicate the illicit manufacture, transfer and circulation of small arms and light weapons, and that their uncontrolled spread in many regions of the world has a wide range of humanitarian and socioeconomic consequences and poses a serious threat to peace, reconciliation, safety, security, stability and sustainable development at the individual, local, national, regional and international levels;

2.   *Recognizes* the urgent need to maintain and enhance national controls, in accordance with the Programme of Action to Prevent, Combat and Eradicate the Illicit Trade in Small Arms and Light Weapons in All Its Aspects, to prevent, combat and eradicate the illicit trade in small arms and light weapons, including their diversion to illicit trade, illegal armed groups, terrorists and other unauthorized recipients, taking into account, inter alia, their adverse humanitarian and socioeconomic consequences for the affected States;

3.   *Emphasizes* the need for States to redouble national efforts to provide for the safe, secure, comprehensive and effective management of stockpiles of small arms and light weapons held by Governments to prevent, combat and eradicate the diversion of those weapons;

4.   *Calls upon* all States to implement the International Instrument to Enable States to Identify and Trace, in a Timely and Reliable Manner, Illicit Small Arms and Light Weapons (the International Tracing Instrument) by, inter alia, including in their national reports the name and contact information of the national points of contact and information on national marking practices used to indicate country of manufacture and/or country of import, as applicable;

5.   *Encourages* all relevant initiatives, including those of the United Nations, other international organizations, regional and subregional organizations and civil society, for the successful implementation of the Programme of Action, and calls upon all Member States to contribute towards the continued implementation of the Programme of Action at the national, regional and global levels;

6.   *Encourages* States to implement the recommendations contained in the report of the Group of Governmental Experts established pursuant to resolution 60/81 of 8 December 2005 to consider further steps to enhance international cooperation in preventing, combating and eradicating illicit brokering in small arms and light weapons;[7]

7.   *Reaffirms* the outcome of the third United Nations Conference to Review Progress Made in the Implementation of the Programme of Action to Prevent, Combat and Eradicate the Illicit Trade in Small Arms and Light

---

[7] See A/62/163 and A/62/163/Corr.1.

Weapons in All Its Aspects, held in New York from 18 to 29 June 2018 (the third Review Conference);

8.   *Endorses* the outcome of the Seventh Biennial Meeting of States to Consider the Implementation of the Programme of Action to Prevent, Combat and Eradicate the Illicit Trade in Small Arms and Light Weapons in All Its Aspects, held in New York from 26 to 30 July 2021;

9.   *Renews its decision*, pursuant to the schedule of meetings for the period from 2018 to 2024 agreed upon at the third Review Conference and recalled by the Seventh Biennial Meeting of States, to convene a one-week biennial meeting of States in 2022 and the fourth United Nations Conference to Review Progress Made in the Implementation of the Programme of Action to Prevent, Combat and Eradicate the Illicit Trade in Small Arms and Light Weapons in All Its Aspects in 2024 for two weeks (20 meetings), to be preceded by a preparatory committee meeting in early 2024 of five days (10 meetings);

10.   *Decides* that the Eighth Biennial Meeting of States to Consider the Implementation of the Programme of Action to Prevent, Combat and Eradicate the Illicit Trade in Small Arms and Light Weapons in All Its Aspects, to be convened in New York from 27 June to 1 July 2022, will consider the implementation of the Programme of Action and the International Tracing Instrument, including means of enhancing modalities and procedures for international cooperation and assistance;

11.   *Underlines* the importance of the full and effective implementation of the Programme of Action and the International Tracing Instrument for attaining Goal 16 and target 16.4 of the 2030 Agenda for Sustainable Development;[8]

12.   *Emphasizes* the need for the equal, full and effective participation of women in all decision-making and implementation processes relating to the Programme of Action and the International Tracing Instrument;

13.   *Encourages* States to take into account recent developments in small arms and light weapons manufacturing, technology and design, in particular polymer and modular weapons, in the implementation of the Programme of Action and the International Tracing Instrument and to strengthen normative frameworks, where needed, and cooperation between law enforcement agencies so as to prevent unauthorized recipients, including criminals and terrorists, from acquiring small arms and light weapons;

14.   *Emphasizes* that international cooperation and assistance remain essential to the full and effective implementation of the Programme of Action and the International Tracing Instrument, while being mindful of the need to ensure the adequacy, accessibility, effectiveness and sustainability of

---

[8]   Resolution 70/1.

international cooperation and assistance measures, including, as appropriate, improved funding arrangements, technology transfer and adequate training and support programmes, as well as strong national ownership;

15. *Also emphasizes* the fact that initiatives by the international community with respect to international cooperation and assistance remain essential and complementary to national implementation efforts, as well as to those at the regional and global levels;

16. *Recognizes* the necessity for interested States to develop effective coordination mechanisms, where they do not exist, in order to match the needs of States with existing resources to enhance the implementation of the Programme of Action and to make international cooperation and assistance more effective, and in this regard encourages States to make use, as appropriate, of the Programme of Action Implementation Support System;

17. *Encourages* States to consider, among other mechanisms, the coherent identification of needs, priorities, national plans and programmes that may require international cooperation and assistance from States and regional and international organizations in a position to do so;

18. *Also encourages* States, on a voluntary basis, to make increasing use of their national reports as a tool for communicating assistance needs and information on the resources and mechanisms available to address such needs, and encourages States in a position to render such assistance to make use of those national reports;

19. *Encourages* States, relevant international and regional organizations and civil society with the capacity to do so to cooperate with and provide assistance to other States, upon request, in the preparation of comprehensive national reports on their implementation of the Programme of Action and the International Tracing Instrument;

20. *Encourages* States to reinforce, as necessary, cross-border cooperation at the national, subregional and regional levels in addressing the common problem of the illicit trade in small arms and light weapons in all its aspects, with full respect for each State's sovereignty over its own borders;

21. *Also encourages* States to take full advantage of the benefits of cooperation with the United Nations regional centres for peace and disarmament, the World Customs Organization, the International Criminal Police Organization (INTERPOL) and the United Nations Office on Drugs and Crime, in accordance with their mandates and consistent with national priorities;

22. *Encourages* all efforts to build national capacity for the effective implementation of the Programme of Action, including those highlighted in the outcome document of the third Review Conference;

23. *Encourages* States to submit, on a voluntary basis, national reports on their implementation of the Programme of Action, notes that States will submit national reports on their implementation of the International Tracing Instrument, encourages those States in a position to do so to use the reporting template made available by the Office for Disarmament Affairs of the Secretariat, and reaffirms the utility of synchronizing such reports with biennial meetings of States and review conferences as a means of increasing the submission rate and improving the utility of reports, as well as contributing substantively to meeting discussions;

24. *Encourages* States in a position to do so to provide financial assistance, through a voluntary sponsorship fund, that could be distributed, upon request, to States otherwise unable to participate in meetings on the Programme of Action;

25. *Welcomes* the establishment of the Saving Lives Entity fund to ensure sustained financing for coordinated, integrated small arms control measures in countries most affected by the illicit trade in small arms and light weapons, and encourages States in a position to do so to make voluntary financial contributions to the fund;

26. *Encourages* interested States and relevant international and regional organizations in a position to do so to convene regional meetings to consider and advance the implementation of the Programme of Action, as well as the International Tracing Instrument, including in preparation for the meetings on the Programme of Action;

27. *Encourages* civil society and relevant organizations to strengthen their cooperation and work with States at the respective national and regional levels to achieve the implementation of the Programme of Action;

28. *Reaffirms* the importance of States undertaking to identify, where applicable, groups and individuals engaged in the illegal manufacture, trade, stockpiling, transfer, possession, as well as financing for acquisition, of illicit small arms and light weapons, and take action under appropriate national law against such groups and individuals;[9]

29. *Requests* the Secretary-General to report to the General Assembly at its seventy-seventh session on the implementation of the present resolution;

30. *Requests* the Secretariat, within existing resources, to present an analysis of implementation trends, challenges and opportunities relating to the Programme of Action and the International Tracing Instrument, including needs for cooperation and assistance, based on information submitted by States, at the Eighth Biennial Meeting of States;

---

[9] *Report of the United Nations Conference on Illicit Trade in Small Arms and Light Weapons in All Its Aspects, New York, 9–20 July 2001* (A/CONF.192/15), chap. IV, para. 24, sect. II, para. 6.

31.   *Also requests* the Secretariat to report on support provided by the United Nations system for the implementation of the Programme of Action and the International Tracing Instrument, including experiences, best practices and lessons learned regarding the efficient use of available resources, for presentation at upcoming meetings on the Programme of Action and the International Tracing Instrument;

32.   *Calls upon* the Secretariat, within existing resources, to develop a good practice document on marking practices for modular and polymer weapons taking into account the views of all Member States and the role of manufacturers;

33.   *Requests* the Secretary-General, within existing resources, to seek the views of Member States, international and regional organizations and other stakeholders for enhancing international cooperation and assistance modalities and procedures in the framework of the Programme of Action and the International Tracing Instrument, taking into account good practice and lessons learned, and to present recommendations for consideration by Member States at the Eighth Biennial Meeting of States;

34.   *Also requests* the Secretariat to present funding and administrative arrangements for a dedicated fellowship training programme on small arms and light weapons in order to strengthen technical knowledge and expertise in areas related to the implementation of the Programme of Action and the International Tracing Instrument, particularly in developing countries, with a view to its expedient establishment, for consideration by Member States at the Eighth Biennial Meeting of States;

35.   *Decides* to include in the provisional agenda of its seventy-seventh session, under the item entitled "General and complete disarmament", the sub-item entitled "The illicit trade in small arms and light weapons in all its aspects".

Action by the General Assembly

Date: 24 December 2021	Meeting: 54th plenary meeting
Vote: Adopted without a vote 144-0-16, p.p. 22	Report: A/76/444

Sponsors

Austria, Bosnia and Herzegovina, Bulgaria, Chile, **Colombia**, Costa Rica, Croatia, Czechia, Democratic Republic of the Congo, Denmark, Estonia, Eswatini, Finland, Germany, Greece, Iceland, Italy, **Japan**, Latvia, Lesotho, Lithuania, Netherlands, Norway, Paraguay, Philippines, Poland, Portugal, Republic of Korea, Republic of Moldova, Slovakia, **South Africa**, Spain, Switzerland

Co-sponsors

Albania, Andorra, Argentina, Australia, Bahamas, Barbados, Belgium, Burkina Faso, Cabo Verde, China, Côte d'Ivoire, Cyprus, Dominican Republic, Equatorial Guinea, France, Georgia, Ghana, Guatemala, Guinea-Bissau, Guyana, Honduras, Hungary, Ireland, Jamaica, Kenya, Liechtenstein, Luxembourg, Malta, Monaco, Mongolia, Montenegro, Namibia, North Macedonia, Papua New Guinea, Peru, Romania, San Marino, Serbia, Slovenia, Sri Lanka, Suriname, Sweden, Thailand, Trinidad and Tobago, Tunisia, Turkey, United Kingdom, Uruguay

Recorded vote

Twenty-second preambular paragraph*

In favour

Albania, Andorra, Angola, Argentina, Australia, Austria, Azerbaijan, Bahamas, Bahrain, Bangladesh, Barbados, Belgium, Bosnia and Herzegovina, Botswana, Brazil, Brunei Darussalam, Bulgaria, Burkina Faso, Burundi, Cambodia, Cameroon, Canada, Central African Republic, Chad, Chile, China, Colombia, Comoros, Congo, Costa Rica, Côte d'Ivoire, Croatia, Cyprus, Czechia, Denmark, Djibouti, Dominica, Dominican Republic, Ecuador, El Salvador, Eritrea, Estonia, Ethiopia, Fiji, Finland, France, Gambia, Georgia, Germany, Ghana, Greece, Grenada, Guatemala, Guinea, Guinea-Bissau, Guyana, Haiti, Honduras, Hungary, Iceland, Iran (Islamic Republic of), Iraq, Ireland, Israel, Italy, Jamaica, Japan, Jordan, Kazakhstan, Kenya, Kiribati, Latvia, Lebanon, Lesotho, Liberia, Libya, Liechtenstein, Lithuania, Luxembourg, Madagascar, Malaysia, Maldives, Mali, Malta, Marshall Islands, Mauritania, Mexico, Micronesia (Federated States of), Monaco, Mongolia, Montenegro, Morocco, Mozambique, Myanmar, Namibia, Nepal, Netherlands, New Zealand, Nigeria, North Macedonia, Norway, Oman, Pakistan, Panama, Papua New Guinea, Paraguay, Peru, Philippines, Poland, Portugal, Qatar, Republic of Korea, Republic of Moldova, Romania, Saint Lucia, Saint Vincent and the Grenadines, San Marino, Senegal, Serbia, Sierra Leone, Singapore, Slovakia, Slovenia, South Africa, Spain, Sri Lanka, Sudan, Suriname, Sweden, Switzerland, Thailand, Timor-Leste, Togo, Trinidad and Tobago, Turkey, Uganda, Ukraine, United Arab Emirates, United Kingdom, United Republic of Tanzania, United States, Uruguay, Yemen, Zimbabwe

Against

None

---

* Subsequently, the delegations of Tunisia and Zambia informed the Secretariat that they had intended to vote in favour.

Abstaining
Algeria, Armenia, Belarus, Bhutan, Bolivia (Plurinational State of), Cuba, Egypt, India, Indonesia, Kuwait, Nicaragua, Russian Federation, Saudi Arabia, Syrian Arab Republic, Tunisia, Venezuela (Bolivarian Republic of)

Action by the First Committee

Date:	2 November 2021	Meeting:	16th meeting
Vote:	Adopted without a vote 152-0-17, p.p. 22	Draft resolution:	A/C.1/76/L.43

Agenda item 100 (u)

76/233 Problems arising from the accumulation of conventional ammunition stockpiles in surplus

Text

The General Assembly,

Mindful of the dangers posed by unplanned explosions at munitions sites and the diversion of materials from conventional ammunition stockpiles to the illicit market, including for the manufacture of improvised explosive devices,

Emphasizing that thousands of people have died and the livelihoods of entire communities have been disrupted as a result of accidental ammunition depot explosions and that diversion from ammunition stockpiles has contributed to the intensity and duration of armed conflict and sustained armed violence around the world,[1]

Recognizing the need to encourage the full involvement of both women and men in ammunition management practice and policy,

Noting that conventional weapons and their ammunition are items for which, in principle, action can be taken to improve the regulation of transfers and prevent their diversion to illicit trafficking,

Recognizing the urgency of addressing the security and safety risks emanating from ineffective stockpile management around the world,[2]

Bearing in mind a through-life management approach to tackle problems related to ammunition in a comprehensive manner, including those related to diversion,

Noting the requirement of the Arms Trade Treaty[3] that States parties thereto shall designate competent national authorities in order to have an effective and transparent national control system to regulate the transfer of relevant ammunition and munitions,

Recalling the report of the Group of Experts on the problem of ammunition and explosives[4] and the report of the Group of Governmental Experts established pursuant to resolution 61/72 to consider further steps to enhance cooperation with regard to the issue of conventional ammunition stockpiles in surplus,[5]

---

[1] See S/2011/255.
[2] See S/2015/289.
[3] United Nations, *Treaty Series*, vol. 3013, No. 52373.
[4] See A/54/155.
[5] See A/63/182.

Welcoming the adoption of the 2030 Agenda for Sustainable Development[6] and its recognition of the relevance for development of a significant reduction in illicit arms flows and of strengthened national institutions for building capacity at all levels, in particular in developing countries, to prevent violence and combat terrorism and crime,

Recalling the recommendation contained in paragraph 27 of the report of the Open-ended Working Group to Negotiate an International Instrument to Enable States to Identify and Trace, in a Timely and Reliable Manner, Illicit Small Arms and Light Weapons,[7] namely, to address the issue of small arms and light weapons ammunition in a comprehensive manner as part of a separate process conducted within the framework of the United Nations,

Taking note of the discussions on munitions management practice in the framework of Protocol V[8] to the Convention on Prohibitions or Restrictions on the Use of Certain Conventional Weapons Which May Be Deemed to Be Excessively Injurious or to Have Indiscriminate Effects,[9]

Noting with satisfaction the work and measures pursued at the regional and subregional levels with regard to the issue of conventional ammunition,

Recalling its decision 59/515 of 3 December 2004 and its resolutions 60/74 of 8 December 2005 and 61/72 of 6 December 2006, its resolution 63/61 of 2 December 2008, by which it welcomed the report of the Group of Governmental Experts established pursuant to resolution 61/72 to consider further steps to enhance cooperation with regard to the issue of conventional ammunition stockpiles in surplus, its resolutions 64/51 of 2 December 2009, 66/42 of 2 December 2011, 68/52 of 5 December 2013, 70/35 of 7 December 2015, 72/55 of 4 December 2017 and 74/65 of 12 December 2019 and its decision 75/552 of 31 December 2020,

Welcoming the conclusion of the work of the Group of Governmental Experts established pursuant to resolution 72/55 and the submission of its report,[10]

Recalling the recommendations of the Group of Governmental Experts established pursuant to resolution 61/72, and encouraging the use, as appropriate, of the voluntary International Ammunition Technical Guidelines to improve the safety and security of ammunition storage sites,

Recalling with appreciation the establishment, within the Secretariat, of the Safe*r*Guard knowledge resource management programme,[11] including its online implementation support tools,

---

[6] Resolution 70/1.
[7] A/60/88 and A/60/88/Corr.2.
[8] United Nations, *Treaty Series*, vol. 2399, No. 22495.
[9] Ibid., vol. 1342, No. 22495.
[10] See A/76/324.
[11] A/63/182, paras. 72–73.

Noting that the voluntary International Ammunition Technical Guidelines are used by national authorities and an expanding network of partners from international and regional organizations, non-governmental organizations and the private sector in an increasing number of States to support ammunition stockpile management efforts,

Emphasizing the need to consider integrating ammunition management measures in accordance with the International Ammunition Technical Guidelines, where relevant, in mandates of United Nations peacekeeping operations and special political missions,

Recognizing the importance of appropriate national ammunition management structures and procedures, including laws and regulations, training and doctrine, equipment and maintenance, personnel management and finances and infrastructure in order to ensure sustainability in ammunition management, and emphasizing in this regard the central role of the provision of technical assistance and capacity-building to Member States, upon their request,

Noting with appreciation the ongoing work of the Ammunition Management Advisory Team to support interested States in the safe and secure management of ammunition through the provision of technical advice and services,

1.   *Encourages* all interested States to assess, on a voluntary basis, whether, in conformity with their legitimate security needs, parts of their stockpiles of conventional ammunition should be considered to be in surplus, and recognizes that the security of such stockpiles must be taken into consideration and that appropriate controls with regard to the security and safety of stockpiles of conventional ammunition are indispensable at the national level in order to eliminate the risk of explosion, pollution or diversion;

2.   *Appeals* to all interested States to determine the size and nature of their surplus stockpiles of conventional ammunition, whether they represent a security or safety risk, their preferred means of destruction, if appropriate, and whether external assistance is needed to eliminate this risk;

3.   *Encourages* States in a position to do so to assist interested States within a bilateral framework or through international or regional organizations, including through activities conducted under the umbrella of the Saf*er*Guard knowledge resource management programme, on a voluntary and transparent basis, in elaborating and implementing programmes to eliminate surplus stockpiles or to improve stockpile management;

4.   *Encourages* all Member States to examine the possibility of developing and implementing, within a national, regional or subregional framework, measures to address accordingly the illicit trafficking related to the accumulation of such stockpiles;

5.   *Notes with appreciation* initiatives at the international, regional and national levels that shed light on improving the sustainable management of ammunition, including through the implementation of the International Ammunition Technical Guidelines, recognizing the relevance of continued discussions and coordination in this regard;

6.   *Welcomes* the release of the updated version of the International Ammunition Technical Guidelines in 2021 and the intention to update the Guidelines on a regular basis, as well as the continued implementation of the Saf*er*Guard programme, managed by the Office for Disarmament Affairs of the Secretariat;

7.   *Also welcomes* the continued application of the International Ammunition Technical Guidelines in the field, including the online implementation support tools and training materials, takes note of the support guides and the availability of translations of the Guidelines in various languages, which encourages States in a position to do so to offer support to the Saf*er*Guard programme, and calls upon all United Nations entities to make full use of the Guidelines when supporting national authorities;

8.   *Encourages* consideration of the integration of ammunition management measures, where relevant, in the mandates of peacekeeping operations, including through the training of personnel of national authorities and peacekeepers, utilizing the International Ammunition Technical Guidelines;

9.   *Welcomes* the ongoing work carried out by the Saf*er*Guard programme to operationalize its quick-response mechanism, which allows ammunition experts to be deployed to assist States, upon request, in the management of ammunition stockpiles, and encourages States in a position to do so to provide technical expertise or financial support to the mechanism;

10.   *Encourages* States wishing to improve their national ammunition stockpile management capacity, wishing to prevent the growth of conventional ammunition surpluses and wishing to implement wider risk mitigation to contact the Saf*er*Guard programme, as well as potential national donors, regional organizations or other organizations, as appropriate;

11.   *Encourages* States, as appropriate, to consider ammunition management as an intrinsic part of their actions for achieving relevant targets of the Sustainable Development Goals related to the reduction of illicit arms flows and the prevention of violence through strengthened national institutions, and to consider, where relevant, developing national, regional and subregional indicators based on this understanding;

12.   *Also encourages* States, where relevant, to develop voluntary national action plans on the safe and secure management of conventional ammunition, and acknowledges the utility of information-sharing and the benefit of good practices among States, as appropriate;

13. *Recalls with appreciation* the series of informal consultations convened within the framework of its resolution 72/55 throughout 2018 and 2019 that focused on matters of conventional ammunition management within the United Nations system and beyond and that sought to identify urgent issues pertaining to the accumulation of conventional ammunition stockpiles in surplus on which progress can be made;

14. *Recalls* the informal paper presented by Germany on the informal consultative process undertaken within the framework of resolution 72/55, as well as the inputs, both written and oral, received from Member States on the same matter;

15. *Welcomes* the report of the Group of Governmental Experts established pursuant to resolution 72/55 contained in document A/76/324 and the substantive recommendations contained therein;

16. *Encourages* States to consider the recommendations contained in the report of the Group of Governmental Experts established pursuant to resolution 72/55, in particular regarding steps to address the safety and security challenges arising from conventional ammunition in a comprehensive manner;

17. *Decides* to establish an open-ended working group to elaborate a set of political commitments as a new global framework that will address existing gaps in through-life ammunition management, including international cooperation and assistance, without prejudice to national legal systems addressing national ammunition ownership, possession and use, and will be part of a comprehensive framework to support safe, secure and sustainable through-life ammunition management at the national, subregional, regional and global levels, building upon and complementing existing frameworks, whereas cooperation at the regional and subregional levels should be considered on a voluntary basis;

18. *Also decides* that the open-ended working group shall take into account the recommendations contained in the report of the Group of Governmental Experts established pursuant to resolution 72/55 and the views of all participating States and be informed by the series of informal consultations convened within the framework of its resolution 72/55 throughout 2018 and 2019, the informal paper presented by Germany on the informal consultative process and the inputs, both written and oral, received from Member States on the same matter;

19. *Further decides* that the open-ended working group shall convene for two 5-day sessions in New York in 2022 and for one 5-day session in Geneva in 2023, preceded by informal consultations as required, within available time frames and with the contribution of relevant international and non-governmental organizations, and shall hold a two-day organizational session in advance of the first meeting;

20.   *Decides* that the open-ended working group shall submit a report on its work, including recommendations on a set of political commitments as a new global framework on conventional ammunition, to the General Assembly at its seventy-eighth session;

21.   *Requests* the Secretary-General to provide the support necessary to convene the sessions of the open-ended working group;

22.   *Reiterates* its decision to address the issue of conventional ammunition stockpiles in surplus in a comprehensive manner;

23.   *Decides* to include in the provisional agenda of its seventy-seventh session, under the item entitled "General and complete disarmament", the sub-item entitled "Problems arising from the accumulation of conventional ammunition stockpiles in surplus".

Action by the General Assembly

Date: 24 December 2021   Meeting: 54th plenary meeting
Vote: 159-0-9   Report: A/76/444

Sponsors

Austria, Belgium, Bosnia and Herzegovina, Brazil, Bulgaria, Canada, Chile, Croatia, Czechia, Estonia, Finland, **France**, **Germany**, Greece, Hungary, Iceland, Italy, Jamaica, Latvia, Lithuania, Luxembourg, Netherlands, Norway, Portugal, Republic of Moldova, Slovakia, Spain, Sweden, Switzerland

Co-sponsors

Albania, Andorra, Argentina, Colombia, Cyprus, Denmark, Georgia, Ghana, Guinea, Ireland, Japan, Malta, Monaco, Montenegro, North Macedonia, Romania, San Marino, Singapore, Slovenia, South Africa, Turkey, Ukraine, United Kingdom, Zambia

Recorded vote*

In favour

Albania, Algeria, Andorra, Angola, Argentina, Armenia, Australia, Austria, Azerbaijan, Bahamas, Bahrain, Bangladesh, Barbados, Belarus, Belgium, Bhutan, Bosnia and Herzegovina, Botswana, Brazil, Brunei Darussalam, Bulgaria, Burkina Faso, Burundi, Cambodia, Cameroon, Canada, Central African Republic, Chad, Chile, China, Colombia, Comoros, Congo, Costa Rica, Côte d'Ivoire, Croatia, Cyprus, Czechia, Denmark, Djibouti, Dominica, Dominican Republic, Ecuador, Egypt, El Salvador, Eritrea, Estonia, Ethiopia, Fiji, Finland, France, Gambia, Georgia, Germany,

---

*   Subsequently, the delegation of Myanmar informed the Secretariat that it had intended to vote in favour.

Ghana, Greece, Grenada, Guatemala, Guinea, Guinea-Bissau, Guyana, Haiti, Honduras, Hungary, Iceland, India, Indonesia, Iraq, Ireland, Israel, Italy, Jamaica, Japan, Jordan, Kazakhstan, Kenya, Kiribati, Kuwait, Kyrgyzstan, Lao People's Democratic Republic, Latvia, Lebanon, Lesotho, Liberia, Libya, Liechtenstein, Lithuania, Luxembourg, Madagascar, Malaysia, Maldives, Mali, Malta, Marshall Islands, Mauritania, Mauritius, Mexico, Micronesia (Federated States of), Monaco, Mongolia, Montenegro, Morocco, Mozambique, Namibia, Nepal, Netherlands, New Zealand, Nigeria, North Macedonia, Norway, Oman, Pakistan, Palau, Panama, Papua New Guinea, Paraguay, Peru, Philippines, Poland, Portugal, Qatar, Republic of Korea, Republic of Moldova, Romania, Saint Lucia, Saint Vincent and the Grenadines, San Marino, Saudi Arabia, Senegal, Serbia, Singapore, Slovakia, Slovenia, Solomon Islands, Somalia, South Africa, Spain, Sri Lanka, Sudan, Suriname, Sweden, Switzerland, Thailand, Timor-Leste, Togo, Trinidad and Tobago, Tunisia, Turkey, Uganda, Ukraine, United Arab Emirates, United Kingdom, United Republic of Tanzania, United States, Uruguay, Viet Nam, Yemen, Zambia, Zimbabwe

Against

None

Abstaining

Bolivia (Plurinational State of), Cuba, Equatorial Guinea, Iran (Islamic Republic of), Myanmar, Nicaragua, Russian Federation, Syrian Arab Republic, Venezuela (Bolivarian Republic of)

Action by the First Committee

Date: 2 November 2021   Meeting: 16th meeting
Vote: 167-0-9   Draft resolution: A/C.1/76/L.47

Agenda item 100

76/234 Promoting international cooperation on peaceful uses in the context of international security

Text

The General Assembly,

Recalling the provisions of the Treaty on the Non-Proliferation of Nuclear Weapons,[1] the Convention on the Prohibition of the Development, Production and Stockpiling of Bacteriological (Biological) and Toxin Weapons and on their Destruction[2] and the Convention on the Prohibition of the Development, Production, Stockpiling and Use of Chemical Weapons and on Their Destruction[3] and the provisions of relevant United Nations resolutions,

Reaffirming the need for all Member States to fulfil their obligations in relation to arms control and disarmament and to prevent proliferation, in all its aspects, of all weapons of mass destruction,

Reaffirming also that proliferation of nuclear, chemical and biological weapons, as well as their means of delivery, constitutes a threat to international peace and security,

Reaffirming further support for the multilateral treaties whose aim is to eliminate or prevent the proliferation of nuclear, chemical or biological weapons and the importance for all States parties to these treaties of implementing them fully in order to promote international stability,

Bearing in mind the potential impact that scientific and technological advances can have on global security,

Recognizing the inalienable right of all States to participate in the fullest possible exchange of equipment, materials and scientific and technological information for peaceful purposes, in accordance with relevant international obligations,

Reaffirming that preventing the proliferation of nuclear, chemical and biological weapons should not hamper international cooperation on materials, equipment and technology for peaceful purposes, while the goals of peaceful utilization should not be misused for proliferation purposes,

Bearing in mind the significant role of international cooperation on materials, equipment and technology for peaceful purposes in facilitating the economic and social development of Member States, in particular the development of developing countries,

---

[1] United Nations, *Treaty Series*, vol. 729, No. 10485.
[2] Ibid., vol. 1015, No. 14860.
[3] Ibid., vol. 1974, No. 33757.

Acknowledging the need to continue the exchange of technologies for peaceful uses, including in accordance with relevant international obligations,

Acknowledging also the importance of technology as one of the key means of implementation in the pursuit of sustainable development,

Noting with concern that undue restrictions on exports to developing countries of materials, equipment and technology for peaceful purposes persist,

Emphasizing that proliferation concerns are best addressed through multilaterally negotiated, universal, comprehensive and non-discriminatory agreements,

Emphasizing also that non-proliferation control arrangements should be transparent and open to participation by all States and should ensure that no restrictions are imposed on access to materials, equipment and technology for peaceful purposes required by developing countries for their continued sustainable development,

Emphasizing further the importance of promoting international cooperation for peaceful purposes,

1. *Urges* all Member States, without prejudice to their non-proliferation obligations, to take concrete measures to promote international cooperation on materials, equipment and technology for peaceful purposes, in particular not to maintain any restrictions incompatible with the obligations undertaken;

2. *Requests* the Secretary-General to seek the views and recommendations of all Member States on all aspects of promoting international cooperation on peaceful uses in the context of international security, including identifying undue restrictions on exports to developing countries of materials, equipment and technology for peaceful purposes, possible measures to achieve a balance between non-proliferation and peaceful uses, and the way forward;

3. *Also requests* the Secretary-General to submit a report containing the views and recommendations to the General Assembly at its seventy-seventh session, for further discussion by Member States;

4. *Decides* to include in the provisional agenda of its seventy-seventh session an item entitled "Promoting international cooperation on peaceful uses in the context of international security".

Action by the General Assembly

Date:	24 December 2021	Meeting:	54th plenary meeting
Vote:	78-53-32	Report:	A/76/444
	75-52-27, o.p. 2		
	74-53-27, o.p. 3		

Sponsors

Belarus, Burundi, Cameroon, **China**, Equatorial Guinea, Eritrea, Ethiopia, Kiribati, Pakistan, Russian Federation, Syrian Arab Republic, Vanuatu, Venezuela (Bolivarian Republic of), Zimbabwe

Co-sponsors

Algeria, Cambodia, Chad, Congo, Cuba, Dominica, Gambia, Guinea, Guinea-Bissau, Kazakhstan, Lao People's Democratic Republic, Nicaragua, Somalia

Recorded vote

As a whole*

In favour

Algeria, Angola, Bahrain, Bangladesh, Belarus, Bolivia (Plurinational State of), Brunei Darussalam, Burkina Faso, Burundi, Cambodia, Cameroon, Central African Republic, Chad, China, Comoros, Congo, Cuba, Democratic People's Republic of Korea, Djibouti, Dominica, Ecuador, Egypt, El Salvador, Equatorial Guinea, Eritrea, Ethiopia, Gambia, Ghana, Guinea, Guinea-Bissau, Indonesia, Iran (Islamic Republic of), Jordan, Kazakhstan, Kenya, Kiribati, Kuwait, Kyrgyzstan, Lao People's Democratic Republic, Libya, Malaysia, Mali, Mauritania, Mongolia, Namibia, Nepal, Nicaragua, Nigeria, Oman, Pakistan, Peru, Philippines, Qatar, Russian Federation, Saudi Arabia, Senegal, Serbia, Singapore, Solomon Islands, Somalia, South Africa, Sri Lanka, Sudan, Syrian Arab Republic, Tajikistan, Thailand, Togo, Turkmenistan, Uganda, United Arab Emirates, United Republic of Tanzania, Uruguay, Uzbekistan, Venezuela (Bolivarian Republic of), Viet Nam, Yemen, Zambia, Zimbabwe

Against

Albania, Andorra, Australia, Austria, Belgium, Bulgaria, Canada, Croatia, Cyprus, Czechia, Denmark, Estonia, Finland, France, Germany, Greece, Honduras, Hungary, Iceland, Ireland, Israel, Italy, Japan, Latvia, Liechtenstein, Lithuania, Luxembourg, Malta, Marshall Islands, Micronesia (Federated States of), Monaco, Montenegro, Nauru, Netherlands, New Zealand, North Macedonia, Norway, Palau, Poland, Portugal, Republic of Korea, Republic of Moldova, Romania, San Marino, Slovakia, Slovenia, Spain, Sweden, Switzerland, Turkey, Ukraine, United Kingdom, United States

Abstaining

Argentina, Armenia, Barbados, Bhutan, Bosnia and Herzegovina, Brazil, Chile, Colombia, Costa Rica, Côte d'Ivoire, Dominican Republic,

---

* Subsequently, the delegation of Myanmar informed the Secretariat that it had intended to vote in favour.

Fiji, Georgia, Guatemala, Guyana, India, Jamaica, Lebanon, Lesotho, Madagascar, Maldives, Mexico, Morocco, Myanmar, Panama, Papua New Guinea, Paraguay, Saint Lucia, Saint Vincent and the Grenadines, Timor-Leste, Trinidad and Tobago, Tunisia

Operative paragraph 2*

In favour

Algeria, Angola, Bahrain, Bangladesh, Belarus, Bolivia (Plurinational State of), Brazil, Brunei Darussalam, Burkina Faso, Burundi, Cambodia, Cameroon, Central African Republic, Chad, China, Comoros, Congo, Cuba, Democratic People's Republic of Korea, Djibouti, Dominica, Ecuador, Egypt, El Salvador, Equatorial Guinea, Eritrea, Ethiopia, Gambia, Ghana, Guinea, Guinea-Bissau, Indonesia, Iran (Islamic Republic of), Iraq, Jordan, Kazakhstan, Kenya, Kiribati, Kuwait, Lao People's Democratic Republic, Libya, Malaysia, Mali, Mauritania, Mongolia, Myanmar, Namibia, Nepal, Nicaragua, Nigeria, Oman, Pakistan, Philippines, Qatar, Russian Federation, Saudi Arabia, Senegal, Singapore, Somalia, South Africa, Sri Lanka, Sudan, Syrian Arab Republic, Tajikistan, Thailand, Togo, Tunisia, Uganda, United Arab Emirates, United Republic of Tanzania, Uzbekistan, Venezuela (Bolivarian Republic of), Yemen, Zambia, Zimbabwe

Against

Albania, Andorra, Australia, Austria, Belgium, Bulgaria, Canada, Croatia, Cyprus, Czechia, Denmark, Estonia, Finland, France, Germany, Greece, Honduras, Hungary, Iceland, India, Ireland, Israel, Italy, Japan, Latvia, Liechtenstein, Lithuania, Luxembourg, Malta, Marshall Islands, Monaco, Montenegro, Netherlands, New Zealand, North Macedonia, Norway, Palau, Poland, Portugal, Republic of Korea, Republic of Moldova, Romania, San Marino, Slovakia, Slovenia, Spain, Sweden, Switzerland, Turkey, Ukraine, United Kingdom, United States

Abstaining

Argentina, Barbados, Bhutan, Bosnia and Herzegovina, Chile, Colombia, Costa Rica, Côte d'Ivoire, Dominican Republic, Fiji, Georgia, Guatemala, Guyana, Lebanon, Lesotho, Madagascar, Mexico, Morocco, Panama, Papua New Guinea, Paraguay, Peru, Saint Lucia, Saint Vincent and the Grenadines, Timor-Leste, Trinidad and Tobago, Uruguay

---

* Subsequently, the delegations of Jamaica and Tunisia informed the Secretariat that they had intended to abstain.

Operative paragraph 3*

In favour

Algeria, Angola, Bahrain, Bangladesh, Belarus, Bolivia (Plurinational State of), Brazil, Brunei Darussalam, Burkina Faso, Burundi, Cambodia, Cameroon, Central African Republic, Chad, China, Comoros, Congo, Cuba, Democratic People's Republic of Korea, Djibouti, Dominica, Ecuador, Egypt, El Salvador, Equatorial Guinea, Eritrea, Ethiopia, Gambia, Ghana, Guinea, Guinea-Bissau, Indonesia, Iran (Islamic Republic of), Iraq, Jordan, Kazakhstan, Kenya, Kiribati, Kuwait, Lao People's Democratic Republic, Libya, Malaysia, Mali, Mauritania, Mongolia, Namibia, Nepal, Nicaragua, Nigeria, Oman, Pakistan, Philippines, Qatar, Russian Federation, Saudi Arabia, Senegal, Singapore, Somalia, South Africa, Sri Lanka, Sudan, Syrian Arab Republic, Tajikistan, Thailand, Togo, Tunisia, Uganda, United Arab Emirates, United Republic of Tanzania, Uruguay, Uzbekistan, Venezuela (Bolivarian Republic of), Yemen, Zimbabwe

Against

Albania, Andorra, Australia, Austria, Belgium, Bulgaria, Canada, Croatia, Cyprus, Czechia, Denmark, Estonia, Finland, France, Germany, Greece, Honduras, Hungary, Iceland, India, Ireland, Israel, Italy, Japan, Latvia, Liberia, Liechtenstein, Lithuania, Luxembourg, Malta, Marshall Islands, Monaco, Montenegro, Netherlands, New Zealand, North Macedonia, Norway, Palau, Poland, Portugal, Republic of Korea, Republic of Moldova, Romania, San Marino, Slovakia, Slovenia, Spain, Sweden, Switzerland, Turkey, Ukraine, United Kingdom, United States

Abstaining

Argentina, Barbados, Bhutan, Bosnia and Herzegovina, Chile, Colombia, Costa Rica, Côte d'Ivoire, Dominican Republic, Fiji, Georgia, Guatemala, Guyana, Jamaica, Lebanon, Lesotho, Madagascar, Mexico, Morocco, Myanmar, Panama, Papua New Guinea, Peru, Saint Lucia, Saint Vincent and the Grenadines, Timor-Leste, Trinidad and Tobago

Action by the First Committee

Date: 3 November 2021   Meeting: 17th meeting
Vote: 75-55-43   Draft resolution: A/C.1/76/L.55
      68-53-37, o.p. 2
      69-54-35, o.p. 3

---

* Subsequently, the delegation of Myanmar informed the Secretariat that it had intended to vote in favour; the delegation of Tunisia informed the Secretariat that it had intended to abstain.

Agenda item 100 (hh)

76/515 Nuclear disarmament verification

Text

The General Assembly, recalling its resolutions 71/67 of 5 December 2016 and 74/50 of 12 December 2019 and its decisions 72/514 of 4 December 2017, 73/514 of 5 December 2018 and 75/516 of 7 December 2020, acknowledging the impact of the coronavirus disease (COVID-19) on the convening of meetings within United Nations premises, noting the impact of COVID-19 on the ability of the group of governmental experts to further consider nuclear disarmament verification issues, established pursuant to resolution 74/50, to convene for two weeks in 2021, as originally scheduled, and recalling the request to the Secretary-General, contained in resolution 74/50, to report to the Assembly on the work of the group upon its completion:

(a)   Decides to request the Secretary-General to hold two additional sessions in 2023 in Geneva to compensate for the two planned 2021 sessions that had to be postponed owing to COVID-19 travel restrictions, for a total of two weeks in 2022 and two weeks in 2023, as well as one additional informal intersessional consultative meeting in New York in 2023 to compensate for the planned 2021 meeting that had to be postponed owing to COVID-19 travel restrictions, for a total of two meetings, one in 2022 and one in 2023;

(b)   Also decides to call upon the Secretary-General to transmit the report of the group of governmental experts to the General Assembly at its seventy-eighth session and to the Conference on Disarmament;

(c)   Further decides to include in the provisional agenda of its seventy-seventh session, under the item entitled "General and complete disarmament", the sub-item entitled "Nuclear disarmament verification".

Action by the General Assembly

Date: 6 December 2021   Meeting: 45th plenary meeting
Vote: 187-0-2   Report: A/76/444

Sponsors

Brazil, Netherlands, **Norway**, South Africa, Switzerland, United Kingdom

Recorded vote

In favour

Afghanistan, Albania, Algeria, Andorra, Angola, Antigua and Barbuda, Argentina, Armenia, Australia, Austria, Azerbaijan, Bahamas, Bahrain, Bangladesh, Barbados, Belarus, Belgium, Belize, Bhutan, Bolivia (Plurinational State of), Bosnia and Herzegovina, Botswana, Brazil, Brunei Darussalam, Bulgaria, Burkina Faso, Burundi, Cabo Verde, Cambodia, Cameroon, Canada, Central African Republic, Chad, Chile, China, Colombia, Comoros, Congo, Costa Rica, Côte d'Ivoire, Croatia, Cuba, Cyprus, Czechia, Denmark, Djibouti, Dominica, Dominican Republic, Ecuador, Egypt, El Salvador, Equatorial Guinea, Eritrea, Estonia, Eswatini, Ethiopia, Fiji, Finland, France, Gabon, Gambia, Georgia, Germany, Ghana, Greece, Grenada, Guatemala, Guinea, Guinea-Bissau, Guyana, Haiti, Honduras, Hungary, Iceland, India, Indonesia, Iraq, Ireland, Israel, Italy, Jamaica, Japan, Jordan, Kazakhstan, Kenya, Kiribati, Kuwait, Kyrgyzstan, Lao People's Democratic Republic, Latvia, Lebanon, Lesotho, Liberia, Libya, Liechtenstein, Lithuania, Luxembourg, Madagascar, Malawi, Malaysia, Maldives, Mali, Malta, Marshall Islands, Mauritania, Mauritius, Mexico, Micronesia (Federated States of), Monaco, Mongolia, Montenegro, Morocco, Mozambique, Myanmar, Namibia, Nepal, Netherlands, New Zealand, Nicaragua, Niger, Nigeria, North Macedonia, Norway, Oman, Pakistan, Palau, Panama, Papua New Guinea, Paraguay, Peru, Philippines, Poland, Portugal, Qatar, Republic of Korea, Republic of Moldova, Romania, Russian Federation, Rwanda, Saint Kitts and Nevis, Saint Lucia, Saint Vincent and the Grenadines, Samoa, San Marino, Sao Tome and Principe, Saudi Arabia, Senegal, Serbia, Seychelles, Sierra Leone, Singapore, Slovakia, Slovenia, Solomon Islands, Somalia, South Africa, South Sudan, Spain, Sri Lanka, Sudan, Suriname, Sweden, Switzerland, Tajikistan, Thailand, Timor-Leste, Togo, Tonga, Trinidad and Tobago, Tunisia, Turkey, Turkmenistan, Tuvalu, Uganda, Ukraine, United Arab Emirates, United Kingdom, United Republic of Tanzania, United States, Uruguay, Uzbekistan, Vanuatu, Venezuela (Bolivarian Republic of), Viet Nam, Yemen, Zambia, Zimbabwe

Against

None

Abstaining

Iran (Islamic Republic of), Syrian Arab Republic

Action by the First Committee

Date:	27 October 2021	Meeting:	13th meeting
Vote:	178-1-4	Draft decision:	A/C.1/76/L.40

Agenda item 100 (cc)

76/516 Countering the threat posed by improvised explosive devices

Text

The General Assembly, recalling its resolutions 70/46 of 7 December 2015, 71/72 of 5 December 2016, 72/36 of 4 December 2017, 73/67 of 5 December 2018 and 75/59 of 7 December 2020, decides to include in the provisional agenda of its seventy-seventh session, under the item entitled "General and complete disarmament", the sub-item entitled "Countering the threat posed by improvised explosive devices".

Action by the General Assembly

Date: 6 December 2021   Meeting: 45th plenary meeting
Vote: Adopted without a vote   Report: A/76/444

Sponsors

France

Action by the First Committee

Date: 2 November 2021   Meeting: 16th meeting
Vote: Adopted without a vote   Draft decision: A/C.1/76/L.45

Agenda item 100 (y)

76/517 Treaty on the South-East Asia Nuclear-Weapon-Free Zone (Bangkok Treaty)

Text

The General Assembly, recalling its resolutions 62/31 of 5 December 2007, 64/39 of 2 December 2009, 66/43 of 2 December 2011, 68/49 of 5 December 2013 and 70/60 of 7 December 2015, as well as its decisions 72/515 of 4 December 2017 and 74/510 of 12 December 2019, entitled "Treaty on the South-East Asia Nuclear-Weapon-Free Zone (Bangkok Treaty)", decides to include in the provisional agenda of its seventy-eighth session, under the item entitled "General and complete disarmament", the sub-item entitled "Treaty on the South-East Asia Nuclear-Weapon-Free Zone (Bangkok Treaty)".

Action by the General Assembly

Date: 6 December 2021   Meeting: 45th plenary meeting
Vote: Adopted without a vote   Report: A/76/444

Sponsors

Brunei Darussalam (on behalf of the States Members of the United Nations that are members of the Association of Southeast Asian Nations and the States parties to the Treaty on the South-East Asia Nuclear-Weapon-Free Zone (Bangkok Treaty))

Action by the First Committee

Date: 27 October 2021   Meeting: 13th meeting
Vote: Adopted without a vote   Draft decision: A/C.1/76/L.57

Agenda item 102 (b)

76/518 Disarmament Commission

Text

The General Assembly, recalling its decisions 75/519 A of 7 December 2020 and 75/519 B of 25 March 2021, decides:

(a)   That the Disarmament Commission will hold a substantive session for a period not exceeding three weeks during 2022, namely from 4 to 22 April, and submit a substantive report to the General Assembly at its seventy-seventh session;

(b)   That the Disarmament Commission will hold its organizational session at the beginning of 2022, before the substantive session, to elect its Bureau and address other outstanding organizational matters;

(c)   To include in the provisional agenda of its seventy-seventh session, under the item entitled "Review of the implementation of the recommendations and decisions adopted by the General Assembly at its tenth special session", the sub-item entitled "Report of the Disarmament Commission".

Action by the General Assembly

Date: 6 December 2021	Meeting: 45th plenary meeting
Vote: Adopted without a vote	Report: A/76/446

Sponsors

Australia

Action by the First Committee

Date: 3 November 2021	Meeting: 17th meeting
Vote: Adopted without a vote	Draft decision: A/C.1/76/L.33

ANNEX

List of reports and notes of the Secretary-General

Agenda item 92

Reduction of military budgets

A/76/129

Objective information on military matters, including transparency of military expenditures: Report of the Secretary-General

Agenda item 93

Implementation of the Declaration of the Indian Ocean as a Zone of Peace

A/76/29

Report of the Ad Hoc Committee on the Indian Ocean

Agenda item 94

African Nuclear-Weapon-Free Zone Treaty

Agenda item 95

Developments in the field of information and telecommunications in the context of international security

A/76/136

Official compendium of voluntary national contributions on the subject of how international law applies to the use of information and communications technologies by States submitted by participating governmental experts in the Group of Governmental Experts on Advancing Responsible State Behaviour in Cyberspace in the Context of International Security established pursuant to General Assembly resolution 73/266

A/76/187

Developments in the field of information and telecommunications in the context of international security: Advancing responsible State behaviour in cyberspace in the context of international security: Report of the Secretary-General

Agenda item 96

Establishment of a nuclear-weapon-free zone in the region of the Middle East

A/76/190 (Part I)

Establishment of a nuclear-weapon-free zone in the region of the Middle East: Report of the Secretary-General (Part I)

Agenda item 97	**Conclusion of effective international arrangements to assure nonnuclear-weapon States against the use or threat of use of nuclear weapons**
A/76/27	Report of the Conference on Disarmament (Suppl. No. 27)
Agenda item 98	**Prevention of an arms race in outer space**
(a)	*Prevention of an arms race in outer space*
A/76/27	Report of the Conference on Disarmament (Suppl. No. 27)
(b)	*No first placement of weapons in outer space*
(c)	*Further practical measures for the prevention of an arms race in outer space*
(d)	*Reducing space threats through norms, rules and principles of responsible behaviours*
A/76/77	Reducing space threats through norms, rules and principles of responsible behaviours: Report of the Secretary-General
Agenda item 99	**Role of science and technology in the context of international security and disarmament**
A/76/182	Current developments in science and technology and their potential impact on international security and disarmament efforts: Report of the Secretary-General
Agenda item 100	**General and complete disarmament**
A/76/130	United Nations Register of Conventional Arms: Report of the Secretary-General
(a)	*Treaty banning the production of fissile material for nuclear weapons or other nuclear explosive devices*
(b)	*Nuclear disarmament*
A/76/117	Nuclear disarmament; follow-up to the advisory opinion of the International Court of Justice on the legality of the threat or use of nuclear weapons; reducing nuclear danger: Report of the Secretary-General
(c)	*Notification of nuclear tests*
(d)	*Relationship between disarmament and development*

A/76/88	Relationship between disarmament and development: Report of the Secretary-General
(e)	*Prohibition of the dumping of radioactive wastes*
(f)	*Regional disarmament*
(g)	*Conventional arms control at the regional and subregional levels*
A/76/92	Conventional arms control at the regional and subregional levels: Report of the Secretary-General
(h)	*Convening of the fourth special session of the General Assembly devoted to disarmament*
(i)	*Nuclear-weapon-free southern hemisphere and adjacent areas*
(j)	*Observance of environmental norms in the drafting and implementation of agreements on disarmament and arms control*
A/76/113	Observance of environmental norms in the drafting and implementation of agreements on disarmament and arms control: Report of the Secretary-General
(k)	*Follow-up to the advisory opinion of the International Court of Justice on the legality of the threat or use of nuclear weapons*
A/76/117	Nuclear disarmament; follow-up to the advisory opinion of the International Court of Justice on the legality of the threat or use of nuclear weapons; reducing nuclear danger: Report of the Secretary-General
(l)	*Implementation of the Convention on the Prohibition of the Development, Production, Stockpiling and Use of Chemical Weapons and on Their Destruction*
A/76/111	Implementation of the Convention on the Prohibition of the Development, Production, Stockpiling and Use of Chemical Weapons and on Their Destruction: Note by the Secretary-General
(m)	*Implementation of the Convention on the Prohibition of the Use, Stockpiling, Production and Transfer of Anti-Personnel Mines and on Their Destruction*
(n)	*Assistance to States for curbing the illicit traffic in small arms and light weapons and collecting them*

A/76/284	Assistance to States for curbing the illicit traffic in small arms and light weapons and collecting them and the illicit trade in small arms and light weapons in all its aspects: Report of the Secretary-General
(o)	*Reducing nuclear danger*
A/76/117	Nuclear disarmament; follow-up to the advisory opinion of the International Court of Justice on the legality of the threat or use of nuclear weapons; reducing nuclear danger: Report of the Secretary-General
(p)	*The illicit trade in small arms and light weapons in all its aspects*
A/76/284	Assistance to States for curbing the illicit traffic in small arms and light weapons and collecting them and the illicit trade in small arms and light weapons in all its aspects: Report of the Secretary-General
A/CONF.192/ BMS/2021/1	Report of the Seventh Biennial Meeting of States to Consider the Implementation of the Programme of Action to Prevent, Combat and Eradicate the Illicit Trade in Small Arms and Light Weapons in All Its Aspects
(q)	*Towards a nuclear-weapon-free world: accelerating the implementation of nuclear disarmament commitments*
(r)	*Promotion of multilateralism in the area of disarmament and non-proliferation*
A/76/90	Promotion of multilateralism in the area of disarmament and non-proliferation: Report of the Secretary-General
(s)	*Measures to prevent terrorists from acquiring weapons of mass destruction*
A/76/189	Measures to prevent terrorists from acquiring weapons of mass destruction: Report of the Secretary-General
(t)	*Confidence-building measures in the regional and subregional context*
A/76/112	Confidence-building measures in the regional and subregional context: Report of the Secretary-General
(u)	*Problems arising from the accumulation of conventional ammunition stockpiles in surplus*

A/76/324	Final report of the Group of Governmental Experts on problems arising from the accumulation of conventional ammunition stockpiles in surplus
(v)	*Transparency and confidence-building measures in outer space activities*
(w)	*Follow-up to nuclear disarmament obligations agreed to at the 1995, 2000 and 2010 Review Conferences of the Parties to the Treaty on the Non-Proliferation of Nuclear Weapons*
(x)	*The Arms Trade Treaty*
(y)	*Treaty on the South-East Asia Nuclear-Weapon-Free Zone (Bangkok Treaty)*
(z)	*Joint courses of action and future-oriented dialogue towards a world without nuclear weapons*
(aa)	*Compliance with non-proliferation, arms limitation and disarmament agreements and commitments*
(bb)	*Follow-up to the 2013 high-level meeting of the General Assembly on nuclear disarmament*
A/76/125	Follow-up to the 2013 high-level meeting of the General Assembly on nuclear disarmament: Report of the Secretary-General
(cc)	*Countering the threat posed by improvised explosive devices*
(dd)	*Humanitarian consequences of nuclear weapons*
(ee)	*Ethical imperatives for a nuclear-weapon-free world*
(ff)	*Implementation of the Convention on Cluster Munitions*
(gg)	*Universal Declaration on the Achievement of a Nuclear-Weapon-Free World*
A/76/91	Universal Declaration on the Achievement of a Nuclear-Weapon-Free World: Report of the Secretary-General
(hh)	*Nuclear disarmament verification*
(ii)	*Treaty on the Prohibition of Nuclear Weapons*
A/76/128	Treaty on the Prohibition of Nuclear Weapons: Report of the Secretary-General
(jj)	*Youth, disarmament and non-proliferation*

Agenda item 101	**Review and implementation of the Concluding Document of the Twelfth Special Session of the General Assembly**
(a)	*Convention on the Prohibition of the Use of Nuclear Weapons*
(b)	*United Nations Regional Centre for Peace and Disarmament in Africa*
A/76/96	United Nations Regional Centre for Peace and Disarmament in Africa: Report of the Secretary-General
(c)	*United Nations Regional Centre for Peace, Disarmament and Development in Latin America and the Caribbean*
A/76/98	United Nations Regional Centre for Peace, Disarmament and Development in Latin America and the Caribbean: Report of the Secretary-General
(d)	*United Nations Regional Centre for Peace and Disarmament in Asia and the Pacific*
A/76/97	United Nations Regional Centre for Peace and Disarmament in Asia and the Pacific Report of the Secretary-General
(e)	*Regional confidence-building measures: activities of the United Nations Standing Advisory Committee on Security Questions in Central Africa*
A/76/274	Regional confidence-building measures: activities of the United Nations Standing Advisory Committee on Security Questions in Central Africa: Report of the Secretary-General
(f)	*United Nations regional centres for peace and disarmament*
Agenda item 102	**Review of the implementation of the recommendations and decisions adopted by the General Assembly at its tenth special session**
A/76/175	Report of the Director of the United Nations Institute for Disarmament Research: Note by the Secretary-General
(a)	*Report of the Conference on Disarmament*
A/76/183	Work of the Advisory Board on Disarmament Matters: Report of the Secretary-General

A/76/27	Report of the Conference on Disarmament (Suppl. No. 27)
(b)	*Report of the Disarmament Commission*
Agenda item 103	**The risk of nuclear proliferation in the Middle East**
A/76/190 (Part II)	Risk of nuclear proliferation in the Middle East: Report of the Secretary-General (Part II)
Agenda item 104	**Convention on Prohibitions or Restrictions on the Use of Certain Conventional Weapons Which May Be Deemed to Be Excessively Injurious or to Have Indiscriminate Effects**
Agenda item 105	**Strengthening of security and cooperation in the Mediterranean region**
A/76/89	Strengthening of security and cooperation in the Mediterranean region: Report of the Secretary-General
Agenda item 106	**Comprehensive Nuclear-Test-Ban Treaty**
A/76/114	Comprehensive Nuclear-Test-Ban Treaty: Note by the Secretary-General
Agenda item 107	**Convention on the Prohibition of the Development, Production and Stockpiling of Bacteriological (Biological) and Toxin Weapons and on Their Destruction**